ORWELL'S REVENGE

THE *1984* PALIMPSEST

■■■■■PETER HUBER

FREE PRESS
New York London Toronto Sydney New Delhi

FREE PRESS
An Imprint of Simon & Schuster, Inc.
1230 Avenue of the Americas
New York, NY 10020

This Free Press trade paperback edition June 2015

FREE PRESS and colophon are trademarks of Simon & Schuster, Inc.

For information about special discounts for bulk purchases, please contact Simon & Schuster Special Sales at 1-866-506-1949 or business@simonandschuster.com.

The Simon & Schuster Speakers Bureau can bring authors to your live event. For more information or to book an event, contact the Simon & Schuster Speakers Bureau at 1-866-248-3049 or visit our website at www.simonspeakers.com.

Manufactured in the United States of America

10 9 8 7 6 5 4 3 2 1

The Library of Congress has cataloged the hardcover edition as follows:

Huber, Peter W. (Peter William)
  Orwell's revenge: the 1984 palimpsest / Peter Huber.
  p. cm.
  Includes bibliographical references.
  1. Orwell, George, 1903–1950. Nineteen eighty-four—Parodies, imitations, etc.
I. Title.
PS3558.U238079   1994
813'.54—dc20   94-22921
                      CIP

ISBN 978-1-5011-2770-0
ISBN 978-1-5011-2773-1 (ebook)

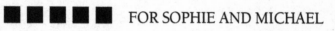 FOR SOPHIE AND MICHAEL

■ ■ ■ ■ ■ GEORGE ORWELL: Since your day something has appeared called totalitarianism.

JONATHAN SWIFT: A new thing?

ORWELL: It isn't strictly new, it's merely been made practicable owing to modern weapons and modern methods of communication.

—"Jonathan Swift: An Imaginary Interview"
[radio broadcast, 1942]

▪▪▪▪▪ CONTENTS

 PREFACE

April 4, 1984 . . . To the future or to the past, to a time when thought is free, when men are different from one another and do not live alone—to a time when truth exists and what is done cannot be undone:

From the age of uniformity, from the age of solitude, from the age of Big Brother, from the age of doublethink—Greetings!

George Orwell, *Nineteen Eighty-Four* (1949)

The date was wrong; the words were in fact written on April 4, 1948, or thereabouts. They were composed by a lonely, iconoclastic genius of English letters, aged forty-four, who was dying of tuberculosis. His book would be published in June 1949, just six months before his death. He chose as a title the year in which the book had been written, with the last two digits interchanged. The writer was George Orwell. The book was *1984*.

It was an immediate, huge success. By July 1949, *1984* had received sixty reviews in American publications. As the *New York Times* reported, 90 percent were "overwhelmingly admiring, with cries of terror rising above the applause." In the *New Yorker*, Lionel Trilling described the book as "profound, terrifying, and wholly fascinating." The *Evening Standard* of London called it "the most important book published since the war."

1

Forty years have passed; *1984* is still the most important book published since the war. Orwell's grimly technotic vision still casts a dark shadow over every advance in telegraphy, telemetry, telephony, and television—which is to say, every facet of teletechnology, every yard of the information superhighway, that is transforming our lives today. No one who has actually read Orwell can go a week without remembering him in one context or another. At any moment, some scene or neologism, which comes from this one short book, is liable to drop into your mind. *Big Brother. The Thought Police. Newspeak. Doublethink. Reality Control.* These were all created by Orwell in *1984. 1984* is not so much a book, it is a world. Even people who affect to disagree with Orwell quote him unconsciously. Through *1984*, Orwell did what very few other writers ever have done: he added not only phrases but his own name to the English language. There are books that one reads over and over again, books that become part of the furniture of one's mind and alter one's whole attitude to life. *1984* is one of them. Whether you approve of him or not, Orwell is there, like the Washington Monument.

And the only trouble with *that* is that Orwell was wrong. Not wrong in the details—Orwell was in fact remarkably right about the little things in *1984*. But he was wrong in his fundamental logic, wrong in his grand vision, wrong in his whole chain of reasoning. Wrong not because he lacked conviction, or industry, or moral integrity—Orwell brought more of those talents to his craft than any other person of his own time, or ours. Wrong, nonetheless, because Orwell built the essential struts and columns, the entire support structure of his magnificent edifice, on a gadget that he did not understand. The gargoyles in *1984* are magnificent. But the architecture beneath is rotten.

I

Begin, as Orwell does in *1984*, with Victory Gin, the opiate of all Oceania that sinks you into stupor every night and floats your mind out of bed every morning. Winston Smith, the hero of the book, sops up gin like everyone else. It is gin that keeps him calm during the Two Minutes Hate, gin that lets him relax even under the eye of Big Brother, gin that stops his mind from straying into the lethal minefields of *thoughtcrime.*

Smith is a miserable little cipher who spends his days falsifying history for the Ministry of Truth. He lives in London, a city filled with posters, propaganda, and all the squalid incidents of Stalinesque Big Brotherhood. The streets are not smashed to pieces, just "a little altered, kind of chipped and dirty-looking, the shop-windows almost empty and so dusty that you can't see into them," marked here and there by an occasional bomb crater. There are "the posters and the food-queues, and the castor oil and the rubber truncheons and the machine-guns squirting out of bedroom windows," slogans and "enormous faces" on posters, "secret police and the loudspeakers telling you what to think."

Life in 1984 is lived without affection, without loyalty, without any shred of real friendship. "Every word and every thought is censored," "free speech is unthinkable," and "in the end the secrecy of your revolt poisons you like a secret disease." "Your whole life is a life of lies, you are a creature of the despotism, tied tighter than a monk or a savage by an unbreakable system of tabus." Your every waking moment is filled with the "hateful feeling that someone hitherto your friend might be denouncing you to the secret police."

As 1984 opens, Winston Smith is about to make a gesture of rebellion: he is going to begin keeping a private diary. The passage I quoted at the beginning of this Preface is one of the first coherent things Winston records. He continues with an account of how he visited a toothless old prostitute, who disgusted him horribly.

The next day, Winston is back at work at the Ministry. He writes in Newspeak, the stripped-down English that is now the official language of all Oceania. An Appendix to 1984 explains its basic grammar, vocabulary, and syntax. By denuding the language of words and texture, the Party is gradually eliminating all possibility of independent thought and communication. Newspeak, to paraphrase Smith's diary, ensures that all men will be the same in what they say, and therefore in what they think. Newspeak communicates nothing, and so forces men to live alone.

The second transcendent political reality in 1984 is the "mutability of the past." There is no such thing as honest history any more; what is done can *always* be undone. Winston's job at the Ministry of Truth is to rewrite old newspaper articles so that every Party prediction is vindicated. "[I]f all others accepted the lie which the Party imposed—if all records told the same tale," Winston reflects, "then the lie passed into history and became truth." The "all" is critical: the Party falsifies not just some records here and there but every record, newspaper, book, and poem everywhere. The past is not merely tampered with; it is rewritten chapter and verse. People thus live in a "shifting phantasmagoric world in which black may be white tomorrow and yesterday's weather can be changed by decree, a nightmare world in which Big Brother controls not only the future but the past as well. If Big Brother says of such and such an event, 'It never happened'—well then, it never happened."

The third key political theme in 1984 is *doublethink*. Doublethink is a "vast system of mental cheating," the "power of holding two contradictory beliefs in one's mind simultaneously, and accepting both of them." To engage in doublethink is to

tell deliberate lies while genuinely believing in them, to forget any fact that has become inconvenient, and then, when it becomes necessary again, to draw it back from oblivion for just so long as it is needed, to deny the existence of objective reality and all the while to take account of the reality which one denies.

Gin makes all of this possible. Silence and Newspeak, forgetfulness and the mutable past, doublethink and the Thought Police: all of life in 1984 is lubricated, all thought dulled, all pain anesthetized, all rebellion dissipated, by Victory Gin. The other fixture of daily life—the other prop that makes the oppression possible, that sharpens the senses rather than dulling them, that creates records rather than destroying them, that enhances memory rather than suppressing it—is, of course, . . .

But I am getting ahead of myself.

II

In 1984, every emotion is transmuted into hate. Winston desires Julia, the dark-haired girl who works just down the hall, but half the time his desire is an evil fantasy of flogging and rape. Then one day, out of the blue, she slips him a note: "I love you," it says. Winston is first astounded, then deliriously happy. The two find a hiding place in a dilapidated room above a junk shop. For a few brief weeks they lust and love. Within their hermetic private world, they are free. Their affair has an achingly poignant desperation to it. They know they're bound to be caught by the Thought Police in the end.

There's one tiny glimmer of hope: Winston has a hunch that O'Brien, a high-ranking member of the Inner Party, is really a secret leader of the underground resistance. So Winston and Julia go to O'Brien and confess all. O'Brien listens sympathetically, then describes a shadowy brotherhood that is plotting to overthrow the Party. He arranges to supply Winston with a copy of *The Theory and Practice of Oligarchical Collectivism*, a seditious book written by the arch-traitor Kenneth Blythe. Some weeks later, the delivery is made.

Blythe's book provides a straight political explanation of the ideology and social structure of Oceania in 1984. Each of the three chapters is titled after one of the three slogans of the Party. Winston avidly reads "War Is Peace" and "Ignorance Is Strength." But he never does get to read the third chapter, "Freedom Is Slavery." Still, the two he gets through make up quite a long tract in the middle of *1984*.

Years ago, Blythe explains, socialism promised men an egalitarian, classless society. The steady advance of technology created abundant new wealth, which could easily have been shared all around. But sharing the wealth threatened power-hungry elites in every nation, and these reactionaries blocked society's natural progress toward humane socialism. Capitalist societies became fascist; socialist ones became communist. On both sides, small states coalesced into large ones. The drift toward superstate totalitarianism occurred everywhere at the same time. Geopolitical stability was thus maintained even while scientific competence and military strength decayed. Blythe's book is the least satirical part of *1984*; it closely tracks Orwell's earlier political essays. This book within a book straightforwardly summarizes Orwell's own views about where the world is headed, and why.

By 1984, the world is dominated by three equally balanced superstates, all with much the same political structure. England is part of Oceania, where English Socialism ("Ingsoc") is the triumphant totalitarian ideology. The other two superstates are Eurasia (which practices "Neo-Bolshevism") and Eastasia (where the political ideology is called "Obliteration of the Self"). With similar systems established by all, the three superstates are in perfect equipoise, and none faces any real threat of outside conquest. The only remaining threats to the power of the Inner Party in each superstate are internal.

There is, first, the problem of the untutored masses—the "proles." An all-around increase in wealth would quickly lead to literacy, which would spark a revolution, so the rulers maintain poverty. They can't simply shut down the machines of industrial production; even the proles would see what was happening and revolt. They can't wage real war either; atom bombs make that unthinkable. So the rulers engage their nations in ceaseless but essentially fake war in the third world, impoverishing society in a psychologically palatable way. Poverty maintains ignorance, which maintains the strength of the ruling oligarchy. Thus, we understand the first two of the Party's three slogans: WAR IS PEACE and IGNORANCE IS STRENGTH.

The one other threat to the ruling elite is rebellion by people like Winston and Julia: members of the Outer Party, the educated, restless middle class. As Blythe explains, "The only genuine dangers [to the ruling elite] are the splitting-off of a new group of able, underemployed, power-hungry people, and the growth of liberalism and skepticism in their own ranks. The problem, that is to say, is educational. It is a problem of continuously molding the consciousness."

Which brings us back to Victory Gin, the opiate and anesthetic of all consciousness in Oceania. And back to the other fixture of daily life in 1984, the thing that extends senses and heightens consciousness, which is, of course, . . .

But I am getting ahead of myself again.

III

O'Brien, it turns out, was a faithful member of the Inner Party all along. Winston and Julia are arrested and taken off to separate cells in the Ministry of Love.

Winston has been imprisoned, rather than vaporized immediately, because O'Brien has decided to save him. The details of the drugs and the pain machine are unimportant; the possibilities and methods of brainwashing were novel in Orwell's day but no longer are now. Suffice it to say that Winston's mind is dismantled, thought by thought. At the very end there remains one last vestige of his identity still to be expunged. O'Brien confronts Winston with his greatest terror: rats. Winston is completely broken, and we are back to gin in the morning, gin at night, and "two gin-scented tears." He no longer cares about Julia, no longer even likes her. Winston has won the victory over himself. He loves Big Brother.

IV

"I have not written a novel for seven years, but I hope to write another fairly soon," Orwell declares in an essay published in 1946. "[I] know with some clarity what kind of book I want to write," he continues. In August he starts work.

Orwell has reason to know what the book will say. He has been composing the drafts and notes for 1984, the scenes, the metaphors, and the images, throughout his literary life. Here is just one small example of what I mean, from a 1946 essay, "Politics and the English Language":

> When one watches some tired hack on the platform mechanically repeating the familiar phrases . . . one often has a curious feeling that one is not watching a live human being but some kind of dummy: a feeling which suddenly becomes stronger at moments when the light catches the speaker's spectacles and turns them into blank discs which seem to have no eyes behind them. . . . The appropriate noises are coming out of his larynx, but his brain is not involved.

The rewrite in 1984 reads:

> His head was thrown back a little, and because of the angle at which he was sitting, his spectacles caught the light and presented to Winston two blank discs instead of eyes. . . . As he watched the eyeless face with the jaw moving rapidly up and down, Winston had a curious feeling that this was not a real human being but some kind of dummy. It was not the man's brain that was speaking; it was his larynx.

There is more of this self-plagiarism in 1984—much more. If you look for it—as I have done systematically, with the aid of a powerful computer—you will find it on page after page.

Orwell knew what he was doing, of course. And gloomy though he was in 1948, it must have amused him to write *1984* with so much reliance on scissors and paste. In *1984* itself, the Ministry of Truth churns out books on its "novel-writing machines" in much the same way. The pornographic stories that Julia helps produce at the Ministry have only six plots, which are swapped around by machine. Sentimental songs are "composed entirely by mechanical means on a special kind of kaleidoscope known as a versificator . . . without any human intervention whatever." Orwell surely must have smiled as he wrote those words, with the litter of his own cannibalized essays and books scattered around his desk.

Happily, however, Orwell's cut-and-pasting worked far better than the book-writing machines mentioned in *1984*. Scissors or no scissors, *1984* is a magnificently original creation. Even today, almost half a century after the book's publication, a decade after the year itself, the mind-numbing, soul-sapping atmosphere of *1984* still seems grippingly real. You can almost feel Big Brother's electronic eye as it monitors every stroke of the pen in your diary, as it watches every slight twitch of facecrime in your living room, as it pursues thoughtcrime into the deepest recesses of your brain. *1984* makes technoparanoia seem completely rational. It makes telephobia respectable.

But—as I have said—*1984* is wrong. Not just wrong as prophecy, but wrong in its architecture, wrong in its mechanics, wrong in its central vision. Exploring why is not just an idle exercise in literary history. In working out just how and why Orwell was so fundamentally mistaken, we learn a great deal about our own present, and perhaps our own future too.

V

I could have worked it out the old-fashioned way, I suppose, but that would hardly have done Orwell justice. Orwell, after all, expected books in our day to be written "by machinery," with "prefabricated phrases bolted together like the pieces of a child's Meccano set." Our books, he promised, would be passed "through so many hands that when finished they [would] be no more an individual product than a Ford car at the end of the assembly line." By now, Orwell predicted, "the surviving literature of the past" would have to be "suppressed or at least elaborately rewritten." Orwell predicted it. I simply delivered.

My crime began with the physical destruction of a book—*1984* itself. I tore off the cover and cut the 314 pages from the spine. I then fed them into my optical scanner, 30 or so at a time, and transferred them by wire into my computer. *1984* lives there to this day, 590,463 bytes of ASCII text. For good measure, I scanned in the rest of Orwell's books, essays, letters, and BBC broadcasts too.* To locate biographical details of Orwell's life, I scanned in Michael Shelden's excellent *Orwell: The Authorized Biography*. Altogether, these writings now reside in 9,546,486 bytes, which is to say a hundred million slivers of magnetized ferric dust glued to the surface of a spinning platter called a hard drive.

Then I set to work. Real names and faces rose up before me from the digitized mists of Orwell's writings and life—Orwell himself most of all, in his several incarnations. Orwell the real-life Winston Smith, the man who ended his broadcasting career at the BBC feeling "like a sucked orange," the man who lived most of his modest life all but unrecognized under his real name, Eric Blair. Orwell again, the man who imagined the hyper-tech Ministry of Love, armed with the technology by which Big Brother is always watching *you*. And Orwell a third time—Orwell the tinkerer, the lover of gadgets, the man who, by his own account, was "perpetually seeing, as it were, the ghosts of possible machines that might save me the trouble of using my brain or muscles."

Around Orwell, Orwell, and Orwell, there congregated real people from Orwell's own lives. Brendan Bracken—"B.B."—who headed Britain's Ministry of Information during Orwell's tenure at the BBC, renamed O'Brien by Orwell in *1984*. Duff Cooper—the man Bracken re-

---

Down and Out in Paris and London (1933; 378,677 bytes); *Burmese Days* (1934; 557,002 bytes); *A Clergyman's Daughter* (1935; 552,502 bytes); *Keep the Aspidistra Flying* (1936; 493,220 bytes); *The Road to Wigan Pier* (1937; 402,951 bytes); *Homage to Catalonia* (1938; 514,313 bytes); *Coming Up for Air* (1939; 465,168 bytes); *A Collection of Essays* (1936-1937; 669,623 bytes); *The Lion and the Unicorn* (1941; 190,422 bytes); *Animal Farm* (1945; 178,574 bytes); selected additional essays from *The Orwell Reader* (254,657 bytes) and *The Penguin Essays of George Orwell* (482,987 bytes) and selected pages from the four volumes of *The Collected Essays, Journalism and Letters of George Orwell* (877,328 bytes).

placed as head of the Ministry of Information. Vaughan Wilkes—the sadistic headmaster who tormented and caned young Orwell during his miserable schooldays at Crossgates. J. D. Bernal—signed up by Orwell to give BBC talks on "the future of science and the position of the scientific worker under Capitalism, Fascism and Socialism." Cyril Connolly—Orwell's fellow Etonian and life-long friend. And Guy Burgess—Orwell's colleague at the BBC, later exposed as a Soviet spy.

As I wrote, I never suffered from writer's block. Whenever I needed to picture Orwell's life through Orwell's eyes, I had his own record instantly at hand. When it suited my purposes, I lifted individual words, images, phrases, entire sentences, occasionally even paragraphs from his own writings. When I felt like it, I rearranged, added, pruned, inverted, reversed, or corrupted. I felt no sense of contrition. I was simply committing the quintessentially Orwellian crime—a crime of plagiarism, forgery, artistic vandalism, and historic revisionism, a crime committed on and by the computer itself. Or was it the other way around? Was the crime really his, and my part simply the punishment?

It hardly matters. When at last I stopped, this book had emerged. Orwell's story had been rewritten. His black had been turned into white. Best of all, it had been done by his own hand.

VI

Or almost so. I said at the outset that Orwell begins with Victory Gin, but I lied. The Gin comes second. What Orwell begins with is the very opposite of gin. And it is in dealing with The Thing That Is Not Gin, the Thing that sharpens the senses instead of dulling them, that Orwell loses his mind.

That thing is, of course . . .

■■■■■■ PART 1: THE MACHINE

CHAPTER 1 ■■■■■

The telescreen was still there. It had always been there, as long as Big Brother himself. Big Brother's black-haired, black-mustachio'd visage still gazed outward from the screen, full of power and mysterious calm. Every minute of every day and night you always knew: BIG BROTHER IS WATCHING YOU.

It was a vile, biting day in March, when the earth was like iron and all the grass seemed dead and there was not a bud anywhere except a few crocuses which had pushed themselves up to be dismembered by the wind. The wind whipped through the leafless trees and flapped the torn posters against the gray walls of the buildings. As Blair pushed his way through the glass doors of Victory Mansions, scraps of paper in the street seemed to scuttle along the walls of the alleys, like rats. The stairs loomed before him, their threadbare carpet a dull green in the light that filtered through the dirty window. The lift wasn't working. The electric power was always shut off for a month during the Nega-watt austerity program that led up to Love Week.

Blair climbed the eight stories to his dingy apartment. The paint on the walls was blistered and peeling from the damp. He stopped on the landing to cough, and doubled up in an agonizing spasm. When he could breathe again, he fumbled in his tattered raincoat for the key, then stepped into the chill, stagnant air of his home. He saw his reflection in the mirror that faced the door. Eric Blair— E. A. Blair—Party Number 503-330-090. He was a pathetic figure: shabby and insubstantial, looking older than his thirty-five years. His otherwise gray skin was red and rough from too frequent applications of a razor blade that had lost its cutting edge weeks ago.

The voice on the telescreen was babbling in his living room about the production of pig iron. It was always pig iron, or the five-year plan, or the latest triumph in the never-ending war against Eastasia. The voice issued from an oblong metal plaque like a dulled mirror, which formed part of the surface of the right-hand wall. The telescreen could be dimmed, but there was no way of shutting it off completely. The device received and transmitted simultaneously. Any sound that Blair made, above the level of a very low whisper, would be picked up by it; moreover, so long as he remained within the field of vision which the metal plaque commanded, he could be seen as well as heard. There was of course no way of knowing whether you were being watched at any given moment. How often, or on what system, the Thought Police plugged in on any individual wire was guesswork. It was even conceivable that they watched everybody all the time. But at any rate they could plug in your wire whenever they wanted to.

Blair turned toward the window, his back to the telescreen. More paint had flaked off the metal frame onto the sill. He looked out over London, chief city of Airstrip One, the third most populous province of Oceania. All around spread endless grimy miles of decayed brick buildings, with gaps like missing teeth, filled with rubble, and patches of waste land where weeds sprouted and rubbish accumulated. Had London always been like this? The building opposite seemed to have once had some kind of dome on it—whatever covered it had been stripped off, leaving a scarred brick infrastructure. The iron railings on the balconies of the buildings had struts missing and misshapen.

A kilometer away the Ministry of Love towered vast and white above the grimy landscape, an enormous pyramidal structure of glittering white concrete. From where Blair stood it was just possi-

ble to read, picked out in elegant lettering on the white face of the
Ministry, the three slogans of the Party:

WAR IS PEACE
FREEDOM IS SLAVERY
IGNORANCE IS STRENGTH

Blair set his face into the expression of quiet optimism it was ad-
visable to wear when facing the telescreen, then turned from the
window. He crossed to the kitchen, poured a teacupful of Victory
Gin, and gulped it down. It burned his throat, and brought tears
to his eyes, but it also loosened the knot of fear in his stomach.
Then, as casually as he could, he walked over to the shallow alcove
to one side of the telescreen. For some reason the telescreen in the
living room was in an unusual position, so that the alcove, once
occupied by bookshelves, was just out of its line of sight. In the alcove stood a small battered table, left there by some former occu-
pant of the flat.

But for the alcove, Blair knew he would never have dared accept
the package. Razor blades would have been bad enough. Nobody
could get razor blades except from the proles, and trading was officially forbidden. Yet somehow his search for blades had produced
this package instead, and Blair knew it contained something infinitely more compromising. The package contained a book—*the
book,* the book without a title, the compendium of all heresies
against the Party, against Oceania, against Big Brother himself. It
was the diary of the archtraitor Winston Smith. Smith had been
hanged, of course—the execution had taken place years ago, in
Victory Square. But somehow his diary had survived.

Blair slid the slim volume out of the brown paper wrapping. It
was amateurishly bound, with no name or title on the cover. The
handwritten text inside had evidently been copied by some photo-
graphic means. The pages were worn at the edges, and fell apart
easily, as though the book had passed through many hands.
Where was the original? Who had found it? A tremor passed
through Blair's bowels. To begin reading was the decisive act. He
opened the book.

At the top of the first page was a date: April 4, 1984. There followed a rambling passage describing a routine piece of newsfilm—something to do with fighting at the eastern front. But at the bottom of the page, printed in bold letters, were the words:

DOWN WITH BIG BROTHER DOWN WITH BIG BROTHER
DOWN WITH BIG BROTHER DOWN WITH BIG BROTHER
DOWN WITH BIG BROTHER

Blair flipped forward in the book. Then he read:

To the future or to the past, to a time when thought is free, when men are different from one another and do not live alone—to a time when truth exists and what is done cannot be undone:

From the age of uniformity, from the age of solitude, from the age of Big Brother, from the age of doublethink—greetings!

He sat back, weak with indecision. A sense of complete helplessness descended upon him. Was this the future that Smith had in mind? Men certainly did not live alone now. In the age of Big Brother no one lived alone. But this was a matter of *doublethink*. Men lived with Big Brother every second of their lives, and they lived alone too—utterly alone, with no empathy, no links of understanding, no connections of any kind, except to the Ministry, which was connected to everyone.

For some time Blair sat gazing stupidly at the page. The telescreen had changed over to strident military music, and he breathed in time with the tinny racket until he felt calmer. It was curious, he thought, how his ability to read Oldspeak had atrophied. The words on the page seemed jumbled and hard to pronounce, though distantly familiar, as if his understanding had been scattered and confounded. He was conscious of nothing except the blaring of the music and a slight booziness caused by the gin. The seconds were ticking by.

He put his hand to his face, and grimaced as he felt the tender surface of his cheek. To be done in by razor blades! It was sublimely ridiculous. For an instant Blair felt an overwhelming desire to laugh. Then his stomach tightened again as he thought of the morning.

It had happened just before eight hundred, if anything so nebulous could be said to happen. The scraping of the six-week-old blade on his raw face had finally been too much. Staring with a wretched frustration at the points of blood appearing on his neck behind the plow of the blade, he had thrown the razor down, wiped his half-shaved face with a towel, and ventured out to the market.

Officially, the market didn't exist. Officially, the parasites and profiteers had been banished, the speculators cleared out, to protect goodthinking people from ruthless exploitation. Unofficially, the proles' market flourished in the very heart of London. There were hundreds, perhaps thousands, of the little stalls and shops inside the four-mile radius of the inner city.

For a long time the market had been confined to one or two narrow streets away from any main thoroughfare. Blair remembered having visited it once years before, in a derelict alley in the east of London. Two miserable stalls were set up, small folding tables that could be quickly removed at any sign of trouble. On one of them were wilted cabbages. But that had been years ago.

This morning, Blair had made his way down Bond Street and the length of Waterloo Road. He passed through Victory Square. There were always a number of prostitutes there—the unsuccessful ones, who couldn't earn enough for a night's bed. One woman who had been lying on the ground overnight was crying bitterly, because a man had gone off without paying her fifty-cent fee. Toward morning some of the girls did not even get that, but only a cup of tea or a cigarette.

By a small bake shop an old, very ugly woman was violently abusing two of the other women because they could afford a better dinner than she could. As each dish was brought out to them she would point at it and shout accusingly, "There goes the price of another fuck! We don't get hash for dinner, do we girls? 'Ow do you think she paid for them kippers? That's that there toff that 'as 'er for a tanner."

Blair headed down toward the river, through one of the most desolate parts of the city. The buildings here were broad and solid, and might once have been imposing, but their window frames

were rotting apart, and the broken windows gaped dark and menacing. Rubbish blew along the deserted street, and a small, dark
form slid into a hole in the wall as his steps approached. In the
middle of a dreary square was an oval building with rectangular
apertures where the windows had been torn out. It had a small
tower in front. The pavement around it was broken and uneven,
and weeds sprouted up through the cracks. He wondered what its
purpose had been. A vague tune came into his head, a singsong
melody about oranges and lemons. Clouds covered the watery sun
and the day darkened.

The wind was stronger now, and blew dust into his face. The
river gave off a thick, sweetish, unhealthy smell, and green slime
clung to the pillars that supported the bridges. There was no rail-
ing to protect the walker from the turbid brown water, though dis-
colored pits on the parapet suggested there once had been.
Eventually the road turned away from the river, and the large dilapidated buildings and wide thoroughfares gave way to rows of brick
houses, huddled shoulder to shoulder, leaning on each other as if
for support.

The streets became narrow alleys, and people appeared again. A
great fat woman with hair sprouting on her lip and chin was peg-
ging washing to a sagging line, shouting in a husky voice to an un-
seen neighbor. A couple of thin children offered cabbage leaves to
a mangy cat, which they held on a string. The cat crouched beside
them sullenly, and turned its face away from their offering with
pointed dislike. In another alley the smell of an overflowing drain
made Blair's stomach turn. He met some men going the other way
with some tools and pipes, and wondered if they could possibly be
doing repairs. Were the proles capable of that? The Ministries were
barely able to keep the plumbing in Party flats in working order.

Blair walked under high brick arches that carried rail lines, his
nose wrinkling at the stench of urine and rotting garbage. He
trailed back southward, knowing he would sooner or later hit
Whitechapel Road. The gray apartments gave way to slums of ter-
raced brown two-story houses.

The scene changed abruptly as he entered the area of the market. Suddenly the sidewalk stalls were so numerous they almost

spilled over on to each other. His nose was assailed by smells of sweat and coffee. He glimpsed the stall he wanted between two great solid females, who beamed at each other and parted. He caught his breath in amazement. There at the top of the stall, lined up against a wooden plank, was chocolate. Real chocolate, eight solid bars, not the Party's dull-brown crumbly stuff that tasted, as nearly as one could describe it, like the smoke of a rubbish fire.

Blair diffidently made his way forward, and was pressed by the crowd against the trestle table that supported the goods.

"'Ullo, mate," the heavy, red-faced stallkeeper said amiably. "Can I 'elp you?"

Blair cleared his throat. His voice, when it came, sounded to him stilted and pedantic. "Well yes," he replied. "The thing is, you see, I need some razor blades. . . . I, ah, have these light bulbs here . . ." Feeling foolish, he pulled a light bulb out of the big pocket of his raincoat.

"Sorry, sir, I just parted with me last ones," the stallkeeper said politely.

The frustration was almost too much to bear. The anticipation of a comfortable shave had become solidly fixed in Blair's mind. The stall owner seemed to understand, even as Blair began to turn away in disgust.

"I can 'ave some for you tomorrow if you like. I'll put 'em aside," he added.

What nonsense! By tomorrow the man would have forgotten all about that promise. Tomorrow, always tomorrow, there would be full employment, exemplary public health, universal education, and free entertainment—Big Brother promised, the Ministry of Plenty solemnly promised. No one ever delivered. No one remembered anything any more. And even if by chance the stallkeeper remembered his promise, why on earth should he bother to keep it? Promises were worth as much as dollars these days, and dollars were worth nothing at all.

As these thoughts flashed through his mind, Blair felt a surge of hate—the kind of blind, gripping hate you felt when the face of Kenneth Blythe leered at you from the telescreen during the Two Minutes Hate. Not hate for this particular stallkeeper, fool though he was, but hate for the Party, hate for the Ministry of Plenty, hate for Love Week, hate for everything that combined to make Blair shave his sore face with a blade that was six weeks old.

And then he had said it. A lunatic impulse had taken hold of him, and the words had shot out of his mouth, faster than he could even think, an ejaculation of bitterness bursting like pus from a boil.

"Like the Jam!" Blair had shouted. "Just like the Jam! We get jam every *other* day, don't we! Jam yesterday, jam tomorrow. But never any jam today, because today isn't any *other* day, now, is it?" Then, in a spasm of sheer insanity he had added: "I suppose Big Brother'll have blades for me tomorrow, too!" A sharp burst of laughter had followed the words out of his mouth, before the horror of what he had said gripped his throat back into silence.

It was exactly at this moment that the significant thing had happened. Blair had caught the stallkeeper's eye. For a fraction of a second when their eyes met, and for as long as it took to happen, Blair knew—yes, he *knew*—that the stallkeeper was thinking the same thing as himself. An unmistakable message had passed. It was as though their two minds had opened and the thoughts were flowing from one into the other. "I am with you," the stallkeeper seemed to be saying to him. "I know precisely what you are feeling. I know all about your contempt, your hatred, your disgust—and about the soreness of your face. But don't worry, I am on your side." A second later the flash of intelligence was gone, and the stallkeeper's face was as inscrutable as everybody else's.

"Don't worry, mate, they'll be here," the stallkeeper said sympathetically. Then, without looking downward, he had reached under the stall and pulled out the package. He had calmly placed it into Blair's hands. And perhaps because his mind had still been reeling at his own outburst, Blair had taken the package without comment, thrust it into his coat pocket, and turned back toward Victory Mansions.

Now, as he sat at the desk in the alcove of his room with the taste of gin in his mouth, Blair felt paralyzed again by the memory of his outburst. He was a dead man.

He stared again at the book in front of him. The gin was

seething in his stomach, and he let out a belch. For a moment he was tempted to destroy the book, quickly and silently. But that was useless. Whether he destroyed it or continued reading it made no difference. The Thought Police would get him just the same. He had committed—would still have committed, even if he had never opened the book—the essential crime that contained all others in itself. *Thoughtcrime*, they called it. Thoughtcrime was not a thing that could be concealed forever. Sooner or later they were bound to get you.

He wondered again: Had it always been like this? Had London always had this horrible atmosphere of suspicion, hatred, censored newspapers, crammed jails, air-raids, machine-guns, enormous food-queues, milkless tea, shortages of cigarettes, and prowling gangs of armed men? Had men always lived under the shadow of the Thought Police? The next moment Blair started violently. There was a knocking at the door.

Already! He sat as still as a mouse, in the futile hope that whoever it was might go away after a single attempt. But no, the knocking was repeated. Blair's entrails seemed to grow cold. The worst thing of all would be to delay. His heart was thumping like a drum, but his face, from long habit, was expressionless. He got up and moved heavily toward the door.

■■■■■ THE MACHINE

The gin is foul, flat, sickly, and oily, like a sort of Chinese rice-spirit. It makes your lips purple and grows not less but more horrible with every mouthful you drink. Still, you drink it in gulps, like doses of vile medicine. You breathe it out of your skin in place of sweat, and cry it from your eyes in place of tears. When you wake with gummed-up eyelids and fiery mouth and a back that seems to be broken, it is impossible even to rise from the horizontal, but for the bottle and teacup placed beside your bed overnight.

Big Brother drinks from a different cup. His thirst is quenched by The Thing that is not Gin. Big Brother has the telescreen.

The telescreen is the key to everything else in *1984*. The word "telescreen" (or "screen") occurs 119 times in Orwell's book, which is to say, on almost every other page. "Big Brother" appears only 74 times. Other related words get far fewer mentions: "the Thought Police," 39; "The Spies" youth group, 14; "spy" in other contexts, 9; "watching" in the context of snooping, 8; "thoughtcrime" or "crimethink," 14; "betray," 24; "slogan," 19; "propaganda," 4. "Newspeak" appears 46 times in the body of the book and another 33 in the Appendix. The three slogans of the Party—WAR IS PEACE, FREEDOM IS SLAVERY, IGNORANCE IS STRENGTH—occur 6, 7, and 6 times respectively. Other related phrases get only occasional mentions: "memory holes," 6; "mutability of the past," 3; "informers," 2; "Thought Police helicopters," 1; "ear trum-pets," 1; "snoop," 1; "eavesdropping," 1. Even the cardinal principle of all Oceania—"doublethink"—appears only 31 times, or about as often as "gin," with 34 occurrences. From a strictly engineering perspective, the telescreen is the scaffold. It is the single, ubiquitous techno-spy that makes possible Big Brother's absolute control.

The political essay set out in the middle of 1984 acknowledges this explicitly:

By comparison with that existing today, all the tyrannies of the past were half-hearted and inefficient. . . . Part of the reason for this was that in the past no government had the power to keep its citizens under constant surveillance. . . . [But] [w]ith the development of television, and the technical advance which made it possible to receive and trans-mit simultaneously on the same instrument, private life came to an end. . . . Every citizen, or at least every citizen important enough to be worth watching, could be kept for twenty-four hours a day under the eyes of the police and in the sound of official propaganda, with all other channels of communication closed. The possibility of enforcing not only complete obedience to the will of the State, but complete unifor-mity of opinion on all subjects, now existed for the first time.

And *that* possibility is what defines reality in 1984. The telescreen connects everyone in England not only to the Ministry of Truth, which spews out the pig-iron statistics and military music, but also to the Ministry of Love, the headquarters of the Thought Police. Day and night the telescreen bruises your ears with Party propaganda. And whether or not you attend to it, the telescreen attends to you. It listens for sedition and watches for *facecrime*, with an ear that never tires and an eye that never blinks. In your home and office, in your bedroom and your lavatory, in private spaces and in public squares, the tele-screen is watching. Big Brother is watching. Not just the foreigners, traitors, saboteurs, and thought-criminals: BIG BROTHER IS WATCH-ING YOU.

But how exactly does the telescreen work? What's connected to what? Where and how do all the people who are watching all the other people select whom they will watch? Orwell never explains. He is in fact remarkably unspecific about the single critical piece of technology on which his book so completely depends. A few privileged members of the Inner Party can turn off their telescreens, but most people can't. Nor do most people have any control over what they watch. The word "dial" (in connection with telescreens) appears only a single time in *1984*, and then as if by accident. Employees in the Ministry of Truth apparently can file a request for documents on their telescreens, but the documents are delivered via pneumatic tubes. If you need some ingenious, revolutionary, high-tech prop to glue your whole book together, you owe it to your reader to explain how the gadget works. Orwell never does.

All we know is that Big Brother has the screens, which convey everything. You have Newspeak, which conveys nothing. Big Brother is watching, always watching, watching everyone, watching *you*. And you? You are blinding yourself on Victory Gin.

CHAPTER 2 ■■■■■

As he put his hand to the doorknob Blair saw that he had left Smith's diary open on the table. It was an inconceivably stupid thing to have done. He drew in his breath and opened the door. Instantly a warm wave of relief flowed through him. A large, stooping woman with wispy gray hair, a sacking apron, and shuffling carpet slippers was standing outside.

"Oh, comrade," she began in a dreary, whining sort of voice. "I thought I heard you come in. Do you think you could come across and have a look at our kitchen sink? It's got blocked up. I've been trying to clear the pipe with a stick. But I can't seem—"

It was Mrs. Wilkes, Blair's neighbor. He followed her down the passage. She had a round pale face, the usual exhausted face of a woman who is twenty-five and looks forty, thanks to miscarriages and drudgery. She looked up and caught his eye, and her expression was as desolate as any he had ever seen. It struck him that she was thinking just the same thing as he was. She knew well enough what was happening to her—understood as well as he did how dreadful a destiny it was to be kneeling on the slimy floor of a cold kitchen in a decaying building, poking a stick down a foul drain-pipe.

The Wilkes's flat was bigger than Blair's, and dingy in a different way. In front of the fire there was almost always a line of damp washing, and in the middle of the room was a big kitchen table at which the family ate. Blair had never seen this table completely un-covered, but he had seen its various wrappings at different times. At the bottom there was a layer of old newspapers stained by Worcester Sauce; above that a sheet of sticky white oil cloth; above that a green serge cloth; above that a coarse linen cloth, never changed and seldom taken off. The kitchen sink was full nearly to the brim with filthy greenish water which smelt worse than ever of cabbage.

It was all so typical, Blair thought. The buildings were falling apart. The electric power was horribly unreliable. Repairs, except those you could do for yourself, had to be sanctioned by remote committees, which were liable to hold up even the mending of a window pane for two years. Blair knelt down and examined the angle-joint of the pipe. Mrs. Wilkes looked on helplessly.

"Of course if my Vaunnie was home he'd put it right in a mo-ment," she said. "He loves anything like that. He's ever so good with his hands, Vaunnie is."

Blair knew that Vaughan Wilkes was nothing of the sort. A low-ranking guard at the Ministry of Love, Wilkes was a fattish but ac-tive man of paralyzing stupidity, a mass of imbecile enthusiasms —one of those completely unquestioning, devoted drudges on whom the stability of the Party depended. He had no ability of any kind, least of all technical.

Blair let out the water and disgustedly removed the clot of human hair that had blocked up the pipe. There was a dreary logic to it all. A decaying pipe, clotted by a decaying human scalp. And with human minds rotting all around, no one knew how to fix anything any more. Nothing worked, nothing was properly maintained.

Except the telescreens. There must have been a time when sci-ence and technology had developed at a prodigious speed to create devices as intricate as these. The electric power might be off—had been off all afternoon, in fact—but the telescreens were still on. What powered them? No one could answer even a question as sim-ple as that any more. Hardly anyone understood anything scientific; engineers worked with the constant knowledge that an error in calculation might take them to prison or the scaffold. Few of the Police Patrol helicopters, once used so widely for snooping into people's windows, could get off the ground. But somehow . . . . somehow the Ministry of Love still functioned, as it always had. It was a curious thing: the giant machine beneath the Ministry kept on working perfectly, in the midst of such universal decay.

All the more curious because the system was maintained by the likes of Vaughan Wilkes. The Party despised anyone of a truly scientific bent. Some people did still know how to use a spanner or a screwdriver—occasionally Blair would see someone at the office with oily hands, who had just done some simple job on a printer. But that was about as much as the authorities could tolerate. The Party attracted people of the opposite temperament, small fat men, a breed of uninquisitive snoops, always watching and listening but quite incapable of real thought. It attracted people who simply swallowed everything. What they swallowed left no residue behind, just as a grain of corn will pass undigested through the body of a bird. Science was knowledge. The Party's strength was ignorance.

Blair took his leave of Mrs. Wilkes and made for the door. Back in the flat, he stepped quickly past the telescreen and sat down in the alcove again. The music from the screen had stopped. Instead, a clipped military voice was reading out, with a sort of brutal relish, a description of the armaments of the new Floating Fortress which had just been anchored between Iceland and the Faroe Islands.

Blair picked up Smith's diary again. He meant to explore it further, but the feel of the book in his hand reminded him of the market. He remembered again the noise and bustle of the morning, the florid, fat faces of the older women, the great bellies of the men under their coarse shirts and aprons. Even the smells returned, the stink of the proles' cigarettes, the reek of fish from a stall nearby, and the whiff of coffee, real, roasting coffee, drifting from some other corner of the market.

He had stumbled away from the razor-blade man, sick with disappointment, stuffing the brown packet into his pocket unthinkingly. The proles shouted and shoved their way around him, and he went where he was pushed, overwhelmed by the loudness of their voices and their sheer dense, smelly humanity.

"Cheer up, ducks!" a woman had said, smiling at him brightly, and he cringed at the sight of her brown teeth and garish red lips.

"Out of me way, there!" bellowed another voice in his ear, and a hulking young fellow strode by with a great box on his shoulder. Blair struggled out of the main stream of traffic, and stared around him. He found a still spot where a board fence met the protruding wall of a house.

Beside him was a steel pillar, dominating the market, but ignored by the proles. He glanced up, then immediately made his face blank. A telescreen was mounted at the top of the pillar. He brought his hand up to his face, and half turned away. It was then that he had seen him, the man they called the phreak. He was wearing an old, tattered tweed jacket with a dark shirt and tie. And without a trace of fear about him, he was facing the screen directly.

"Wotcher doin'?" a prole had shouted cheerfully at the phreak from down the street. "Tryin' to bust something open?" The phreak had just grinned.

Only the Thought Police were supposed to touch the telescreens, but the phreak obviously wasn't one of them. He was a tall, big-headed man, with pale-blue, humorous eyes, and a working-class look. His young face was pinched by deprivation, but sharp and inquisitive, not the dull look of a Party functionary. His wretched clothes were a far cry from Party-blue overalls. He appeared to be in his early twenties, a bit disheveled, a hieroglyphic of a man, with too many bends in his body, and not enough body. His hair was not quite combed, his face not completely shaved, his shirt not fully tucked in. He looked like a lavatory brush, with bristles of black hair on top of a gaunt face and skeletal frame.

Blair had stared at him with fascination. There he was, his face right up to the screen, fearless. He was working on the device with some tool. He bent down to Blair.

"Could yer pass up me screwdriver from me bag, please?" he asked civilly. Blair obliged him, and stared a moment longer. Then he remembered where he was, lowered his head, shrugged his raincoat up around his neck, and plunged back into the shelter of the crowd.

Afterward, on his way home with the terrible book in hand, Blair had passed by the phreak again. Their eyes had almost met as Blair worked his way back up the street, though the phreak seemed to focus a bit beyond where Blair was standing. As he passed, the phreak had said: "We shall meet in the place where there is no darkness." Or at least that was what Blair thought he had said. It had been said quietly, almost casually—a statement, not a command. The phreak had not paused. He had walked on, looking slightly lost, like an overgrown three-year-old, embarked on a busy day before he had quite finished with dressing and breakfast.

What was curious, Blair thought, was that at the time the words had not made much impression on him. It was only now that they seemed to take on significance. There had been a link of understanding between the two men, more important than affection. *We shall meet in the place where there is no darkness*, the phreak had said, and in a surprisingly cultured voice with no trace of accent. Blair did not know what it meant, only that in some way or another it would come true.

The telescreen struck fourteen. Then a trumpet call, clear and beautiful, floated from the wall. "Attention! Your attention, please! A newsflash has this moment arrived . . ."

The chiming of the hour seemed to put new heart into him. He was a lonely ghost, reading a forbidden truth that would change nothing. But so long as he read it, in some obscure way the continuity was not broken.

■■■■■ BRAIN IN A BOTTLE

"[T]he logical end of mechanical progress," George Orwell declares in *The Road to Wigan Pier*, "is to reduce the human being to something resembling a brain in a bottle." Orwell hates the thought. Though a socialist himself, Orwell disdains the machine worship of socialism, the dismal "socialism-progress-machinery-Russia-tractors-hygiene-machinery-progress" of the 1930s. Humans don't really have to do anything but eat, sleep, and procreate, Orwell observes gloomily, and when machines have advanced far enough, that is all there will be left for humans to do. Mechanical progress may be a necessary development, but it should not become a religion. Orwell is repelled by the "glutinously uplifting" view of machines put forward by a writer like H. G. Wells. "The thought he dare not face," Orwell says of Wells, "is that the machine itself may be the enemy."

The machine itself may be the enemy. That's what Orwell believes, first and last. The machine, Orwell continues in *Wigan Pier*, is "getting us into its power" at "sinister speed." Machines produce a "frightful debauchery of taste"—in food, furniture, houses, clothes, books, and amusements. "The machine," Orwell predicts, will "even encroach upon the activities we now class as 'art'; it is doing so already, via the camera and the radio." Aldous Huxley got it right in *Brave New World*: the machine leads to "the paradise of little fat men." Countless more pages of machine-and-fat-men invective are scattered throughout Orwell's books, essays, reviews, and letters. The "machine age" is responsible for "disgusting" artists like Salvador Dalí. The "forces of the machine age are slowly destroying the family." The "machine age" is one of "ugliness and spiritual emptiness." "In a healthy world there would be no demand for tinned food, aspirins, gramophones, gaspipe chairs, machine guns, daily newspapers, telephones, motor-cars, etc., etc."

Ah yes, gramophones, telephones, machine guns. Orwell dislikes all machines, but he hates instruments of electronic communication the most.

Until 1984, Orwell aims most of his techno-loathing at the gramophone. He alludes to the instrument dozens and dozens of times in his writings, and always with revulsion. In 1934, Orwell even composes a horrible poem, "On a Ruined Farm Near the His Master's Voice Gramophone Factory," blaming gramophones for the demise of farming. The gramophone keeps popping up all the way through his 1939 novel, *Coming Up for Air*, where the instrument symbolizes the ruin of George Bowling's beloved Lower Binfield. Time and again in other books and essays, Orwell's favorite insult for party hacks who spout canned propaganda is "the gangster gramophone." "[W]hether or not one agrees with the record that is being played at the moment," Orwell writes in the preface to *Animal Farm*, "[t]he enemy is the gramophone mind."

Films—the "synthetic pleasures manufactured for us in Hollywood"—are just as bad. Gordon Comstock, Orwell's semiautobiographical hero in *Keep the Aspidistra Flying*, "hated the pictures," "the flickering drivel on the screen," the "drug for friendless people." "Why encourage the art that is destined to replace literature?" Comstock wonders. Orwell the essayist dismisses films as "treacly rubbish;" politically speaking "they are years behind the popular press and decades behind the average book." For a period, Orwell writes film and theater criticism for *Time and Tide*; he later characterizes the film critic as one who "is expected to sell his honour for a glass of inferior sherry." One of Orwell's film reviews begins, not atypically, "This fairly amusing piece of rubbish . . ."

Radio is the worst of all. Orwell describes his own wartime BBC productions as "rubbish" and "bilge." *Coming Up for Air* has an "intolerable woman" whose only recorded sin is to have purchased a wireless set. Indeed, the shallow, superficial, materialistic, or simply hateful types in Orwell's novels all love gramophones and radio. "There are now millions of people," Orwell reflects contemptuously in *Wigan Pier*, "to whom the blaring of a radio is not only a more acceptable but a more normal background to their thoughts than the lowing of cattle or the song of birds."

For Orwell, then, the electronic media are ugly, oppressive, mind-numbing—the enemies of quiet and the wreck of civilization. He ranks them right beside gambling as "cheap palliatives" for oppressed people. He ridicules "the queer spectacle of modern electrical science showering miracles upon people with empty bellies," his two specific examples of this "electrical science" being the telegraph and radio. Radios and gramophones invariably figure on Orwell's frequent lists of things the modern world would be better off without, alongside bombers, tanks, syphilis, and the Secret Police.

And just how bad might the machines become? For a man who loves privacy and solitude as much as Orwell does, the answer is obvious. "The most hateful of all names in an English ear," Orwell announces in "England, Your England," is "Nosey Parker." The key to English liberty is "the *privateness* of English life," the "liberty to have a home of your own, to do what you like in your spare time, to choose your own amusements instead of having them chosen for you from above." For Orwell, then, the end of freedom will be the ultimate in electronic Nosey Parkers—a machine used by Big Brother to drown out the song of birds with tinny music and to spy on the citizenry with a tinny ear and eye. It's the gangster-gramophone pushed to the limit— the phonograph, film camera, and radio transmitter rolled into one. The telescreen is the logical end of the machine age, the age of Salvador Dalí and ruined families, the age of debauched tastes, the Dneiper dam, and the latest salmon canning factory in Moscow. The telescreen is the eye in the glass. It is the brain in the bottle.

And what will it do to the human mind? It will weaken consciousness, dull curiosity, and drive people nearer to the animals. In fact, it will cleave the brain in two, and so impel humans to engage in . . .

CHAPTER 3 ■■■■■

Doublethink. Blair had been dreaming of the word, and it continued echoing through his fractured consciousness when he woke. He crawled out of bed, stumbled into the living room, and spread his exercise mat out on the floor in front of the telescreen.

"Thirty-to-forty group," bellowed a grating woman's voice on the screen. Blair stood up wearily. The torn underpants and ragged pullover in which he slept chafed his arms and thighs as he flung his fists out and back over his shoulders. The woman began lunging left and right in the next exercise, her sinews snapping back and forth under her skin. Blair followed, his spine cracking loudly at every turn. How could this be doing him or the Party any good? He desperately tried to recapture his waking dream, the few fantastical moments before consciousness, when he was oblivious to the bedsprings poking into his back, the rough wool of the blanket, and the cold draft from the window.

What was it? ("Lean to your right, further, now left . . .") He had been in an enormous building, brightly lit and warm, had been wandering in a kaleidoscope of colors and smells, aromas he could not describe or recognize, objects whose purpose he did not understand. He ran his fingers along in the air like the fins of a fish, waving them as he swam, touching the things around him with feather-light contact, the way a fish might brush an anemone. He had a feeling of tremendous safety. Then a woman had spoken, and her voice had been the most beautiful thing he had ever heard.

He strained his neck around at the order of the telescreen, failing miserably to touch his chin to his shoulder. His pulse throbbed uncomfortably in his neck.

"Stretch a little further, think of our soldiers at the front, get your head *right* round, again, again," the instructress shouted. There had been something extraordinary about the woman who had bent over him in his dream. He seemed to know the feel and smell of her skin as well as he knew his own. He floated along behind her; then the beloved voice had come again.

The woman on the screen was bellowing something about straighter knees. Was it a memory of some time past? He had no conscious memories of childhood; he only knew from his school training that it had been a period of "social reconstruction," when corrupting influences had been stamped out and the glorious dicta of Big Brother introduced. What was it about the dream that was so warm and comforting, even now, as he clung to the last shreds of it? It was something about the voice, its intimate, direct quality. And with a sudden wave of warmth in his chest and stomach he understood what he had loved so much about it. The voice had been meant for him, only for him—him alone, in all creation.

His thoughts switched abruptly to the Ministry of Love. Surrounded by barbed wire, steel doors, and towers, the Ministry was guarded by dogs and gorilla-faced guards with bulging jacket pockets and jointed truncheons. This was where all the telescreen wires converged. They passed through giant tunnels just above the sewers, and were routed into the three thousand basement rooms of the Ministry. There were said to be great bundles of multi-colored wires, twisted and braided like the cables of a suspension bridge. From the basement, individual wires peeled off from the cables and terminated on towering frames, like millions of threads leading to looms to weave enormous tapestries. Then there had to be massive switches, racks upon racks of electronics. No human ever worked with this end of the system; it would have been hopeless even to try. The machines, it was said, directed the sounds and pictures up to the higher terraces of the pyramid, up to the Thought Police.

Probably none of this was true. Many of the telescreens, Blair knew, had no wires. They were just bolted to the wall. But somehow or other they still connected with the Thought Police. From the Ministry of Love, towering, massive, central, and omnipotent, hearing all, watching all, Big Brother controlled everything.

When had he last been spoken to as a person rather than a Party instrument—he, Blair, the thin man with the bad back and the cough? He could not recall. Blair's vapid exchanges with the Wilkeses or his colleagues were mechanical, emotionless. There was no heart in conversation any more, there was no such thing as conversation. Crowds produced rhythmic chanting, feral roars of rage, wild beastlike sounds that rose uncontrollably from thousands of throats. Private communication, if it occurred at all, depended on talking by installments, on tiny snatches of conversation squeezed into any quiet space that might be found.

It was the same with music and poetry. The Party loved songs, loved the crowds roaring out "Oceania, 'tis for thee," songs in processions, songs to martial music, brassy female voices squalling patriotic songs from the telescreens. But the lyrics came straight from the electronic versificators, composed without any human intervention at all. The words were often clever, gnomic, or sententious, but even at their best they were always graceful monuments to the obvious. They helped you to remember, but what you remembered was always trite. Party verse supplied ready-made thought, vulgar thought vigorously expressed. No individual Party member ever sang alone, just for the joy of it. The Party likewise churned out reams of official books and papers and records, but if individuals wrote to each other they relied on faint scribbles on lavatory walls. Every human connection had been severed, and yet the one, all-important connection to the Party was more perfect than any despot before had ever dreamed possible.

The woman on the telescreen continued her graceless movements, her muscles knotting and sliding under the loose skin. Blair now lay on the floor, breathing in the dust, his cheek off the edge of his mat on the cold linoleum. He desperately tried to do a push-up, wearing on his face the look of grim enjoyment that was considered proper during the Physical Jerks.

"Stand up!" the woman barked, her figure redolent of hockey fields and cold baths. Blair complied awkwardly, wheezing slightly. His thoughts reverted to the dim period of his early childhood. It was extraordinarily difficult. At best, you remembered bits and pieces, without context, without meaning. He knew that Airstrip One had once been called England, though London, he felt fairly certain, had always been called London. But it was impossible to say for sure. Memories faded quickly; this too was Party policy. To remember was to communicate privately with another time and place. But private communication was illegal. So no one was allowed to remember.

Except the Party—the Party remembered everything. It made records, and then it remade them at will. Blair himself did this sort of thing every day at the Ministry of Truth. The heroic Comrade Ogilvy, who had never existed in any present, would spring into existence in the past, and would then exist just as authentically, and upon the same evidence, as Charlemagne or Julius Caesar. Blair had used Ogilvy many a time to replace Winston Smith, who had once had a present but who now had no past, who had been wiped out, deleted, and erased from every record. The past was not merely altered but destroyed—*reformatted*, as they said in Newspeak. Eliminating the past eliminated one more standard of comparison—a dangerous one, since the average level of material comfort was constantly declining. It also safeguarded the infallibility of the Party. The Party always produced as much chocolate today as it had promised yesterday; the official records of yesterday's promises always confirmed it. "Who controls the past," ran the Party slogan, "controls the future: who controls the present controls the past."

As Blair lunged painfully in the direction of his toes, a brick-red shade flowed upward from his neck and congested his face with a threat of apoplexy. The sweat gleamed on his chest. Stick it out, stick it out! A healthy enthusiasm for physical fitness always stood you in good stead with the Party. Blair had gone through these contortions for years, every morning the same senseless sacrifice to the exacting god behind the screen. Now the instructress was staring right at him. She always did, Blair thought. Or at least she always managed to make him feel that way. Somehow, the telescreens, or the people behind them, knew exactly where to find you.

"Stand easy!" said the woman, a little more genially. Blair sank his arms to his sides and refilled his lungs with air.

"And now let's see which of us can touch our toes!" bellowed the woman. "Right over from the hips, please, comrades. One-two! One-two! . . ." Blair loathed this exercise, which sent shooting pains all the way from his heels to his buttocks. The marvel was that they could still make him do this every morning, in the solitude of his own home, that for a decade or more it had never even seriously crossed his mind that he might avoid this nonsense and linger in bed instead. They would have learned it at once. The Party always learned, always knew.

How did they do it? The telescreens watched, but what could they possibly see? To look skeptical at the wrong moment was *face-crime*, but almost everyone had learned by long habit to look completely expressionless. This was not difficult, and even your breathing could be controlled, with an effort. True, you could not control the beating of your heart, and it was said the telescreen was quite delicate enough to pick it up. But hearts beat fast for all kinds of reasons; a shot of Victory Gin usually sent Blair's soaring just before it settled him into a deep calm.

Had Big Brother somehow learned to read the human mind, then? Could he see behind the masses of blank faces? It was known that Party functionaries were working tirelessly to penetrate the skull itself. They studied with extraordinary minuteness the meaning of facial expressions, gestures, and tones of voice, and tested the truth-producing effects of drugs, shock therapy, hypnosis, and physical torture. But everyone also knew that these bastard psychologists, inquisitors, and executioners were not real scientists. None of their projects ever went anywhere.

They never would. The Party consisted of people like Wilkes, the obedient drudges, the stupid and the uninquisitive. Scientific and technical progress had ceased; the empirical habit of thought could not survive in a strictly regimented society. As private communication had eroded, scientists had lost their ability to check up on each other, to record their findings and compare results. In any event, science had been abolished. The Party made the laws of nature by decree; its control over the physical world was absolute. What was commonly called "reality" was an illusion, a fraud: outside man, outside the human skull there was nothing at all. At the will of the Party a man could float off the floor like a soap bubble, ice could be heavier than water, two plus two could make five. Being omnipotent, the Party had no need for science.

And yet . . . and yet, somehow they watched, somehow they knew. In a world with no memory, the Party remembered all; in a society with no records, the Ministry of Truth churned out records in endless supply; in a city with no directories, where it was impossible even to discover where anyone lived except by personal inquiry, Big Brother always knew exactly where you were. Big Brother was able to inspire only abstract, undirected emotion, love or hatred, anger or jealousy, which could be switched almost randomly from one object to another like a plumber's blow-flame; but when the Thought Police came after you they found you, found you alone, and destroyed you with quick, perfectly directed efficiency. In a city of no real human contact, no links, no loyalties, no reliable connections of any kind, the Party maintained perfect connections with everyone, everywhere, all the time. It was as if the laws of physics and engineering had succumbed to *doublethink*, the Party's vast system of mental cheating.

The hot sweat had broken out all over Blair's body. His face remained completely inscrutable. He stood watching while the instructress raised her arms above her head and—one could not say gracefully, but with remarkable neatness and efficiency—bent over and tucked the first joint of her fingers under her toes.

"There, comrades! That's how I want to see you doing it. Watch me again. I'm thirty-nine and I've had four children. Now look." She bent over again. "You see my knees aren't bent. You can all do it if you want to," she said as she straightened herself up. "That's better, comrade, that's much better," she added encouragingly as Blair, with a violent lunge, succeeded in touching his toes with knees unbent, for the first time in several years.

■ ■ ■ ■ ■ THE MINISTRY

For all its remarkable powers, the telescreen is really impressive at only one point in all of *1984*. While Winston Smith is doing his morning exercises, his mind begins to wander. It doesn't get very far:

> "Smith!" screamed the shrewish voice from the telescreen. "6079 Smith W! Yes, you! Bend lower, please. You can do better than that. You're not trying. Lower, please! That's better, comrade."

This is indeed unsettling. Smith, among tens of thousands of Londoners aged thirty-something, is apparently being watched personally by Jane Fonda.

She is watching from the Ministry. The Ministry of Truth is responsible for all books, periodicals, pamphlets, posters, leaflets, films, soundtracks, cartoons, photographs, telescreen broadcasts, and so on. The other telescreen Ministry—"the really frightening one"—is the Ministry of Love, headquarters of the Thought Police.

Miniluv, as it is called, towers over central London, "vast and white above the grimy landscape, . . . [an] enormous pyramidal structure of glittering white concrete, soaring up, terrace after terrace, three hundred meters into the air." It contains "three thousand rooms above ground level and corresponding ramifications below." The Ministry of Truth occupies an identical building next door. Every broadcast, every news report, film, and documentary, emanates from one government building, and every return signal, from every telescreen in every lavatory, living room, and public square, returns to another. The terror of the telescreen isn't the message or the newfangled two-way medium; the real terror is the Ministry. The word itself—"Ministry"—gets 75 mentions in *1984*.

Orwell has been anticipating the arrival of such monoliths of centralization all his life. Take the problem of dirty crockery, for example—the problem of "cleaning out a frying-pan which has had fish in it." Orwell's little 1945 essay on the subject is lighthearted, but the self-parody is nevertheless quite unconscious: "Every time I wash up a batch of crockery I marvel at the unimaginativeness of human beings who can travel under the sea and fly through the clouds, and yet have not known how to eliminate this sordid time-wasting drudgery from their daily lives." What is to be done? The thought of private, automatic dishwashing machines never even surfaces. Orwell considers paper plates but rejects the idea in favor of something better. We must "devote as much intelligence to rationalising the interiors of our houses as we have devoted to transport and communications." Dishwashing is like communications? Anyone who has read *1984* suddenly knows what's coming next: "I see no solution except to do [the washing up] communally, like a laundry." Orwell isn't joking. He really means it: "Every morning the municipal van will stop at your door and carry off a box of dirty crocks, handing you a box of clean ones (marked with your initial, of course) in return." The problem of dirty dishes, in short, is going to be solved by . . . Yes! A Ministry of Crockery.

What holds for crockery holds even more for mass communications; Orwell has been predicting centralization here for years. The English press in 1938 is appallingly concentrated. Monopolists lurk behind such politically vital things as two-penny postcards and *Boys' Weeklies*. The film industry is "virtually a monopoly"; so are the daily papers, "and most of all," the radio. Even gramophone needles have been cornered by a conniving monopolist.

For Orwell, the centralization of powerful machines is inescapable economic destiny in the industrial age. "The processes involved in making, say, an aeroplane are so complex as to be only possible in a planned, centralised society, with all the repressive apparatus that that implies," Orwell declares in a 1945 book review. The book he is reviewing maintains that advanced machines can be reconciled with efficiency and individual freedom. Orwell doesn't believe it. For Orwell, the road to industrial efficiency leads straight to the Ministry. Immutable economic laws dictate that industrialism "must lead to some form of collectivism." Only governments can raise the "enormous sums" needed to modernize vital industries like coal mining.

For Orwell, modern weapons raise the same basic issues, albeit with more unpleasant implications, as coal mining or the greasy frying pan. As he reasons in "You and the Atom Bomb," "tanks, battleships and bombing planes are inherently tyrannical weapons, while rifles, muskets, long-bows and hand-grenades are inherently democratic weapons." Expensive, complex weapons make the strong stronger; simple ones "give claws to the weak." Regrettably, civilization is moving steadily away from private weapons toward collective ones. Nothing is more complex, more expensive, and therefore more centralizing than a nuclear bomb. Such weapons inevitably imply some monstrous, all-consuming Ministry of Peace behind.

Which leads in turn to collectivist nations, collectivist maps, a collectivist planet. The atom bomb fits perfectly with a vision of "two or three monstrous super-states . . . dividing the world between them." Little nations are to be absorbed into big ones, just as the grocer and the milkman are to be swallowed by trusts. Orwell has been saying this for years too, and when he revisits the issue in 1945, neither Hitler's recent immolation nor Stalin's imminent mummification has changed his views at all. The likeliest development is an armed peace, with power concentrated in fewer hands than ever before. The world is "heading not for general breakdown but for an epoch as horribly stable as the slave empires of antiquity." "[T]he general drift is unmistakable, and every scientific discovery of recent years has accelerated it."

The acceleration is not about to end. As Orwell knows, after radio, gramophones, and film there will come . . .

CHAPTER 4 ■■■■■

The telescreen in Blair's office had been behaving erratically for days. Three times already, to his intense irritation, Blair had lost a full morning of meticulously rewritten history. And all because the dark-haired girl from the Fiction Department had happened to walk by his cubicle one morning during the Two Minutes Hate. Blythe's leering face had filled the screen, his voice had been bleating out some new piece of treason. The girl had flushed, her chest had swelled, her arm had quivered, and then, unable to contain herself, she had begun crying out "Swine! Swine! Swine!" Before he knew it, she had picked up a Newspeak dictionary and flung it at the screen. The unit had been acting up ever since.

With a deep, unconscious sigh, Blair pulled the decrepit chair up to his desk. Every day, he thought to himself, he became more and more like a sucked orange.

He worked in the Records Department of the Ministry of Truth. The largest section of the Department consisted simply of persons whose duty it was to track down and collect all copies of books, newspapers, and other documents which had been superseded and were due for destruction. Blair had a far more delicate job, of creating new histories to replace old ones. It was never called forgery. All errors due for correction were blamed on prior tele-screen malfunction.

Blair glanced across the hall. In the corresponding cubicle on the other side a small, precise-looking, sharp-faced man named Connolly was working steadily away, with a folded newspaper on his knee. He kept his mouth as close to the screen as possible, and spoke in a low voice as though trying to keep what he was saying a secret. He looked up, and his spectacles darted a hostile flash in Blair's direction.

"Display mail," Blair said to his own screen, in a carefully mea-sured tone.

Four messages materialized on the screen, neatly arrayed by time and date, with a ten-digit source code at the top. Each was only one or two lines long. Miniplenty projections of chocolate production for this month were to be corrected, certain unpersons were to be replaced in last month's *Times* . . . routine matters, though the first would require some tedious wading through lists of figures. Blair was good at these things.

The Records Department had become much more efficient in recent years, just as Orwell had planned. A curious figure, Orwell. Blair was probably one of the few left who even remembered him any more. Some years before, Blair had worked for many months expunging Orwell's name from official Party histories, and the man was now almost completely forgotten. But Blair remembered. The act of erasing every memory of Orwell had imprinted Orwell's story indelibly on Blair's own mind. The telescreen, the network, the Ministries of Truth and Love: Orwell's brilliant mind had creat-ed them all.

For years, Orwell had been a member of the Outer Party, though often suspected of being ambivalent in his love for Big Brother. Long after his disappearance, the Party hacks had continued to build the network exactly as Orwell had planned. The speak-writes—dictation machines that converted spoken words into written text—had been manufactured precisely according to Or-well's original design, then incorporated in the telescreens them-selves. Now, everything moved through the telescreens. Orwell himself had been vaporized, of course.

In the cubicle across the way Comrade Connolly was still growling hoarsely into his screen. It was quite possible that Connolly was working on the same job as Blair. Some master brain in the Inner Party would eventually select among several independent rewrites; other drafts would be consigned to the memory holes. Orwell had invented those too. There was a hole beside every desk, a large oblong slit protected by a wire grating. The memory holes still existed in tens of thousands throughout the Ministry, not only in every room but at short intervals in every corridor. It was said they led down to giant furnaces in the basement.

"Back numbers," said Blair to his telescreen. "*Times*. One-four dash two dash nine-four. *Times*. Three dash twelve dash eight-three." After a moment's delay, the front page of the corresponding issues appeared in a window on his screen.

Blair set to work. When he had finished compiling each set of corrections, the revised document would be dispatched by telescreen to higher authority. His work would be reviewed and probably approved, the back issues of the *Times* would be systematically destroyed, and corrected copies placed on file instead. Similar processes of continuous alteration were applied to every conceivable kind of record. Day by day and almost minute by minute the past was brought up to date. After a while, it was not even forgery any more, just the substitution of one piece of nonsense for another. Garbage in, garbage out, Blair thought to himself. Somewhere or other, far away and quite anonymous, members of the Inner Party coordinated the whole effort, decreed that this fragment of the past should be preserved, that one falsified, and the next rubbed out of existence. Every time records were revised they were also brought into line with the latest edition of the Newspeak dictionary. This meant the records got a little shorter each year, as the vocabulary shrank. The deliberate denuding of the language had been going on for years.

A puzzling thing, Blair reflected, was that Newspeak had at one time been growing richer. He was quite sure of it. There had been a day when Newspeak had been even smaller than it was now, when the wonder of it all was how quickly the language was expanding. Intelligent people had taken pride in mastering its latest subtleties, and had shown off the breadth of their Newspeak vocabulary. Newspeak hadn't been quite the rich, mellifluous Oldspeak that the proles still used, but it hadn't had the vapid emptiness of modern Newspeak either. The language had been clipped, precise, but also powerfully expressive. Now, Newspeak was just a foolish affectation, simple to the point of being dysfunctional. Like everything else controlled by the Party, Newspeak had been overtaken by decay.

Blair was an hour into his work when the technician arrived to replace his screen. Burgess was a slow, flabby, dark man with eyes like black buttons set wide apart in his face. His skin had a greasy sheen, like the cuticle of an insect. He reminded Blair of one of the shiny black beetles that he had seen patrolling the areas of waste ground, moving with predictable, dull progress across the stones. For years Burgess had toiled as a petty engineer, going back and forth along the halls with a stack of manuals in hand. He had so distinguished himself by unfailing devotion to duty, lack of inquisitiveness, and absence of imagination, that he had finally been promoted to work on the screens, as an Assistant Sub-Deputy System Agent. This meant he was allowed to help carry replacement screens around the Ministry. Now, his mettle proved by years of acting as a porter, he had been promoted to the rank of Deputy System Agent.

Connolly, small and suspicious, and Burgess, ponderous and loyal: the Party belonged to men like these. The machines, it was said, made such men possible, even necessary. Ever since Orwell's day, the Party had promised machines and more machines—machines to save work, machines to save thought, machines to save pain, machines for hygiene, efficiency, organization, more hygiene, more efficiency, more organization, more machines. And where did it all end? In a paradise of little fat men.

In the Party's day-dreams, of course, the little fat men were neither fat nor little; they were men like gods. But in a world from which physical danger had been largely banished the men like gods had turned out to be men like beetles. Technological progress had eliminated danger, and physical courage had not survived. There was no need for physical strength in a world where there was never the need for physical labor. Loyalty and generosity were irrelevant—almost unimaginable—in a world where nothing went wrong. The mechanized world had grown safe and soft, and the men in it had found it impossible to remain brave and hard. Mechanical progress had produced a foolproof world—which had turned out to mean a world inhabited by fools. The Party had tied itself to electronic efficiency, and so tied men to the ideal of softness. But softness was repulsive. The Party had reduced man to a kind of walking stomach, without hand, or eye, or brain. Men had ceased to use their hands, and had lopped off a huge chunk of their consciousness.

Burgess gave Blair a stupid, malignant glance, then beckoned brusquely to two of his five assistants. He waved Blair out of the cubicle, and the team squeezed in. Three other assistants were unwrapping the new screen in the hall. Burgess carried the blue box.

The screen was about the size of an unfolded newspaper, an oversized dull mirror about five centimeters thick. The men lifted it nervously into Blair's cubicle. A minute or two later they had unbolted the old screen, and mounted the new one in its place. There were no wires to attach, not even a power cord. One of the managers peeled a sheet of sticky paper from the front surface. Another few minutes passed, then the screen flickered into life. Almost immediately, an announcer's fruity voice could be heard. It appeared there had been demonstrations to thank Big Brother for raising the chocolate ration to twenty grams a week. Only a month ago, Blair seemed to recall, the ration had been thirty grams.

Burgess elbowed his way to the screen, and shoved his assistants out of the cubicle. He propped two thick instructional binders on Blair's desk. He opened the first with meticulous care, and stared at it intently for several minutes. Then, glancing at the manual every few seconds, he positioned the blue box in front of the screen. The man obviously had no idea what he was doing, and was terrified of missing some crucial step.

With agonizing slowness he pressed one and then another of the dozen or so buttons mounted on the front of the blue box. The box emitted a series of atonal whistles as each button was pressed. Burgess paused to turn a page in the binder; then the whistling resumed. Abruptly, the fruity voice clicked off. On the screen there appeared instead a view of the Laseprint room fourteen stories below.

"All set, comrade," said Burgess, his face gleaming with sweat. He was quite genial now, obviously relieved to have made it through the installation without a hitch. "Good to be back in touch again, eh, Blair?"

"Capital, capital!" Blair replied, with a weak grin. One always sought to convey a certain vapid eagerness when speaking to a member of the Outer Party. Burgess was an idiot, Blair thought behind his smile. An absolute idiot, venomously orthodox, typical of the types who controlled everything of any importance these days. The man had without exception the most stupid, vulgar, empty mind that Blair had ever encountered. He had not a thought in his head that was not a slogan, and there was no imbecility, absolutely none, that he was not capable of swallowing if the Party handed it out to him. "The human sound track" Blair nicknamed him in his own mind.

It was always the Burgess types who got promoted. People like Burgess and Connolly, across the hall. The smart ones, the ones with any spark of real technical skill, got vaporized. Bernal, for example. Bernal and his Hush-a-Screen.

Blair glanced back at his rival. Something seemed to tell him with certainty that Connolly was busy on the same job as himself. Connolly obviously suspected the same. He was doing his utmost not to let his voice carry, addressing his screen in a sort of hoarse whisper. But that never worked; the screen then picked up stray sounds from other cubicles. It was in fact a constant problem in the long, windowless hall, with the double row of cubicles and the ceaseless background drone of voices. Sometimes the noise level got so high your screen recorded complete gibberish.

Bernal, Blair reflected bitterly, had solved the problem, and had been immediately vaporized for doing so. It was appalling! Bernal, the closest thing to a friend Blair had ever had at the office, Bernal with his mocking eyes, with his irrepressible interest in the technicalities of everything—vaporized, because he had lacked discretion and the saving stupidity needed to survive within the Party.

He had arrived in the office one day hugely pleased, and announced that he had the solution to the whole problem. It was a sort of rigid plastic tent—Bernal had even built a prototype—that fitted neatly over the rim of the telescreen, creating a small zone of quiet. The "Hush-a-Screen," he had called it. Bernal had vanished soon after. A morning came, and he was missing from work. Despite himself, Bernal had ended up a perfect member of the Party. Orthodoxy was unconsciousness.

And short of death itself, the best orthodoxy of all was a belligerent, anti-intellectual stupidity, of the kind that Burgess had been born with. Small wonder that all the useful arts in the world were either standing still or going backward. The Party dimly understood that it still needed the telescreens, still needed science for war and police espionage, and so tolerated empirical approaches in these two areas. The Party's managers all ended up like Burgess anyway.

Blair felt a sense of helplessness take hold of him. *If there is hope*, Smith had written in the diary, *it lies in the proles*. But there was no hope. A prole's loyalty extended only as far as a prole could see, and for only as long as he could remember. Their market was just a rubbish heap of detail, tiny things that would stay forever tiny. A prole saw no further than the stalls in the marketplace, and remembered nothing bigger than razor blades. A prole was like an ant, which can see small objects but not large ones, simply another species of insect. Only Big Brother was an eagle. He alone saw everything.

This, Blair thought in despair, was the Party's real triumph. There were electronic files but no records, telescreens but no human contacts. Everything was connected, the past with the present, the people with Big Brother, yet all the connections ended in the empty basement of a single, huge Ministry. There were no humans anywhere, only insects, the machine, and the Ministry.

As Blair settled back in his chair, he took a last look at Connolly across the hall. The little men who scuttled so nimbly through the labyrinthine corridors of Ministries were never vaporized. One of these days, thought Blair with sudden deep conviction, Connolly will be a System Manager.

■■■■■ THE ENEMY

So for Orwell, hypercentralized Ministries are economically inevitable, and nothing will slip more naturally into their adhesive hands than radios, gramophones, films, and the combination of them all, the telescreen. With that, *1984* falls into place.

One can indeed watch Orwell's thoughts about telescreen totalitarianism evolve in other writings he publishes while *1984* is crystallizing in his mind. Those thoughts take shape most clearly in Orwell's pre-*1984* dialogue with another writer and political theorist of his day, James Burnham. The rest of the world has largely forgotten Burnham, but it has not forgotten Orwell. The principal reason is Orwell's telescreen.

In his "Second Thoughts on James Burnham," published in 1946, Orwell agrees with Burnham on many major points. "Capitalism is disappearing, but socialism is not replacing it," Orwell writes. Coming instead is "a new kind of planned, centralised society" ruled by an oligarchy of "business executives, technicians, bureaucrats, and soldiers." Small nations will coalesce into "great super-states grouped round the main industrial centers in Europe, Asia, and America." "Internally, each society will be hierarchical, with an aristocracy of talent at the top and a mass of semi-slaves at the bottom." This is Orwell summarizing Burnham, but it is also Burnham summarizing Orwell.

For almost a decade before Burnham, in *Wigan Pier*, *Coming Up for Air*, and countless earlier essays, Orwell has been making identical predictions—and in better prose than Burnham's.

In his "Second Thoughts" essay, Orwell accepts Burnham's thesis that "a planned and centralised society is liable to develop into an oligarchy or a dictatorship." Indeed, Burnham's conclusions on this point "are difficult to resist. . . . The ever-increasing concentration of industrial and financial power; the diminishing importance of the individual capitalist or shareholder, and the growth of the new 'managerial' class of scientists, technicians, and bureaucrats . . . all these things seem to point in the same direction." The many details of Burnham's prewar predictions that have *not* been fulfilled (Hitler's inevitable triumph, for example) "do not disprove Burnham's theory."

And yet, at the end of his essay on Burnham, Orwell declares that Burnham is fundamentally mistaken after all. The most astonishing thing about this pronouncement is its timing. The essay is published in 1946. Orwell is just beginning to write *1984*, the novel that will persuade millions of readers that Burnham's geopolitical vision is correct. But when he reviews Burnham head on, Orwell concludes that Burnham has missed the one critical point. Which one? "[T]he 'managers' are not so invincible as Burnham believes," says Orwell. Burnham has ignored "the advantages, military as well as social, enjoyed by a democratic country." "[O]ne should have been able to see from the start that such a movement as Nazism could not produce any good or stable result. . . . [C]ertain rules of conduct have to be observed if human society is to hold together at all."

This is a perfectly sensible criticism of Burnham; the one remarkable thing about it is that it comes from *Orwell's* pen, a pen that is about to write *1984*, a pen that has been writing exactly the same kind of thing as Burnham for a long time. Only a few years earlier, Orwell had reviewed Bertrand Russell's *Power: A New Social Analysis*. In that book, Russell argues that tyrannies eventually collapse because they depend on lies. "[W]e cannot be sure that this is so," Orwell replies. "It is quite easy to imagine a state in which the ruling caste deceive their followers without deceiving themselves. . . . One has only to think of the sinister possibilities of the radio, state-controlled education and so forth."

Does Orwell then agree with Russell, that tyranny is self-destructive, or with Burnham, that tyranny is durable and strong? In 1940, when he reviews Russell, Orwell is with Burnham. In 1946, when he reviews Burnham, he is with Russell. In 1948, when he finishes *1984*, he is with Burnham once again. What's going on? The answer is "the radio . . . and so forth." The answer is the telescreen.

In 1946, Orwell is (temporarily) sure that Burnham is wrong. As a responsible critic, Orwell takes pains to explain why. Burnham has relied on Machiavelli, but Machiavelli's theories, valid enough when "methods of production were primitive," are now obsolete. World politics have been transformed. By what? By "the arrival of the machine." Industrialism has made human drudgery "technically avoidable." "In effect," says Orwell, "Burnham argues that because a society of free and equal human beings has never existed, it never can exist. By the same argument one could have demonstrated the impossibility of aeroplanes in 1900, or of motor cars in 1850." Burnham's key mistake has been to misunderstand the political implications of new technology.

And having written that, Orwell puts Burnham to one side and sets to work on *1984*. As he writes, Orwell finds himself thinking again about just where it was that Burnham went wrong. He thinks about machines—Orwell is *always* thinking about machines. And then it hits him: Burnham's geopolitical prophecies are right after all! The Orwell of the 1930s, who anticipated all of Burnham's ideas by years, was right too. Superstate totalitarianism is coming again. Burnham didn't correctly understand why; he blamed it all on the Machiavellian instincts of the ruling oligarchy. But Orwell now grasps the real reason. Big Brother is coming because of the advent of a new machine. He is coming by telescreen.

And indeed, Orwell has being saying *that* for years, too. Perhaps he reaches back into his files to refresh his memory. To his 1940 review of Bertrand Russell, the one pointing to "the sinister possibilities" of radio and so forth. Or to another book review Orwell published in 1936. "You can't ignore Hitler, Mussolini, unemployment, aeroplanes and the radio," Orwell had written then. Or to another review he published in 1939: "The Inquisition failed, but then the Inquisition had not the resources of the modern state. The radio, press-censorship, standardised education and the secret police have altered everything. . . .

Mass-suggestion is a science of the last twenty years, and we do not yet know how successful it will be." Or perhaps Orwell remembers his wartime broadcasts for the BBC, and pulls from the shelf his "Imaginary Interview with Jonathan Swift":

> GEORGE ORWELL: Since your day something has appeared called totalitarianism.
> JONATHAN SWIFT: A new thing?
> ORWELL: It isn't strictly new, it's merely been made practicable owing to modern weapons and modern methods of communication.

There it is again: *modern methods of communication*. The new telemedia are what give modern totalitarianism an altogether new power, never before seen or even imagined. *1984* is not just a rewrite of Burnham, or a variation on H. G. Wells' *The Sleeper Awakes*, Jack London's *The Iron Heel*, Zamyatin's *We*, Aldous Huxley's *Brave New World*, Arthur Koestler's *Darkness at Noon*, or E. M. Forster's "The Machine Stops," all of which Orwell has read and written about many times. Like the others, *1984* is a book about power. But what is politically new about Orwell's book—radically, brilliantly new—is the combined power of oligarchy and the communicating machine. In *1984*, Big Brother speaks to everyone, and Winston Smith speaks to no one. Public propaganda is everywhere; private discourse is nowhere. It's the same with memory: the Ministry stores, collects, and rewrites everything; the private individual forgets, and forgets again. The Thought Police know every private thought; private thought itself ceases to exist. All of this hinges on the technology of telecommunications.

And what's most chilling about *1984* is that it seems so plausible. The Ministry installs all telescreens, and the telescreens project Big Brother's face and voice, his eyes and ears, the Ministry incarnate. In fact, "[n]obody has ever seen Big Brother in the flesh. He is a face on the hoardings, a voice on the telescreen." Yes, that's it: Big Brother is sense, sound, and image inside the electronic machine itself. He is the Brain in the Bottle. *The machine itself is the enemy*.

Except that that's impossible. Even the most evil of machines require evil men behind them.

CHAPTER 5 ■■■■■

The lifts worked, silently and fast. White-jacketed servants still hurried about on the softly carpeted passages in the building. The smells were of good food and good tobacco, as they had always been. But the cream-papered walls with white wainscotting, once exquisitely clean, were now beginning to show the grime of long contact with human bodies. The dark-blue carpet, rich as velvet, was now distinctly frayed.

O'Brien sat alone in the room, by a table under a green-shaded lamp. The telescreen was dimmed to a murmur. He had once been a monstrous man, with a mane of greasy gray hair. His face, pouched and seamed, coarse, humorous, and brutal, had suggested a certain charm of manner. The charm was gone now. Nothing remained but the size and brutality.

O'Brien stretched a great, flabby arm over the desk, and picked up a memorandum. Idiots, he thought, they were all idiots and incompetents, every last one of them. He was surrounded by fools. It went to show what happened when you left things to others. The helicopters, the telescreens . . . now a pathetic little diary—they bungled everything.

It had been different in the old days. O'Brien remembered how he had personally taken charge of breaking Winston Smith. Smith

59

had confessed, recanted, and learned to love Big Brother. The business had been handled with dispatch. O'Brien had particularly enjoyed the hanging afterward. The Party had abolished the drop, of course. People were hanged by simply hauling them up and letting them kick and struggle. Smith had taken almost fifteen minutes to die. The Party was good at this sort of thing.

Yet now—now O'Brien's own Thought Police couldn't even find Smith's diary. Agitators and traitors were probably paging through it at this very moment. It was outrageous, a fundamental threat to Party hegemony. The Party had taught this from the very beginning: *Every citizen shall be kept for twenty-four hours a day in the sound of official propaganda, with all other channels of communication closed.* Yet despite all the Party's efforts, other channels of communication remained open.

O'Brien thought of Smith again. It had been an amusing case. After breaking and releasing him, O'Brien had ordered Smith rearrested some months later. It was proved at the trial that Smith had engaged in fresh conspiracies from the very moment of his release. The execution had been performed in Victory Square, as a warning to posterity. But somehow, through an unfortunate mix-up, Smith's diary had escaped the memory holes.

Worse still was the problem of the telescreens. That no one knew how to fix a broken unit was manageable. The Eastasian prisoners were perfectly capable of producing new ones as fast as the old ones broke down. But now the entire system seemed to be acting up. Perhaps the network was just aging, but it was impossible to say for sure. Orwell would have known, but Orwell had been purged years ago. And if the network failed, what then? At stake was the Party's second cardinal principle of control: *Every citizen worth watching shall be kept for twenty-four hours a day under the eyes of the police.*

O'Brien stared wearily at the enormous map spread out on the table in front of him. For several minutes his formidable, intelligent face hung motionless and baleful above the desk; then at last he leaned back in his chair again.

The map had always reminded him of the old underground subway. Many of the wires ran through the train tunnels. Years ago,

O'Brien had even climbed down a long access ladder for a quick inspection. He had seen the orange cables suspended like rubber vines from hangers along the walls. Orwell had said a word or two about the enormous capacity of the system, but O'Brien had not cared to linger underground. The tunnels were home to millions of rats.

The network consisted of several dozen rings and serpentine lines, wandering aimlessly across London, each marked on the map in a different color. There were two or three larger central rings, circling from Kensington to Liverpool Street, and some peripheral ones around Harrow in the west, and Woodford in the east. Across these straggled the other lines, from Morden to High-Barnet, from Hounslow to Cockfosters, from Watford to the East-End, from Waterloo Road across the river to Tower Hill, from the center of the city eastward to Pennyfields, and from Wapping to Whitechapel. Two major rings intersected at the Embankment not far from Waterloo Bridge. The network was densely interlinked in the heart of the city; out toward the suburbs it grew progressively thinner.

O'Brien knew he'd never be down in the tunnels again. He was too old for that now. It didn't bother him—he had lived well. A Party member from the beginning, he had survived the great purges and then risen to consume the best food, the best wine, the best women. His one pleasure now lay in Party affairs. The decay of his own body was tolerable. What was not tolerable was the decay of the Party itself.

O'Brien had known—had known instinctively—that the new design of the network was a mistake. The old network had consisted of simple lines connected to simple screens. Dumb terminals, the engineers had called them; idiot boxes. Just as they should be, O'Brien had always thought. The screens had attached directly to the wires, simple copper things, easy to understand, easy to fix, easy to replace. And the wires had led directly to where wires were supposed to lead. O'Brien remembered how he had admired a map of the old system years ago, the million capillaries connected directly to a single, massive brain in the Ministry of Truth, a single, undauntable Heart in the Ministry of Love. Not at all like the tangled mess on the map in front of him now. The old network had been a formal garden of classicism. The new was a wild romantic jungle, full of stupendous beauty, and also of morasses and sickly weeds.

He had been the last to agree to the conversion, O'Brien recalled with bitter satisfaction. The Ministry of Peace had led the charge, terrified that a single well-placed rocket bomb might bring down the whole network. Then the Ministry of Plenty had weighed in: it could no longer ensure supplies of electric power on which the old network had depended. Then the Ministry of Truth: it had demanded a system powerful enough to reach every room, to revise every record, to overwhelm every other form of communication.

But it had been O'Brien's own Thought Police who had finally persuaded him. It had been Orwell, in fact, the master architect of it all. Orwell had explained the logic of the new design, explained it patiently, and then explained it again. The old system was overloaded. It hadn't been designed to handle the cataract of information that would flow from the offices and homes and public squares, and course through the tunnels to the Ministries. Only the new design could carry the load.

And so, against his better judgment, O'Brien had capitulated. The old wires had been ripped out, vast bundles of them, tons and tons of useless copper, replaced by a few dozen of the new, orange-rubber rings. The basements of the Ministry of Love, like the main tunnels, now seemed cavernously empty. A new generation of telescreens had been deployed all over London. And for a decade, O'Brien had to admit, the system had performed just as Orwell had promised. The telescreens had worked. *Every citizen shall be kept for twenty-four hours a day under the eyes of the Thought Police and in the sound of official propaganda, with all other channels of communication closed.* Orwell had promised it would be so. Orwell had delivered.

Yet O'Brien still sometimes wondered: Did the Party really need telescreens? He remembered how he had caught Winston Smith, caught him the old-fashioned way, without all the gadgets. O'Brien had done what he always did—he had inspired trust and invited confidence. The likes of Smith needed to confide, to expose their souls even at the peril of their lives. Enemies of the Party were always like that. They couldn't trust Big Brother, so they put their trust in other men. All you had to do was offer a sympathetic ear, a flash of understanding, a suggestion of intimacy, some small hint that you were an ally and friend. At first O'Brien hadn't even known whether Smith was angling to join the Inner Party or the traitorous brotherhood. So he had waited, listened, and in the end Smith had told him. It was almost too funny to believe. O'Brien had gently persuaded Smith to write his seditious diary for O'Brien's own personal enlightenment.

No telescreen could ever have achieved that. People feared the telescreens, avoided them, obeyed them—but never willingly confided in them. Even if some poor fool had tried to confess to a telescreen, he would have been disappointed. The overwhelming odds were that no one would even have turned up to arrest him. People were of course encouraged to believe that the Thought Police watched everybody all the time, but that was obviously impossible—there were far too many people to watch. Fortunately, maintaining the illusion served almost as well. At random intervals during the Physical Jerks, for example, the Ministry would broadcast something that sounded terribly personal. "Smith!" the announcer would scream. "Yes you, Smith! Shape up there!" Every Smith in London would assume they meant him and every Baker and Jones would suppose his turn would come next. It worked, O'Brien grudgingly admitted to himself. So long as people believed they were being watched they behaved accordingly.

And if Big Brother couldn't watch everybody all the time, the telescreen did at least allow everybody to watch Big Brother. The Ministry of Truth used the telescreens to anesthetize people with prurience and cheap violence, to keep them believing that they lived lives like those on the telescreens, and that life had never been so good. It was a queer spectacle, O'Brien reflected, this modern electrical science, showering miracles upon people with empty bellies. The proles might shiver all night for lack of bedclothes, but in the morning they could gaze at news transmitted from San Francisco or São Paulo. Twenty million people were underfed, but literally everyone had access to a telescreen. What they had lost in food they had gained in electricity. Whole sections of the working class who had been plundered of all they really needed were being compensated by cheap luxuries which mitigated the surface of life. It was a very satisfactory arrangement. Telescreens were efficient palliatives for a half-starved people.

Day and night the machines bruised their ears and gripped their eyes. The people lost their ability to concentrate, to pursue any train of thought, to articulate anything for themselves. They were never alone, never out of the sound of music or Party propaganda. The music—it was always the same music for everybody—was the most important ingredient. Its function was to prevent thought and conversation, and to shut out any natural sound, such as the song of birds or the whistling of the wind, that might otherwise intrude. The telescreens were never turned off; they played all through meals, and people talked just loudly enough for the voices and the music to cancel out. The music prevented the conversation from becoming serious or even coherent, while the chatter of voices stopped one from listening attentively to the music and thus prevented the onset of that dreaded thing, thought. That was the aim—to narrow the range of human consciousness. The peoples' interests, their points of attachment to the physical world and the day-to-day struggle, had to be as few as possible.

Like it or not, O'Brien reflected, the telescreens were essential. Orwell's design had worked well—still did for the most part. As promised, the network was now entirely self-powered. And for years it had seemed quite reliable. Orwell had in fact rambled on and on about this. The system was "robust," Orwell had said, it was "fault tolerant," it operated "peer-to-peer." No single screen, no single cable, could bring down the whole network if it failed. It had all been meaningless jargon to O'Brien, but jargon draped in the one kind of authority—scientific—that O'Brien had never dared contradict. O'Brien had hated it.

He had hated even more the thought of ripping out the old system he had spent so many years building. O'Brien looked back at the map on the table, and he knew *that* was what he hated most of all. There was no order to it. The cables snaked independently around the city, intersecting almost at random, it seemed. The map reminded him of one of those hideous bubble-like structures from the 1960s, the geodesic domes, every rib connected to every other, a shapeless globule with no central spine, no omniscient brain. The map was an abomination. On the map, the Ministry of Love seemed almost irrelevant. It was not the center of anything.

And now, with Orwell purged, with the old-guard engineers dead or lost in forced labor camps, and the few who had survived too terrified to think, with the Ministry's Laboratories in complete decay, the network was beginning to act up. Screens were failing in unusually high numbers. Not simply dying, but behaving erratically. Suppose things got worse. Suppose the screens went completely out of control. Without telescreens, the Party was finished.

O'Brien resettled his monstrous body in the chair. He wondered idly when it was that he had grown so fat. It seemed to have happened suddenly, as if a cannon ball had hit him and got stuck inside. One night he had gone to bed still feeling more or less young, with an eye for the girls and so forth, and the next morning he had woken up in the full consciousness that he was hugely fat. He was proud of his fatness now—he saw the accumulated flesh as the symbol of his greatness. He who had once been obscure and hungry was now fat, rich, and feared. He was swollen with the bodies of his enemies, a thought from which he extracted something very near poetry.

But he was also old, and he knew he would soon be dead. He felt a numb weariness creeping up from his feet toward his knees. This happened every few days now. Some day, he knew, it would keep on creeping until it reached his chest. Until then, he had one great mission left—to save the Party. He had already convened the right people. He had spoken to Cooper. A competent System Manager of unquestioned loyalty would be found to investigate and correct the problems in the network.

For perhaps twenty seconds O'Brien sat without stirring. Then he pulled his chair over to the telescreen and barked out a message in the hybrid jargon of the Ministries:

COMM-ONE-OPEN. Items one comma five comma seven approved fullwise stop. Transmit. Item six doubleplus ridiculous verging crimethink stop. Delete. COMM-ONE-CLOSE. COMM-TWO-CLOSE.

The telescreen faded into darkness.

■■■■■ DOUBLETHINK

The machine itself is the enemy. But whose? For Orwell, the answer is obvious. The telescreen empowers evil men in the Inner Party, like O'Brien and Charrington, and enslaves decent people in the Outer Party, like Winston and Julia. The telescreen is a two-way device *but with one-way control*. The ordinary lovers whisper and wait, helpless innocents who will inevitably be discovered and destroyed. The Thought Police watch and listen, evil brains behind the glass eye of the bottle.

There are two obvious objections to all this, however. Orwell has thought through the first with some care. It is the objection Bertrand Russell set out in *Power: A New Social Analysis*. Tyrannies, according to Russell, depend on a "huge system of organised lying," which "tends to put them at a disadvantage as against those who know the facts." To put it in *1984* terms, tyrannies can't build telescreens. The second objection is more important. Telescreens will not abide tyranny.

Start with Russell's objection. How can a state in which "two and two will make five when the Leader says so" maintain such technically complex things as telescreens? Orwell has asked himself that question many times. His review of Russell's book includes a capsule summary of his answer. In *1984* terms, the answer is *doublethink*. It is "quite easy to imagine a state in which the ruling caste deceive their followers without deceiving themselves." "Do you suppose it is beyond us to produce a dual system of astronomy?" O'Brien asks Winston Smith in *1984.* "The stars can be near or distant, according as we need them," O'Brien himself replies. "Do you suppose our mathematicians are unequal to that? Have you forgotten doublethink?"

Now this requires a bit of a mental stretch, but it's not completely implausible. Perhaps Orwell is right: tyrannies might conceivably develop technologies as advanced as telescreens. This would require rigid isolation of a privileged and comparatively free community of scientists and engineers. Still, one can imagine that happening, particularly after *Sputnik.*

But will telescreens abide tyranny? Orwell addresses only one small part of that question seriously. Even with doublethink, science inside a totalitarian state is not going to advance as it will in liberal societies. Freedom will thus develop more powerful weapons and in time will overwhelm Slavery from the outside. Or will it? Long before *1984,* Orwell had developed his answer. It appears, among several other places, in his 1943 essay, "Looking Back on the Spanish Civil War."

Orwell's answer is quite simple: "Fascism, or possibly even a combination of several fascisms, [will] conquer the whole world" simultaneously. Thereafter, the need to preserve military efficiency and defend against faster scientific advance in more liberal societies will no longer exist. This is what has happened in *1984.* Oceania is indistinguishable from the world's two other totalitarian superstates, Eurasia and Eastasia. The political cultures of the three superstates have different names: Ingsoc (English Socialism), neo-Bolshevism, and Eastasia's "Obliteration of the Self." But "the three philosophies are barely distinguishable, and the social systems which they support are not distinguishable at all." The result is perfect balance: the three superstates "prop one another up, like three sheaves of corn." Science atrophies, but it atrophies everywhere at the same rate, so military balance is maintained.

Orwell thus seems to have covered his intellectual flanks. With doublethink, even tyrannies can develop telescreens. With sheaves-of-corn geopolitics, military stability can be maintained thereafter. Everything hangs together. Totalitarianism, once established worldwide, endures forever. The birth of the telescreen is the death of free speech.

Which—if you think about it for just a second more—is still a very curious thing. After all, the telescreen—like the radio, gramophone, and the film camera it supersedes—is a medium of expression. It is the newfangled printing press, just vastly more powerful than the old. It is the supernova among far dimmer stars in what Marshall McLuhan called *The Gutenberg Galaxy*. And what do we find? The development of a fantastically capable new printing press means the end of literature, the end of art, the end of intellectual freedom, the end of thought itself. And *that*, all in all, is hard to swallow.

■

Part of Orwell's pessimism about the telescreen derives from the medium itself. "[T]he English are not gifted artistically," Orwell confidently declares in "England, Your England." "They are not as musical as the Germans or Italians, painting and sculpture have never flourished in England as they have in France." But "there is one art in which they have shown plenty of talent, namely literature." In sum, pictures, sounds—all media other than the written word—are not really British. This quaint (and, for all I know, correct) cultural reductionism has obvious implications for a man who plans to take on the telescreen. Telescreens in the office for the convenience of insect men? Certainly. Telescreens for Wagnerian music or semipornographic Botticelli nudes? No doubt. But telescreens, being picture machines, obviously have nothing to add to the artistic freedom of England.

That's basically what Orwell concludes, but Orwell himself knows better. Pictures and art, even English art, belong together. Again and again in his books and essays he uses the simile of the glass walls of an aquarium to illustrate problems of separation and communication. "Good prose is like a window pane," Orwell writes in a 1946 piece. "When one reads any strongly individual piece of writing, one has the impression of seeing a face somewhere behind the page," he says in his brilliant 1939 essay on Charles Dickens. Seeing the picture, seeing the face—the images are all important for Orwell and his writing. The first, most horrifying propaganda scene in *1984* is a film clip in which helicopters are machine-gunning a woman and child in a lifeboat. "If you want a picture of the future," O'Brien offers at the end of the book, "imagine a boot stamping on a human face—forever." At the end of *1984*, as at the beginning, it is the *picture* that tells it all.

Indeed, a complete one-line answer to Orwell's disdain for the artistic and expressive value of telescreens is set out in Orwell's own classic essay, "Politics and the English Language." Orwell is explaining the art of good writing. He is emphasizing how important it is not to rush things down onto paper, especially in a day when language is dilapidated and stock clichés often substitute for hard thought. "When you think of something abstract," Orwell explains, "you are more inclined to use words from the start, and unless you make a conscious effort to prevent it, the existing dialect will come rushing in and do the job for you, at the expense of blurring or even changing your meaning. Probably it is better to put off using words as long as possible and get one's meaning as clear as one can through pictures." Yes, *pictures*.

But there is no other sign Orwell ever imagined that picture machines might empower the artist, liberate the press, and expand intellectual freedom all around. Orwell never does manage to grasp the connection between his own vivid word-pictures and the picture-words of the telescreen.

◼

For Orwell, the other thing irredeemably wrong with the picture-machine is that it's a *machine*. Try as he may—and he *does* try—Orwell simply cannot persuade himself that machines will ever enhance personal freedom.

In one part of his brain, Orwell understands perfectly that science, technology, and empirical thought are the very antithesis of oligarchy, collectivism, and Big Brother. In a 1943 essay, for example, Orwell—the man with his own pet theory about "English art"—scorns Nazi distinctions between "German Science" and "Jewish Science." Science, Orwell recognizes, is one of the great enemies of totalitarian government, the most potent antidote to systematic lying. He says this explicitly in several early essays and repeats it in *1984*. In *1984*, the word "science" has been completely abolished, "any meaning that it could possibly bear being already sufficiently covered by the word Ingsoc."

Orwell is equally certain that machines are essential to reduce human drudgery and raise standards of living. Indeed, "human equality cannot be realised except at a high level of mechanical civilisation." He thinks it a great shortcoming of capitalism that free markets develop only those machines that are commercially valuable; he is sure that "the rate of mechanical progress will be much more rapid once Socialism is established." In *1984*, as in earlier essays, Orwell assures us that minimum standards of decent living are now "technically possible" for all, because machines have made them possible. Orwell firmly believes that a certain level of machine-supplied plenty would be a blessing.

He is equally fascinated by other good things that machines might accomplish. Though a writer himself, he scorns "hostility to science and machinery" that stems from "the jealousy of the modern literary gent who hates science because science has stolen literature's thunder." As a BBC broadcaster, Orwell commissions a series of talks that include "Science and the People" and "Science and Politics"; one of the first speakers is a specialist on the newfangled technology of television. "The Western man invents machines as naturally as the Polynesian islander swims," Orwell writes in *Wigan Pier*. "Give a Western man a job of work and he immediately begins devising a machine that would do it for him; give him a machine and he thinks of ways of improving it. I understand this tendency well enough, for in an ineffectual sort of way I have that type of mind myself. . . . I am perpetually seeing, as it were, the ghosts of possible machines that might save me the trouble of using my brain or muscles."

Orwell, far better than most of his contemporaries, has brilliant insight as to what those ghosts might some day accomplish. At a technical rather than a political or sociological level, Orwell is tremendously prescient about technology. His *1984* telescreen is a practical reality today, already widely used for teleconferencing. Orwell's "speakwrites"—machines that transcribe the spoken word into electronic text—are now being perfected. These things are familiar to us, but Orwell described them all when primitive, one-way television was the high-tech marvel of the day. All of the technological props and gadgets that Orwell describes were in fact made possible by the transistor. Yet the transistor was discovered at Bell Laboratories only in 1947, the year Orwell completed his first draft of *1984*.

When he gets beyond describing the capabilities of his ghosts, however, and tries to anticipate how new machines will transform art, politics, and society, Orwell sinks back into visceral pessimism. In all his writings I have found only four, halfhearted attempts in which Orwell looks to the brighter side of what he calls "modern electrical science." Orwell *does* try—he's too honest a man not to—but he just doesn't get very far.

Consider two letters Orwell writes while working at the BBC. He is commissioning a talk on microfilm, which he thinks may "have very important effects." How? Microfilm just might prevent "libraries from being destroyed by bombs or by the police of totalitarian regimes." Microfilm, after all, makes huge amounts of text portable and easy to replicate. Thus, it both improves memory and facilitates communication. Push the logic just a bit further, and you find that civilization's defense against bombs and the Thought Police is . . . the telescreen! But Orwell doesn't push it.

Then there's an unpublished essay that Orwell wrote in 1940, titled "New Words." Words are invented, Orwell argues, on the basis of common experience. That experience is usually visual. Primitive man gestured and cried out; eventually the cry came to substitute for the gesture. First the thought must be given an objective existence; only then can it be given a name. But for many things—dreams, for example, and other complex emotions—the first step is very difficult. "The thing that suggests itself immediately," says Orwell, "is the cinematograph." "A millionaire with a private cinematograph, all the necessary props and a troupe of intelligent actors could, if he wished, make practically all of his inner life known." Perhaps this is just idle speculation on Orwell's part, but one can hardly ignore it, coming as it does from a man whose greatest writings concern the shrinkage of vocabulary and the dilapidation of language. In fact, push the logic of "New Words" a little further and you find that the answer to Newspeak is . . . the telescreen! But Orwell doesn't push it.

How about radio's power to carry culture across class and national boundaries? Once or twice, Orwell is grudgingly optimistic about this too. Radio programs "are necessarily the same for everybody," films "have to appeal to a public of millions," and these new media thus tend to erode class differences. National differences too. "I believe this is the most truthful war that has been fought in modern times," Orwell writes in a 1941 essay. "[T]he radio, especially in countries where listening-in to foreign broadcasts is not forbidden, is making large-scale lying more and more difficult." A law forbidding people to listen to foreign stations "will never be enforceable." And in 1946 Orwell is pleased to report that "after years of struggle" the BBC has agreed "to set aside one wave-length for intelligent programmes." "[T]here are in the BBC, mostly in its lower ranks, many gifted people who realise that the possibilities of radio have not yet been explored."

Perhaps so, but Orwell doesn't explore them either. And elsewhere he scoffs at "shallowly optimistic" books announcing "the abolition of distance" and "the disappearance of frontiers":

> It is nonsense to say that the radio puts people in touch with foreign countries. If anything, it does the opposite. No ordinary person ever listens in to a foreign radio; but if in any country large numbers of people show signs of doing so, the government prevents it either by ferocious penalties, or by confiscating short-wave sets, or by setting up jamming stations. The result is that each national radio is a sort of totalitarian world of its own, braying propaganda night and day to people who can listen to nothing else.

Finally, there's Orwell's hopefully titled 1945 essay, "Poetry and the Microphone." Orwell is reflecting on his wartime broadcasting work for the BBC. "[T]he formula we usually followed was to broadcast what purported to be a monthly literary magazine." On Orwell's show, the editorial staff of this magazine were sitting in their office, discussing what might go in the next number. They would read poems, essays, and so on and then discuss them. A promising start, one might think: the radio doubling as the *Times Literary Supplement*.

Orwell then turns to what he sees as the larger problem: "how to imagine the radio being used for the dissemination of anything except tripe." People have come to associate radio exclusively with "dribble," "roaring dictators," or "genteel throaty voices announcing that three of our aircraft have failed to return." But Orwell makes a big concession:

> Nevertheless one ought not to confuse the capabilities of an instrument with the use it is actually put to. Broadcasting is what it is, not because there is something inherently vulgar, silly and dishonest about the whole apparatus of microphone and transmitter, but because all the broadcasting that now happens all over the world is under the control of governments or great monopoly companies.

Well then, there's hope after all! Just cut government control and abolish the monopolies, and all will be well. Free speech will flourish through the telescreen, and despots will wither. Turn the page, however, and Orwell is certain again that the outlook is "bleak":

> Something of the same kind [i.e., monopolization] has happened to the cinema, which, like the radio, made its appearance during the monopoly stage of capitalism and is fantastically expensive to operate. In all the arts the tendency is similar. More and more the channels of production are under control of bureaucrats. . . . [T]he totalitarianization which is now going on . . . must undoubtedly continue to go on, in every country of the world.

Orwell blames all this on a huge reactionary conspiracy to "prevent the common man from becoming too intelligent" and "to destroy the artist or at least to castrate him."

Orwell makes one last effort to end "Poetry and the Microphone" on an optimistic note, but he writes without conviction. The "huge bureaucratic machines" are getting too big, he says. The modern state aims "to wipe out the freedom of the intellect" but needs intellectuals to do so; it needs "pamphlet-writers, poster artists, illustrators, broadcasters, lecturers, film producers, actors, song composers, even painters and sculptors, not to mention psychologists, sociologists, biochemists, mathematicians and what-not," to run its propaganda machines. And "the bigger the machine of government becomes, the more loose ends and forgotten corners there are in it." So "in countries where there is already a strong liberal tradition, bureaucratic tyranny can perhaps never be complete."

In other words, an occasional rebel like Winston Smith may worm his way into the Ministry, and thus seditious art "will always have a tendency to appear." To be sure, it is still "harder to capture five minutes on the air in which to broadcast a poem than twelve hours in which to disseminate lying propaganda, tinned music, stale jokes, faked 'discussions' or what-have-you. But that state of affairs may alter." The best Orwell can say at the very end of "Poetry and the Microphone" is this: "The radio was bureaucratized so early in its career that the relationship between broadcasting and literature has never been thought out." "[T]hose who care for literature might turn their minds more often to this much-despised medium, whose powers for good have perhaps been obscured by the voices of Professor Joad and Doctor Goebbels."

This one halfhearted little essay is the nicest thing Orwell ever writes about radio. Yet it would have been so easy to write more. Maybe the Ministry monopolies won't be maintained. Maybe there will be more loose ends to the network than even Orwell supposes— loose ends that multiply and reproduce, with each new end creating a new electronic outlet for protest and sedition. Maybe the freedom of telescreens in private hands will overwhelm slavery maintained by a telescreened Ministry.

In fact, push Orwell's own logic just a bit further, and you find that the answer to Professor Joad and Doctor Goebbels may be . . . the telescreen itself! But Orwell never does push the logic of the telescreen quite far enough.

Which raises two questions. What if he had? And why didn't he?

▪▪▪▪▪▪ PART 2: THE MARKET

CHAPTER 6 ■■■■■

It was early evening when Blair came out of the Ministry and headed back toward the market. The day's clouds were dispersing, blown in ragged dark strands across the sky, and pale blue showed between. The wind still made him shiver in his badly made raincoat. He put his hands in his pockets and hunched his shoulders, but the evening sun shone intermittently and brightened his mood. The night before, fearful and alone in the dark, Blair had resolved to slip Smith's diary into a memory hole, and never to set foot among the proles again. By the morning he had changed his mind. As he walked, he felt absurdly cheered by the thought of a comfortable shave.

If there is hope it lies in the proles, Smith's diary declared. It was an astonishing idea. When Blair thought of the proles he thought mostly of how they smelled. Their homes, their shops, and their streets all smelled, not of dust but of coffee and cigarettes, chocolate, bacon, sweat, and sex. The sex was the most unsettling part. Blair was accustomed to the red sash of the Anti-sex league, the hygienic ugliness of Party overalls, the brisk androgyny of the Party women. The prole women had red mouths, and blue lids, and an arch manner that he found both horrifying and tantalizing. They smelled of glutinous roses, and sugary violets, which failed to conceal the heavy underlying musk of their unwashed, lavishly used bodies. Their sinuous young shapes swelled with many pregnancies and collapsed like overripe fruit, as their teeth rotted and their hair fell out, yet still they preserved the inviting manner and salacious glances of their youth.

Did they know—did the stallkeepers and the small clerks, the shop-assistants, the commercial travelers, and the tram conductors know—that they were only puppets dancing when the Party pulled the strings? If they did, they didn't care. They were too busy being born, being married, begetting, working, dying. Their lives were founded on greed and fear, but in the lives of proles, the greed and fear were mysteriously transmuted into something nobler.

Two huge women were talking outside a doorway. The one facing him wore an apron the size of a tablecloth, and her enormous bust hung down over the waistband to meet her great round abdomen. Her rough hands were planted on her hips, and she nodded her head assertively at her companion. Blair caught scraps of conversation as he approached.

"So I says to 'er: 'a promise is a promise. You come back 'ere with the flour and the eggs,' I says, 'and I'll take care of 'em jest like I said I would. You and me, we got the same problems,' I says. 'We've to look out for each other.'"

"Ah," said the other, nodding in complete understanding. "That's the truth."

He felt they looked at him with mild contempt as he passed—these confident matriarchs, contemplating him as a miserable example of the Party male.

"So if she don't bring the eggs, she won't get no cake," the woman concluded, turning back to her friend as Blair drew away.

The razor blades would be waiting for him when he arrived. That realization had gradually dawned on him during the day, and Blair was utterly certain of it now. In matters the size of razor blades, the proles knew how to remember. The proles kept their promises. Blair couldn't fathom why, but he knew with deep conviction that they did. *The proles are governed by private loyalties which they do not question,* Smith had written. *The proles are not loyal to a party or a country or an idea, they are loyal to one another.*

The words kept coming back to Blair, a mystical truth and a palpable absurdity.

The street into which Blair had turned ran downhill. From somewhere ahead there came a din of voices. He passed three men standing by a table, deep in conversation.

"Not a bad day," said one. "Not bad at all."

"'S'right," said the second. "And I've been addin' 'em up together, all of 'em over the last fourteen months. Back 'ome I got the 'ole lot for over two years wrote down on a piece of paper. I takes it down reglar as the clock."

For a moment Blair thought they must be discussing the lottery. At one time gambling had been the cheapest and most ubiquitous of the proles' luxuries. Even people on the verge of starvation had bought a few days' hope by having a penny on a sweepstake. Organized gambling had risen to the status of a major industry. But it hadn't lasted for long. The Party had rigged the system of course. It had assumed that in the absence of any real intercommunication between one part of the country and another it could simply announce that prizes had been paid even though they never were. Somehow the proles had learned about the fraud in short order, and this attempt at doublethink had failed abysmally. The proles seemed to have found other pursuits. As he walked by the men in conversation, Blair realized they must be stallkeepers too.

"We've now sold two hunner' of 'em," continued the second man. "An' I tell you, another few months like this and we can all bleedin' well retire!"

Soon the air was filled with a hubbub of similar human exchange. The passers-by were increasing in number, and instead of shuffling along, they strode firmly down the road. The mutter and clatter and shouting rose toward Blair like the bubbling of a stream. He was thrust onward with the human current, which increased and became more turbulent as they approached the main road, and with a feeling of tumbling over a cliff into the wild vortex he moved into the throbbing whirlpool of the market. The street was so crowded that you could only with difficulty thread your way down the alley between the stalls. The stuff on the stalls glowed with fine lurid colors—hacked, crimson chunks of meat;

piles of oranges and green and white broccoli; stiff, glassy-eyed rabbits; live eels looping in enamel troughs; plucked fowls hanging in rows, sticking out their breasts like guardsmen naked on parade. His spirits rose at the sight of all the activity. It was delightful—the noise, the bustle, the vitality. For a moment the sight of the street market persuaded him there was hope for England yet.

That was a curious thought, Blair reflected—hope for England, hope for Airstrip One, because the proles still dared to maintain their stalls. In the midst of all the bustle, he marveled at the civility of the place. It was deliberate Party policy to tolerate, perhaps even promote, every manner of vice and criminality among the proles. Proles were expected to be thieves and prostitutes, crack peddlers and racketeers—it was their natural condition. Yet among themselves, the proles seemed to agree quite readily who owned the cornucopia of wealth that spilled over the edges of the stalls and was often piled on the street itself.

Officially, no one owned it. Private property had been abolished long ago. Factories, mines, land, houses, transport—everything had been seized. Party histories taught that in the days of the capitalists, private property had been an obstructive nuisance. The very thought of private property was inimical to Ingsoc. Property depended on a system of reliable memory, on deeds and records, or at least recollections, to track who had cleared the land, or planted the corn, or built the oaken chest. The Party's business was to burn books—deed books along with all the others—and so obliterate private memory. Only the Party could build an oaken chest, so a carpenter who claimed it as his own must have stolen it. Private Property Is Theft, the Party taught. It was just one more piece of the Party's vast scheme to rewrite history at will.

Even if people did maintain hazy records of who had created what, "ownership" was an empty concept in the absence of loyalty, reciprocity, and a culture of mutual promises to respect tomorrow what each had accomplished today. Private promises had been abolished by the Party; they had in fact been the first thing to go. Building Societies had been denounced as a huge racket, and shut down. Private insurance had been officially labeled a swindle. A private contract of any kind represented a subversive attempt to control a private future. The future, like the present, like the past, belonged to the Party.

Blair threaded his way through the press of people, retracing his steps from the day before. A minute later he was back at the stall. He saw the razor blades at once, carefully set to one side on the top shelf. For an instant he felt a surge of affection for the stallkeeper.

Unable to suppress a smile, Blair handed over a bag containing three light bulbs. The bulbs worked; they had come from the hall outside Blair's office at the Ministry. Blair had removed them, one by one, over the space of several months. Each good bulb had been carefully replaced with a dead one. Blair took the blades and thrust them deep into the pocket of his overalls.

"Might I get some more from you when I run out?" he asked casually.

"Any time, guv. We can always get some sent down. Wiv the screens," he added amiably.

"With the screens?" Blair said blankly.

"Yeah, them telescreen gadgets. That feller comes along to turn it on, and then I tells me mate in Ipswich what I need, see, then his bruvver drives down wiv it next day. It's got the business movin' nicely." The stall owner glanced back at the pillar and grinned. "Don't exactly know the feller's name. Some calls 'im 'Fronky.' Others call 'im the phreak. But 'e's an exceptional bloke orl right. One day 'e jes arrives, and next thing we know, 'e's doing amazin' things with them gadgets. Saved me no end of time, 'e did. I had them blades sent down for you special this morning, all the way from Ipswich."

Blair stared back at him. The proles didn't use telescreens. And even if they did, a telescreen could not deliver razor blades from Ipswich.

"Ah-h-h," said the stallkeeper, reading his look. It was a long, drawn-out sound, a sound of satisfaction with just a hint of conspiracy behind. "You'd have to be asking 'im about that now, woun' ya. I coun' begin to tell you 'ow it works, but it does. Used it last night. I says to me mate Fred, I need them blades tomorrow morning sharp—told him over the gadget, y'a see—an' I'll pay for 'em in bulbs later. And Fred sent 'em right down."

Another prole elbowed his way to the front of the stall. With a wink and grin, the stallkeeper turned away.

Blair stepped back and allowed himself to be carried along by the crowd. As he drifted down the street he saw other traders exchanging odd items just as he had done—an old hammer, a piece of cloth, things salvaged and stolen from who knew where. They received in exchange eggs, sugar, white crumbly stuff that must be cheese, and little paper packets, the contents of which he did not recognize. He went to a trestle table where the packets lay, and timidly picked one up.

"That's first class sage, the missus'd love some for 'er cooking," said the stallkeeper helpfully. "Have a sniff."

Blair opened the little flap at the top. Inside were a few brittle gray-green leaves. He put his nose to them tentatively, and was surprised by the strong aroma.

"First class," he agreed, and retreated, leaving the sage on the table. How did the proles know about things like sage? Blair was not aware that any Party canteens used it, and the food that Mrs. Wilkes cooked never smelled of anything but cabbage.

He wandered on. Some of the proles did not seem to offer anything to the stallkeepers. They exchanged a few words, and goods were handed over. As he passed the chocolate stall he saw a man open the silver wrapping of a chocolate bar and break off a small square. Blair could smell the rich, dark chocolate, and his empty stomach contracted with longing.

He reached the niche between fence and building where he had paused the other day. There was the telescreen above him. Was it really connected to Ipswich? How could the proles know anything about the telescreen when it was clearly a mystery to a trained technician like Burgess? He noticed that the screen was opaque—another one broken.

Blair turned to find the elongated, tweed-jacket-clad youth beside him, climbing up on to the fence again. The man was so thin that his shabby trousers seemed about to fall down, just suspended by his protruding hip bones. His elbows stuck out, knobbly and pale, as he lifted himself up. When he was balanced on the fence, he leaned down and took the bag. Nobody was taking any notice. The phreak was a silhouette against the yellow evening sky, perched on the fence with his arms raised and his head turned upward.

Clutching his blades, Blair headed back toward home. Out of the proles' part of town, the bustle, grime, and conversation of the market gave way to gray dust and gray people, hurrying silently past the decaying buildings. As Blair pushed through the glass doors into his building, a syrupy voice was reading out a list of figures over the telescreen.

He arrived back in his apartment and checked the drawer of his desk. Smith's diary was gone.

■■■■■ THE MARKET

No, the market in *1984* has no stalls glowing with fine lurid colors; no hacked, crimson chunks of meat; no piles of oranges; no green and white broccoli; no stiff, glassy-eyed rabbits; no live eels looping in enamel troughs; no plucked fowls sticking out their breasts like guardsmen naked on parade.

There are, admittedly, little shops: stationers' shops, junk shops, cafés, and so on. There's even a street market, which is "generally crowded and noisy." But *1984*'s market is a dismal place. The men are interested in nothing but the lottery. For millions of proles, the lottery is the principal reason for remaining alive. Where the lottery is concerned, "even people who could barely read and write seemed capable of intricate calculations and staggering feats of memory." There is "a whole tribe of men who ma[ke] a living simply by selling systems, forecasts, and lucky amulets."

And the women? Winston Smith walks down a crowded street and hears "a tremendous shout of hundreds of voices—women's voices." It is "a great formidable cry of anger and despair, a deep loud 'Oh-o-o-o-oh'" that goes "humming on like the reverberation of a bell." Smith's heart leaps. It has started! The proles are rioting, breaking loose, rising up against the Party! But no. It is only a mob of several hundred women fighting over some stallkeeper's cooking pots. "Two bloated women, one of them with her hair coming down, had got hold of the same saucepan and were trying to tear it out of one another's hands. For a moment they were both tugging, and then the handle came off."

And that's all there is to the market in *1984*—no friendly intercourse, no mutual benefit, no shared profit, nothing but covetous greed. Orwell hates it, of course. Elsewhere in *1984* he satirizes the anticapitalist Party propaganda, which portrays the shoeless poor, seven-year-old factory workers, cruel masters, servants, frock coats, and top hats. He reminds us repeatedly that *1984* is a world in which shopping means rations and vouchers, not cash and carry. In *1984*, private property has been abolished. The dollar (which has replaced the pound sterling) buys almost nothing.

This is not to say that Orwell likes the alternative. He hates the degenerate socialism of *1984*, but he hates the free market just as much. His essays and his other books are littered with criticism of markets, money, and every form of private wealth. Orwell wants people to have what they need; he just doesn't want them to work or compete or sell to get it. Orwell wants people to consume things—in moderation and in roughly equal amounts—but not to own them.

Keep the Aspidistra Flying, for example, is an unrelenting diatribe against (in Orwell's overhyphenated prose) money-stink, the money-sty, the money-god, the money-world, the money-priesthood, the money-code, money-civilization, money-business, and money-morality. In Orwell's other books we learn that Building Societies (savings and loan banks) are a "huge racket," insurance is "a swindle," a competing merchant is a "tapeworm," and the ruin of modern life is the "everlasting, frantic struggle to sell things." All private property "is an obstructive nuisance." Indeed, "the right to private property means the right to exploit and torture millions of one's fellow creatures." "Corpses" should not have the "irresponsible power" to "interfere with living people by means of idiotic wills." "I don't believe that capitalism, as against feudalism, improved the actual quality of human life," Orwell writes in a 1940 letter. "[W]e are all groaning, or at any rate ought to be groaning, under the shackles of the capitalist system," he declares in a 1946 essay. Capitalism is a "tyranny"; fascism and capitalism are in fact "Tweedledum and Tweedledee." The "nature of the relationship between a man earning £50,000 a year and one earning fifteen shillings a week" is "that the one is robbing the other."

The market robs the worker of his mental freedom too. Salvador Dalí's "diseased and disgusting" paintings, Orwell informs us, stem from the capitalist affluence of his patrons. Writers required to "tickle money out of the pockets of tired businessmen" produce nothing but "saleable drivel." The freedom of the press in Britain is "something of a fake" because "money controls opinion." In any event, the press has been ruined by the malignant influences of commercial advertising, "the dirtiest ramp that capitalism has yet produced." Thus, "[a]ny writer or journalist who wants to retain his integrity finds himself thwarted by the general drift of society, . . . the concentration of the press in the hands of a few rich men, the grip of monopoly on radio and the films." "[I]f the news is not distorted by businessmen it will be distorted by bureaucrats, who are only one degree better." Because of "centralised ownership," the "much-boasted freedom of the British press is theoretical rather than actual." The businessman, just like the bureaucrat, censors the news: "the fact that most of the press is owned by a few people operates in much the same way as a state censorship."

As Orwell sees it, the free market despises intelligence, suppresses science, and undermines free thought. England's "years of investment capital . . . produced like a belt of fat the huge blimpocracy which monopolises official and military power and has an instinctive hatred of intelligence." Free markets "slow down the process of invention and improvement, because under capitalism any invention which does not promise fairly immediate profits is neglected; some, indeed, which threaten to reduce profits are suppressed almost as ruthlessly as the flexible glass mentioned by Petronius." Only the rich "can afford to be intelligent," Gordon Comstock reflects bitterly in *Aspidistra*. "The first effect of poverty is that it kills thought."

Yes, that's it! Capitalists, like the Thought Police, kill thought. The machine is the enemy. *The free market is the enemy too.*

■

What Orwell wants instead of capitalism is "democratic socialism"— basic economic security for everyone and a reasonably high degree of economic equality. Occasionally Orwell does use "democracy" in what he terms the "narrow nineteenth-century sense of political liberty, independence of the trade unions and freedom of speech and the press." More often, however, he insists that "democracy" necessarily includes "economic justice." In his standard list of Orwellian horribles, unemployment typically lands midway between Hitler and the radio, right beside censorship or the Secret Police. In Orwell's view, no political system that tolerates sharp disparities of wealth can be called "free" or "democratic."

Laissez-faire capitalism, Orwell argues, has delivered real freedom only once, and then only for a short while, in early nineteenth-century America. That America, unlike the industrial America that was to follow, had a "wildness of spirit," "not only innocence but a sort of native gaiety, a buoyant, carefree feeling." It was the America in which "the great plains were opened up, when wealth and opportunity seemed limitless, and human beings felt free, indeed were free, as they had never been before and may not be again for centuries." Young artists did not starve, nor were they "always tethered to safe jobs," so they spent their youths "in adventurous, irresponsible, ungenteel ways." In that America, "the twin nightmares that beset nearly every modern man, the nightmare of unemployment and the nightmare of State interference, had hardly come into being."

At first these paeans to frontier America seem strange, coming as they do from Orwell's left-wing pen. But the old America Orwell admires is really quite like the new democratic-socialist England he dreams of: a land of natural, unmachined abundance, where minds are free because food, jobs, and all other basic essentials are there for the taking. Freedom cannot possibly involve commerce, banks, insurance, merchants, or private property. Freedom simply does not include traditional "economic liberty." It does, however, include what socialists always include: enough wealth in every man's pocket to cover all basic necessities and wealth spread around evenly enough to ensure social equality. Peace, freedom, flowers, happiness, and art flourish when economic times are so good that people don't have to worry about money at all. One can almost hear Orwell, who loved biblical allusions, reading the lesson from Matthew 6:28: "Behold the lilies of the field, they toil not, neither do they spin, yet even Solomon in all his glory was not arrayed like one of these."

And who will tend the lilies in Orwell's socialist garden? Well, the government, of course. The Ministry.

CHAPTER 7 ■■■■■

The door was opened silently by a small, dark-haired servant in a white jacket. A second man followed behind, with a look of vapid wonder on his face.

"Come in Burgess, come in." O'Brien's expression was grim, but he spoke the words gently. He rose deliberately from his chair and walked across the soundless carpet. His visitor clutched his hands together in uncertain embarrassment.

O'Brien moved closer, so that his solid form towered over the smaller man. The seconds marched past. Burgess was standing silently, his opaque black eyes fixed unblinkingly at a point somewhere below O'Brien's collar. The man was solid Party timber, O'Brien thought, the kind of man who got a servile pleasure from lumbering deferentially forward when something was wanted by the Party, the kind of man who would suck up whenever he had the chance to suck up, whose hatred would always turn into a sort of cringing love at the first smile. Circus dogs jumped when the trainer cracked his whip, but the really well-trained dog turned his somersault when there was no whip.

"Burgess, thank you. Thank you for coming. I have asked you to come here because—"

O'Brien paused, realizing for the first time the vagueness of his own motives. He did not in fact know what kind of help he expected from Burgess. He went on, conscious that his words must sound remarkably tentative, coming as they did from a high-ranking member of the Inner Party.

"We believe there may be some kind of conspiracy to sabotage the network. The Party would like you to investigate." O'Brien gave a faint smile.

Burgess took his cue. He spoke eagerly, saliva flicking from his lips, his fat cheeks wobbling.

"If there's anything going on, Blythe's behind it! I've said it for years: it's time for the complete and final elimination of Blytheism." This last sentence was barked out very rapidly, all in one piece, like a line of type cast solid. "And now he's after the network, eh? What we need are sterner measures against thought-criminals and saboteurs!" His head was thrown back a little, and because of the angle at which he was sitting, his spectacles caught the light and presented to O'Brien two blank discs instead of eyes. "What lessons do we learn from such treachery? The lessons . . ."

"Burgess," said O'Brien quietly. "Shut up."

A look of fear flitted across the man's face.

"The Party knows you're a good man, Burgess. This is not a test of Party loyalty." O'Brien turned back toward his chair and sat down heavily. A cough rumbled in his chest, and he suppressed it. "There really does seem to be some sort of problem with the network. We need to find out what it is. And if there is a problem, we need to fix it."

O'Brien gestured toward a chair, and Burgess sat with an air of abject deference. He carefully did not look at the delicate, polished surface of the desk. To stare covetously at such a luxurious item would be suspect in a Party member. Exactly right, thought O'Brien. The man's whole life was playing a part. Burgess understood it would be dangerous to drop his assumed personality even for a moment.

"I need first to understand a bit more about these telescreens," O'Brien continued gently. "Perhaps you can help me." He resettled his glasses on his nose, then continued. "Most telescreens are on permanently, of course. Tell me first, Burgess, how is it that members of the Inner Party are able to switch off their telescreens?"

Burgess brightened visibly. Something like eagerness moved across his face.

"Ah, that's really quite straightforward. It's in the manual, in fact. I can leave you a copy. You just approach the screen, and carefully say: 'COMM-ONE-CLOSE, COMM-TWO-CLOSE,' quite slowly and clearly, and that does it. Marvelous, really. It took me a while to get the hang of it too," he added as a confidential afterthought.

For a moment O'Brien was certain he would send Burgess straight to the cells in the basement of the Ministry. It would be worth it—worth silencing one last pedantic fool, whatever the cost. But the thought passed. The Party needed Burgess, at least for the moment.

"Yes, yes, I know about that. You'll notice that I've shut down my own unit." O'Brien gestured toward the dark screen on the wall. "I also know that 'COMM-ONE-OFFICE, COMM-TWO-HOME' connects me from here to my office in the Ministry. What I'm trying to understand is why some units work like this and others don't."

O'Brien paused again, to let the thought register. "The screens in Victory Square, for example—the ones around the monument. No one can turn those on or off. From room 101 at the Ministry, we watch the people in the square. The people in the square of course see the Big Brother channel—news from the front, that sort of thing. What is it exactly that makes those telescreens work differently from mine? Are they different units?"

"No, they're the same units," Burgess replied slowly. "We install them differently. It's all part of the installation. It's in the manual, of course. The one B.B. wrote for us."

"And how exactly do the installations differ?"

Burgess twitched, and his face drooped. "Well, it has to do with the blue box, you see. After the screen's mounted, we use the box. To get the unit started, you understand. This part's really quite complicated. But it's in the manual—all in the manual." Burgess brightened. "I could get you a copy. There aren't many, but I don't suppose we'd have much trouble locating one for someone in your position." He chuckled hoarsely.

O'Brien felt the anger rising in his throat. Again he swallowed the urge to obliterate the man at once. "That might be helpful. Yes, certainly, I'm sure it would be. But do fill me in a bit more first. My men in the Ministry—how exactly do they go about selecting which screen they're going to monitor? Suppose, for example, I was at the Ministry now, and I wanted to check up on—" O'Brien glanced down at his desk—"on comrade Blair, let us say, a chap who's been having a spot of trouble with crimethink lately. Now if I were in the Ministry at this very moment, how would I arrange to take a quick look round Blair's living room?"

Burgess looked gloomy. "It would be done with the blue box, I think. I'm really not exactly sure. It's a very specialized application."

"Then how about the offices?" O'Brien gestured again at his own telescreen. "My unit here connects up to the Ministry. I can also link up with Cooper, my personal secretary. Most people in the Ministry can connect with one or two other offices. How do you take care of that?"

"I think—" Burgess hesitated for a long moment. "I think we look after that part during the installation." He stopped again, deep in thought. "They send us the order forms, you see. There are two numbers on them—it's two most of the time at least. Then we follow the manual. That's extremely complicated. But toward the end we use the blue box and enter the two numbers. Sometimes it's more than two." He looked uneasy. "I once did a unit in the Ministry with six!" he added brightly.

O'Brien sat silently. He found himself thinking of Orwell. Orwell had sat in this same room, in the same chair now occupied by Burgess. The memory came back to O'Brien with a sort of crystalline clarity, the kind of vivid memory of things long past that he had often had of late. Orwell had been trying to persuade O'Brien to approve the new network. He'd gone on and on about the technical details. And unlike this fool Burgess, Orwell had known what he was talking about. He had loved the gadgets, loved their complexity, loved the whole network. Orwell had an inventive faculty;

he invented machines as naturally as the Polynesian islander swam. He also had a doggedly empirical habit of thought. Orwell had been a singlethinker, no doubt about it.

"These manuals that you use—" O'Brien hesitated again. "I wonder if there might be some simpler explanation of it all. Something for a nontechnical chap like me. Or do you suppose—better still—that we might locate one of the engineers who helped to write it? Someone from the '80s, perhaps?"

Burgess gazed back expressionless. "We could look. Can't say I've ever met any of the old guard. Most of them turned out to be saboteurs. Until the manuals were perfected those types did almost anything they liked with the network." He spoke with increasing vigor, and the spittle began to gather at the corners of his mouth. "Completely unreliable, most of them. Not really Party men at all. Probably Blythe . . ."

"Thank you Burgess." O'Brien spoke quietly, but his words again carried an unmistakable note of warning. Burgess froze, leaning forward on his seat, his arm stuck in mid-gesticulation.

"I know exactly what you mean," O'Brien continued. "Still, if we could find one of the old engineers, we might perhaps be able to extract something useful from him. Find out a bit more about this blue box you use, ask him how it all fits together." O'Brien resettled his weight in the chair. Burgess stared with obsequious concentration. "Perhaps you could pursue the matter. My aide at the Ministry will see to it that you are given whatever assistance you might need."

"Certainly, certainly," Burgess replied with sickly enthusiasm. "Be happy to. I'll get right to it. And whoever it is that's causing the trouble—well, I'm sure we'll catch the swine. After all, B.B. has said—"

Burgess caught O'Brien's look, and his mouth snapped shut. After only the shortest pause, O'Brien held out his hand. Burgess leapt to his feet. A moment later, he was gone.

A man of small intellect, O'Brien reflected, but tenacious, of unquestioned loyalty. He'd plod along, dig through the archives and the records, and in the end find what was needed. This kind of investigation required no real originality.

O'Brien turned back to the writing table with its green-shaded lamp and the wire baskets deep-laden with papers. His glance fell on the memorandum he had received the day before about Blair, and Winston Smith's elusive diary.

■ ■ ■ ■ ■ THE MINISTRY

O'Brien works in the Ministry of Love, which houses the Thought Police. Nearby stands the Ministry of Truth, which spews out propaganda and falsifies history. Orwell of course despises ministerial Love and Truth more than anything else, except perhaps ministerial Peace. He knows that the Ministries of Love, Truth, and Peace deliver nothing but hate, lies, and war. When it comes to the marketplace of ideas, Orwell is as laissez-faire as Adam Smith.

The Ministry of Plenty, however, is another matter. Such a ministry really could deliver Plenty—or so Orwell firmly believes, until the day he dies. Collectivism, Orwell knows, is far more efficient than the free market.

How does he know? First, the economics of "the machine" require it. As we've seen, the process of washing crockery, making an aeroplane, or building an atom bomb is "so complex as to be only possible in a planned centralised society." When a new invention threatens profits, capitalists suppress it "as ruthlessly as the flexible glass mentioned by Petronius." "Establish Socialism—remove the profit principle—and the inventor will have a free hand. The mechanisation of the world . . . could be enormously accelerated." One can almost hear Orwell add: "Indeed, by 1984 . . ."

Second, Orwell cites modern economic experience. Capitalism, Orwell observes time and again in his many writings, is "in decay," "dissolving," "disappearing," "doomed," and "dead"—and it "will not return." Businesses are collapsing into monopoly all around, and the rot of monopoly spreads year by year. "[T]he march of progress is going in the direction of always bigger and nastier trusts," Orwell writes in 1928. "The combines" have squeezed the grocer and the milkman out of existence. "[P]rivate capitalism—that is, an economic system in which land, factories, mines and transport are owned privately and operated solely for profit—does not work. It cannot deliver the goods." "There is little question now of averting a collectivist society," Orwell announces in 1940. "[A] return to small-ownership is obviously not going to happen and in fact cannot happen." "I don't believe economic liberty has much appeal any longer," he writes elsewhere. "A collectivised economy is bound to come," he announces to the world in a BBC broadcast. Indeed, by 1984 . . .

Orwell's third piece of evidence, and for a while his trump card, is—of all people—Hitler. Orwell sets out this argument for the efficiency of central planning in a strange little book published in 1941, *The Lion and the Unicorn*. Orwell loves socialism and hates fascism, but he believes—in 1941, at least—that fascism "borrows from Socialism just such features as will make it efficient." Hitler's conquest of Europe, says Orwell, "was a physical debunking of capitalism." A fascist state, like a socialist one, "can solve the problems of production and consumption. . . . The State simply calculates what goods will be needed and does its best to produce them. . . . The mere efficiency of such a system, the elimination of waste and obstruction, is obvious." This isn't sarcasm. Orwell really believes it.

"Shopkeepers at War," the second chapter of *The Lion and the Unicorn*, argues that England is certainly going to lose World War II unless it, like Hitler, embraces a form of socialism. The fields of Norway and Flanders have proved "once and for all . . . that a planned economy is stronger than a planless one." Orwell concludes this argument with the following astonishing passage:

> However horrible [fascism] may seem to us, it works. . . . British capitalism does not work. . . . Hitler will at any rate go down in history as the man who made the City of London laugh on the wrong side of its

face. . . . [T]he ghastly job of trying to convince artificially stupefied people that a planned economy might be better than a free-for-all in which the worst man wins—that job will never be quite so ghastly again.

The only trouble (for Orwell) is that a few years later it's clear that fascism doesn't work after all. Hitler goes down in history as the symbol of collectivist efficiency only in matters of mass murder, whereas the City of London survives pretty much unchanged, laughing as it always did—all the way to the bank. In a 1944 essay Orwell confesses how wrong his predictions were, most notably his "very great error" in believing that England would certainly lose the war unless it too established a collectivist economy. A year later, with the embers on Hitler's funeral pyre scarcely cool, one might have supposed that Orwell's faith in the "efficiency" of collectivism would have been shattered forever.

But it hasn't been. Orwell has not revised his basic views about collectivism, only his timetable. Britain is still "moving towards a planned economy." "[T]here will be no return to laissez-faire capitalism." Civilization will *not* "revert again towards economic chaos and individualism. Whether we like it or not, the trend is towards centralism and planning and it is more useful to try to humanise the collectivist society that is certainly coming than to pretend . . . that we could revert to a past phase." The ordinary people "have become entirely habituated to a planned, regimented sort of life" and actually "prefer it to what they had before." History hasn't unfolded as fast as Orwell expected, but it's still unfolding. "Socialism, in the sense of economic collectivism, is conquering the earth at a speed that would hardly have seemed possible sixty years ago," he writes in 1948.

And by 1984? By 1984, four huge Ministries will govern all of England.

CHAPTER 8 ■■■■■

Blair woke up to the shrill whistle of the telescreen. Groggy with sleep, still sodden in the atmosphere of a dream, he stumbled out of bed and began his Physical Jerks before he remembered.

He had not bothered to get undressed the night before. They always came for you at night, and there was no sense in trying to flee. So he had stretched out on the bed, fully dressed, and resolved to wait for them calmly. It was as though England had slid back into the Stone Age, he thought. Human types supposedly extinct for centuries—the dancing dervish, the robber chieftain, the Grand Inquisitor—had reappeared, not as inmates of lunatic asylums, but as the masters of the world. And now they were coming after him.

Quite unexpectedly, he had fallen into a deep sleep, and had dreamed vividly, as though his brain was determined to anesthetize itself against what lay ahead. He had dreamed a vast, luminous dream, in which his whole life seemed to stretch out before him like a landscape on a summer evening after rain. He was floating in space, under the glass dome of the sky. He saw his mother gesture, as if to surround him in her embrace. He was with a beautiful naked woman again, the one he had once dreamed of flogging with a truncheon. Now they were sitting together under the spreading branches of a flowering chestnut tree, and every touch was of unconditional love. He was floating in an ocean of strange, pink, convoluted coral, as delicate as a sea anemone, dividing and subdividing again, each arm joined to two others, growing ever finer and more intricate. Everything was flooded with clear, soft light in which one could see into interminable distances. Everything was connected. He was overwhelmed with a sense of perfect unity. His life had become whole.

And then he had woken. They had apparently decided not to arrest him quite yet. He wondered why, as he flapped his arms up and down in time with the bossy woman on the telescreen. It suddenly struck him that he had no reason to submit to this nonsense any more. He walked resolutely to the door of his apartment, and stepped out.

By pure instinct he turned in the direction of the Ministry. Halfway there he wondered whether he shouldn't just spend whatever time he had left in the spring air, strolling through the proles' market once again. But habit proved too strong—habit and a tiny glimmer of hope that somehow, for some convoluted reason, they had decided to leave him alone. He spent his day at work in a daze, moving mechanically from one task to the next, waiting for the inevitable. By evening they still hadn't arrived.

When he left work he turned away from the bus stop once again. He had intended at first to return to the stallkeeper and seek his help, but then changed his mind. He moved roughly southward—through the wastes of Camden Town, down Tottenham Court Road. It grew dark. He crossed Oxford Street, threaded through Covent Garden, found himself in the Strand, and crossed the river by Waterloo Bridge. With night the cold had descended.

He passed a cluster of prostitutes, shivering in their skimpy clothes. London was full of these women. Many of them, he knew, could be bought for a bottle of gin. He walked along aimlessly, inhaling the chilly air of the evening. It had been like this for several days now—warm spring afternoons, followed by near freezing nights. He thrust his hands in his pockets. After a time, he found himself in front of the junk shop he had passed twice before in search of razor blades.

It was then that he heard the girl singing from down the alley. The thin sound filled the air like the song of a bird, and brightened the drab walls of the gray street. It was a strange thing to hear singing, especially by a woman—like smelling scent. Party women never sang. It wasn't exactly forbidden; it was just unthinkable that any member of the Party would ever sing, except in unison, in crowds. This girl sang alone. The sound floated up the alley, the words belied by an incongruous note of defiance:

> *As I write this letter*
> *Send my love to you*
> *Re-mem-ber that I'll always*
> *Be in love with you.*

The girl sang the same words again, and then again, with undiminished conviction each time. Once she inserted an "Oh-oh-oh" at the end of a line.

The song obviously hadn't been composed by the versificators at the Ministry of Truth. None of the machines there would ever have included a line about writing letters; no one wrote letters any more. By a routine that was not even secret, all letters were opened in transit. For the few messages still needed, there were preprinted postcards, bearing either canned sentiments or long lists of phrases, so you could strike out the ones that were inapplicable. No one remembered anything much either, least of all love.

He saw her as she stepped out of the doorway under the street lamp just a few yards down at the end of the short alley. She was a bold-looking girl of about twenty-seven, with a wildrose face and long thick hair, the color of autumn leaves. Beneath the thin silky raincoat, belted at the waist, her youthful flanks showed supple and trim. Her freckled face was partly turned. She hadn't seen him.

For a moment Blair's gaze lingered on the shapeliness of her hips.

> *As I write this letter*
> *Send my love—*

She gave him a quick sidelong glance and stopped. Was she another one of them, Blair wondered, another prole, running another stall, with her merchandise between her legs? He couldn't quite tell, but it didn't matter. In a flash of wild inspiration, he finished the line for her.

"To me?" he said.

She tossed her head and made no reply.

"What song is that?" he asked.

"Dunno," she said. "Mum used to sing it years ago." A small smile brushed across her face. She moved up the alley toward him. Her lips were deeply reddened, her cheeks rouged, her nose powdered; there was even a touch of something under the eyes to make them brighter. It was not very skillfully done, but Blair's standards in such matters were not high. He had never seen or imagined a woman of the Party with cosmetics on her face, and the girl seemed intensely feminine. A wave of synthetic violets flooded his nostrils. He remembered the half-darkness of a basement kitchen and a woman's cavernous, toothless mouth. It was the very same scent that she had used; but at the moment he didn't care. The young woman paused, as if about to say something to him, but didn't. Then she tossed her head again, and turned back into the doorway.

Blair felt a pang of sadness. She had sung the song—perhaps she had been singing it just for him. He wondered how he might have drawn out the conversation. Was she selling her body, like so much smooth chocolate on a stall? It didn't matter, he thought again. She was a prole, she was pretty, he wanted her, and that thought alone filled him with an unexpected contentment. The Party of course taught that sex was a despicable appetite for men, a frigid duty for women. But a man who was not entirely dead inside could still feel desire and not be ashamed of it.

"Cripes, it ain't 'alf fucking cold out 'ere," said a short, powerful, jolly man with a grin as he passed. Blair walked aimlessly on down the street, thoughts of the girl's face and body filling his mind. He would not let his desire for her be dirtied by the Party. Sex was part of the human condition, and coupling was connection. In a world of unfathomable loneliness, connection of any kind was good. Proles like her still understood. A prostitute might sell what should not be sold, but it was the selling that was wrong, not the sex.

Among the proles—even among their prostitutes—men and women tangled and strove, lusted and loved, all fleeing from solitude, all searching for something larger—searching for desire certainly, but mostly searching to sate a hunger that rose from their loins to fill their hearts. It didn't matter if the freckle-faced girl was a prostitute. She was beautiful, and he wanted her, and he wanted her to want him; he wanted to see desire rising in her eyes and melting in her face; he wanted her to unfold her thighs beneath his touch and become a part of him.

Two men were standing in an alley talking loudly but amiably.

"Scrumping's what yer want," one of them said. "All them rows of turkeys in the winders, like rows of fucking soldiers with no clothes on—don't it make yer fucking mouth water to look at 'em. Bet yer a tanner I 'ave one of 'em afore tonight."

"I know where I can flog it for a keypad," the second replied.

Blair thought again of the song the girl had been singing. It struck him that a song, like an idea, like thought itself, could take on a life of its own after it had been composed. The words might change, the composer might be forgotten, the tune might be used to celebrate different things in different cultures, yet the song continued to live. It went through the ages remaining the same in itself but getting into very different company.

He had walked a long way, now, five or seven miles perhaps. His feet were swollen from the pavements. He was in a slummy quarter where the narrow, puddled streets plunged into blackness at fifty yards' distance. The few lamps, ringed in a frosty mist, hung like isolated stars illuminating nothing save themselves. He went under some echoing railway arches and up the alley on to Hungerford Bridge. On the miry water, lit by the glare of skysigns, the muck of East London was racing inland. Corks, lemons, barrel-staves, a dead dog, hunks of bread. He walked along the Embankment to Westminster. The wind made the plane trees rattle. Up Tottenham Court Road and Camden Road it was a dreary drudge. He slowed, dragging his feet a little. There was a penetrating chill in the air.

He thought of turning back, of seeking her out again. "I love you," he would say. He would say that first, before anything else. He would explain that he had committed thoughtcrime from which there could be no reprieve, that he was now already numbered among the dead, that it was only a matter of time, but that in the time he still had he needed her, he needed her desperately, he couldn't stand the thought of living for even a moment without her. But he didn't turn, he kept on walking. He lost track of the time.

Then somehow, without apparent design, Blair was back in the alley where the girl had been. It seemed he had moved in a wide circle. An icy rain had begun to fall, and a stiff wind was blowing. Before him, at the corner of the alley, he recognized the junk shop. Although it was nearly twenty-three hours the shop was still open. With the feeling that he would be less conspicuous inside than hanging about on the pavement in the rain, he stepped through the doorway.

He saw the phreak at once, in a back corner of the room, rummaging through shelves of metal boxes, discarded radios, and dusty electronics. The room was lit by a single flickering oil lamp, which gave off an unclean though friendly smell. By the dim light, Blair could see that most of the room was dominated by ragtag pieces of furniture, china, glass, picture frames. One corner contained the hardware—discarded speakwrites, some ancient computers of no conceivable value, bits and pieces of every description. The phreak was picking through them methodically.

Their eyes met again, but only for an instant. And once again, as had happened before, Blair felt sure that a message had passed, that they had a link of understanding between them, that their two minds had opened and thought had flowed from one into the other. Then the phreak turned back to the shelves. A moment later he seemed to have found what he wanted—a sort of keyboard with twelve or so flatish white buttons. The man picked them up, nodded to the proprietor, and headed for the door. And again as he passed, Blair heard, or thought he heard, him say: *We shall meet in the place where there is no darkness.*

There was nothing else of any interest in the shop. For a moment Blair toyed with a lunatic idea of renting a room somewhere in the area, and living there with the girl. Yes, he would do that! He would ask if he could join her. He would become a prole, erect an obscure stall in the market, and simply disappear from the Party rolls. For a moment the pleasure of the daydream filled his thoughts. He didn't even notice the telescreen mounted on the wall beside the shop.

A moment later they were upon him. Four or perhaps five men in black uniforms. For a moment he thought he recognized his neighbor Wilkes, his tongue protruding slightly from his mouth, grinning sadistically. But before Blair could even make a sound, he was on his knees, and the first kick landed squarely in his testicles. Vomit spewed from his mouth. He felt his ankle crack under another kick as he rolled on the pavement. A truncheon smashed into his two front teeth, and everything exploded into yellow light. Inconceivable—inconceivable that one blow could cause such pain. As he lost consciousness Blair felt himself floating back to a schoolhouse and cowering once again under the lash of a schoolmaster's cane. He badly wanted to urinate, and felt a faint surprise, because he had done so only two or three hours before.

CHAPTER 9 ▪▪▪▪▪

Gasping for breath, O'Brien shifted his bulk into the back seat of the car. He was unaccustomed to walking more than a few yards any more, and even the trip down the hall from his apartment had been a challenge. Still, he was glad to be on the move again. Another hour with the network manuals would have been unbearable.

He had left them stacked around his desk, great piles in hopeless disarray. Plowing through a dozen of them that afternoon had been the most tedious thing O'Brien had ever done. The manuals seemed to treat him like a six-year-old, with page after page of painfully detailed instruction about things either obvious or trivial. Then, when finally he arrived at something important, the explanations were completely opaque. It was Orwell—Orwell, reaching out to infuriate him even from the grave.

Fortunately, Burgess had already located one of the engineers, an original, who had worked with Orwell in the early days. The man's cooperation was assured, of course. Sooner or later, everyone cooperated with the Party.

The car moved slowly through the dilapidated streets of London. It was headed to a pub in one of the seedier parts of town. This was unpleasant, but necessary. The engineer had served time in a labor camp, and men with that kind of experience simply froze

when confronted by official authority. The beer and the casual surroundings of a pub would put him at ease. If that failed, they
could always try sterner measures.

The manuals hadn't been altogether useless. The network itself
was almost annoyingly simple. The cables ran through the tunnels,
with branches leading off into the apartments and offices. Directly
or indirectly, every point on the network was connected to every
other. One could say that the cables all connected to the Ministry
of Love, but it was equally true that they all connected to any telescreen anywhere on the network. No, they didn't quite connect.
Over the last few hundred yards to the telescreens, the signals
often traveled by radio.

Everything important apparently happened in the telescreens
themselves. Messages traveled primarily through the rubber-coated
glass cables in the tunnels, but up to a point, it seemed, telescreens could communicate directly by radio with each other.

Each telescreen had four principal layers. The front side converted sound and light into electrical signals. The back converted
electrical signals into either radio waves, to be transmitted
through the air, or intense beams of light, for transport through
glass. Ordinary light and sound went in at the front; laser light or
radio signals went out the back. It all operated in reverse too, with
incoming light or radio waves converted into pictures and sound.
The front end was both a camera and screen; the back, both a
transmitter and a receiver. All the parts functioned independently
and simultaneously.

The power and brain of the telescreen were lodged in the middle. Just below the front surface lay a battery, an inch thick, as
broad and wide as the screen itself. Charge was maintained by an
array of cells incorporated in the front surface of the screen, which
transformed light or loud sound into electricity. When fully
charged, each unit converted any additional energy it picked up
into amplified light or radio signals and shared the excess power
with other units on the network.

The third layer of each telescreen was a calculating device that
processed and stored information. It was apparently here that spoken commands were converted into machine instructions. But the

manuals said nothing about this function at all. After diligently searching for the information, O'Brien was quite sure it wasn't there. He was equally sure the omission had been deliberate.

The best hope now was with the engineer. The man had managed to survive the great purge and ended up in a camp. He had spent ten years there, and then finally had been released into the slums of London. O'Brien found himself hoping almost desperately that the engineer would understand how telescreens really operated. Surely he would. A bit of Orwell's genius must have rubbed off on his assistants.

Somehow or other, O'Brien knew, it was possible to control from where telescreen pictures were received and to where they were sent. Most telescreens just received Big Brother's standard broadcasts from the Ministry of Truth. But in the Ministry of Love there had to be a straightforward way to choose which pairs of screens were connected at any given instant. The manuals even explained how this was done, but in a completely mechanical way ("Hold blue box up to screen, press button NXX, then press button NYY . . .") that provided no insight at all into what was really going on. The telescreens in the offices, like those in the Ministry of Love, could also be set to receive information from one place (a back issue of the *Times*, say, from the Records Department) and send it to another (the same issue after revision, sent on to higher authority for review). O'Brien had even sent for one of the blue boxes, but it hadn't helped. He had stood in front of his own screen, pressing buttons at random. Nothing had happened at all.

O'Brien's car stopped in front of a low-looking pub on a corner in a side street. The windows appeared to be frosted over but in reality were merely coated with dust. He pulled himself out of the car and stepped heavily down the stairs. A sour cloud of beer seemed to hang about it. The smell revolted him. The landlady, a tall grim woman with a black fringe, looking like the madam of a brothel, stood behind the bar, her powerful forearms folded, watching a game of darts. The players were proles, with calloused dirty hands, wearing grubby overalls and heavy work boots. They stared at the darts board with casual concentration, let the darts fly in a single, deft movement, and stood back to lift their thick glass

mugs of beer to their lips once again. There was a moment's hush
as people glanced inquisitively at O'Brien. He pretended not to notice that they were staring at him.

O'Brien saw his man almost immediately—a very old man,
bent but active, with white mustaches that bristled forward like
those of a prawn. He was wearing a decent dark suit and a black
cloth cap pushed back from very white hair. O'Brien approached.
The man's face was scarlet and his eyes were blue and laughing.
He reeked of gin.

As O'Brien stood watching, it occurred to him that the old man,
who must be eighty at least, had already been middle-aged when
the network had been deployed. He and a few others like him were
the last links that now existed with the vanished world of technical
knowledge. Scientists had been wiped out almost completely in
the great purges. If there was anyone still alive who could give you
a truthful account of how the network had been built, it could
only be someone like this, someone old enough to have worked
with Orwell from the beginning.

The man was standing at the bar, having some kind of alterca-
tion with the landlady. His white-stubbled face flushed pink. The
old man turned away from the bar, muttering to himself. O'Brien
moved heavily up beside him, and touched him on the arm.

"May I offer you a drink?" he said.

"You're a gent!" said the other, straightening his shoulders.

The barlady swished two liters of dark-brown beer into thick
glasses which she had rinsed in a bucket under the counter. The
game of darts was in full swing again, and the knot of men at the
bar had begun talking about black market deals. O'Brien's presence was forgotten.

There was a free table under the window where he and the old
man could talk. O'Brien carried their drinks over to it. The glasses
were thick and cheap, thick as jam jars almost, and dim and
greasy. It crossed O'Brien's mind that this beer had been sucked
up from some beetle-ridden cellar through yards of slimy tube, and
that the glasses had never been washed in their lives, only rinsed in
beery water. O'Brien swallowed a mouthful or so and set his glass

gingerly down. It was typical London beer, sickly and yet leaving a chemical aftertaste. O'Brien thought of the wines of Burgundy.

"She could've drawed me off a pint," grumbled the old man as he settled down behind his glass. "A 'ole liter's too much. It starts my bladder running." The man reminded O'Brien of many prisoners he had dealt with over the years. Either out of fear or disease, they used the chamber-pots half a dozen times during the night.

"You must have seen great changes since you were a young man," said O'Brien tentatively.

The old man's pale blue eyes moved from the darts board to the bar, and from the bar to the door of the Gents, as though it were in the barroom that he expected the changes to have occurred.

"The beer was better," he said finally. "And cheaper!" He took up his glass. "In those days beer cost twopence a pint, and unlike the beer nowadays it had some guts in it. 'Ere's wishing you the very best of 'ealth!"

In the man's lean throat the sharp-pointed Adam's apple made a surprisingly rapid up-and-down movement, and the beer vanished. O'Brien went to the bar and came back with two more half-liters.

"You worked with Orwell, I believe. On the network."

The man seemed to stiffen a bit, and his shoulders straightened again.

"You can remember what it was like in the old days," O'Brien continued. "There aren't many like you left. Few people even understand how it was built any more. We can only read about the network in manuals, but they don't explain very much."

The old man brightened suddenly. "The manuals!" he said. "Funny you should mention 'em. The same thing come into my 'ead only yesterday, I dunno why. I was jes thinking, I ain't seen one of 'em in years. I remember Orwell working on 'em. Ever so careful with 'em he was. And that was—well, I couldn't give you the date, but it must 'a been thirty years ago."

"It isn't very important about the manuals," said O'Brien patiently. "The point is, can you tell me how the network operates? The Ministry, Members of the Party—they live like the lords of the earth. They watch whatever they like. The whole thing works for their benefit. You—the ordinary people, the workers—you're always under their eye. They can use the network to do what they like with you. They can watch you at work and at home, in your lavatories and in your bedrooms. But you can't even turn off your telescreen. You can't choose . . ."

The old man peered at O'Brien, his white eyebrows bristling up on his forehead. "Orwell could," he said insistently. "'E knew 'ow they worked. Always laughed about that one. Can't choose indeed!" The man grinned widely. "They 'ad the television. With the television, you couldn't choose. You jes listened to ol' B.B. But it weren't enough for 'em. Oh no! The people at the Ministries, they wanted more. That was the joke, see? It was the blokes at the Ministries that wanted more. And Orwell gave it to 'em. 'E found it ever so funny."

The man chuckled and took another long drink.

"And Orwell gave it to them?" O'Brien said after a moment.

"Oh, 'e gave it to 'em all right. He gave 'em the network they wanted. Everyone connected to everyone. Made the Thought Police 'appy, 'e said. 'Cos now they could watch you all the time, see. And t'other Ministry got the systems for rewriting all them papers, see, so they was 'appy too. And Orwell said, if that's what the idiots want, that's what the idiots'll get. A telescreen in every 'ome, in every office." The old man chuckled, and drank some more beer. "If that's what the idiots want, says Orwell, that's what the idiots'll get." He was laughing again—a sort of weak wheezing laugh, but the man obviously found the memory deliciously rich.

"Why was it funny for the Ministries to get what they wanted?"

"'Cos the screens really worked."

"How exactly did they work?"

The old engineer appeared to think deeply. He stroked his face with a palsied finger before answering.

"It wos done with the blue box," he said vaguely. "I recollect it as if it was yesterday. Orwell knew 'ow it worked. Quite a gent, Orwell was, though he never dressed the part. Dressed almost like a tramp, 'e did. Always pretendin' to be down and out. But he weren't, not a bit of it. Went to Eton, I don't doubt. A real gentle-man, 'e wos, and 'e knew the network. Well, I was young in them days, and I was 'appy to 'elp, only—"

A sense of helplessness took hold of O'Brien.

"Perhaps I have not made myself clear," he said. "What I'm try-ing to understand is this. How can the screens be so selective? You have been alive a very long time; you worked with Orwell on the network. Can you explain to me just how the network decides which pictures will show up where?"

The old man looked meditatively at the darts board. He finished up his beer, more slowly than before.

"Follow the manual. That's wot Orwell taught them Party mem-bers, when 'e was done. That's wot 'e told 'em. Take the blue boxes, 'e said, and follow the manual. The Party don't need noth-ing more than that."

O'Brien was about to buy some more beer when the old man suddenly got up and shuffled rapidly into the stinking urinal at the side of the room. The liter was already working on him. O'Brien sat for a minute or two gazing at his empty glass. It was no use going on. The huge and simple question—"How does a telescreen work?"—had ceased once and for all to be answerable. The few scattered survivors from the ancient world were incapable of ex-plaining it any more. They remembered a million useless things—the color of the boxes, the clothes Orwell used to wear—but all the important facts were lost.

O'Brien leaned back against the wall and felt an enveloping tiredness settle on his brain. A minute or two later the engineer was rambling on again, but O'Brien had stopped listening. It struck O'Brien for the first time that though slightly drunk, the man was filled with some deep joy that made all the other griefs of his life bearable.

O'Brien shut his eyes, and his thoughts began to drift. Dimly, as though muffled through a wall, he heard the old man repeating:

"'Cos the screens worked. 'E said so, didn't 'e? 'E said so all along. Trust the screens, 'e said."

O'Brien's thoughts began to drift. If the network still worked, it was only because Orwell, who had been dead for years, still allowed it to. The Party survived at the pleasure of a single man it had vaporized long ago.

A moment later, despite the hubbub of the surroundings, O'Brien was asleep.

CHAPTER 10 ■■■■■

Blair was dreaming. He was walking along a pitch-dark street and the air was unspeakably cold. Then through the blackness he saw a full moon that seemed so extraordinarily bright it looked like a white-hot coin in the cold night sky, its brilliance making the stars invisible. He looked up through the branches of a tree, which the moon seemed to have changed into rods of silver. The light lay thick, as though palpable, on everything, crusting the earth and the rough bark of trees like some dazzling salt, and every leaf seemed to bear a freight of solid light, like snow. He was desperately cold.

He dreamed of a golden country, where the slanting rays of the sun gilded the ground of an old pasture, and the elm trees moved faintly in the breeze, their leaves swaying in dense masses like women's hair. He saw horses, and ducks in flight at dawn, and he remembered it was forbidden to dream of such things. The cold penetrated into the deepest recesses of his unconsciousness.

He dreamed of sitting among enormous, glorious, sunlit ruins, with a woman—not doing anything, merely sitting in the sun, talking of peaceful things. He dreamed of the world as it would be when Big Brother had vanished, a world of privacy, love, and friendship, when the members of a family would stand by one another without needing to know the reason, when people would live together according to a conception of loyalty that was private and unalterable. He dreamed of a just society, a Golden Age, of things that could not be put into words, a stream of nameless things, of thoughts, images, and feelings. He had the sense of being drawn upward through enormous and gradually lightening abysses.

He was dreaming, but he was also conscious of his surroundings and the bitter cold. There was a chorus of varying sound—groans, curses, bursts of laughter, and through them all the uncontrollable chattering of teeth. He realized that all these sounds were issuing from his own mouth. And he felt a desperate longing to reach out to the woman, and to know her as well as he knew himself, to connect with her, body and soul, before he died.

After some time—several more hours, he thought—he dreamed of the sea and the seashore, and of enormous, splendid buildings or streets or ships, in which he had lost his way. He had a peculiar feeling of happiness and of waking in sunlight. He felt a sort of rich warmth creep up his limbs and reach for his brain. He dreamed that he desperately wanted to sleep.

But he didn't dare sleep. At the very back of his skull, almost in his neck, he knew that if he slept he would never awake. With a convulsive effort, he opened his throat and tried to howl. Somewhere, as if from several yards away, he heard himself groan.

A moment later, a woman was coming toward him. The gesture of her arm filled him with overpowering happiness. In a single movement she reached down toward his face and touched him, more softly, he thought, than he had ever been touched before. She drew her arm round him, and he was enveloped in the cheap scent of violets.

■■■■■ DOUBLETHINK

The free market is the enemy too. But whose? For the young Orwell, the answer is obvious: the free market is the enemy of the working man. Capitalism is Slavery. Collectivism is Freedom.

Not just economic freedom, but individual freedom too. Through the 1930s, Orwell remains confident that "democratic socialism" will not merely tolerate but actually promote art and civil liberty. Collectivism will be much more efficient than capitalism, artists will get a goodly share of the new socialist abundance, and free thought will prosper every bit as much as the economy. This is the lilies-of-the-field Orwell. This is the Orwell who in 1938, in all seriousness, can write: "The only regime which, in the long run, will dare to permit freedom of speech is a Socialist regime."

Then Hitler scorches the bloom off Orwell's socialist lily. By the beginning of World War II, Orwell has begun to appreciate that economic collectivism requires a Ministry, and that once people get used to a Ministry of Plenty they may accept Ministries of Truth, Peace, and Love too.

In his 1940 essay "Literature and Totalitarianism," Orwell takes a hard look at his lily daydreams for the first time. He is still quite sure "that the period of free capitalism is coming to an end." It's what comes next that (for Orwell) is new. Until now, Orwell admits, "[i]t was never fully realised that the disappearance of economic liberty would have any effect on intellectual liberty." Socialism "was usually thought [by Orwell] as a sort of moralised liberalism." The state was going to take charge of your economic life but wasn't going to touch your personal freedom. The arts were going to flourish far more than under liberal capitalism, because artists would no longer have to worry about money. In this 1940 essay, Orwell concedes he was probably wrong. "Now, on the existing evidence, one must admit that these ideas have been falsified."

From then on, Orwell never can quite decide how civil liberties will survive the demise of the free market, which he still hopes for, or the rise of socialism, which he still desires. "Mechanisation and a collective economy," Orwell states firmly in 1940, lead to "endless war and endless under-feeding for the sake of war, slave populations toiling behind barbed wire, women dragged shrieking to the block, cork-lined cellars where the executioner blows your brains out from behind." But only a few months later Orwell will write to his (left-wing) publisher: "You are perhaps right in thinking I am over-pessimistic. It is quite possible that freedom of thought etc. may survive in an economically totalitarian society. We can't tell until a collectivised economy has been tried out in a western country." Orwell's uncertainty about this endures for the rest of his life. In a 1945 book review he criticizes another author for mistakenly "assuming that a collectivist society would destroy human individuality." Yet in a letter written soon after *1984* is published, Orwell summarizes his book as "a show-up of the perversions to which a centralised economy is liable."

■

Orwell had doublethoughts about socialism from the beginning. *The Road to Wigan Pier*, an underrated and often misunderstood book published in 1937, sets out some of these at length. In the first half of the book, Orwell paints a chilling picture of life in the slums of a coal-mining town. In the second half, he reproaches his comrades of the left for making a religion out of machines, which threaten to transform man into "a kind of walking stomach" without hand, eye, or brain. This is a perfectly cogent argument against too many machines. It is also a cogent argument against the idle side of socialism, and in my view is plainly intended as such. Lazy men, Orwell is telling us, can come to depend on industrious neighbors quite as easily as on industrial machines. A free market forces people to work productively, which may mean killing labor in the Wigan Pier coal mines. Socialism forces people to share, which for those on the receiving end may mean brain-in-a-bottle dependency.

So, as a good socialist, Orwell believes that the race ought not be to the swift, nor the battle to the strong, neither yet bread to the wise. As an honest man, Orwell also recognizes that the problem of the swift, strong, and wise is also a problem of the slow, lazy, and foolish. It is no small irony that *Wigan Pier*, which begins with a horrifying description of the working life of a coal miner in the 1930s, ends with Orwell arguing that there is no real difference between work and play, and that hard work is fundamentally good for body and soul. Nonetheless, Orwell's early attempt in *Wigan Pier* to doublethink machine collectivism is oddly ineffectual. It is presented so elliptically that few casual readers will even grasp his point.

Animal Farm, by contrast, published after the war and just before *1984*, is perfectly clear. Overthrowing the farmer's economic tyranny is a good thing. But the hard part is to make sure that honest pigs who mastermind the revolution don't then become neo-farmers themselves. The pig who frees the other animals may end up eating them, just as the machine that liberates the coal miner may end up changing him into a walking stomach. Orwell has recognized all along that socialism tends to swallow up those it sets out to save.

Orwell's political prescriptions, once so confident, now become more and more ambivalent. An unintentionally hilarious paragraph in a 1947 essay, "The Cost of Letters," illustrates what I mean. To understand the full irony of this little piece, keep in mind that it was written while Orwell was smack in the middle of writing *1984*.

Under "full Socialism," Orwell declares, writers will be supported by the state, and should "be placed among the better-paid groups." In present circumstances, however, "the less truck a writer has with the State, or any other organised body, the better for him and his work." Why so? "There are invariably strings tied to any kind of organised patronage." But it's also "obviously undesirable" for a writer to rely on the patronage of any individual plutocrat. "By far the best and least exacting patron is the big public." That sounds suspiciously like the mass market. But unfortunately, Orwell says, the average citizen refuses to spend as much on books as on tobacco or alcohol. By way of taxes, then, the common man "could easily be made to spend more without even knowing it." The government must simply "earmark larger sums for the purchase of books." But government must of course avoid "taking over the whole book trade and turning it into a propaganda machine." In sum, the market ("the big public") is better than the alternatives. But still not good. The government (which is worse) could be better. So long as it doesn't take us to *1984*. Which it probably will.

But whether it ends well or badly, collectivism is still coming. Orwell is sure of it. The "ghosts" of the new machines that Orwell is always imagining are still dragging society straight to the economic ministry, the Ministry of Plenty. And collectivism, says Orwell, can still "be made to 'work' in an economic sense." Indeed, in 1945 Orwell calls on England's new Labour government to nationalize land, coal mines, railways, public utilities, and banks. He still ranks class privilege under English capitalism side by side with hierarchy in the Soviet Union. In the same letter in which he describes *1984* as showing "the perversion to which a centralised economy is liable," Orwell writes: "My recent novel is NOT intended as an attack on Socialism or on the British Labour Party (of which I am a supporter)."

So by this point, Orwell can only be described as thoroughly unhappy about the political options that history seems to have offered him. Capitalists are as bad as ever. The collectivists who are bound to displace them are no good either. "Bureaucrats" now rank alongside "press lords and film magnates" as "enemies of truthfulness, and hence of freedom of thought." Now the writer's freedom is threatened not only by "concentration of the press in the hands of a few rich men, [and] the grip of monopoly on radio and the films," but also by "the encroachment of official bodies" like Britain's Ministry of Information. "[T]he BBC and the film companies buy up promising young writers and geld them and set them to work like cab-horses," but totalitarian countries are killing the arts too. Capitalism "is doomed and is not worth saving anyway," but "the independent status of the artist must necessarily disappear with it."

At the end, the best hope Orwell offers on how economic collectivists might somehow avoid instituting the Thought Police is much along the lines of "Poetry and the Microphone." Maybe, somehow or other, Western civilization will muddle through. "[L]iberal capitalism is obviously coming to an end," he says in a 1941 BBC broadcast, but freedom of thought is not "inevitably doomed," at least not in the Western democracies. "I believe—it may be no more than a pious hope—that though a collectivised economy is bound to come, those countries will know how to evolve a form of Socialism which is not totalitarian, in which freedom of thought can survive the disappearance of economic individualism. That, at any rate, is the only hope to which anyone who cares for literature can cling."

In other words, Orwell piously hopes that when you hand over your purse to the Ministry of Plenty, you may still somehow avoid handing over your pen to the Ministry of Truth and your thoughts to the Ministry of Love. The Ministry of Plenty is coming in any event: the Machine requires collective management, and so does common decency, which is to say democratic socialism. The only thing Orwell now understands better—and fears more—is that when you get one Ministry, you probably get them all.

■

Does Orwell, the consummate doublethinker, have anything at all good to say about the free market? Yes, but not much.

His *Keep the Aspidistra Flying* is a diatribe against money and commerce. But what do we find at the very beginning of the book? A beautifully painted scene of a street market. It is filled with the "bellowing of street hawkers"; the place is so crowded "you could only with difficulty thread your way down the cabbage-littered alley between the stalls." There are "crimson chunks of meat, piles of oranges and green and white broccoli, stiff, glassy-eyed rabbits, live eels looping in enamel troughs," alongside "stalls of cheap art-silk undies." Gordon Comstock suddenly feels more cheerful. "Whenever you see a street-market you know that there's hope for England yet," he reflects.

Hope for England in *the market*? Has Orwell forgotten *Coming Up for Air* and his own scathing contempt for the "everlasting, frantic struggle to sell things"? Is this just some slip of a socialist writer's pen in *Aspidistra*'s otherwise unrelenting attack on "money-stink"? Apparently not. At the end of *Aspidistra*, Orwell says it again: "Our civilisation is founded on greed and fear, but in the lives of common men the greed and fear are mysteriously transmuted into something nobler." The lower classes live by the "money-code," and yet they also "contrive to keep their decency." In all his writings, this is the nicest thing Orwell ever has to say about free market economies.

Yet the man who dreamed up the ubiquitous telescreen could so easily have said more. As we've seen, he simply cannot imagine a world in which fancy gadgets like movie cameras ("cinematographs") are owned by the masses. In *1984* itself, the junk shop owner explains the absence of a telescreen on his premises with the words "too expensive." Winston Smith apparently finds this quite plausible. But if one thing is evident in *1984*, it is that telescreens are *not* expensive any more. The "too expensive" line brings to mind Lenin's boast that he would use the capitalists' gold to line the public urinals. What is "too expensive" for any private owner in *1984* has become all but costless when taken over by Big Brother. Telescreens are everywhere; communication has become instantaneous, automatic, and ubiquitous, too cheap to meter.

And what does that imply? Perhaps—perhaps in a world of cheap telecommunication—monopoly won't survive after all. Orwell has said as much himself, in a column published in 1944: "[W]hen a commodity is not scarce, no one tries to grab more than his fair share of it. No one tries to make a corner in air, for instance. The millionaire as well as the beggar is content with just so much air as he can breathe. . . . So also with any other kind of goods. If they were made plentiful, as they so easily might be, there is no reason to think that the supposed acquisitive instincts of the human being could not be bred out in a couple of generations."

Yes, surely that's it! Substitute "airwaves" for "air" here, and you are describing a telescreened society in which JunkNet is the private network for dealers in curios and antiques, and "Dr. Goebbels" is a situation comedy aired Wednesday nights on Fox Television. The mental frontiers of the cheap telescreen will be like nineteenth-century America, filled with a wildness of spirit. Young minds will be able to wander; there will be a sort of native gaiety, a buoyant, carefree feeling; there will be room for everybody. The telescreen will do for the mind what the prairie did for the body: give people room, and easy affluence too, and with those, a real sense of being free.

■

But Orwell never did push the logic of the telescreen quite far enough. And the question still is: Why not? Why didn't Orwell ever imagine that the freedom of telescreens in private hands might overwhelm even the slavery of a telescreened Ministry? Or, to put the same question another way: Where is the missing chapter in *1984*?

Because one chapter *is* indisputably missing.

With the machine and the Ministry firmly in place, the political logic of *1984* is simple. The proles' ignorance of their own exploitation permits the ruling oligarchy to remain in power. Thus, IGNORANCE IS STRENGTH. To prevent education from gradually dispelling proletarian ignorance, the Party must maintain poverty, and that is done by waging ceaseless, wealth-devouring war. And so, WAR IS PEACE.

Ignorance isn't really strength, however, nor is war really peace. So Orwell also supplies a picture of what strength and peace might be. The proles' strength lies in their private loyalties and their procreative persistence. Sooner or later their "strength [will] change into consciousness," and they will "blow the Party to pieces." *Real* strength, then, is proletarian consciousness. And *real* peace is simply peace. There is no economic reason for war any more; natural resources are plentiful, and slave labor can be replaced by machines.

But how about FREEDOM IS SLAVERY, the third slogan of the Party? *That's* the missing chapter. Orwell never does get around to supplying us with a positive vision of freedom. Blythe's book—the book-within-a-book in the middle of *1984*—supposedly contains one, but Winston Smith is arrested before he gets to read it. Winston's love affair with Julia is not Freedom either; it's just a daydream of sex, coffee, and chocolate, lived by two lost souls who are still collecting their paychecks from the Ministry of Truth. The prison scenes in Part 3 of *1984* add nothing more. We are told how Slavery is Freedom within the twisted, collectivist logic of the Party. But we learn nothing more about what real freedom might be.

Where then is Orwell's missing chapter? If Freedom isn't really Slavery, what is it?

■■■■■■ PART 3: FREEDOM

CHAPTER 11 ■■■■■

"'Cos the screens worked. 'E said so, didn't 'e?" Now, five months later, the memory of the old engineer's words had slipped back into O'Brien's thoughts.

It was a sweltering summer afternoon, and the air-conditioning had failed in his office. He was at his desk again, the map of the network spread out before him. Beads of sweat rolled off his chin on to the paper, smearing the colored lines where they fell.

London had been transformed. Once subdued and secretive, the stallkeepers now openly touted their goods everywhere but in the immediate vicinity of the Ministries. Where there had been only the stamp and shuffle of feet, and surreptitious whispers in between telescreens, the noise of the market now filled the streets. The shelves were piled high with scarves and colored bolts of cloth, soaps and scents stacked in profusion, chocolate, coffee. Even O'Brien had found himself marveling at the abundance. The most remarkable thing was that no one would accept the Party's dollars and ration books any more; the proles seemed to have created their own private currencies. Somehow they maintained private accounts, an elaborate set of intersecting books to track each other's debts and credits. O'Brien couldn't imagine how it was all coordinated.

The network was behaving worse than ever. Was it sabotage? Was some technical wizard working his way across London, vandalizing thousands of telescreens? O'Brien felt a spasm of fear in his entrails. Perhaps the man had even found some electronic fuse to the whole thing, which when lit would cause a complete collapse of communication. Without warning, the screens would go dark all across London. The network would die. Big Brother would be left blind, deaf, and mute. There would be a great uprising. It would be over in an instant.

There came a soft knock at the door.

"Come in, come in," growled O'Brien.

Burgess entered, as oily and shiny as ever. His shirt showed two large damp patches at the armpits. He gave a kind of awkward bob in greeting, and made his way across the room.

"Well?" said O'Brien.

"They found it last March, but no one told me! Not a word! A thought criminal from the Ministry of Truth . . . it was in his apartment." The words gushed out. "When I finally got hold of it I handed it to the technical types at the Ministry, of course. They did nothing with it for all this time!" Burgess was white with anxiety. "So then I took a look myself. Didn't really read it of course. I saw at once that it was treason, so I didn't really read it." He looked at O'Brien fearfully.

"I take it this is about the network," O'Brien said acidly.

Burgess had obviously finished his prepared speech and was now at a loss for words. Breathing heavily, he undid the straps of his briefcase. He pulled out a slim black volume and almost dropped it on the desk in front of O'Brien. "It does say things about telescreens," Burgess replied at last.

O'Brien opened the book to the first page. The words were written in pen, in clumsy letters. His eyes skimmed down the page. Toward the bottom, the letters grew bolder, and the handwriting was no longer cramped or awkward. Printed in large, neat capitals were the words:

DOWN WITH BIG BROTHER DOWN WITH BIG BROTHER
DOWN WITH BIG BROTHER DOWN WITH BIG BROTHER
DOWN WITH BIG BROTHER

O'Brien looked up at Burgess.

"Get out."

Burgess scuttled to the door.

For a moment O'Brien's eyes wandered around the room. He was alone, he was safe, the telescreen was off. Yet for some reason he was possessed by a nervous impulse to glance over his shoulder and cover the page with his hand. The room was stifling, but for an instant there seemed to be a chill in the air. He leafed forward into the book. On the third page he came across a bold title, and began to read:

THE THEORY AND PRACTICE OF NETWORKED INDIVIDUALISM

1. Ignorance Is Strength

Among all the Party's lies there is one great truth: Strength in numbers. To survive a war a nation must be united. Patriotism—blind patriotism—is the single most important source of national power. As a positive force there is nothing to set beside it. What is critical is emotional unity. . . .

Suddenly, as one sometimes does with a book of which one knows that one will ultimately read and reread every word, O'Brien opened it at a different place and found himself in a new section. He went on reading:

3. War Is Peace

If the enemy had not fired the rocket bombs at London we would have fired them at ourselves. War is essential to destroy the products of human labor. By destroying goods we maintain poverty. By maintaining poverty we prevent education. By preventing education we preserve the Party's control. Because of the war all records must be centralized under a unified command. The consciousness of being at war, and therefore in danger, makes the handing over of all power to a small caste seem the natural, unavoidable condition of survival. By keeping our subjects at war, we ensure they will never rise up against us. WAR IS PEACE.

The Party recognizes that other things being equal in war, the side with the better arms will win. We consequently cannot ignore external reality in ways that impair military efficiency. In philosophy, religion, ethics, or politics, two and two might make five, but when one is designing a rocket or a bomb they have to make four. So the Party maintains communities of scientists, who must continuously develop various devices connected with warfare—better explosives, stronger armor, new and deadlier gases and disease germs, or a device for focusing the sun's rays through lenses suspended thousands of kilometers away in space. Yet all this is only idle daydreaming; the art of war is not in fact advancing at all.

It doesn't have to. Oceania, Eurasia, and Eastasia are evenly matched in their military incompetence. They prop one another up, like three sheaves of corn. The ceaseless wars they fight are mostly frauds, waged on vague frontiers in the third world. They involve very small numbers of people, mostly highly trained specialists, and cause comparatively few casualties. The wars swallow up prosperity, but aside from that they are just an illusion, like all else in the age of doublethink.

To maintain the illusion, we must rigidly maintain our cultural integrity. The average citizen of Oceania never sets eyes on a foreigner, never even learns a foreign language. If it were otherwise, he might discover that foreigners were not so very different, nor so very much to be feared or hated. War would then end. Cut off from contact with the outer world, and with the past, the citizen of Oceania is like a man in interstellar space, who has no way of knowing which direction is up and which is down.

Or that, at least, is the Party line; that is the teaching of English Socialism, INGSOC. But none of INGSOC is true. It is war that is coming to an end, because technical progress is now continuous. War will soon be abolished. The telescreen will abolish it.

O'Brien stopped reading for a moment. He was sure that he had already read what was coming next. A small band of brave partisans would storm the Ministry of Love and seize control of the network.

There would be a bloody struggle. It was all rubbish, of course. The Ministry was impregnable. He turned back to the book.

The telescreen abolishes cultural integrity. It erases interstellar space. Culture can now cross frontiers a million times faster than a rocket bomb. Not just cultural garbage, not just films oozing sex and violence—these things are not important, and in any event are the same in every country. The culture that will now pour across national boundaries is the culture of commerce. With the telescreen, trade can reach anywhere.

The economic motives for war will also disappear. The Party maintains that war still makes sense to win control of cheap labor. But in a world where value consists mostly of information, labor can move instantly across frontiers. The age of the telescreen is the age of the nowhere man, in a nowhere land, pouring value into nowhere plans that can be conveyed anywhere to anybody. Armed with a telescreen the human mind can escape faster than any soldier can pursue. Linking peoples and nations by telescreen offers far better prizes than taking away other peoples' provinces or lands, or grinding them down in exploitation.

Suppose the Party manages to start a real war anyway. Neither side will dare use atom bombs, weapons conceived in the image of the Party itself, sweeping, gross, and indiscriminate. How then will the war be fought? Nations are not in fact sheaves of corn, and anyone able to use his eyes knows that human behavior differs enormously from country to country. Sooner or later we will confront an enemy that has not only mastered but maintained the art of communicating at a distance. That enemy's telescreened rocket bombs will rain down upon us with an accuracy never before imagined. They will land with relentless precision on our four Ministries. Perhaps, in an excess of zeal, the enemy will also decide to knock out our principal bridges and highways, our central bank, and even our electric power plants and reserves of fuel.

Then the war will be over, and we will have lost. Without its communication system, without its electronic eyes and ears and tongue,

the Party ceases to be an enemy of any account. The next war will indeed involve only small numbers of people, mostly highly trained
specialists. But the casualties will not occur out of sight, on distant
frontiers. Our dead will lie buried in the rubble of our Ministries.

Only one kind of society can survive such an attack: a society with
no central brain, no all-powerful Ministry in the heart of its capital
city, no single place where all the wisdom of the state can be lost in
an instant to a bomb addressed as precisely as a postcard. The only
society that can survive the telescreened bomb is one in which people rule themselves.

This, then, is how the last war will be fought, if it is fought at all.
Not against individuals, nor against their possessions. It will be
fought against what coordinates a nation—against its ideas, its slogans, its propaganda, the instruments of its Thought Police, and the
machines of its centralized Ministries. War will be Satyagraha, a
nonviolent struggle by which the enemy is defeated without being
hurt. The word used to be translated as "passive resistance," but
what it really means is "firmness in the truth." For the first time in
history, war will be fought against the state itself, against what
unites a people. If all that unites a people is Big Brother, war will be
fought against Big Brother alone.

O'Brien shut his eyes again. He had grown unaccustomed to
reading a book of any length. For the first time in years he experi-
enced an unpleasant feeling of solitude. He had always lived in
comfort and safety, always enjoyed the luxury of complete privacy,
which was reserved only to the highest-ranking members of the
Inner Party. And yet now, unexpectedly, silence seemed oppressive. He found himself wishing for a gentle touch against his cheek
and the sound of children laughing at their play.

CHAPTER 12 ■■■■■

The preparations for Love Week were unfolding all around. Processions, meetings, lectures, telescreen programs—all had to be organized. The Fiction Department of the Ministry of Truth was rushing out a series of pamphlets on the victimization of the weak. A new poster had suddenly appeared all over London. It had no caption and represented simply a group of cowering women and children ("oppressed peoples," the Party called them), staring in terror at a monstrous male figure, three or four meters high, striding forward with an expressionless white face and enormous boots, a submachine gun pointed from his hip. Encylopedias had to be rewritten. Airplanes and radio, the Ministry had recently discovered, had been invented not by the Party (as had previously been recorded) but by the ancient Hindus, who afterward dropped them as being unworthy of their attention.

None of this mattered to Blair any more. He was in a new world, a world he had never known before. He was extravagantly happy. When he walked with Kate in the country, they fell into absurd enthusiasms over everything they saw: over a jay's feather that they picked up, blue as lapis lazuli; over a stagnant pool like a jet mirror, with boughs reflected deep down in it; over the fungi that sprouted from the trees like monstrous horizontal ears.

For many days after the beating, he had lain half conscious on a mattress in the corner of her room. He dimly remembered other men coming and going, their silhouettes and coarse grunts drifting in and out of his fractured dreams. Then at last he'd been able to stagger to his feet.

The next morning she had made him a cup of coffee—richly perfumed, market coffee—and had mentioned quite casually that she'd grown tired of the streets.

"If you wants to stay for a bit, I can put you up," she added. "Why'd you get done over, anyway?"

"Thoughtcrime," Blair answered solemnly.

"Yeah, but whacha do?"

He pondered. He had read a few pages of Smith's diary, of course. Why they had left him alive in the street he could not explain.

Perched on a wooden stool opposite him, she accepted his silence as an answer. Her steaming mug was cradled in both hands, her hair in glorious bright disarray, her lacy petticoats showing under a long flowered skirt. She wore less makeup now, though vestiges of black liner shadowed her lids. Her skin was milky white and translucent.

And that night, it was hard to say by whose act, he had been in her arms. At the beginning he had no feeling except sheer incredulity. The youthful body was strained against his own, the mass of tumbled red hair was against his face, and yes! actually she had turned her face up and he was kissing the wide red mouth. She had clasped her arms about his neck. He had held her with a fierce passion, she utterly unresisting, he could do what he liked with her. Wherever his hands had moved it had been all as yielding as water. In the morning, just before dawn, he had lain beside her looking at her face, until she woke and stretched herself with voluptuous, sleepy writhings, half smiling, half yawning up at him, one cheek and bare arm rosy in the early morning light.

In the weeks that followed he had watched the changes in the city with amazement. There was always a terrific hullabaloo in the market nowadays: dogs barking, pigs squealing, chaps in tradesmen's vans who wanted to get through the crush cracking their whips and cursing. The down and out still slept on the benches and urinated in the shadows of the buildings; in some ways, the poverty stood out even more now, against the rising wealth. The vegetables in the stalls were fresh and abundant. The black market chocolate had a rich creaminess Blair had never tasted before. And only the day before Blair had seen an astonishing new poster. The colors were fresh. It displayed several loaves of steaming bread, and the smiling faces of a mother and two small children.

"Fresh bread! Penny a lump! Taste before you buy!" a stallkeeper had cried from nearby.

"Cockles and whelks," another had replied. "Buy my cockles and whelks! Jellied eels! Cockles and whelks!"

"Bargain time! Bargain time!" sang another voice. "Loose strawberries going cheap, bargain time!"

"Last batch of pork sausages, finish up my pork sausages!"

How was the trading maintained, without dollars or coupons? As far as Blair could tell, it worked on well-documented trust. *The proles are governed by private loyalties which they do not question,* Smith had written. *The proles are not loyal to a party or a country or an idea, they are loyal to one another.* Blair understood now. Money was just another medium of trust, and the proles could make it almost as easily as fresh bread. Their market was a civilization of its own, a tradition and a shared understanding. Their currencies, their property, their laws evolved spontaneously from their loyalties. And the telescreens were now extending those private loyalties across all of London and beyond. Selling good bread was the greatest revolt of all. It was a political act.

The Party, it seemed, dimly understood the danger. Day by day telescreens denounced the "grave threat to our new happy life." Free speech, it was reported, was under attack by a conspiracy of wealthy private interests. Money was being used by subversive groups to undermine Party policies. Mysterious plutocrats were said to have infiltrated London and were using their wealth to drown out the voices of honest citizens. There were even shadowy rumors that rich capitalists were planning to seize control of the network and cut themselves off from the rest of society entirely. The agents of Blythe were at work again. It was obvious to any thinking man that London was being turned upside down, but the Party seemed determined to continue with its purges and directives, like a fish bashing its nose against the wall of an aquarium again and again, too dimwitted to realize that glass and water are not the same thing.

The proles ignored the Party. They seemed concerned only about little goods and evils, but in attending to those they somehow took care of the big ones too. If you didn't pay your debts or keep your promises, every shopkeeper soon knew it. The cardinal punishment was to be exposed as a deadbeat and sent back to grub for food and clothes in the Party's empty emporiums.

In response, the Party had launched another virulent campaign against what it called the corrupt currency capitalists. That one comrade should report on another's habit of paying his bills was a criminal invasion of privacy. Any comrade who desired credit was to apply through normal channels at a government bank. After the first announcement had aired, the telescreen had crashed into "Oceania, 'tis for thee," which was always a sign that the matter was considered to be serious.

"There'll be a purge," Kate predicted. "Mass arrests. Cart 'em off and shoot 'em. Nothing changes."

"The network is changing," Blair had answered. She had ignored him. She tolerated his network daydreams with feminine amusement, but she refused to treat any of it seriously. Her preoccupations were more earthy.

"Stop dreaming about tomorrow," she said. "You've got me now. Forget about the rest."

But he hadn't been able to. He dreamed now of a world with neither solitude nor Big Brother, a world in which thought was free, and men were different from one another, and yet still did not live alone. One had to imagine the telescreen without the Thought Police behind it. That now seemed possible. He had seen the young man again, standing by the telescreen, looking somewhat frail, a tall fellow with a fawn jacket and a mac. His strong cord trousers gave a massivity to his legs oddly in contrast to his emaciated torso. His pale, china-blue eyes still had a mischievous, amused look.

"Didn't I see you working on the telescreens?" Blair had asked.

The phreak had grinned. "Marvelous things. Bloody marvelous!"

"Was the screen broken?"

"Broken from the day it was put in," he had replied with a laugh. "I fixed it."

Blair had told Kate about it after they made love in the belfry of an abandoned church. She had been both amused and annoyed by Blair's fascination with the phreak. "He plugs wires together instead of fucking," she had said offhandedly, as if this was obvious and beyond dispute. Then she had arched her back under the blanket and curled up like a cat. She adored cats.

"I don't imagine that he can alter anything in our own lifetime," Blair had replied. "But suppose he really does get control of a few screens. One can imagine little knots of resistance springing up here and there—small groups of people banding themselves together, and gradually growing, and even leaving a few records behind, so that the next generation can carry on where we leave off."

"I'm not interested in the next generation, dear. I'm interested in us."

"You're only a rebel from the waist downward," he told her.

She thought it brilliantly witty and flung her arm round him in delight. But Blair knew now that it was possible. *Sooner or later it will happen*, Winston Smith had written. *The proles' strength will change into consciousness. A race of conscious beings must one day come.*

That afternoon they had wandered out of town into the country lanes. There was a golden glow over the countryside. The flat fields were full of ripening grain, and bluebells and forget-me-nots and Queen Anne's lace clustered along the hedgerows. Bees buzzed and fumbled around the flowers, independent vagabonds. In the clear blue dome of the sky, a lark twittered and soared. After a while they had found their way as they always did back to the belfry, and into each other's arms.

They had awoken with the sun streaming in through the stone pillars. It was perfectly silent. And then a single green bird had fluttered down and perched on the windowsill. It did not know it was being watched. It was a tender thing, smaller than a tame dove, with a green back as smooth as velvet, and a neck of iridescent colors. Its legs were like pink wax. The bird rocked itself backward and forward on the bough, swelling out its breast feathers and laying its coralline beak upon them. It burst into a torrent of song. In the afternoon quiet the volume of sound was startling. They had clung together, fascinated. Then the bird took fright and fled with a clatter of wings, and once again all was silence. They lay perfectly still. The silence engulfed them like a mother's embrace.

Later he talked to her about it. To her amused annoyance, he tried to explain how it was all connected, the thrush and the sex, the market and the telescreen, and the glorious silence of the warm afternoon. The idea that the phreak might have given him a profound insight into their passion made her laugh out loud. She had stretched out languorously beside him again and had listened quietly as he talked. After a while she had closed her eyes. A moment later she had been asleep.

Now the shadows were lengthening. They were nearing the huddle of streets where they lived. Their paces were matched, and they walked hand in hand. Women leaned out of their windows in the clear evening light, gazing at the street, or stood on their front doorsteps talking casually to neighbors. Through their open doors he could see into little back yards, where washing hung on lines and children played. He felt a warm familiarity and safety. E. A. Blair had disappeared from the Party and was no more. He had become a prole, in a prole's clothes, living in a prole's home. They had lost interest in him.

Blair thought again of his conversation with the phreak.

"How does one escape it?" he had asked.

"You turn it off," the phreak had replied.

"But you can't," Blair had said.

The phreak had laughed. "Any machine can be turned off," he had said. "You just have to find the switch."

It was a gigantic thought, which seemed to verge on doublethink. Silence was oppression; silence was also freedom. Freedom was solitude; freedom was also the company of others. The difference between slavery and freedom was nothing more than a switch on the front of a screen. Freedom was the power to choose.

The sun began to set. The pavement turned pink, and even the pitted street and ramshackle houses seemed radiant. Abruptly, from the far distance, there came a hollow ringing sound, floating through the evening air and echoing over the roofs of London, filling the sky and the street with a rhythmic resonance. It started in only one place, far in the east, but in a moment it had surrounded them.

It was the sound of church bells. At first he thought he had never before heard church bells ringing. Then, with a rush of remembrance, he knew that once, long ago, when he had still been a child, church bells had often spoken to the community, ringing out sounds of danger and warning, worship and love.

"Oranges and lemons, say the bells of St. Clements," he said. To his surprise, Kate immediately capped the line:

"You owe me three farthings, say the bells of St. Martins. When will you pay me? say the bells of Old Bailey—"

With a sort of grave courtesy, Blair completed the stanza:

"When I grow rich, say the bells of Shoreditch."

For a moment they stood quite still in the street. The pealing of the bells slowly died away, and then the echoes too. The light was golden, the sky a prussian blue. As they watched, the crimson ball of the sun sank from view, the scarlet fleece of clouds slowly changed hue, and the air was filled with a crimson silence.

CHAPTER 13 ■■■■■

The sound of bells, O'Brien reflected, had not been heard in London for years. He wondered idly how the proles would react. They probably wouldn't. Proles were animals.

The bells had woken him from a light doze. As his mind cleared, a deep sense of misgiving crept through him, which he could not explain. Was he hanging someone he knew today? Was his chest bad again? His eyes fell on Smith's diary, which had slipped off his lap and lay closed on the floor. He looked at the book dully for a moment, then painfully reached down and picked it up. He opened it back at the third page and began to read again.

1. Ignorance Is Strength

Among all the Party's lies there is one great truth: Strength in numbers. To survive a war a nation must be united. Patriotism—blind patriotism—is the single most important source of national power. As a positive force there is nothing to set beside it. What is critical is emotional unity, a people's tendency to feel alike and act together, at least in moments of supreme crisis. *The nation must be bound together by an invisible chain*. It must have its private language and its common memories, and at the approach of an enemy it must close its ranks. The whole nation must swing together and do the same thing, like a herd of cattle facing a wolf, prepared for swift, unanimous action, in perfect unison.

War is unique, but the need for unity is not. All great achievements of human civilization are creations of communities. A man with a woman, a child with his parents, a family among neighbors—all are stronger because they are together. Numbers are the strength of the town market. The community is the spirit of the church. Industrialism requires coordinated control. Philosophers, writers, and artists not only need encouragement and an audience, they need constant stimulation from other people. The best nonsense poetry is produced gradually and accidentally, by communities rather than by individuals. For any work of art there is only one test worth bothering about—survival, which is entirely an index to majority opinion. Language itself is a creation of common experience, and beauty of any kind is meaningless until it is shared. Science, the pinnacle of peaceful civilization, exists only in the collective consciousness of a self-disciplined community. The Party is right about this at least: In science, truth is indeed statistical.

Sanity is not. A man may be alone in holding a great belief, and if alone, then a lunatic. But the thought of being a lunatic need not greatly trouble him. The horror is that the belief might also be wrong. Like salvation, like charity, like love, sanity survives or perishes inside the individual brain. All scientific truths are statistical. Not all statisticians are truthful.

And it is on individual sanity that all else depends. The market is no more robust than its individual farmers and craftsmen, the culture no more creative than its solitary artist, the Army no more courageous than the soldier at the front line. Great prose must be written in solitude. Science, above all, depends on solitary observation and the flash of insight within a few cubic centimeters of a single human skull.

Whom then shall we trust: The individual for his sanity, or the community for its numbers? What shall it be: the Darwinian horrors of unfettered competition, or a dedicated sect of central planners serving as eternal guardians of the weak? A city teeming with police patrols, or a city in which every armed citizen is a police force of one? Autocrats, who govern everything, or Anarchists, who govern nothing? The Communist's centralism and cutthroat efficiency, or the Anarchist's liberty and cutthroat equality? The single-minded unity essential to a nation in times of war, or the suicidal herd instinct of the Gadarene swine in times of peace?

O'Brien wiped his eyes and turned away from the book. It was appalling how Smith's diary had been found. With all the telescreens, with the whole gigantic array of the network behind them, it had taken the frumpish wife of Blair's neighbor to spot the book and mention it in all innocence to her half-wit husband. And then, instead of bringing the diary straight to O'Brien, the idiots from his own Ministry had gone out and beaten Blair to a pulp. Granted, it was standard procedure to soften up a thought criminal before an arrest, so that he might then run to friends for help. A whole gang of saboteurs could often be rounded up this way. But there was no use in beating a man so hard he could barely be lifted off the street by a passing whore. With an exasperated grunt O'Brien turned back to the diary.

Until recently, collectivist oligarchy or something much like it was stronger than any of the alternatives. The successful state was a beehive, a world of rabbits ruled by a handful of stoats. People needed a king to promote stability and act as a sort of keystone. The real power, of course, belonged to unprepossessing men in bowler hats: the creature who rode in a gilded coach behind soldiers in steel breastplates was really a waxwork, a ventriloquist's dummy. But he was also the voice of the nation, and a nation needed a single voice. Government by Big Brother was not only inevitable but desirable: inequality was the price of civilization. People gained more by anointing a king than they lost by submitting to his will. They were capable of wonderfully coordinated action, but only because they submitted absolutely to the will of their rulers. They lost their freedom, but they gained unity. No other social arrangement was as powerful. Every new political theory, by whatever name it called itself, led back to hierarchy and regimentation.

In the countries that now comprise Oceania, the great autocracies eventually gave way to commercial oligopolies. At first, the new social structures were not very different from the old. Small businesses proliferated but then quickly merged into large ones; and great monopoly companies swallowed up hosts of petty traders. The giant corporation became a big brotherhood in itself, a homogeneous community dominated by a single, all-powerful leader, whose commands were followed unquestioningly by obedient drones. The clerks and typists, looking so unpleasantly like ants, streamed over London Bridge at the rush hour every morning, into their steel and concrete nests. They were employed by collectivist commercial autocracies. These organizations inspired their workers with a drumbeat of simple slogans. They demanded uniformity of attire, appearance, habit, locution, and culture. Yet in their time, the great corporations proved stronger than what had come before. They eventually reached their apex in what we now call Eastasia—in the culture known by a Chinese word that translates roughly as "Obliteration of the Self."

The old autocracies all thrived because they solved a single, critical problem: how to unite and coordinate many people across time and space. The only really effective systems of memory and communication existed within a single human skull, or in small hermetic councils with access to central repositories of vital records; communication among larger, more dispersed groups was too slow and unreliable. So mankind turned to kings, oligarchs, or plutocratic captains of industry, and lodged all important thought in a single dominant city or palace, a single citadel, a single executive suite, often a single human brain. All superfluous communication was avoided because it was just too inefficient. The masses were not to question, negotiate, or respond; they were to follow orders. Industrialism meant oligarchical collectivism. The only practical alternatives were slave-state socialism and slave-state fascism, which were in fact identical.

The slave state remains the essence of Party rule. The slavery is not physical, of course—machines now do most of the menial work—

the slavery is of the mind. What is required of the individual is utter submission, escape from his own identity, and complete submergence in the Party. The individual's ignorance is the Party's strength. IGNORANCE IS STRENGTH.

O'Brien's thoughts turned back to the engineer in the pub.

"'Cos the screens worked," the man had said. What could he possibly have meant? At first, O'Brien hesitated even to crystallize the thought in his own mind. He began reading again.

The Party's pursuit of ignorance began in schools, which were staffed by loyal Party drones. We inculcated in our children a sense of desolate loneliness and helplessness, of being locked up not only in a hostile world but in a world without good or evil, where the rules were such that it is actually not possible to keep them. We taught history as a series of unrelated and unintelligible facts. Our universities studied the oral traditions of lesbian headhunters in New Guinea, not the great classics on human freedom. Whatever students did—whether they laughed or sniveled or went into frenzies of gratitude for small favors—their only true feeling was hatred.

At all levels, our educational system neglected mathematics and did not teach science in any form. Empirical thought was opposed to the most fundamental principles of Ingsoc. For Party purposes the earth was the center of the universe. The Party conceded that to navigate the ocean it was often convenient to assume that the earth went round the sun, but Party mathematicians and astronomers were quite capable of producing a dual system of astronomy. Outside our steadily shrinking scientific communities, all talk of science disappeared.

By cutting off memory, the Party halted the accumulation of knowledge. By cutting off communication, the Party prevented its spread. To that end, the Party limited travel, outlawed private meetings, suppressed love, and condemned sex. Instead, it filled the air with official sights and sounds: mass rallies, posters, lectures, and the ceaseless jabber from the telescreens, so as to crowd out every competing private thought or communication.

To crown it all, the Party had Newspeak. Newspeak served Party purposes perfectly. By stripping the English language of its subtle texture and richness, the Party deprived people of their power to think and communicate. By controlling language and all ancillary means of communication, the Party controlled the ends.

But now there is the telescreen.

O'Brien looked up from the book. He found himself thinking again that he knew what was coming next: a sort of anarchistic utopia, another tired exhibition of machine worship in its most vulgar, ignorant, and half-baked form. The individual will be set free from the sordid necessity of living for others. There will be no want and no insecurity, no drudgery, no disease, no ugliness, no wastage of the human spirit in futile enmities and rivalries. There will be no disorder, no loose ends, no wildernesses, no wild animals, no weeds, no poverty, no pain—and so on and so forth. The telescreened world will be above all things an ordered world, an efficient world. Telescreens to save work, telescreens to save thought, telescreens to save pain, hygiene, efficiency, organization, more hygiene, more efficiency, more organization, more telescreens.

It would never happen. The people at the Ministry, even idiots like Burgess, still knew how to make the network serve the Party's will. The proles weren't interested in telescreens. With a steady diet of indifferent food, sex, and violence, the proles wanted nothing more. Only the elite of the Inner Party understood the pursuit of power. Telescreens offered power only to those with the will to use it.

O'Brien rose stiffly from his chair, dragged his vast bulk to the side table, and poured a glass of wine. Almost as an afterthought, he made his way over to the telescreen. "COMM-TWO-OFFICE," he growled. And a few seconds later: "Cooper—double the guard around the Ministry." He walked slowly back to his chair, sat down heavily, and turned back to the diary.

But now there is the telescreen. When Orwell proposed the new machine the Party was ecstatic. Private life could now come to an end. For the first time in history, it would be possible to enforce not only complete obedience to the will of the State but complete uniformity of opinion on all subjects. The tele-ocratic Ministry would be the Party's new citadel and palace, its center of power. The telescreen would forge Party unity as no instrument of governance had ever forged unity before.

But the Party was wrong about the telescreen. What fools you were! You, the technological determinists, you who maintained that technology was destiny, that machines made history, that all politics and economics revolved around the means of production! The Party, which believed in machines above all else, completely failed to understand the most revolutionary machine of all. The masters of doublethink neglected to doublethink the machine itself.

The important medium of communication is no longer Oldspeak or Newspeak—it is Viewspeak, the telescreen. While you denuded the language of its adjectives and verbs, of its texture and color, Orwell filled the tunnels with a new power of expression richer than ever before imagined. While you destroyed hundreds of words, Orwell created millions of pictures.

You idiots! You fantasized that with boundless power to communicate, you could somehow end all communication. You dreamed that if the Party could watch, listen, and connect with everyone all the time, no one else would be able to watch, listen, or connect at all. But the telescreen Orwell designed was not imprinted with your faith in oligarchical collectivism. It couldn't have been; it wouldn't have worked if it had.

The Party understood that telescreens could connect the Ministries to the people. But it failed to grasp that telescreens could equally well connect people to each other, to form new communities, new alliances, new collaborations of every kind outside the Ministry. The telescreen contains the power to forge a new kind of brotherhood, an equal dignity among people who choose freely to collaborate among themselves.

With the telescreen in hand, mankind has finally solved the age-old problem of human isolation. We have reached a time when thought can be free, and when men can be different from one another and yet still not live alone. The tenet is wrong which says that a man is the quotient of one million divided by one million. The telescreen creates an altogether new kind of arithmetic based on multiplication: on the joining of a million individuals to form a new entity which, no longer an amorphous mass, will develop an individuality of its own, a consciousness increased a millionfold, in unlimited yet self-contained space. Strength no longer requires ignorance. For the first time in history, it is possible to have brotherhood without Big Brother.

O'Brien felt a cold sweat start out on his backbone. For a moment he was afraid—afraid that something was about to break. For some wild reason, his fear at that instant was that it would be his own spine. With a sense of growing panic he turned to the next page of the diary.

Party texts recognized four ways in which a ruling group can fall from power. Either it is conquered from without, or it governs so inefficiently that the masses are stirred to revolt, or it allows another strong and discontented group to come into being, or it loses its own self-confidence and willingness to govern. Ultimately the determining factor is the mental attitude of the ruling class itself. This is why the Party's paramount mission is to suppress the growth of liberalism and skepticism in its own ranks. This is why we have the Thought Police. But in a telescreened world, the Party is doomed.

You can still be conquered from outside. You have easily averted slow demographic changes in our society, but alien cultures no longer invade by land or sea—they invade through the ether. You have persuaded yourselves that your natural defenses are too formidable, that Eurasia will be forever protected by its vast land spaces, Oceania by the width of the Atlantic and the Pacific, Eastasia by the fecundity and industriousness of its inhabitants. But land masses and oceans are irrelevant; the images on a telescreen can circle the globe in one-seventh of a second. Fecundity is irrelevant; telescreen signals can reach any number of people. What is relevant now is not the power of a Party but the power of the ideas that unite a nation.

With the telescreen, no Party state is safe from attack by a new way of thinking.

The second danger is graver still. So long as they are not permitted to have standards of comparison, the masses may remain unaware that they are oppressed. But the telescreen, like a telescope, exposes what otherwise would not be seen. Before the telescope, people might believe that Mars, like Earth, had artificial canals, or that every celestial body revolved around our planet, but after the telescope they could not. A telescreen is a gigantic telescope that allows men to see other men. It supplies standards of comparison. And like a telescope, it builds memory. A telescope peers into the past, even into man's own past, when light that left the earth a million years ago is bent back on its own path by a massive object in the great nebula in Orion. Like Orion, the telescreen creates memory by dispersing and reflecting information. It builds collective memory.

And it compels us to learn. With the telescreen, the masses will discover that the lottery is a fraud, and understand that members of the Inner Party live vastly better than they do. With the telescreen, oppression will inevitably have political consequences, because discontent can now become articulate.

The third threat to Party rule is that a strong and discontented group will arise from the lower ranks of the bureaucrats, scientists, technicians, trade union organizers, publicity experts, sociologists, teachers, journalists, and professional politicians. The Party has made these groups the targets of all its indoctrination, all its relentless propaganda. But with the telescreen, political alliances can be as fluid and changeable as pictures in a glass bottle. Now the voice and visage of any rebellious member of the Outer Party can travel as far and wide as Big Brother himself.

The last threat to the Party comes from within. The strength of the Party is determined ultimately by its mental attitude. The Party dies when its members lose their self-confidence and willingness to govern. Today, the Party's confidence depends on the telescreen, the machine that allows you to see all, hear all, and reach everywhere. But your confidence will not last; sooner or later you will recognize

that the masters of doublethink cannot also be the masters of telescreens. Orwell's network cannot be maintained by people committed to mental cheating. You may assert that black is white, but no
act of antiscientific will can make a color picture materialize on a
screen. You may deny the existence of objective reality, but you cannot master reality without facing it squarely every hour of the day.

The essence of Party rule is doublethink, the linking together of opposites. The essence of the telescreen is the linking together of identities: one telescreen displays exactly what another views, and does
so with perfect fidelity. If telescreens function at all, they function
truthfully. Science itself depends on singlethink—pure, rigorous, in-
corruptible. Science *is* singlethink. Without singlethinkers, there
will be no telescreen. With singlethinkers, there will be no Party.

Today, the Party no longer reads books. But sooner or later you will
read this one. Your self-confidence will evaporate. The outside powers will not need to invade. The proles will not need to revolt. The
new groups from within will not need to grow strong. Once you recognize you have lost control of communication in your society, the
Party will collapse in an instant.

You have asked: "What is it, this principle that will defeat us?" It is
the principle that the past does not belong to the present. It is the
principle that what is inside a man is separate from what is outside,
and that what is believed does not determine what is. It is the principle that two plus two equals four.

O'Brien sat slumped in the armchair. Perhaps Smith had
glimpsed revolutionary possibilities, but what of it? No one else
would even conceive of such things. Orwell's network might even
have a capacity for revolution built into its wires, but what was still
missing was the will. The network would not set the proles free
until they understood its power. But they could not understand its
power until they were free. However explosive the telescreen might
be, it would not explode without a spark of understanding. And
there was no spark.

The face of Winston Smith floated back into O'Brien's mind. He found himself remembering how he had broken the man. In the end, there had been nothing left in Smith except sorrow for what he had done, and love of Big Brother. It had been touching to see such love. O'Brien glanced again at the slim black volume of Smith's diary. There were undoubtedly other copies of it in circulation, he thought.

And then it struck him: the diary was the spark. When the proles read it, they would understand the power of the telescreen. And once they understood that power, it would be over.

O'Brien turned to his telescreen. "COMM-TWO-OFFICE," he barked. The screen flickered into life. "Get me Cooper."

O'Brien noticed with some surprise that his voice was breaking as he spoke the name. He turned back to Smith's book. He had still not learned the ultimate secret. He understood why; he did not understand how. The why was obvious now: the network was dangerous because it might bring consciousness to the masses. But how it would do so was still a mystery. The first part of the diary, like the third, had not actually told him anything that he did not know; it had merely systematized the suspicions he had long possessed. He flipped the page and began to read again, in a desperate hurry.

> There is one question which until this moment I have almost ignored. What is it about Orwell's telescreen that makes freedom inevitable?

> Here we reach the central secret. As we have seen, the mystique of the telescreen, and above all the Thought Police, depends on the telescreen's power to watch every citizen at every moment of time. But behind that power lies the original structure of the device itself, the never-questioned design that made it possible to place telescreens everywhere, and to monitor any screen at will from any other place. The secret of the telescreen is . . .

A soft buzz issued from O'Brien's own screen. He heaved his vast bulk from the chair. A moment later, a face came into focus on the screen.

"Cooper," said O'Brien, "Destroy the underground press. Locate and eliminate every last copy of Winston Smith's diary. This is of the utmost urgency."

The face on the screen said nothing.

"Surely we have some leads," O'Brien exclaimed, his voice rising unexpectedly. "What about Blair? What about the whore? Does she have anything to do with it?"

"I don't believe so," Cooper answered slowly. "We've been watching them both."

O'Brien stared back at the screen. Perhaps the time had come. O'Brien had long prepared for this day, though he had always hoped it would never arrive.

He turned and shuffled painfully back to his armchair as his telescreen faded into darkness. A white-jacketed servant moved silently across the room, picking up a glass and emptying an ashtray.

Suddenly the telescreen burst into sound again. O'Brien looked up, startled. Five men in black uniforms had appeared on the screen. In front of them, apparently unaware of their presence, shambled an insubstantial figure, his slight frame frail in his oversized overalls. O'Brien had a vague feeling he had seen the man before. In a moment, the others had fallen upon him and were beating him mercilessly with their truncheons. O'Brien felt a faint but definitely pleasant thrill. A kick landed squarely in the man's groin, and vomit spewed from his mouth.

The picture abruptly froze, with the face of one of the black-coated men filling the screen. The man's tongue was protruding slightly from his mouth, and he was grinning sadistically. After a few seconds, there appeared at the bottom of the screen, like a noose around a condemned man's neck, the words:

THE PROLES ARE WATCHING YOU

CHAPTER 14 ■■■■■

It happened on the sixth day. On the sixth day of Love Week, after the processions, the speeches, the shouting, the singing, the banners, the posters, the films, the sit-ins, the demonstrations, the sensitivity sessions, the consciousness raisings—after six days of celebrating Big Brother's all-embracing love, his nurturing of the young, his caring for the old, his generosity to the poor, his feeding of the hungry, his ministrations to the sick, when the great orgasm was quivering to its climax and the general revulsion of all oppression and exploitation, all callousness and insensitivity, had boiled up into delirium—at just this moment it was announced that Big Brother had been overthrown. Big Brother was a renegade and backslider, a traitor and a spy. Kenneth Blythe had returned.

There had not exactly been an admission that any change had taken place. Merely it became known, with extreme suddenness and everywhere at once, that Big Brother was gone. It was night, and the white faces and scarlet banners were luridly floodlit. The square had been packed with several thousand people, including a block of about a thousand schoolchildren in the green uniform of the Huggers. On a scarlet-draped platform stood an orator of the Inner Party, an androgynous woman with wire-rimmed glasses and thin brown hair dragged into a bun. She bent over the micro-

157

phone, her black overalls loose on her bony frame. Her voice, made metallic by the amplifiers, whined forth an endless catalog of oppressions and iniquities, harassments, discriminations, and deportations, a never-ending account of supercilious wealth, lying propaganda, unjust aggressions—a vast litany of injustice.

The speech had been proceeding for perhaps twenty minutes when a messenger hurried onto the platform and a scrap of paper was slipped into the speaker's hand. She unrolled and read it without pausing in her speech. Nothing altered in her voice or manner, or in the content of what she was saying, but suddenly the names were different. The next moment the face of Kenneth Blythe, the former Enemy of the People, flashed onto a giant screen behind the speaker. Blythe looked different now. His once-lean face had filled out; the great fuzzy aureole of white hair was tamed, brushed back, silvery; the small goatee was gone; the old look of cleverness had given way to a new one of wisdom. He was now full of power and mysterious calm.

Without words said, a wave of understanding rippled through the crowd. Big Brother had betrayed them! Blythe had resumed his rightful position. But the Love continued exactly as before, except that the name of the great protector, the fount of all Oceanic love, had been changed. The orator, still gripping the neck of the microphone, her shoulders hunched forward, her free hand waving in the air, had gone straight on speaking. The Fascist octopus had sung its swan song, the woman said, the jackboot had been thrown into the melting pot. All laws had been abolished; nothing was forbidden any more, and the only arbiter of behavior would be public opinion. Oceania would be governed by love and reason. The thing that impressed Blair in looking back was that the speaker had switched from one line to the other actually in midsentence, not only without a pause but without even breaking the syntax.

She was a mean, hollow woman, a skeletal frame fleshed out with words, clothed in sallow skin and shooting out slogans. What was she doing? Quite deliberately, and quite openly, she was stirring up hatred. Yes, she was talking of love, of course. Love, love, love. But in fact, she was doing her damnedest to make you hate anyone who disagreed with her. The grating voice went on and on, and another thought struck Blair. She meant it. Not faking at all— she felt every word she was saying. She was trying to work up hatred in the audience, but that was nothing to the hatred she felt herself. If you cut her open all you'd find inside would be Democracy-Fascism-Democracy. Interesting to know a woman like that in private life. But did she have a private life? Or did she only go round from platform to platform, working up hatred? Perhaps even her dreams were slogans. Blair reached for Kate's hand and smelled a whiff of violets from her hair.

The cadence of the woman's speech slowed. There were to be great changes in government, she was saying. Responsibility for the network had been reassigned to the Ministry of Plenty. The authorities asked for the people's commitment, their toil, their energy; it asked them to lose their identities, and if necessary, to devote the rest of their lives to building a new and glorious future.

"Down wiv Big Bruvver!" shouted a man in a green shirt just ahead of Kate. A few people turned and stared. The man's back looked unpleasantly familiar. "'Ooray for Blythe!" the man shouted.

"'Ooray for Blythe! 'Ooray for Blythe!" other voices echoed, and soon the square was filled with shouts and cries, cheers and pleas, and gradually a deep, rhythmical chant emerged, "BLYTHE! BLYTHE! BLYTHE!"

The speech continued, in a stern, businesslike tone. The woman was lapsing into the kind of political lecture Blair had attended hundreds of times before, during which your soul writhed with boredom.

She was speaking about telescreens. It appeared that owning a telescreen was to be a new right of citizenship. It was now the official policy of Blytheism that every prole would be entitled to watch telescreen programming at least eight hours a day. There would be universal service, round-the-clock entertainment. Fabulous statistics poured out of the woman's mouth. The phrase "our new, happy life" recurred several times. The crowd responded like pigs hearing the rattling of a stick inside a swill-bucket.

Providing these things would require a great new government endeavor, the speaker admitted. Resources were limited. Radio waves were in short supply. There was scarcity in the tunnels as well: too many wires, too little room. The telescreens for the masses could only be one-way devices, capable of receiving but not transmitting. Nevertheless, the Ministry of Plenty would meet all legitimate public needs. Her voice rose. The future was glorious. There would be equality, abundance, freedom. "One Policy!" she shouted. "One System! Universal Service!"

Only the announcement of free telescreens had drawn any kind of response from the crowd. Kate looked up at Blair with a knowing smile and gave him a wink.

The woman on the platform was back at it. Hyena, hangman, cannibal, petty bourgeois, lackey, flunky, mad dog, . . . the same old invective, a huge dump of worn-out metaphors, meaningless phrases tacked together like the sections of a prefabricated hen house. Her voice hardened.

A grave danger lay ahead. What danger, dear comrades? The danger of backsliding and corruption. Traitorous elements of the old regime would attempt sabotage. The fight against them might entail the death of hundreds of innocent people, but the cause of the revolution was just. Other elements would conspire—were already conspiring—to capture the network and seize it for their selfish private interests. They would attempt to monopolize the wires. They would charge people for telescreen films and sports programs, for all the simple pleasures that even the old Party had distributed for free. These rich men, these lackey-flunky-mad-dog-jackal-hyena-hydra-headed capitalists, would attempt to control the network, and through the network all the land, all the houses, all the factories, and all the money. "Cynical betrayal . . . stab-in-the-back . . . blood-bath," the woman was saying. The great mass of people in London would be silenced and cut off from each other, severed from the lifeline of the network.

Then, abruptly, she was back at it again. "Defense of Democracy . . . firm stand . . . indignation of all decent peoples . . . oppressed peoples . . . racists . . . hideous outbursts of sadism . . . indignation of all disempowered elements . . . Fascism . . . Democracy . . . Fascism . . . Democracy . . ."

It was all horribly familiar, like a malfunctioning old gramophone. Turn the handle, press the button, and it started. It was a ghastly thing, really, to have a sort of human barrel-organ shooting propaganda at you by the hour. The same thing over and over again. Love, Love, Love, which somehow always meant Hate, Hate, Hate. It gave you the feeling that something had got inside your skull and was hammering down on your brain. She didn't go into details. Left it all respectable. But what she was seeing was something quite different. It was a picture of herself smashing people's faces in with a spanner. Fascist faces, of course. Smash! Right in the middle! The bones cave in like an eggshell, and what was a face a minute ago is just a great big blob of strawberry jam. You could hear all that in the tone of her voice.

The man in the green shirt had been fidgeting for several minutes. "Lackeys," he muttered at last, as if unable to restrain himself any longer. And then, louder: "Lackeys of the bourgeoisie! Flunkies of the bourgeoisie! Parasites! 'Yenas!"

Nobody heard him. The speaker on the podium was droning on. Steps were already being taken to protect the public from the reactionary capitalists. Private networks had been outlawed. There was to be no private spending on advertising; the authorities would sponsor suitable public service announcements as needed. All telescreen programming would be funded by the Ministry. Whenever one view of a controversial subject was aired on the network, an opposing view would follow—the Ministry of Plenty would select a suitable one. What she really meant was Quick! Let's all grab a spanner and get together, and perhaps if we smash in enough rich faces they won't smash our poor ones.

For a moment Blair was thinking of Kate, of how they had made love that morning, how he had explored her body, how she had cried out with pleasure. Then the woman on the podium was bellowing again, impossible to ignore. She had slipped into a familiar style, at once military and pedantic, asking questions and then promptly answering them. What lessons do we learn from this fact, comrades? The lessons—which is also one of the fundamental principles of Blytheism—that, etc., etc. It was unbearable. And she had this horrible habit of shrieking out a point just as your mind had begun to drift toward something more pleasant. The crowd was impassably thick; there was no escape.

"I must speak to you finally about the problem of hate," said the woman over the grating static on the loudspeakers. "Hate! What it comes down to is Hate!" she shouted. "Hate is a sickness, a disease, a corruption of the mind! Remember, fellow citizens, the years of our oppression, the years of Hate! The stinking corpse of Hate was the poison of our lives, the cancer of our society. Comrades, the brotherhood has abolished Hate. Hate will be liquidated." Her voice was filled with a sort of treacly sorrow. And behind the sorrow, the same old malevolence.

"But it grieves me to report, ..." the woman paused, as if to control her emotion, and her voice grew angry. Hate was still among us. Wealthy commercial interests were peddling hateful products at inflated prices, degrading women with prurience and pornography, harassing members of oppressed races and classes. The capitalists behind these things were corpse poisons, disgusting offal from a rentier class. They were a direct assault on sanity and decency, and even—since their filth poisoned the imagination—on life itself.

"Citizens, we shall banish hate!" The loudspeakers crackled, and her voice began to rise. "We shall rip hate with knives out of the bowels of our society." And then she was off and running again. "Megalomaniac and satanic regime . . . monstrous octopus . . . revolting cynicism . . . liberated from the evil yoke . . ." Another filthy stew of words.

One thousand Huggers rose in unison chanting, "No more Hate! No more Hate!" "Wipe 'em out! Stamp 'em out!"

"No more 'ate!" shouted the man in the green shirt.

The crowd picked up the chant and then abruptly began to march in place, feet stamping together in rhythm with the words. "No more Hate! No more Hate! No more Hate!" The chanting grew louder, the stamping feet stronger, the woman at the podium pounded her fist in the air, in rhythm with the shouting.

It was during the moment of disorder that a man whose face he did not see tapped Blair on the shoulder and said very close to his ear, "Excuse me, I think you've dropped something." Blair looked down, and somehow the press of the crowd around him brought him to his knees. Kate reached to help, and then there was a scuffle and a green shirt was beside him, where Kate should have been. For some reason Blair found that his tongue was exploring his broken teeth. And then he knew where he had seen the man in the green shirt before—outside the junk shop, among the black-coated guards and the rain of truncheons.

"Kate!" he cried struggling to his feet. He reached for her in desperation, but the press of the crowd was too thick. "Kate!" he cried again. No one noticed. A sea of bodies closed in upon him and flung him from side to side, bumping his ribs and choking him with their animal heat. He saw a tight group of people and a flash of red hair passing through the crowd, like a disturbance in long grass. He struggled forward with an almost dreamlike feeling. It was a fearful labor—it was like wading neck deep through a viscous sea. "Kate! Kate!"

His voice was lost in the booming of the loudspeakers and the roaring of the crowd. The woman on the podium was contorted again; she gripped the neck of the microphone with one hand while the other, enormous at the end of a bony arm, clawed the air menacingly above her head.

An overpowering loneliness gripped his mind. In the distance behind the speaker, the floodlights lit up the enormous pyramidal structure of the Ministry of Plenty. The concrete glittered and shimmered in the glaring white lights. Then the lights dimmed again, and shaded into colors, and suddenly there came into focus on the wall of the Ministry, in immense red letters, the three slogans of the new brotherhood:

SCARCITY IS PLENTY
WEALTH IS POVERTY
SILENCE IS SPEECH

CHAPTER 15 ■■■■■

The filtered light, bluish and cold, lit up the prisoner's tall, bony figure with unmerciful clarity. What was most startling was the emaciation of his face. It was like a skull. Because of its thinness the mouth and eyes looked disproportionately large.

"2714!" roared the voice from the telescreen. "2714 Stand Up!"

The man stood.

"Remain standing where you are," said the voice. "Face the door. Make no movement."

The man obeyed. His bony arms hung loosely by his side like dry sticks.

The door swung open, and for a minute or so O'Brien faced the prisoner. "Leave this man alone until I'm ready for him," he said at last. He turned and walked heavily out of the cell. In the old days O'Brien had always worn heavy boots, so that prisoners would hear him coming. Now he could barely manage a shuffle.

They had the man at last. He would confess to all his sabotage. He would explain exactly what he had done to the wires and the screens, and then he would be hanged. There was a certain satisfaction in that, but to his surprise, O'Brien felt no exultation. He was growing too old for the business—the groveling on the floor, the screaming for mercy, the bloody clots of hair, the drugs, the delicate instruments, the gradual wearing down by sleeplessness, solitude, and persistent questions.

O'Brien stepped into the lift and was whisked silently up to his office. Had the Party been defeated at last? It still owned the Ministries, but did Ministries matter any more? Even Blythe's meticulously choreographed reappearance had attracted little interest. The usual crowd had been rounded up for the rally, but most of the proles had ignored it. Since then, surveillance from the Ministry of Love had collapsed. O'Brien still didn't understand what had happened. Nobody in the Ministry did. All he knew was that the network had developed a will of its own.

As he entered his office, O'Brien looked stupidly at the map on the wall. The network was an ugly thing, he thought to himself for the hundredth time. There was no order to it, no discipline. It was the product of an unruly mind. The colored lines snaked here and there, intersecting all over the place. They looked as if they had just been thrown down at random.

Smith's diary lay closed in the middle of O'Brien's desk. O'Brien had never finished it. With a vague sense of foreboding, as someone invited to read about a distant and unwelcome future he would never live to see, he opened it in the middle and began to read again.

2. Freedom Is Slavery

There is one question which until this moment I have almost ignored. What is it about the telescreen that makes freedom inevitable?

Here we reach the central secret. As we have seen, the mystique of the telescreen, and above all the Thought Police, depends on the telescreen's power to watch every citizen at every moment of time. But behind that power lies the original structure of the device itself, the never-questioned design that made it possible to place telescreens everywhere and to monitor any screen at will from any other place. The secret of the telescreen is the power of choice.

No society before has ever been able to vest that power fully in its citizens, not even within the marketplace of ideas. Even the freest markets require defenses against theft, trespass, and coercion. In matters of discourse, that means keeping the peace between the quiet and the loud, the retiring and the intrusive, the decent and the vulgar. It means maintaining some sort of control over the noisy and the nosy. And that requires government.

The essential problem is that free speech involves two individuals simultaneously, not just one. Speech is truly free only when there is mutual consent to it on both sides. Consent spells the difference between nudity in the bedroom and in a public park, between pillow talk and dirty words on the public radio.

But half a loaf of consent is easier to find than a whole. My handbill is your litter, my political soundtruck your interrupted rest, my radio broadcast your static, my street art your ugly graffiti, my cross burning your intimidation, my inept wooing your sexual harassment, my copyright your right to publish denied, my privacy your inability to listen, my pillow talk your vulgarity, my autoerotic flashing your indecent exposure. Every right to speak collides with some reciprocal right not to listen, not to speak, not to watch, not to give away your own words, images, or thoughts.

And so, to maintain a fair balance between those who wish to watch, listen, or speak and those who do not wish to be watched, heard, or bothered, even the most liberal governments have always relied on City Hall to license parades, on the courts to enforce copyrights, on employment commissions to proscribe sexual harassment, on public censors to suppress indecency, hate, and incitement, on the police to cut off fighting words, on the state to protect the softly spoken from the loud, and the retiring from the nosy. Who then protects privacy? Big Brother. Who protects free thought? The Thought Police.

But now there is the telescreen. It offers a new, and altogether different power: the power of private choice, the power to control not only what you say and show, but also what you see and hear. The telescreen supplies the power of choice. It has to. It couldn't work otherwise.

O'Brien began to cough. He heard, to his surprise, an unspeakably repellent sound, a foul bubbling and retching as though his bowels were being churned up within him. It was a cough that almost tore him open. When it was finally over he noticed some blood-streaked mucus on his hand.

Consider what a telescreen is expected to do. It must be capable of watching every citizen at every hour of the day, capable of filling every home and office, every pub and public square, with words, sounds, moving pictures, photographs, news bulletins, and ledgers. The machine must transmit pictures as well as receive them. It must send the right signals to precisely the right place. And it must be compact enough for mass production.

All of this became technically possible in the 1980s. A telescreen would be built of transistors, and at that time the technology was improving at an astonishing pace. Engineers learned to shrink transistors into unbelievably compact arrays. The speakwrites, the novel-writing machines, the versificators—all of the Party's familiar calculating machines that once filled entire rooms—collapsed into chips the size of beetles.

A grave new problem then became apparent. Even with the old television technology operated by the liberal capitalists, the airwaves were impossibly crowded. The Party required that every individual telescreen in every home and office become a full-fledged broadcast station in its own right. This was impossible with the old, high-powered broadcast transmitters. The millions of signals would have interfered with each other. The airwaves would have ended up filled with meaningless static.

Wires could be used instead of the airwaves, but this created other difficulties. Millions of wires would have to be routed for miles under the streets, to converge at the Ministry of Love in the heart of London. It was still hopelessly impractical to funnel a Niagara of information through a single faucet in the center of the city.

The telescreens themselves helped up to a point. Words, sounds, and pictures all contain vast amounts of information that is wasted on the sluggish eyes and ears of humans. Efficient coding can compress telescreen pictures by factors of a thousand or more, with no loss apparent to human senses. Compression requires fantastic mathematical calculations to distill what is sent and then reconstitute the original at the receiving end, but the telescreen chips developed in the '80s contained those capabilities. The carrying capacity of even the old, copper-wire network could have doubled and doubled again, year after year, for as long as chips increased the telescreen's power to squeeze gallons of information into cupfuls of compressed digits.

At the same time the engineers were radically improving the wires. Light-transmitting glass proved to be vastly more capacious than electricity-conducting copper. The engineers developed single-mode transmission methods, built new lasers, perfected frequency modulation, and deployed erbium-doped amplifiers. Every four years the transmission capacities of the optical fibers increased tenfold. Thus, the wires in the tunnels shrank a thousandfold in size, and increased a millionfold in carrying capacity. Scarcity again gave way to plenty. The tunnels, once filled with great bundles of metal wire, were soon all but empty.

The last step was to cut the glass umbilical, so that telescreens could be deployed even where the wires could not follow. At first the problem of scarcity in the airwaves seemed intractable: if millions of transmitters sent signals through the air simultaneously, there would be a cacophony of interfering radio noise. Then the engineers hit upon an ingenious solution. The idea was to slash the power of every transmitter—to reduce its range, down to a mile, down to a hundred yards, down to a hundred feet, less still if necessary. When every personal television broadcast studio operates at low enough power, there is no interference. Space is divided into thousands of · tiny broadcast "cells," each controlled by a single telescreen.

How then are signals carried over larger distances? Adjacent telescreens relay them one to the next, or hand the signals off to the glass network underground. Every telescreen supervises, relays with, and connects to its neighbors. With cellular technology there is no practical limit to how much information can be moved through the air. As new telescreens are added to the network, the number of possible pathways between any pair increases. The more crowded the system gets, the more capacious it becomes, and the better it functions.

A cellular system of course requires massively complex coordination. At any instant, the signal from one telescreen must be tracked by its immediate neighbors. As the signal strength varies, each telescreen must monitor where its neighbors are moving. Connections are handed off from one cell to the next as units move, or are turned on or off. Coordination of this complexity was completely infeasible—until the arrival of the new calculating chips in the telescreens themselves. Then it became easy.

There remained one final problem. The network permitted—in fact required—that every telescreen be able to communicate with every other. But in front of each screen is a person. And the human eye can only assimilate one picture at a time.

So every piece of information, whether traveling as light in a glass wire, or as a radio signal through the air, must be preceded by an electronic address, specifying where the signal came from and where it is to be displayed. Every telescreen must be able to dispatch outgoing signals and select among incoming ones correctly. The telescreens themselves must have the power to "screen"—to select what comes in and what goes out—or the human viewer in front of the unit will be utterly overwhelmed by an excess of information. This power to select signals, to tune one in and others out, is not a luxury, still less a device for sabotaging Party control. Without such capabilities, telescreens as powerful as Orwell wanted cannot be made to work. With them, the telescreen becomes possible.

No other network architecture could ever have supplied the capabilities the Party demanded. A network able to watch everywhere, all the time, every hour of the day and night, must operate without hierarchy, without central control. Telescreens must be linked as one technological peer to the next, with each unit equally autonomous and powerful. Whatever one telescreen can transmit, another can receive; whatever one can store, another can retrieve. It is impossible, and in any event useless, to build a network of infinite capacity without matching power to direct the flow of information. *If it is to function at all, a telescreen must incorporate the power to choose.*

Yes, the power to choose! The power to select, as your telescreen company, other flower lovers, stamp collectors, pigeon fanciers, amateur carpenters, coupon snippers, darts players, and crossword puzzle fans. The power to build private communities, to assemble network equivalents of the pub, the football match, the back garden, the fireside, and the "nice cup of tea." The power to choose your own company and your own amusements, instead of having them chosen for you from above.

O'Brien rubbed his eyes, then reached over and adjusted the green lampshade on the light beside his chair. From the large window that ran the length of his office he could look out over the vastness of London. It was a moonless night, and the sky outside was now pitch black. Nearby, only the monstrous pyramids of the other three ministries, brightly lit, stood out against the black shadows of the night. But toward the east he could see the glow of the proles' market. He turned back to the diary.

Even the telescreen might have changed little if the Party had been right about the proles. The proles, the Party believed, aspired to material equality more than anything—or would have aspired to it had they not been too crushed by drudgery to be more than intermittently conscious of anything outside their daily lives. The Party would appeal to their prurience with rubbishy newspapers filled with sport, crime, and astrology, sensational novelettes, vapidly sentimental songs, films oozing with sex. The pornography section of the Ministry of Truth would churn out "Spanking Stories" or "One Night in a Girl's School," to be peddled furtively to their youths.

The proles had the numbers to brush the Party aside, of course, like a horse shaking off flies. With a broader vision, with standards of comparison, with higher levels of education, the proles might become aware that they were oppressed and might then rebel. Left to themselves, however, they would continue from generation to generation without any impulse to rebel. They might remember a million useless things—a quarrel with a workmate, a hunt for a lost bicycle pump, the expression on a long-dead sister's face, the swirls of dust on a windy morning seventy years ago—but all the larger issues would stay outside the range of their vision.

Except in one place—their market. Yes, their *market!* It is in the market, after all, that humans learn to assemble, to write, to count, to compare, to remember, to interact, to cooperate, to plan—and thus, ultimately, if they must, to conspire. The market requires no autocrat, no queen bee, no central planner, no citadel, no all-powerful executive suite. Communication across the span of a market occurs through the accumulation of small, face-to-face deals. The market, like the currency on which it depends, is a network—a system for communicating across time and space. The market creates the strength of numbers outside Party control.

The Party's road to serfdom was built on the rubble of the free market. Private markets—money itself—were inimical to Party control. The Party abolished private property and condemned individual enterprise. It degraded the currency and substituted for it fistfuls of special coupons and ration tickets.

And yet the Party could never completely eradicate the proles' market, and never really bothered to try. Their market was efficient at discovering that one family needed a blanket, and that another had some food to spare. But it still depended on roads and bridges and the creeping movement of people and things. Currency could streamline everything—but currency was controlled by the Party. So the proles' market depended intimately on Big Brother. Their loyalty, their trust, their efficiency, depended on the Party's; the most valuable item in their market—the dollar bill—in fact had no value at all. For their market to reach any farther than their legs could carry them, the proles had to trust the Party's dollar—which the Party could short-weight, inflate, and corrupt at will.

Even when the Party kept the currency reasonably stable, the proles' market failed at every turn. Even the capitalists of the old days rejected the market within their own corporations, because it was too inefficient to negotiate a contract each time a letter had to be typed or a waste basket emptied. Internally, a corporation had to operate as an oligarchical collective. The proles faced similar problems. Their market could not supply them with highways, bridges, parks, or lighthouses. It thus depended on all sorts of shared goods which, like currency, had to be owned and managed collectively. The Party was confident that these problems would protect Party rule forever.

And then the Party lost its senses. It directed Orwell to deploy the telescreens.

O'Brien looked up from the book. A feeling of weariness had overwhelmed him—weariness mixed with repulsion and bewilderment. The weariness was penetrating the depths of his bones. He began to read again.

And then the Party lost its senses. It directed Orwell to deploy the telescreens. Any prole who buys razor blades or sells chocolates will someday discover how much he needs the network. The proles will learn to use telescreens sooner or later. The proles have incentives to learn useful things. The proles have a market.

Imagine the world that awaits now—a world shaped by perfect communication over any distance, between any pair, or any cluster, of telescreens. It is a world in which records can be maintained and manipulated, combined and merged, moved and processed, effortlessly and at almost no cost.

In a telescreened society, free markets will be irrepressible. The genius of a market is that it elicits information about what people have and what they want. That information, however, becomes powerful only when it is communicated to others. The invisible hand has no power unless guided by visible eyes and ears. Guided by telescreen, the most powerful eye and ear ever imagined, nothing can stop it.

What are the essential ingredients of a market? Communication, to connect together the willing buyer and the willing seller. Promises, so that trades begun today can be consummated tomorrow. Memory, so that promises will be kept. More memory, to record what belongs to whom. More promises, to create all other rights beyond property rights, because all social norms depend on a shared commitment to enforce them. Promises again, by which honest traders agree to ostracize cheats, deadbeats, and thieves. Promises and memories, trust and loyalty: these are the essentials on which all else in the marketplace is constructed. And the telescreen is the greatest of all communicating machines, an electronic scribe of records and memory, a laser-light weaver of trust and loyalty.

The Party has abolished private property. The telescreen will recreate it. Private property is an idea, built around a memory and a promise. In their day, the capitalists maintained vast records to track who owned which parcel of land. That was the memory. And they committed among themselves to defend each other's claims and possessions. That was the promise. Now we have the telescreen, the most powerful machine ever imagined for recording memories and communicating promises.

With private property resurrected and the telescreen at hand for trading it, the market will create prosperity beyond anything ever before imagined.

The giant trusts and corporations that evolved in the early days of capitalism will not reappear. The old corporation operated in the image of Big Brother, as a homogeneous, collectivist autocracy, dominated by a single, all-powerful leader. In the age of the telescreen no such structures can survive. They will be replaced by independent but tightly interconnected business groups, linked by telescreen but disciplined in all their relationships by market forces. In the telescreened world, people will be paid because they work, not because they show up daily on the factory floor or in some glass-walled office. Services delivered over the new network will be metered with absolute precision. Specialists will specialize as never before.

Labor supplied over the network—which is to say, most labor—will be valued with scrupulous precision. People who really produce will be in high demand, and no one will care at all about their race or religion, their sex, social graces, physical appearance, or how they smell. Quality services will be purchased wherever they can be found, across the street or across the ocean. Inferior services will be priced accordingly, and incompetence will not be bought at all, however much employment commissions may protest. No government agencies will even be able to keep track of what is being supplied where, still less dictate who should be employed or on what terms.

The factory will be irrevocably changed. A car manufacturer will become a truly efficient assembler of parts provided by hundreds of independent suppliers. Secretaries, accountants, designers—most of the enterprise's support services—will be replaced by independent outsiders, knitted together into an efficient whole by intercommunication over the network. Suppliers, assemblers, distributors, and customers will coordinate themselves with meticulous precision. Even the largest factory will operate with no inventory, no warehouses, no fitful starts and stops caused by shortage of supply or excess of output. A customer's order will be conveyed instantly up the chain of production to the assembly line, and back further still to the factory's suppliers of paint, tires, and radios, and hence back to their suppliers of rubber and steel. There will be little waste, few unsold goods, almost no friction. Industrialism no longer requires collectivism. In every collectivist society of the past, the aim was to make men resemble insects in the hope that they would cooperate as effectively. With the telescreen, the insect-men are dead; the ants are now in the chips. An almost anarchistic form of society is now completely compatible with industrialism and a high level of technical development. Freedom and organization can be reconciled. Cooperation can be by consent.

The old systems of marketing will be transformed beyond recognition. In primitive societies, the market operates with tiny stalls and without reliable currency; trading extends only as far as goods can be carried. In a barter economy, the seller exchanges the pig directly for a dozen chickens. Payment is assured, but the process is terribly cumbersome. In societies that are stable enough to issue currency and imbue it with value, money marks a great advance. It records value in a standardized form that is widely understood; it conveys value without any need to transport pigs or chickens. The paper itself is worthless, except for the information it conveys. Money, then, is just another network—a system of communication, a record of past effort and a promise of future return. With money, the record is on paper, a primitive, inefficient, and vulnerable medium of communication. And a single, master record keeper, the government treasury, with a single, centralized printing press, has absolute power to determine value.

But there is ultimately only one valuable currency: the currency of reputation, of stable, honest, reliable loyalty. Once it is established of a man, or a leader, or a nation's central banker, that his word is his bond, he can issue currency at will. Once it is established that he is a chiseler, a deadbeat, or a thief, no amount of currency will do him much good, for his paper will be shunned wherever he tries to peddle it. The value of money thus depends on trust and promises among the people who control the records.

If the network is powerful enough, nobody controls the records, or at least no central authority does. Trust begins among individuals; then it coalesces among larger groups; then it coalesces in larger groups still. At their peak, the old capitalists trusted a thousand different private currencies in varying degrees: personal checks, stock certificates, bonds, credit card slips, futures contracts, green stamps, patronage accounts of every kind. Even the primitive network at their disposal enabled them to confirm that an account had assets, that a business was functioning, or that an individual faithfully paid his bills. Private enterprises were already issuing countless private currencies, by verifying credit, clearing checks, evaluating investments, dealing in futures, and insuring risks.

All this was done on a network that was pitifully slow and unreliable by comparison with Orwell's. Even then, the capitalists knew that governments could never be trusted, that even in the best of times the Treasury was corrupt and melted down the official currency a little bit every year, and that in the worst of times governments would simply repudiate their debts, deny their memories, and disclaim their banknote promises. But with perfect memory and communication the government bank is no longer needed—currencies of every imaginable description will be created by the market itself, like all other goods. With the telescreen, virtually every kind of good can become the equivalent of a banknote, available for inspection, conveyance, and storage at any distance. The telescreen spells the end of our worthless dollars, ration books, and coupons.

Money is just one example among many. Almost everything that now belongs to Big Brother can be returned to the market. Lighthouses for ships? With advanced communication, ships can be tracked and guided privately. Air traffic control for planes? Planes, like pedestrians, can avoid colliding on their own, if they can see far enough ahead and communicate fast enough among themselves. Pollution of natural resources? This too is ultimately a failure of private dialogue and negotiation, as to who is willing to pay how much for air, water, or land. Prisons for criminals? The most pathologically violent will still need to be confined, but most antisocial citizens can simply be ostracized, or tracked by means of electronic collars, or credit reports, or private references.

Today, nothing is illegal in Oceania because there is no law. Thoughts and actions which, when detected, mean certain death are not formally forbidden; a Party member is required to have not only the right opinions but the right instincts. The rule of law will be reborn spontaneously in a telescreened society. Law is created by consensus. Consensus is created by communication. The telescreen, the most perfect communicator, is also the most perfect police force. Not because the wires lead to a Ministry, but because free and honest people will always take up the hue and cry against brigands and thieves when the alarm is sounded. Our ancestors relied on branding and mutilation—crude records of past transgression, crude promises of future ostracism. An advanced network can brand people too, but with infinitely finer calibration and far less cruelty.

That is what you must fear most, comrades, the branding and the punishment. You may fear that the proles will turn your own tools of torture and violence against you. They will do worse: they will leave you to yourselves. And comrades, among yourselves you will starve, because you produce nothing of any value at all.

The proles' education did not matter so long as it came in our schools, from our teachers. Science did not matter, so long as we could isolate scientists in a few government laboratories and occupy them with useless military research. Private property did not matter, so long as it was protected by Party police. The market did not matter, so long as trade was conducted over our roads, using our currency. Now there is the telescreen. In the age of the telescreen, freedom will no longer be slavery. Freedom will be freedom.

O'Brien felt coarse and worn. His shoulders surrendered to their weariness; he slouched forward. It was almost as if he could feel the pouches under his eyes and tired lines from nose to chin. He turned back to the book with a mounting sense of despair.

The telescreen will bring about the greatest liberation in the most important marketplace of all, the marketplace of ideas. In the age of the telescreen, men's thoughts will be freer than even the utopian dreamers of yesterday ever imagined was possible.

In the best days of the old capitalists, freedom of the press still belonged only to the few who owned one. The telescreen will give voice to the average man, the man who has never before owned a printing press or a broadcast station. It will mobilize public opinion, giving every man a stake in free speech itself. Once large numbers of people have their own, private interests in freedom of speech, there will be freedom of speech, even if the law forbids it. By giving people the power to speak freely, the telescreen will also give them the right. No law, no Thought Police, will be able to change that.

Amid all our memory holes, the telescreen will resurrect memory too, and expand it indefinitely. The Party thought that history could be obliterated in a telescreened society; in fact history will be more accurately preserved, memory will be more constantly and widely refreshed, than ever before. Every act of communication creates a new memory, if only inside another human skull. With the telescreen, any document of importance, any title or deed, any record of science or business, any poem or book, any newspaper or photograph, can be replicated at will, and distributed far and wide, thus creating new memories far faster than any Ministry can alter or incinerate them.

Ignorance—or at least rigid, class ignorance that endures generation after generation—cannot survive the telescreen. Not simply because wealth creates leisure, and leisure creates literacy; as often as not, leisure in fact creates passive ignorance. But ignorance will be attacked by the telescreen itself. People will now educate themselves and their children, if they wish to. The Party may continue to own the public schools—the stone and mortar—but the telescreen can create a school out of any pair of desks. The great universities, the great libraries, will no longer be in places; they will reside in cyberspace, securely out of reach of the Party torches and bonfires. Heresy can no longer be eradicated by fire. Heresy is now fire itself, pulses of light in a network of glass.

The telescreen creates the one freedom that matters in the realm of free expression: the freedom to choose. When men lived as crowded as ants, they quarreled endlessly about who could make noise and who was entitled to quiet, who could watch and who had a right to close his curtains against prying eyes. The telescreen gives man eyes and ears that can see at any distance, so that thoughts and words and gestures can inhabit infinitely spacious parks. It frees his senses, and so frees his intellect and his conscious mind. It gives him the power to hear, see, and speak, to be heard and seen, in the company of his own choosing. Now men can create new assemblies, new congregations, new cities whenever they need them, in the capacious light beams of the network and the airwaves of the stratosphere.

The network is boundlessly public but also as private as the womb. The owner of the telescreen designates who may receive his transmissions. He designates which signals he wishes to receive. He can broadcast to the world from his bedroom, or reserve his great novel for the enjoyment of a few choice friends. He can exclude all racists, sexists, pornographers, drug peddlers, or others whose message he finds hateful. Distance was once privacy but also isolation, peace but also loneliness. The network erases distance, or creates it, precisely as directed by the owner of each telescreen. The network is the true master of distance: it can maintain distance as easily as it can cross it. The power is in the individual's hands, and his alone.

In the old days of the capitalists, the press, the film industry, radio, and television, were all stagnant oligopolies, dumping the same mind-numbing rubbish into every home. The owners of those media pitched their programs at what the great mass of people share in common—their prurience, their neurotic fears—and relied on crude polling to estimate how many people were attracted by sex and violence to endure advertisements for sugared cereal and laundry soap. All of this will now disappear. Every hobby and pastime— cage birds, fret work, carpentry, bees, carrier pigeons, home conjuring, philately, chess—will have at least one telescreen channel devoted to it, and often several. Gardening and livestock keeping will have at least a score between them. Then there will be the sporting channels, the radio channels, the children's comics, the large range of channels devoted to the movies and all more or less exploiting women's legs, the various trade channels, the women's soap opera channels, the needlework channels, and countless others. These dimestore novels of the telescreen will exist because there is a definite demand for them, and they will reflect the minds of their viewers as a single national network cannot possibly do. Ours will become, once again, a nation of flower lovers and stamp collectors, pigeon fanciers, amateur carpenters, coupon snippers, darts players, and crossword puzzle fans. The days of mindless broadcast to the mindless masses are at an end.

Amid all this freedom there will still be prurience, violence, necrophilic reveries, and the disgusting art of Salvador Dalí. Yet in the universe of the telescreen, speech in public spaces no longer needs to be regulated. Public spaces—or at least the ones of any importance—are no longer surrounded by walls or gates. Bulletin boards, auditoriums, theaters, schools, stadiums, squares, subway walls—electronic replacements for all the traditional public forums—can be created upon demand. The network gives the pamphleteer and soapbox orator not just a place in Speaker's Corner but the whole of Hyde Park. There is room for the Pacifist, the Communist, the Anarchist, the Jehovah's Witness, and the Legion of Christian Reformers who have declared Hitler to be Jesus Christ. Temperance reformers, Communists, Trotskyists, the Catholic Evidence Society, Freethinkers, vegetarians, Mormons, the Salvation Army, and any number of plain lunatics: all will be able to speak out over the network; all will receive a good-humored hearing from anyone who chooses to listen. The network will be Alsatia, where no opinions are outlawed. There has never been any place like it before in the physical world.

The network will supply room enough for every sight and sound, every thought and expression that any human mind will ever wish to communicate. It will make possible a wildness of spirit, where young minds can wander in adventurous, irresponsible, ungenteel ways. It will contain not innocence but a sort of native gaiety, a buoyant, carefree feeling, filled with confidence in the future and an unquenchable sense of freedom and opportunity. It will be capitalist civilization at its best. It will be the new frontier, and also the last frontier, for it extends as far as any human mind may wish to range. People will assemble in any numbers, at any distance, in groups that are infinitely variable. They will be able to cry fire whenever they wish: the theater will no longer be crowded.

O'Brien leaned back in his chair and gazed for a moment at the handwriting in the diary. How had the pages even been reproduced, he wondered. A dim recollection of a science called xerography floated into his mind. He was certain the copying machines had all been confined to secure rooms inside the Ministry, but a traitor had apparently gained access to one anyway. Perhaps Winston Smith himself. The man had worked in the Ministry, after all, and had undoubtedly had access to these machines. It had probably taken him no more than a few hours to produce a hundred copies of his diary. And any other traitor with a copy, and access to a machine, could produce a hundred more. There were always traitors about, O'Brien reflected. Always traitors . . . always. His shoulders sagged, and he turned back to the diary.

Armed with the telescreen, the proles will leave you to yourselves and return to their own private pursuits. That is how the English always escape from Party gangsters; they sell their souls in public, then buy them back in private, among friends, among their fellow flower lovers or stamp collectors. The proles will rediscover English liberty, which is the liberty to have a home of your own, to do what you like with your time, to choose your own employment and your own amusements instead of having them chosen for you from above. Freedom—the right to choose your associates and friends and live with them as you please—is now at hand.

The Party believed that with the telescreen it could close man's eyes and ears, that it could deliver an incessant stream of pictures and sound, of Party propaganda emerging from the larynx, not the brain, of noise uttered in unconsciousness, like the quacking of a duck. The Party believed that the telescreen would drown out all other discourse, that it would be every man's hearty companion and insinuating spy.

But the Party was wrong. The telescreen does not destroy communication; it creates it. The Party wanted perfect communication to repress all independent thought. But with perfect communication, independent thought is irrepressible. Without the telescreen, there can be no Big Brother. With the telescreen, there can be no Big Brother either.

The Party saw the telescreen and imagined a world of slavery. The Party was right about that—right on this point alone. Every communication is an act of surrender, a loss of privacy, a confession of dependence on others. Freedom is indeed Slavery, because it is when we are free that we confide our secrets, confess our sins, and give away our love. The essence of being human is that one does not push one's privacy to the point where it makes friendly intercourse impossible, and that one is prepared in the end to be defeated and broken up by life, which is the inevitable price of fastening one's love upon other human individuals. The essence of freedom is that the surrender, when it occurs, is voluntary, and the defeat is embraced gladly, as the essence of love itself.

CHAPTER 16 ■■■■■

A torn petticoat lay on the floor, and broken makeup pencils littered the dressing table. Their room, once so warm, now looked shabby and stark. It looked like a room where a whore took her clients. Blair sat on the bed, wretched without her. They were right, of course. She was in the Ministry.

He had wandered the streets of London through the night, searching for her aimlessly. About midnight he had downed five pints of beer and a quarter bottle of gin. For a brief time his brain had seemed marvelously clear. He had seen as something far, far away, like something seen through the wrong end of a telescope, his wasted life, the blank future. He seemed immediately to sink into some immense abyss from which he rose again more gradually and with only partial consciousness of what he was doing. He was gliding smoothly through darkness stained with lights. Or were the lights moving and he stationary? It was like being on the ocean bottom, among the luminous, gliding fishes. The landscape in hell, he fancied, would be just like this. Ravines of cold evil-colored fire, with darkness all above.

He had walked through the seedier parts of London again. The appalling faces of tarts, like skulls coated with pink powder, peered meaningfully from several doorways. He became aware of two hard yet youthful faces, like the faces of young predatory animals, that had come close up to his own. They had blackened eyebrows and hats that were like vulgarer versions of Kate's. As he approached the Palace Theater a girl on sentry-go under the porch marked him down, stepped forward, and stood in his path. A short, stocky girl, very young, with big black eyes. She looked up at him and broke out into a broad-lipped smile.

A short while later they were in a smallish, darkish, smelly hallway, lino-carpeted, mean, uncared for, and somehow impermanent. An evil-looking chambermaid appeared from nowhere. She and the girl seemed to know each other.

Another young woman came mincingly down the stairs, buttoning on a glove; after her a bald, middle-aged man, who walked past them with small mouth tightened, pretending not to see them. Blair watched the gaslight gleam on the back of his bald head. His predecessor. In the same bed, probably.

Then Blair heard himself say, in a suicidally loud voice, "Wharr-I-shay is, perfijious Big Brother! You heard that? Perfijious B.B. Never trust Big Brother! You can't trust the bastard. You wanna do anything 'bout that?" He remembered sticking his face out like a tomcat on a garden wall as he spoke. The man with the bald head had hit him across the legs with a walking stick. Through his private mist, Blair saw in the man's face a curious blend of fear and sadistic exaltation.

A moment later, Blair and the girl were on the landing. There was a smell of slops in the air, and a fainter smell of stale linen. They entered a dreadful room. He seemed to be lying on the bed. He could not see very well. Her youthful, rapacious face, with blackened eyebrows, leaned over him as he sprawled there.

"How about my present?" she had demanded, half wheedling, half menacing.

Never mind that now. To work! Come here. Not a bad mouth. Come here. Come closer. Ah!

In the morning he had emerged from some long, sickly dream. He remembered the feel of more gin after the girl, as it flowed down his throat, bitter and choking. A frightful spasm of nausea overcame him. He rolled over and was violently sick, three or four times. His face was close to a brick wall, and at first he thought he was in a prison cell. But he was lying on the pavement.

"I'm going to be sick!" he had muttered as he tried to stand up. And as he began to fall, a strong arm went round him.

A moment later the stallkeeper—the razor-blade man—had handed him a mug.

"'Ja do with a cup of tea?" the stallkeeper had said.

"Please," Blair had replied weakly.

"You'll have to go get her," the man had said. "It's 'cos of you and me, mate," he had said. "'Cos of the diary."

Blair had stared back uncomprehendingly.

"They get Kate, they get you nervous, you come to me, I go to me mate that copies the diary, to me friends that works on the screens—they get all of us. Lucky for us you just wandered around and got drunk."

Blair's head had slowly cleared. As it did, the first thing he had seen, towering above him in the distance, was the vast, glittering white, windowless pyramid that was the Ministry of Love.

Then he had set off again, in search of the phreak.

CHAPTER 17 ■■■■■

The camp bed was still in the corner of the room. Two small tables, covered with green baize, stood against the wall. Behind the spare brown desk was a high-backed, red-leather swivel chair. O'Brien was seated in it, rocking slowly. He had been immensely strong; now his great body was sagging, sloping, bulging, falling away in every direction. He seemed to be breaking up, like a mountain crumbling.

The prisoner sat on a wooden chair directly in front of the desk. There were no chains, no ropes. He had a forlorn, jailbird's face with a knobby forehead running back into a bald scalp, a crooked nose and battered-looking cheekbones above which the eyes were fierce and watchful.

For several minutes O'Brien sat quite still looking thoughtfully at his victim. He felt unable to keep his own mind from wandering. It was easy enough, O'Brien reflected, but it was still a serious matter to kill a man. It was comparable to destroying an intricate and costly piece of machinery.

"I would like to make this as easy for you as possible," O'Brien said at last. "Please cooperate. I do not wish to waste time with hypodermics and the pain machine."

The prisoner stared back with the same hooded, fierce gaze. His eyes had sunk deep in their sockets, and the thin blue membranes of his lids drooped down over them. Ravaged grooves ran down his face from cheek to chin.

"Please remember, throughout our conversation, that I have it in my power to inflict pain on you to whatever degree I choose. Do you understand that?"

"Yes," came the hoarse whisper.

O'Brien looked down at the papers in front of him. "You are a member of the Inner Party." It was a statement, not a question, as though he were reading from a record that was already complete.

"Yes."

"You have betrayed the Party."

"Yes."

"You have been sabotaging the network."

"Yes."

"You have read Winston Smith's diary."

"Yes."

"You believe in the secret accumulation of knowledge, a gradual spread of enlightenment—ultimately a proletarian rebellion—the overthrow of the Party. You believe Orwell's network will bring about universal liberty, fraternity, and equality."

There was a pause. "No," the prisoner replied.

O'Brien looked up.

"No?"

The prisoner seemed to gather himself for an effort. "The network will bring liberty but not equality."

"And fraternity?"

"Up to a point," the prisoner whispered.

It struck O'Brien that in almost any revolt the leaders would tend to be people who could pronounce their aitches. For a moment the old pleasure was back. The prisoner would certainly be hanged, but first there would be good conversation. It was a privilege to explore an intelligent mind before obliterating it, a bit like deflowering a virgin or shooting a great elephant. For a moment at least, you owned the thing. You knew it was yours to possess forever, that no one else would delight in precisely the same pleasure again.

He reached for the decanter of wine at the side of his desk, poured a glass, and handed it to the prisoner. "I shall enjoy talking to you," he said. "Your mind appeals to me. It resembles my own mind except that you happen to be insane." He resettled his spectacles thoughtfully. When he spoke again his voice was gentle and patient. He had the air of a doctor, a teacher, even a priest, anxious to explain and persuade rather than to punish.

"The Party has always understood the danger of machines. From the moment when the steam engine first made its appearance it was clear to all thinking people that the need for human drudgery had disappeared. Within a few generations, those machines might have eliminated hunger, overwork, dirt, illiteracy, and disease. They produced wealth. You understand that, of course."

"Yes."

"The living standards of the average human being improved steadily. If we had allowed the process to continue, the all-round increase in wealth would have destroyed the hierarchical society, and our favored position in it. Once it became general, wealth would confer no distinction. Given leisure, the poor would become literate. Sooner or later they would realize that the privileged minority had no function, and they would sweep it away. In the long run, a hierarchical society was only possible on a basis of poverty and ignorance."

O'Brien paused, slightly surprised at how much he had said. "You agree?"

The prisoner looked at the floor, his head drooping farther. Then, very carefully, he lifted the glass O'Brien had given him, and holding it in both hands like a child, he sipped it. He seemed to have difficultly swallowing. He sipped again, then drank greedily, emptying the glass. His eyes closed, and his face seemed to relax.

"Do you agree?" O'Brien repeated.

"No," the man answered, in a firmer tone. He seemed to be collecting thoughts that had once been coherent, but had become fragmented and broken.

"Why not?" said O'Brien.

The prisoner took a long breath. His eyes wandered around the room, then he looked straight at O'Brien and replied with a soft resignation.

"Inequality is the unalterable law of human life. Liberty is incompatible with equality." The prisoner seemed to ponder. His eyes burned under the transparent lids.

"Please explain," said O'Brien. "There is no hurry."

The prisoner looked back, and for an instant his stillness seemed full of strength.

"Even at the apex of the old machine age, human equality had not become technically possible. Men were still not equal in their native talents." His words seemed to give him new energy. "Functions still had to be specialized in ways that favored some individuals over others. There were still sharp distinctions in ability, in achievement, in accomplishment, and thus in social standing and wealth. None of the industrial engines of mass production changed any of that. They steadily reduced drudgery and increased wealth. But they could not abolish inequality."

He sat back against the chair. O'Brien reached once more for the wine, and refilled the man's glass. "I am surprised to hear you say this," he said with a smile. "But you are quite right, of course. The division of humanity into rulers and ruled is unalterable. In their capabilities, as in their desires and needs, men are not equal. There is an iron law of oligarchy, which would operate even if democracy were not impossible for mechanical reasons. So you agree that Smith was wrong? We are not entering a new age of human equality?"

"Not material equality," the prisoner answered in a low voice. "Not equality of intellect, achievement, or material success." There was another pause. The prisoner looked at O'Brien with a curious kind of reservation, as if he could not understand why he asked these questions.

"What kind of equality then?"

"Equal opportunity. Equal dignity. Equal freedom to succeed or fail."

"And what will bring that about?"

"The machine."

"You have just said that the machine will not bring about human equality."

"I mean Orwell's machine. The telescreen."

"What will it do?"

"It will give every man equal power to choose."

O'Brien felt a twinge of annoyance. Was it all so obvious? He wiped his eyes. When he spoke his voice was even softer than before. "You know a great deal about the network. Far more than I do. I should like—" He paused, unsure for a moment just what it was he wanted. "I should like to understand. Explain to me please how the telescreen will bring about equality of any kind."

The man gazed back hollowly; for a moment his eyes seemed to be sinking back into the shell of his skull.

"I am starving," he said at last. "I am terrified of my own body. I am a skeleton; my knees are thicker than my thighs. My spine is curved; my neck can hardly support the weight of my skull."

O'Brien sat still, expecting the plea for food, or perhaps just for the bullet. He wondered vaguely how the man would conduct himself on his way to the gallows. He remembered one man in particular, who had urinated all over the floor of his cell. Another had clung desperately to the bars, and it had taken six guards to pry him loose.

"I wish I were free," the prisoner said. "I wish I were free of hunger and disease, and free to leave this evil place."

O'Brien sat quietly. He had learned years ago that in some interrogations the trick was to say less, not more. The prisoner continued.

"But you are not free either. You are free to be a drunkard, an idler, a coward, a backbiter, or a fornicator, but you are not free to think for yourself. Your opinion on every subject of any conceivable importance is dictated for you by the Party's code. Every kind of freedom is given to you except the one that counts most. Your whole life is a life of lies. As a member of the Inner Party you are tied tighter than a monk or a savage by an unbreakable system of tabus."

The man was obviously mad, O'Brien thought. A raving lunatic, and suicidal too. The prisoner continued to speak.

"Real freedom is now at hand. The telescreen gives man the power to decide for himself whom he will approach or avoid, what he will divulge or conceal, by whom he will be entertained or employed, what he will say or hear, show or see, think or believe. Man now holds in his hands the power to share his own thoughts precisely as he pleases, with friends near or far and with no one else."

For a moment, the prisoner seemed to subside and grow feeble again. In the silence O'Brien saw the man's body melt out of focus, and then split into two. What was remarkable was that the two images were seated a couple of feet apart and were quite distinct. O'Brien shook his head, bringing on a burst of pain. A single body reappeared in front of him again. He looked at it with contempt.

"Suppose your fantasy comes true," O'Brien said. "Suppose you do create a world of perfect communication, with telescreens at the disposal and under the control of every individual citizen. What then? If the private citizen can communicate at will, so too can the Thought Police. If eyes can see they can also watch. Improve your power to communicate and you improve your power to spy."

The prisoner shook his head. "Improve your power to communicate and you improve your power to create privacy and solitude. If a spy can see a hundred miles, his target can range farther still. When communication is poor, a man must deal with the same small group of neighbors and associates day after day. He cannot move, so he cannot hide. The telescreened world offers the ultimate privacy—the privacy of distance and the crowd."

One had to admire the man's impudence, O'Brien thought. His life was running down, like seconds ticking off a clock, and yet he was not afraid. "Even with the telescreen, your privacy will still be at the mercy of every nosy neighbor and officious tradesman," O'Brien replied. "Sellers will track your every purchase of carrots and condoms. Bankers will record your every visit to the brothels in Soho. Your electronic footprints will be followed by every peddler of disgusting American breakfast cereal."

"You are wrong," the prisoner replied in a low voice. "When people shop face to face in a small town there is no privacy. With the telescreen, they can do business with complete strangers a thousand miles away, who have no interest in anything but the sale. The telescreen supplies the privacy of the metropolis on demand, even to residents of small communities. When cash becomes a reliable medium of exchange once again, the telescreen will support cash machines next to every brothel, casino, or opium den. The power to communicate is the power to keep your distance and cover your tracks. The telescreen does not destroy privacy; it gives people the power to mold their own privacy at will." He looked up at O'Brien again. He seemed calmer, and his voice no longer cracked at every syllable.

"The telescreen will become the instrument of extortion, blackmail, fraud, and libel," said O'Brien. "If someone denounces you as a deadbeat, you will be commercially ostracized. If your spiteful neighbor whispers into the network that you thrash your wife, the entire world will hear it at once. Whatever empowers honest people also empowers criminals."

The prisoner shook his head again. "The telescreen makes possible new forms of lies, deceits, and frauds, but it also offers vastly more choice, and creates new standards of comparison. When one credit company falsely denounces you as a deadbeat, its competitors will quickly expose the lie; the market punishes sellers of bad credit reports just as it punishes sellers of bad eggs. Libel of any kind will be corrected quickly, because the responsible and well intentioned gain more from truths than the irresponsible or malicious can gain from lies."

"You are a fool," O'Brien replied sharply. "The market itself will not survive the telescreen. In your telescreened utopia most property will consist of information. But there can be no private ownership of expression, no true marketplace of ideas, in a world where words, sounds, and pictures can be copied effortlessly by anyone. The first buyer of your film or software program will flood the market with pirated copies. Books will get cheaper and cheaper, and the cheaper they become, the less money will be spent on them. You will have to choose between art and money. Cheaper communication spells disaster for every publisher, compositor, author, and bookseller."

The prisoner looked back. His emaciated face seemed hungrier than ever, but to his amazement O'Brien now saw a shadow of contempt under the yellow skin of his eyes. "Do you really suppose that the power to communicate will destroy the market for thought and speech? If the telescreen makes it easier to steal art, wisdom, or entertainment, the telescreen is what imbues those things with value to begin with. A printing press can be used to steal a book, but it is the press that makes the copyright valuable to start with. And in any event, there are defenses against pirates and bootleggers. With a machine as powerful as the telescreen, information can easily be encoded. The honest seller can sell openly in the mass market created by the network, while pirates who follow have to lurk in the electronic shadows. Theft and dependence always trail behind industry and wealth, but they never catch up."

The man had a drizzly voice, O'Brien reflected. Listening to his monologues, with all their rambling speculations, was very English in a way. Hearing his monotonous voice was like walking down a wet street. And O'Brien was finding it increasingly difficult to concentrate—his head seemed to be throbbing in time with his heartbeat. He grimaced at the prisoner and rubbed his forehead.

"You will be astounded at how quickly your new world of free choice becomes ugly and depraved," O'Brien said. "People will claim, on behalf of the so-called artist, a kind of benefit of clergy. The artist will be exempt from the moral laws that are binding on ordinary people. Just pronounce the magic word 'Art' and everything will be O.K. Rotting corpses with snails crawling over them will be O.K.; kicking little girls in the head will be O.K.; a film of a woman defecating will be O.K. So long as you can paint or sing or write well enough to pass the telescreen test, all shall be forgiven you. Your artists will spend on public sodomy what they have gained by private sponging."

O'Brien leaned back in his chair but continued to speak. "The greatest impoverishment of your world will be self-inflicted. Free choice on the telescreen will bring about a frightful debauchery of taste; it will do for the mind what mechanization has already done for the human palate. Thanks to tinned food, cold storage, synthetic flavorings, and so on, the palate is almost a dead organ. Machines will kill human thought too. There are already millions of people to whom the blaring of a telescreen is not only a more acceptable but a more normal background to their thoughts than the lowing of cattle or the song of birds. Place every telescreen under private control, and the masses will wallow in filth far worse than the rubbishy entertainment and spurious news the Party supplies today."

O'Brien stopped, breathing heavily. His head was hurting more and more. It felt as if something was pushing his eyes out, and expanding behind his ears.

"You are right," the prisoner said intensely, leaning forward. "On the telescreen, everything shall be forgiven, whether or not called art. Some forms of telescreen expression will be unspeakably vile. They will be tolerated not because all art is beautiful but because all Thought Police are ugly. There is room enough on the network for every form of diseased intelligence. Freedom includes the freedom to be foolish, to be sick. Free choice includes the freedom to choose badly."

"For others as well as yourself?" said O'Brien. "Your free choice of women defecating will appear in my living room too."

"With the telescreen, people can create their own censors and keep their own thought police on private retainer," the prisoner replied. "The editors of the *Times* will serve as private censors employed at the pleasure of their readers. A credit company will supply private protection against fraud. Copyright will be protected not by laws and courts but by private encryption. For every possible private fraud, for every private oppression, there will be private protection. With the network, people can join together to coordinate private police forces as they never could before."

For the first time in their conversation, O'Brien felt himself smile. "So instead of one censor in the Ministry of Truth, you will now have a censor in every household. People will no longer be able to proselytize or persuade, to solicit, canvas, or agitate. Prudes will assemble only with other prudes, racists with other racists. Today you must confront the homeless soliciting in the subways and seeking shelter in the public libraries. Tomorrow, your libraries will all be electronic, and your subways will consist of fiber-optic glass. The hungry will starve unnoticed outside." O'Brien leaned back into the red leather of his chair. His weight seemed so great, he found it difficult even to sit without support. "If liberty means anything at all, it means the right to tell people what they do not want to hear."

"If liberty means anything, it means the right not to listen," the prisoner replied. "Freedom is sometimes intolerant and unwise. Some people will use the telescreen to close their minds. Some will stop listening to unwelcome ideas. But silence and calm solitude, even the silence and solitude of bigots and fools, are as much a part of freedom as sound and furious assembly. Freedom is sometimes bland. Free people sometimes live in little box houses just like their neighbors', sometimes dress up in uniforms, sometimes eat only pallid, spiceless food. But more often, free people choose variety."

The prisoner paused, then continued. "Some, as you predict, will anesthetize their minds with visual opiates peddled over the network. But others will use their new power to choose wisely. The obscene caller will no longer enjoy the shock and fear of the elderly widow. The reformed alcoholic will no longer have to watch advertisements for fortified beer. Parents will be able to insulate their children from vulgarity. The deeply religious will be able to surround themselves with others of similar conviction. In the cataract of information of the telescreened world, the most important right will be the right not to listen, not to speak, and not to share one's thoughts, words, or gestures. Freedom of thought, freedom of assembly and religion, copyright and privacy, all pivot on a single, higher right: the right to communicate by mutual consent with other individuals possessing the same dignity, the same power of choice. That is the promise of the telescreen."

O'Brien stared into the distance.

"There will always be bullies," he said at last. "The mass of people will always worship them. And if one must worship a bully, it is better that he should be a policeman than a gangster. Civilization rests ultimately on coercion."

"It rests on consent—the consent of the governed," the prisoner answered. "What holds society together is not the policeman but the goodwill of common men."

"That goodwill is powerless unless the policeman is there to back it up."

"The policeman is powerless without public backing."

"Any government which refused to use violence in its own defense would cease almost immediately to exist, because it could be overthrown by any body of men, or even any individual, that was less scrupulous," said O'Brien. "Whoever is not on the side of the policeman is on the side of the criminal."

"Consensus is the master of both the criminal and the policeman," the prisoner replied. "The only durable law is common law, law forged by custom and molded by tradition. Law is ultimately what most people in a society agree that it should be. Agreement is built by communication. It is built by telescreen."

O'Brien shrugged. "With or without agreement, every utterance, every thought crystallized inside a human skull, has public consequences. Whatever is heard or seen or fantasized, even in utter solitude, may become transformed into an attack on others. By encouraging necrophilic reveries, a depraved artist may do quite as much harm as by picking pockets at the races. Private pornography inspires public violence. Private scheming and conspiracy culminate in fraud, extortion, or blackmail. The individual's freedom becomes the community's slavery. Freedom is slavery."

"Freedom is sanity," the prisoner replied. "The telescreen will give us necrophilic reveries, but it will also create room for the art of angels. It will supply passion but also reason. It will spread propaganda but also private discourse. It will give us spies but also distance to elude them. It will carry the proclamations of generals before battle, the speeches of führers and prime ministers, the solidarity songs of public schools and left wing political parties, national anthems, temperance tracts, papal encyclicals and sermons against gambling and contraception—and it will also carry the chorus of raspberries from all the millions of common men to whom these high sentiments make no appeal. The network empowers electronic thugs at one end and the Thought Police at the other. But in the middle stand the great mass of men, simple, honest, and sane. So long as common men use the network too, their basic sanity will prevail. Freedom will be freedom."

"But not equality?"

"No."

O'Brien scarcely heard the answer. The man would be flogged before he was hanged, he was thinking. His skin would be stripped from his back as neatly as a skinned rabbit. O'Brien thought of how the corpse would look, scarlet and blue—devilish. But instead of a sense of power, the thought filled him with unexpected disgust. A look of ineffable sadness had appeared on the man's face.

"Only one kind of human equality will survive the telescreen," the prisoner said. "The only kind of equality that men have the power to affirm. It is equal opportunity—an equal chance to converse, trade, and collaborate with others by mutual consent. The telescreen offers equal dignity, nothing more. All other kinds of equality belong to Big Brother."

"So your glorious fantasy is not so glorious after all." O'Brien felt a brief surge of triumph. "Why are you so pessimistic?" he said contemptuously. "Your telescreen will create wealth, it will distribute culture, it will educate the masses. Equality is therefore inevitable. A socialist utopia is at hand. Why do you stubbornly insist that equality will not come?"

"Education will still not put an end to hierarchy," the prisoner replied calmly. "Men are still unequal in their native talents. Some men will use their telescreens for education, others for lotteries. The talented or industrious will embrace the new opportunities; the lazy or foolish will sink into tele-induced stupor. Hierarchies will not disappear. They will simply come to mirror inequalities among men themselves."

"Do you not see, then, what kind of world you are creating?" O'Brien said angrily. "It is the exact opposite of the stupid hedonistic utopia that Winston Smith imagined. Your society will be founded upon nothing but market greed and technocratic wizardry. The strong will devour the weak."

The prisoner shook his head slowly. "The telescreen will do all that man can do about equality of human thought and human minds. It will affirm the equality of true equals. Victims of foolish prejudice will do well in the telescreened society, because they will no longer have to confront prejudice face to face. In a telescreened community, it will be economically ruinous to discriminate against the Buddhist, the Anabaptist, or the Jew, the man in the wheelchair or the woman with the thick spectacles, because competitors from far afield will bid for their talents and welcome their business. But a telescreened market will always discriminate between quality and rubbish. The telescreen will amplify every native difference in our abilities to entertain, educate, design, provoke, amuse, or inspire, every difference between the industrious and the lazy, between the competent and the incompetent, between the provident and the improvident, between truthful people and liars, between honest people and thieves. The telescreen lets people see and compare and choose. It punishes mental cheating of every kind."

O'Brien found himself thinking again of the hanging to come. There would be six guards. The prisoner would be handcuffed, his arms lashed tight to his side. The guards would crowd very close about him, with their hands always on him in a careful, caressing grip as though all the while feeling him to make sure he was there. It would be like men handling a fish which is still alive and may jump back into the water. It was always a good spectacle. But O'Brien's head still throbbed. He felt as if his nose were going to bleed. Where did this shrivelled man find such a fountain of words? O'Brien gripped the leather arms of his chair.

"Do you suppose that democracy will emerge from all of this?" O'Brien said. "Do you think that government by the people will still be possible among the mountains and valleys of wealth and achievement that your network will create?"

"No. The network will destroy democracy, or at least our last illusions about it. Democracy is only a polite name for capitalism. True government by the people will never be attained anywhere but in tiny, homogeneous communities. Even in the old days of liberal capitalism, political power belonged to the wealthy and articulate, those with the time and inclination to organize and participate. Most people didn't even bother to vote. Political power has always flowed to the great orator, to the tireless stuffer of envelopes, to the indefatigable canvasser, to the obsessive baker of fund-raising cakes. It always will.

"But with the network we will come closer to democracy than anyone has before," the prisoner continued. "The mass media will lose the vast political power they once exercised. The wealthy will have influence only to the extent they engage society and interact productively with other people. Power will lie in constantly shifting communities of shopkeepers, housewives, old Etonians, fruit-juice thinkers, nudists, sandal wearers, sex maniacs, Quakers, Nature Cure quacks, pacifists, and phesbian leminists of England. All of society will be shaped by the accumulation of individual decisions to meet or stay apart, to buy or sell, to speak or to remain silent. The political and social hermit will have no more political power tomorrow than he did yesterday. People who choose lives of parasitic dependence will be disenfranchised, not by any government decree but by their own passivity. In politics, as elsewhere, the telescreened society will discriminate fiercely—on the basis of conviction, talent, and effort."

"Then you will recreate the Party," O'Brien said sharply. "Political power will converge once again in the hands of the wealthy, the articulate, and the technically sophisticated."

The prisoner nodded. In his hollow eyes there also seemed to be a faint, secret glow. "Yes, up to a point that will happen. But the inequalities created by the network will have nothing to do with Party rank. They will spring up among the wealthy and the poor, among fathers and sons, siblings and cousins. The ancient hierarchies of blood or ancestry, the plutocracies that endured from generation to generation, will be swept aside. The new hierarchies will always be changing, because they will be hierarchies of talent and nothing else."

"Freedom and organization cannot be reconciled," O'Brien said. "Without Ministry coordination you will never maintain the air-conditioned, chromium-plated, gadget-ridden existence that is now considered desirable and enlightened. The processes involved in making an aeroplane or running a network are so complex as to be possible only in a planned centralized society. Liberty and efficiency pull in opposite directions."

For the second time a shadow of contempt seemed to move across the prisoner's yellowing face. "The telescreen will decentralize authority and simplify all of life. Inhuman entities like the modern city will disappear. The telescreen resolves the apparent contradiction between decentralization and electric power, air transport, the division of labor, or industrial efficiency. With the telescreen, individuals and voluntary groups can work at any distance for each other's mutual benefit."

O'Brien thought again of the condemned man who had clung to the bars. The man had screamed and screamed, and then he had fouled his pants. O'Brien remembered how he had laughed afterward, laughed quite loudly. Everyone had laughed.

Now, throatily at first, then with great gasps and wheezes, O'Brien was laughing again. He threw his head back. The sagging jowls on his face were shaking. His laugh was a disgusting bubbling sound deep down in his belly. "Do you really believe that telescreens can function without a Ministry?" Finally his voice settled back to a strained hoarseness. "Whatever you call it, the authority that controls the network will be a collectivist oligarchy of bureaucrats, scientists, technicians, trade union organizers, publicity experts, sociologists, teachers, journalists, and professional politicians. It will be the Party. It will be Big Brother."

"The network requires no central authority behind it," the prisoner replied. "In ordinary markets, sausages and sweaters move through dozens of intermediate owners on the way from producer to consumer, without central planning, without coordination from above. Electronic networks link together in the same way. Connections add up. Individuals link into small networked communities, small communities into larger ones, and higher-level networks are overlaid on lower ones, one tier above the next. There are no central planners; central planning is in fact impossible. There will be no Party behind the network. There will be no Big Brother. It is when Big Brother seizes control that the network atrophies and dies."

The prisoner slumped back into his chair, exhausted. It had been a remarkable performance, O'Brien reflected. The man was too intelligent to imagine he could escape. And yet he had spoken with detached, intellectual interest, and with no hint of fear.

For some time O'Brien sat immobile, gazing again at the broken figure in front of him. Filthy grime covered the prisoner's entire body. There was dirt between his toes. He had a vile sore running up his right leg.

"You are rotting away," O'Brien said with contempt. "You are falling to pieces. What are you? A bag of filth. Perhaps with the network you might some day have created markets, memories, money—whatever else you imagined were necessary in your new utopia. Perhaps you really did know how to control the network. But the Party controls you. You will be lifted clean out from the stream of history. We shall turn you into gas and pour you into the stratosphere. The network may perhaps belong to you. But you are my prisoner. You belong to me."

The prisoner's hollow eyes flitted round the walls, as though he half expected to find a window somewhere.

"Yes, I belong to you."

"You are dead."

"Yes, I am dead."

"Your dream will die with you."

"No. Others will carry it forward."

"You are wrong. Winston Smith's diary is of no consequence. You are alone, and soon you will be dead."

O'Brien felt wearier than ever. The pounding in his head was almost unbearable. His chest felt tight. Somehow, interrogations had been easier in the old days, a challenge which his massive intellect had met with greedy anticipation and enjoyment.

The prisoner reached toward his collar, and adjusted the rough cloth of his prison uniform where it had chafed against his neck. It was curious, but 'til that moment O'Brien had never realized what it meant to destroy a healthy, conscious man. The man's nails would still be growing when he stood on the drop, when he was falling through the air with a tenth of a second to live. He and O'Brien were seeing, hearing, feeling, understanding the same world; and in a few minutes, with a sudden snap, one of the two would be gone.

It was time to put an end to the farce. The pain machines would not be needed. O'Brien knew the prisoner would cooperate.

"We know that you have helped stallkeepers connect their telescreens directly to each other."

"Yes," the prisoner answered dully.

"You have discovered some new way to control the telescreens."

"Telescreens were designed to be controlled by their owners."

"That is impossible. Telescreens are controlled by the Ministry."

"No. People can control the connections themselves."

"Do you mean—" the thought was so monstrous that O'Brien could hardly utter it. "Do you mean that any telescreen in London can be connected to any other?"

"Yes."

"That people can stop watching Big Brother whenever they like?"

"Yes."

"That they can disconnect from the Ministry of Love at will?"

"Yes."

"You could send any picture you liked to the telescreen in my own apartment?"

"Yes. I would need to know your number. And your screen would have to be programmed to accept my call."

"How is that done?"

The prisoner shifted on his hard chair. "The most reliable way is with a multifrequency generator. It is a small device that generates certain simple tones. Each tone represents a number. Each telescreen has its own number."

O'Brien slumped back in his chair.

"But this is very complicated? It requires great technical ingenuity?"

"No."

"The tone generators are in very short supply?"

"I don't know. But the tone generators aren't needed."

"Why not?"

"A telescreen can also be programmed with appropriate voice commands."

"How?"

"The screen responds to a simple vocabulary of spoken words. Each word has an exact meaning. The choice of words has been cut down to a minimum, to avoid all possibility of ambiguity or confusion. Each word is simply a staccato sound expressing one clearly understood instruction."

The prisoner paused, as if wondering whether he would say any more. Then, with a shrug, he added: "The command set used to be called BASIC. Now it is known as Newspeak."

Newspeak. The word echoed in O'Brien's brain, and for a moment he wondered stupidly how the language was used. Then with a great effort, with the feeling of deadness creeping up into his belly, O'Brien spoke again.

"You are the only one who knows how to do this?"

"No."

"Who taught you?"

"I don't know his name. The proles call him the phone phreak."

"But you are the phreak."

The prisoner looked back, surprised. Then, for a second, a smile flickered across his hollow face. For a ghastly moment O'Brien thought the man was going to laugh at him. O'Brien's whole life had been one long struggle not to be laughed at.

"I would have earned my phreaking credentials soon enough," the prisoner said after a moment. "There are thousands of phreaks out there already. But you arrested me too soon. I've only just learned how to use the box."

O'Brien thought again of the hanging he had attended years ago. The hangman had fixed the rope round the prisoner's neck, and O'Brien had stood with the warders in a rough circle round the gallows. And then, when the noose was fixed, the prisoner had begun crying out to his god. It was a high, reiterated cry of "God! God! God! God!" not urgent and fearful like a prayer or cry for help, but steady, rhythmical, almost like the tolling of a bell. Now, for a reason he could not understand, O'Brien found himself chanting the same words himself. But his tongue seemed to cleave to the roof of his mouth, and he made no sound.

He heard the vessel bursting in his head even before he felt it. It was a sound like water rushing angrily through a drain, and into the center of his skull. He felt a tremendous pressure. It was as if a bullet had penetrated his brain.

He climbed with desperate slowness to his feet and stood weakly upright, with legs sagging and head drooping. Every line of his body had altered. His mouth slobbered. An enormous senility seemed to have settled upon him; one could have imagined him thousands of years old. At last, after what seemed a long time, he sagged flabbily to his knees. Even in falling he seemed for a moment to rise, like a huge rock toppling. Thick blood welled out of his cavernous mouth like red velvet. He fell forward, and his great fleshy face crashed into the desk. The blood dripped out of his nose and slowly formed a viscous pool on the map of the network spread out in front of him.

CHAPTER 18 ■■■■■

Blair smelled the rats long before he saw them. It was a foul, musty smell of fetid droppings and wet fur. He heard them scuffling evilly behind the bricks. The small flashlight cast only a tiny pool of light on the floor of the tunnel at his feet; everything else was darkness. Occasionally he raised the beam to check on the rubbery orange cables. They were to his right, about shoulder high, just under the curved roof of the tunnel.

"Follow the cables," the phreak had said.

For a moment Blair wished he had not listened to him. He would have forgotten Kate in time, consigned her to the memory holes of his mind. He had gone about a mile in the tunnel now, and it had taken the best part of an hour. It had been bad going underfoot—thick dust and jagged chunks of rock, and here and there the mud as deep as in a farmyard, and viciously slippery. At the start the stooping had not been too difficult, but now it was almost unbearable. At some points in the tunnel he had to bend double, but all the while he also had to keep his head up to watch for the tunnel arches and dodge them when they came. He had a constant crick in his neck, but that was nothing to the pain in his knees and thighs. After half a mile it had become unbearable agony.

At first, as he crept into the dark, stinking tunnel, a terror had risen in his throat, an unreasoning fear that he could not understand. He knew that in the darkness was something unendurable, something too dreadful to be faced. And then he had known. Rats. Somewhere, near him, they were rustling, scurrying, gnawing. He felt blind and terrified. Of all the horrors in the world, he despised rats the most.

He shone his flashlight up onto the cables. Every third or fourth hanger was dislodged, and the cables dangled limply downward like decaying vines in a dying forest. The rats had been at the orange insulation, and in many places it was entirely stripped away. Every few feet the pale beam of the flashlight picked up a glint of glass threaded through the tattered rubber shielding.

The tunnel was curving to the right now, and seemed to be sloping slightly upward. He had just passed through a low stretch of about a hundred yards and a succession of arches which had forced him to a crawl. Getting down on all fours had been a relief after the stooping, but when he came to the end of the arches and tried to get up again, he found that his knees refused to lift him. He rested for a minute or two, before painfully rising again to his feet. A large patch of muddy water appeared in the pale light of his flashlight. He reached up with his left hand to steady himself against the wall.

For a moment he felt the dank hairiness under his hand, and then a piercing pain shot through the tip of his index finger. He swung his flashlight toward the wall, and the animal seemed to leap at his face. It was enormous, an old scaly grandfather of the sewers with pink hands, fierce whiskers, and yellow teeth. It was at the age when a rat's muzzle grows blunt and his fur brown instead of gray, and it seemed to shoot out toward his face like a bullet. In an instant Blair knew that it was going to attack his eyes and burrow through his cheeks and devour his tongue.

He saw his flashlight arch through the air toward the blur of fur, moving by its own will. The light crashed against the brick wall of the tunnel, and a black darkness enveloped him. He felt the blood dripping off the end of his hand. Behind the walls of the tunnel, not far from where the flashlight had struck, there was an outburst of squeals. The sound seemed to reach him from far away. The rats were fighting.

He heard a wild singing in his ears, and he was overcome with a feeling of utter loneliness. He was in the middle of a great empty plain, a Rat desert drenched with sunlight, across which all sounds came to him out of immense distances. He stood hunched in the tunnel, rigid with terror. A succession of shrill cries now appeared to be occurring in the air above his head. There was a violent convulsion of nausea inside him. Panic took hold of him.

He turned violently, striking his head against the roof, and scrambled back up the tunnel. Now he was insane, a screaming animal. Kate didn't matter any more. He hated her. She was a syphilitic whore. She was not young and soft as he remembered, but old and hard, with paint plastered thick on her face, with white hair and a cavernous black mouth with no teeth. Kate didn't matter. Nothing mattered, except escaping the rats. And then he was falling backward, into enormous depths, away from the rats, through the floor of the tunnel, through the earth, through the oceans, through the atmosphere, into outer space, into the gulfs between the stars, always away, away, away from the rats.

His eyes gradually adjusted to the darkness and he saw the lights—tiny filaments of light, jensen blue and ruby red, suspended near the upper edge of the tunnel. Immediately to his side was a hairlike thread of red about a yard long, a sort of deep, glittering red, like blood spilled on an illuminated piece of cut glass. For a moment he thought the color came from his bleeding hand. A bit farther ahead was a short line of blue, the richest blue imaginable, as if drawn in the air with a fine-tipped, luminous fountain pen. He forgot his terror and marveled at the beauty. Perhaps he was hallucinating, but the terror was gone. All that remained was the crystal revelation of light, beautiful light, after the tomblike darkness. He thought what a good thing it was to be alive in a world where such beautiful things could be found.

He remembered lying on the street before Kate had found him; he remembered his dream of the sea and the seashore, of enormous, splendid buildings and streets and ships, and his peculiar feeling of happiness. He knew that these thoughts meant death, but he could not understand why death had to appear to him in these various disguises, for he was no longer afraid of dying.

He thought of the phreak. He remembered when he had first seen him, an overgrown child, tinkering with the wires in the market. *We shall meet in the place where there is no darkness*, the phreak had said. Blair turned around and reached up with his right hand. Delicately now, without fear, he touched the red light and saw it sway gently under his hand. He felt the tattered rubber insulation of the cable where the red beam disappeared back into the darkness. So long as he had regarded himself as an individual, his attitude toward death had been one of simple resentment. But now Kate was a part of him too. She was alive and he was going to get her.

He began to move forward again, splashing through the puddles and the mud. The smell of rats was still heavy in the air, and the blood still dripped from his hand, but he clutched at the lifeline of the cable and pressed on. He reached a stretch of a couple of hundred yards where the tunnel was exceptionally low, and he had to work himself along in a squatting position. He felt only a tremendous longing to finish the journey, an agonized desire to reach the end, and a dreamlike certainty that it was possible. Suddenly the roof opened out and he could stand upright. The relief was overwhelming.

The tunnel continued to curve toward the right and slope upward. After a few minutes more, the red and blue filaments faded from his sight again, and the pitch black of the tunnel became a shadowy gray, and then a weak yellow. A moment later Blair found himself looking through a grating into a musty basement room.

It was a long, rectangular cellar, lit by a single bulb. About a dozen other tunnel entrances were cut into the four walls. The orange rubber cables issuing from each tunnel were routed on large, gray steel trays and converged at the far end of the room. The trays were massive—far too big, it seemed, for the slim orange cables they supported. At the very corner of the room, a single tray curved toward the ceiling, and the cables disappeared through a hole. Next to it, an iron ladder was bolted to the wall. Blair pushed the grating open and climbed into the basement room.

He looked at his watch. It was four-fifteen in the morning. Wait until five, the phreak had said. Wait until five—then go in and get her. They won't stop you. The phreak had promised.

Blair sat down on the floor. The minutes crawled by. To his surprise, he felt a pleasant sort of calm creeping along the length of his limbs. He stretched out his legs, and even imagined that if he had wanted to he could have slept. He ran his tongue over his broken teeth, and wondered abstractly whether he would soon be in the hands of the Thought Police.

It occurred to him that there would always be Thought Police. So long as there were thugs of any kind, there would be thugs of the mind. And the most ruthless would always end up in the ministries. If there was hope, it lay with the proles, with their families, their private loyalties and their market. There was a strength there, far deeper than the Party's, immeasurably more powerful than Big Brother's. *Sooner or later it will happen*, Smith had written. *The proles' strength will change into consciousness. In the end their awakening will come.* As the memory of Smith's words drifted through his mind, Blair imagined he heard Big Brother again, the deep voice full of power and mysterious calm, speaking words of wisdom, the sort of words that are uttered in the din of battle, not distinguishable individually but restoring confidence by the fact of being spoken.

It was five o'clock. Blair moved to the ladder and began to climb. There was a metal trapdoor at the top. He pushed it up and lifted himself into the room above. It was enormous and brightly lit with fluorescent fixtures built into the low ceiling. From one end to the other, the room was filled with rack after rack of gray-painted metal boxes. There was a quiet hum of fans and electric transformers. The cable tray ran the length of the wall. Every few yards, one of the orange cables rose from the tray and snaked up the side of the wall, along the ceiling, and then down into one of the metal racks.

Thousands of hair-thin glass strands branched out from each rack and on to a great vertical metal frame, like the warp of a huge loom. They gleamed and glistened, the colored lights iridescent, slicing through the air like hair-thin icicles, indescribably rich in red and blue colors. The room was a giant pink, convoluted rose, a sea anemone of cut glass, an enormous piece of fluorescent coral plucked from the Indian Ocean, alive with strands of light.

At the far side of the room there was a door, and from behind it came the low sound of a single voice, a voice full of calm, and confidence, and quiet authority. It was Big Brother. Trust me, the phreak had said. And now Blair understood.

He walked across the room and opened the door. He saw the telescreen. He saw on the screen the face of Big Brother, as he had known he would, and heard his resonant voice fill the room with a sort of languorous calm. Three uniformed guards sat on decrepit wooden chairs in front of the screen. They seemed anesthetized, as if their brains had somehow been disconnected from their limbs. They looked at Blair when he entered, but made no move to stop him.

"Await further instructions, comrades," said the face on the telescreen. "Follow instructions. Assist our agents as they move through the Ministry. Follow instructions, stand by the Party, and all will be well. Follow instructions. Cooperate with my agents. Follow instructions . . ."

"Good morning comrades," said Blair.

One of the officers reluctantly pulled his gaze away from the telescreen and stared at him with an air of passive expectation.

"I shall need your help, Wilkes," said Blair. "Please come with me."

Wilkes rose obediently from his chair. His amphibian face was composed and had even taken on a slightly sanctimonious expression. The other two guards sat unmoving. Blair and Wilkes moved across the room and stepped through the door.

"I'm looking for a prisoner. A young woman."

They walked along a featureless corridor of gray cement and up a flight of stairs. A similar corridor lay above the first. Concealed lamps flooded the halls with cold light. They moved down another long corridor, then through another room. On the right was yet another room where more guards sat, staring at a telescreen with the same expression of unthinking absorption. "Follow instructions, comrades," Big Brother was saying. "Assist my agents . . ."

He saw her first through the spy hole in the bolted steel door. The cell had a bench, or shelf, just wide enough to sit on, that ran round the wall, broken only by the door. She sat alone, hunched down, her dress in shreds. Her face was bruised and expressionless. The steel door clanged open as he walked in.

At first she seemed not to recognize him. Then a look of desperate sadness filled her face, and two tears formed at the edges of her eyes and slid down her dirty cheeks.

"I betrayed you," she said baldly.

Blair thought of the youthful, rapacious face, with blackened eyebrows, and of the tunnel, and the rat.

"I betrayed you too," he said.

She still sat frozen on the bench.

"Sometimes," she said, "they threaten you with something—something you can't stand up to."

"Yes," he said. "Sometimes you're afraid."

"And then you're defeated. They break you up."

"Yes."

"After that, you don't feel the same toward the other person any longer," she said.

He walked over to her and with a single finger touched the side of her cheek. "But I still do," he said.

She stared at him, unbelieving.

"I'm not a prisoner," he said. He reached down with both hands, and touched her shoulders, and gently made as if to lift her from the bench. She rose under her own strength. She looked up at him an instant longer, and then buried her face in his breast as suddenly as though ducking from a blow. She wept, clinging to him like a child. And as he led her gently toward the door, he felt her waist, still sweet, still soft, still warm.

They walked out of the cell, and made their way down the corridor and past the guard posts.

"Assist my agents . . ." droned the confident, smooth voice from the telescreen.

"Lead us out, Wilkes," Blair said. They climbed three more sets of stairs and emerged in the great white foyer of the Ministry of Love.

At the iron doors were two more guards, hulking gorillas hung with weapons, grimacing outward toward the courtyard. They fell back as Blair and Kate passed.

Wilkes followed them to the main gates. They walked by the last of the guard posts. Big Brother was still on the telescreen. The guards were still watching, passive, silent, and immobile. "Await further instructions," said the calm voice. "Do not interfere with my agents . . ."

Blair remembered the phreak again. Trust me, the phreak had said. We own the network now. It was all right, everything was all right, the struggle was finished. And for the first time in his life, Blair knew that he loved Big Brother.

■

And now, in the age of doublethink, in the age of the telescreen, there is choice. It is so simple. One keystroke: DEFINE. A second keystroke: DELETE. One page is gone, the other remains. Which shall it be? After *1984*, all history is a palimpsest, scraped clean and reinscribed exactly as often as is necessary. History is yours to erase. But not yours alone. And whatever your choice may be, mine may be different. What you may erase, I may save. So the ending is yours to choose. And mine. And theirs . . .

I

They stepped out of the Ministry together into the dawn. There was a mist in the air; the light was still dim. And for a moment he thought it was the end of the day rather than the beginning. He shut his eyes and saw their children clustered around him, and heard their voices distant and choked with pain, their faces blurred and wet. He saw himself smile when he heard them. He heard himself trying to say something to comfort them, while his gaze stayed locked on hers. He saw that her face was old, her eyes tired, her flesh wrinkled, and her teeth gone, and he saw that she was more beautiful now than ever before. And he knew that without Kate's face close to his the separation from all else would be too painful to bear. He knew that only with Kate beside him would he ever see the face of God.

He opened his eyes, and saw her face again, not in his imagination now but alive and young, and no longer grieving. The fog was rising and the sun was just beginning to creep down the glistening wet streets of London. The first narrow streaks of gold, like swords slitting the darkness, were cutting through the mists. The light was growing, and behind, seas of carmine cloud stretched away into inconceivable distances.

He took her hand, and saw the light of the city and the beauty of her face. He remembered, or thought he remembered, what the first man in the world had learned, after searching all of creation for a friendship deep enough to pierce the ineffable loneliness of dying. And he knew now that even the network could never reach everywhere, that man alone was too small to reassemble the dispersed sparks of creation, that only God is infinite, that only God transcends all, not through power but through love. And he knew that where Eve is, there too will always be Eden.

II

"That should do it," said O'Brien. He flicked off the novel-writing machine and pulled the pages from the tray. "Send it on down to the printer."

And as he heaved his bulk from the room, he reflected that this would surely be the end of all the trouble Smith's diary had caused. It had been remarkably simple. O'Brien had supplied the new template, the new plot; the machine had done the rest. It was just a matter of rearranging a paragraph here and a sentence there, changing a name, and substituting some suitable antonym from the thesaurus. He knew it was a rubbishy book put together with scissors and paste, but it would do the job.

"Nowadays there is no mob, only a flock," Orwell had written. "Nitwits wanting only to be doped." Orwell was right of course. The proles would feel better about it all now, the few who still bothered to read. Most just sat stupefied in front of their screens.

In any event, the traitor's book now had a happy ending, one suitable for the telescreen itself. Just the sort of thing the mob always demanded.

And with the book rewritten, nothing else would have to change. This was the essence of doublethink. No need to change the world or even to see it clearly, no need to worry about the future, no need to atone for the past. Rewriting history would always be enough.

■■■■■ DOUBLETHINK

So it's Christmas 1931, and Orwell has decided to get himself sent to prison. He wants to write about the experience, you see. While other old Etonians sip brandy at their country homes, Orwell gets roaring drunk and (with some difficulty) achieves his goal. The prison cell he is locked up in reappears in *1984*, but Orwell's original description is in his 1932 essay "Clink."

"One remark made by these men [fellow cellmates] struck me," Orwell reports. "I heard it from almost every prisoner who was up for a serious offence. 'It's not the prison I mind, it's losing my job.' This is, I believe, symptomatic of the dwindling power of the law compared with that of the capitalist."

It's a typical Orwellian aside, so casual, so neatly fitted to the context of his story, that you read another paragraph or two before it hits you. The force of law is giving way to the power of the capitalist! What a disgrace. And then you read on.

Or perhaps you think about it some more. Pushed to the limit, the force of law is . . . the Ministry of Love. And the power of the capitalist? Push that to the limit and of course you end up in . . . well, it depends who's doing the pushing. Orwell is quite sure that the capitalist becomes a monopolist and in due course ends up running the Ministry of Plenty. But in 1943, while Orwell is imagining *1984*, another

Londoner is finishing up an equally challenging book that proposes a different answer. The man is Friedrich Hayek; his new book is titled *The Road to Serfdom*. What Hayek argues, roughly speaking, is this: in a free society the market *should* be more important than the prison.

Central economic planning, Hayek reasons, requires coercive government. The Ministry of Plenty (or whatever else it may end up being called) must treat people as means, to be directed for the achievement of a plan, rather than as ends, to be treated equally under law. The Ministry is typically occupied at first by moderate and well-meaning socialists—men much like Orwell perhaps. But ministries attract men who love power of every kind—men like O'Brien. Well-intentioned plans for progress and social equality thus lead straight down the road to totalitarianism. In Orwell's political vision, decent socialism triggers a neofascist reaction, which leads to Big Brother. Hayek paints a simpler picture: decent socialism decays into a Big Brotherhood directly.

Is economic anarchy the only alternative, then, to economic planning through a Ministry of Plenty? Hayek sets out the answer a few years after *1984* is published, in *The Constitution of Liberty*. The essentially Orwellian choice between central planning, in which the Ministry controls everything, and anarchy, in which the strong prey on the weak without restraint, is false. There is a middle ground between the polar alternatives of planned and wholly unplanned economies. The alternative is the free market.

Market mechanisms are rational and efficient: the market is orderly, bounded by rules, and well adapted to private, individual purposes. Yet the order of the market is spontaneous too, not centrally planned, a product of human action, not human design. Commonly accepted rules evolve over time and embody far more wisdom than any central planner can incorporate in a decree. Free markets and free speech can supply coordination of any scope and complexity. A planned society, by contrast, is inherently limited by what the minds of the planners can grasp. Small bands of hunter-gatherers could perhaps be led efficiently by a single headman. But advanced industrial society is possible only if humans are guided by rules rather than commands. Those rules—the rules of free societies and free markets—were not invented consciously, or ever even fully articulated. They exist by common consent, like the rules of grammar.

Rules of grammar? Funny that Hayek should point to language as another example of the kind of spontaneous order that can develop without central planning. Orwell looks at the English language and sees dilapidation and decay—clear signs (he might have said) of a nation sliding down the road to serfdom. Hayek looks at language and rejoices in its spontaneous, consensual order—clear evidence (he might have said) of the possibility of civilization without Big Brother. Prophecy aside, however, Hayek and Orwell would have agreed about language: there is a middle ground between the meaningless babble of infants—"unplanned" language, perhaps—and Newspeak—a language so "planned" that it culminates in *duckspeak*. The middle ground is the English language itself—Oldspeak, that is—subtle, expressive, delicate, and alive, created and maintained by consent and common usage rather than by coercion and central planning. Though Orwell believes that Ministries operate better coal mines and more efficient railroads, he understands clearly that central planners would wreck the tool of his own trade, the English language. Hayek understands that coal mines and the English language are really much the same.

Except on the subject of language, Orwell has sounded like Hayek only once in his life—at the end of *Keep the Aspidistra Flying*, in words I've already quoted: "Our civilisation is founded on greed and fear, but in the lives of common men the greed and fear are mysteriously transmuted into something nobler." The lower classes live by the "money-code," and yet they also "contrive to keep their decency." Hayek could hardly have said it better. The difference is that Hayek really believed it; Orwell didn't. On economic matters, as we've seen, Orwell believed sincerely in the efficiency of socialism.

1984 would have been rather different if Orwell had ever read *The Road to Serfdom*. In fact, it might never have been written at all. Except that Orwell *had* read *The Road to Serfdom*, and he wrote *1984* anyway. Orwell even wrote a book review of *The Road to Serfdom* in 1944, though he died before *The Constitution of Liberty* was published.

His review of Hayek displays Orwell's economic theories at their gloomy, fuzzy best. To begin with, he reviews Hayek's book—which Orwell describes as "an eloquent defence of laissez-faire capitalism"—alongside another book by K. Zilliacus, who has written "an even more vehement denunciation of it." "[E]ach writer is convinced that the other's policy leads directly to slavery," Orwell observes cheerfully, "and the alarming thing is that they may both be right." What pleasure it must have given Orwell to write that sentence! He is not often handed such a perfect opportunity to play the capitalist off against the communist and pronounce a plague on both their houses. Nonetheless, Orwell finds "a great deal of truth" in the "negative part" of Hayek's thesis, which is that socialism leads to despotism by way of Ministries. "[C]ollectivism," Orwell agrees, "is not inherently democratic, but, on the contrary, gives to a tyrannical minority such powers as the Spanish Inquisitors never dreamed of." This is the Orwell most people remember today. But what comes next is Orwell too:

> [What Hayek] does not see, or will not admit, [is] that a return to "free" competition means for the great mass of people a tyranny probably worse, because more irresponsible, than that of the State. The trouble with competitions is that somebody wins them. Professor Hayek denies that free capitalism necessarily leads to monopoly, but in practice that is where it has led, and since the vast majority of people would far rather have State regimentation than slumps and unemployment, the drift towards collectivism is bound to continue if popular opinion has any say in the matter.

For Orwell, the only dim hope is that "a planned economy can be somehow combined with the freedom of the intellect." Just how, Orwell doesn't know.

And what happens when economy and intellect converge, when the market and the mind become one, as they do in the commercialization of such things as radio, films, and television? Then, Orwell has always replied, the prospects are bleak. Gramophones inevitably lead to Goebbels. The Ministry is bound to end up owning all the airwaves. It is a law of economics, as obvious and immutable as the law of gravity.

■

Unless, perhaps, you believe another Londoner of Orwell's day—another great thinker to whom Orwell himself will introduce you if you follow him far enough.

In June 1950, five months after Orwell's death, the literary magazine *World Review* dedicates its issue to Orwell's works, with commentary by Bertrand Russell, Aldous Huxley, and Malcolm Muggeridge, among others. The back pages of the magazine contain the usual assortment of book reviews, including one of a new book by Ronald Coase. So far as I can tell, this juxtaposition of Orwell and Coase is pure coincidence. If the editors knew it was important, they certainly didn't let on. But what a perfect coincidence it is: Orwell, the man of fuzzy economics but brilliant vision set up against Coase, a future Nobelist in economics whose interest happens to be the telecommunicating machine. Coase's book is titled *British Broadcasting: A Study in Monopoly*.

Coase's book is Hayek for the telescreen. The BBC, Coase recounts, has fought for years to retain monopoly control of British airwaves. All along, the need for monopoly has been assumed, not proved. Technicians claimed monopoly was necessary because of the problem of airwave "scarcity" and radio interference. The press welcomed government monopoly to freeze out a rival outlet for advertising. Power-hungry politicians of both parties fell into line readily enough. But the economic and technical argument for a broadcast monopoly is wrong, and irreconcilable with venerable principles of free speech. The monopoly argument's "main disadvantage is that to accept its assumptions it is necessary first to adopt a totalitarian philosophy or at any rate something verging on it."

For Orwell, the telecommunicating machine necessarily leads to the Ministry. In the jargon of economists, Orwell believes wholeheartedly in efficient "natural monopoly." For Coase, it is the Ministry that monopolizes the communications system; the monopoly is neither natural nor efficient. Orwell is certain that complex machines cannot be owned and managed effectively by small capitalists. Coase knows that private property and markets can manage even something as ephemeral as the ether. Orwell believes that Ministry-owned machines are more efficient in theory, though Ministries often go bad in practice. For Coase, theory and practice are the same: the Ministry is rotten from the outset. Orwell thinks that the Ministry-controlled machines will in theory produce Abundance and Truth, though not always in practice; Coase knows that giving the airwaves to the Ministry produces Scarcity and Lies. Give the airwaves to the market, Coase says, and you get more Plenty and more Truth, because markets always produce more goods. You will also get advertising, capitalism, Salvador Dalí, and all the other free market things Orwell despised. But you will not get Big Brother.

I have not come across any indication that Orwell ever read anything by Coase, but he surely would have reacted to Coase in much the same way as he did to Hayek. To be sure, small ownership avoids Big Brother, but the small owners don't last; they get swallowed up into trusts, and still larger trusts, and then the Ministry. Just look at the grocer and the gramophone needles. Monopoly, the Ministry, centralization of one kind or another is stronger, avoids waste, is more efficient, and so always takes over in the end—and nowhere more certainly than in connection with complex machines like steam engines and radio transmitters. Coase just hasn't grasped the modern economic realities. Little shopkeepers and big science belong to different eras, different generations. They coexist only in fiction.

In the fiction of H. G. Wells, for example. As a boy, Orwell loved Wells, but as a man he finds him ridiculous. Wells "writes about journeys to the moon and to the bottom of the sea, and also he writes about small shopkeepers dodging bankruptcy. . . . The connecting link is Wells's belief in Science. He is saying all the time, if only that small shopkeeper could acquire a scientific out-look, his troubles would be ended." But who could seriously believe that shopkeeping and science—the market and the machine—might save the world? Wells could. Hayek could. Coase could. But Orwell can't. When Orwell thinks of the radio and the market, he invariably thinks of Goebbels and the Ministry.

■

Suppose, however, that Orwell had somehow overcome his distaste for gramophones, radios, and films. And suppose he had also understood that telescreens might some day end up as consumer goods in the hands of the masses. Where then might his doublethoughts about the telescreen have led him?

First, to a fundamentally different understanding of the machine itself. Remember the Physical Jerks and Jane Fonda? Winston Smith, among tens of thousands of Londoners aged thirty-something, gets screamed at personally when he doesn't bend low enough. But there is really no other comparable display of two-way telescreen powers anywhere else in *1984*. At only two other points in the book do telescreens talk back: once in a prison cell and once in a room that is used by Charrington, a member of the Thought Police, to entrap people like Winston and Julia. Neither of these displays of telescreen technology is very impressive. Even in 1948, it wasn't all that hard to spy on one designated target in one specific room.

Orwell was on the mark when he imagined that two-way television might some day become practical. But what he never grasped was that the telescreen he envisioned was more telephone than television. (Telescreens appear 119 times in *1984*, microphones 7 times, gramophones once—and telephones never once.) Yes, the telescreen has pictures, but so far as politics, propaganda, and spies are concerned, that's secondary. What's important is that the telescreen is a two-way device—it can transmit as well as receive—and that means that it has to be *addressable*. It has to work like a letter, not a poster. Missing that point is Orwell's biggest mistake. Televisions are collectivist; they broadcast indiscriminately to everyone, just as a Ministry of Crockery would do everyone's washing up. Broadcast television is the collective farm of communications, perfect for Goebbels and the Ministry of Truth. But a telephone can't work unless it is personal, individual, and specific. Same with a telescreen. And for that reason, both are seditious.

If he had ever grasped the telescreen's power to spread people out and disaggregate their affairs, Orwell would have had to rethink all his views about history and memory. When the Caliph Omar destroyed the libraries of Alexandria, Orwell notes sadly in a 1944 essay, he kept the public baths warm for eighteen days with burning manuscripts, and great numbers of tragedies by Euripides and others perished. Ever since the Spanish Civil War, Orwell has been horribly fascinated by an even more chilling possibility: the despot's power not simply to destroy what has been written but to rewrite it. By falsifying every paper, every news clip, every photograph, a Franco or a Stalin might perhaps recreate history itself. As Orwell puts it in *1984*: "[I]f all records told the same tale—then the lie passed into history and became truth." The key assumption here is contained in a single word: "all."

In a telescreened society, records multiply far too fast to be systematically falsified. Caliphs can irrevocably transform Greek tragedy into warm bath water only when there is a single, central repository where the never-copied manuscripts of Euripides are stored. In the hyper-centralized, Ministry-dominated society that Orwell is always imagining, the idea that every single record might be falsified is vaguely plausible. But records can in fact exist simultaneously in many places, and communication can multiply records without limit. The tele-screened society, then, should be one in which the collective memory is better than ever, constantly refreshed and expanded as information is transmitted and shared. Orwell recognized microfilm's capacity to "compress a very large amount of information into a very small space" and saw here a possible protection against "bombs [and] the police of totalitarian regimes." Today the technological successors to microfilm are in tens of millions of hard drives and compact optical disks built into millions of modem-equipped personal computers.

What next? The cheap, ubiquitous, decentralized telescreen re-shapes society in its own image. Orwell knows this too—or half knows it at least. In *The Lion and the Unicorn*, for example, Orwell sees great significance in the rise of a new group "of indeterminate social class." These people are living in townships made economically viable by "cheap motor cars." In a major 1944 essay, "The English People," Orwell argues that England needs to be "less centralised," less dominated by the urban culture and economy of London. He sees more efficient cross-country bus service as an important part of the solution. The future England, Orwell writes, lies "along the arterial roads." So Orwell understands: society is defined by how people connect. Cars, buses, and arterial roads move people.

Telescreens move pictures. If you move the pictures efficiently enough, you'll completely reverse the world's dreaded slide toward centralized monopoly. Orwell has been telling himself for years that whether it is benignly socialist, or malignly fascist, centralized control is much more powerful than decentralized capitalism: it eliminates waste, invents better machines, and wages war more effectively. It is easy to smile at Orwell for believing that, but in fact all he is really saying is that cooperation is good and that he can't imagine men cooperating on a large scale except through Ministries. Yet with the gadget he *did* imagine, even the enormous levels of coordination required to transform aluminum and glass into an airplane can be maintained far from the shadow of any central Ministry. The "tele" in telescreen, after all, means "distance." The telescreened society has no need for marble edifices to house either Captains of Industry or Ministers of Plenty. Instead of towering huge and high above the antlike masses, as they did before the telescreen, corporations and ministries now thin down and spread out. The pyramid of Cheops gives way to the geodesic dome, the fisherman's net of the telescreen network. Telescreens make possible collectivism by choice—a commonwealth society based on individual willingness to share and cooperate.

Daydream about the telescreen a while longer, and you revise all your notions about the wealth of nations. England's only alternative to thieving colonialism, Orwell writes in Wigan Pier, "is to throw the Empire overboard and reduce England to a cold and unimportant little island where we should all have to work very hard and live mainly on herrings and potatoes." Thus, Orwell writes off the entire wealth of the British people—the people who gave the world Shakespeare, Newton, Darwin, Adam Smith, H. G. Wells, Coase, and the glories of the English language—on the assumption that wealth comes mostly from potato farming. The man who conceived of the telescreen and understood perfectly the impoverishing effects of a Thought Police should have known better. In the age of the telescreen, an island as small as Japan, or even a waterless piece of rock like Hong Kong, can still amass the wealth of Croesus.

The curious thing is that Orwell had almost certainly heard and studied just that argument in 1943, the same year he first thought of writing 1984. Winston Churchill had presented it in a speech given at Harvard University. For a nation like England, Churchill had said, there are "far better prizes than taking away other people's provinces or lands, or grinding them down in exploitation. The empires of the future are the Empires of the Mind." By a double irony, Churchill also discussed the 850-word "Basic English," which he hoped to promote as the world's universal second language. Basic English became a very fashionable concern around then, and Orwell himself was an enthusiast for a while. The advantage of Basic—the part Orwell liked—was that it eliminated pedantry. It also placed the Ministry of Information in full control, a thought that eventually led Orwell to 1984's

Newspeak. But Newspeak aside, Churchill's Empires-of-the-Mind speech was a great breakthrough. Today we know that the empires of the mind are conquered not by Newspeak but by telescreen.

Come to think of it, what can we really expect of the English language in the telescreened world? In some respects, no doubt, further dilapidation of just the kind that Orwell always feared. Pictures, which are easy, allow people to get lazy about words, which are comparatively hard. But Orwell knew that a world of pictures offers something to language too. As we have seen (i.e., read), Orwell's unpublished "New Words" argues that the "cinematograph," with its power to make thought visible, may be the best hope we have for expanding our vocabulary. "A millionaire with a private cinematograph [and] all the necessary props," Orwell reflects, would be able to transform thought into visual reality and so develop new words. And yet half of what Orwell called a telescreen is the "cinematograph"—today's videocamera. If Orwell was right in "New Words," the migration of the rich man's cinematograph into millions of private homes will end up adding more to language than it subtracts.

In any event, artists will thrive in a telescreened world in which communication is too cheap to meter. Remember *Keep the Aspidistra Flying*, in which the rich like Ravelston get to run nice little magazines, while the poor like Comstock sell their souls to horrible American PR firms? Remember Orwell's years of invective against the plutocrats who have monopolized all the major presses and publishing houses, and the advertisers whose money soils every commercially successful piece of writing? Remember Orwell's 1944 column on capitalism and art, the one in which the BBC and the film companies "buy up promising young writers and geld them and set them to work like cab-horses"? Remember Orwell saying that capitalism deserves to die and surely will, but Orwell knows the artist will die along with it, though he deserves to live? "I have never yet seen this dilemma solved," says Orwell, though he is sure that "there must be a solution."

Well there is. It's called the telescreen. Capitalism is not doomed; the telescreen has saved it. The telescreen saves the artist too, by giving the artist a boundless, cheap new medium of expression. It used to be said that freedom of the press belongs to those who own one, just the sort of crack that might have come from Gordon Comstock. But in the age of the ubiquitous telescreen, everyone will own a video-press. That should mean vastly more freedom of expression, not less. The telescreened world is fragmented, competitive, fluid, and richly textured, a world filled with the electronic equivalents of *Boys' Weeklies*, farthing newspapers, microphoned poetry, and the comic art of Donald McGill. The starving artist may still starve, but he will be able to reach an audience anyway, at least if his poems, songs, or pictures are good enough to interest anyone outside the south-side garret he occupies in Brewer's Yard.

If the telescreen can let almost any artist be heard or seen, it can equally easily create as much privacy as any hermit could desire. By overcoming distance, the telescreen contains the power to create solitude. You don't, of course, get to that conclusion by assuming that telescreen technology can be operated only from a single giant Ministry. But once you get beyond that mistaken idea, you soon imagine would-be snoopers exhausted and dispirited by distance alone. As Orwell himself has written, the two keys to privacy are distance and crowds. London offers privacy because it is vast and anonymous. The remote Scottish island of Jura, where Orwell retreats to write 1984, offers privacy because it is far from everything. Orwell's farmhouse there becomes his office, restaurant, pub, and inn. As a writer, Orwell could make that move with just a typewriter; a telescreen offers a similar escape to professionals of almost every kind. It lets you live in one place and work, shop, or entertain in another. And at the same time, it creates communities as crowded, and therefore as anonymous, as the largest metropolis. With the telescreen, the privacy of London converges with the privacy of any wind-swept island off the coast of Scotland.

With the telescreen, it is thus possible to have brotherhood, or at least as much brotherhood as free individuals can stand, without Big Brother. And if little brother remains on the scene, the telescreen can do much to keep him in line too. Orwell dimly anticipates some of the possibilities in a 1947 column that discusses "Cooper's Snoopers," the social survey unit recently established by Britain's (Labour-run) Ministry of Information. "[S]ome people do seem sincerely to feel that it is a bad thing for the government to know too much about what people are thinking," Orwell acknowledges, "just as others feel that it is a kind of presumption when the government tries to educate public opinion."

Well, yes, some people do sincerely feel that, including (one might have supposed) the author of *1984*. But as Orwell points out—quite correctly—democracy "is only possible when the law-makers and administrators know what the masses want, and what they can be counted on to understand." It's the sort of line Orwell could easily have handed to O'Brien in *1984*. But it also happens to be true. So long as governments exist and derive their just powers from the consent of the governed, the consent must somehow be conveyed to those in power. The telescreen, properly used, can do just that, far better than any number of social surveys or by-elections.

All of Orwell's gloomy visions about hypercentralized society look equally bright in the glow of the doublethought telescreen. Orwell dislikes "standardised education"; the telescreen has the power to put a private school on every desktop. Orwell hates xenophobia; the telescreen, despite Orwell's doubts, moves "Dallas" from Los Angeles to the Alsace Lorraine. Orwell despises atom bombs, mustard gas, and weapons of mass destruction; the telescreened rocket bomb, guided by videocamera and electronic maps, flies straight down the air shaft of the enemy's Ministry of Peace.

The telescreened world, which we see unfolding around us today, is thus the complete opposite of *1984*. It is a world in which the power of communication is decentralized, with control dispersed, the entire apparatus far beyond the reach of the insect men in the Ministry. It is a world in which state propaganda is a joke—albeit a filthy one—a complete flop, volumes of nonsense shot into the stratosphere and listened to by no one. It is a world in which the Thought Police are driven to distraction by telephones, facsimiles, handheld video cameras, and all the other variations on the telescreen that have become so familiar in the decade since 1984. If Orwell had doublethought his telescreen to its logical conclusion, he would have foreseen the day in which the proles do the watching, and the Party is whipped into submission. As Ithiel de Sola Pool would record in 1983, telescreens are the technologies of freedom.

∎

Not for Orwell. His dislike of fancy machines is visceral, almost atavistic. It slices down between the two lobes of his brain and cuts deep into the recesses of his mind.

It is 1944, a year after he first thought of writing *1984*. Orwell writes an essay for *Partisan Review*. "We are living in an age," Orwell declares, where "[t]he most intelligent people seem capable of holding schizo-phrenic beliefs, of disregarding plain facts, of evading serious questions with debating-society repartees, or swallowing baseless rumours and of looking on indifferently while history is falsified." And what accounts for this "schizophrenic" thinking? "Fear, I suppose," Orwell replies. Fear and "the ghastly emptiness of machine civilisation."

So there it is, the primal traitor, the Enemy of the People, the original defiler of civilization's purity. It is *the machine* that cleaves the human mind, the machine that causes schizophrenia, the machine that impels men to engage in . . .

■ ■ ■ ■ ■ ■ PART 4: DOUBLETHINK

Even in using the word doublethink it is necessary to exercise double-think. For by using the word one admits that one is tampering with reality; by a fresh act of doublethink one erases this knowledge; and so on indefinitely, with the lie always one leap ahead of the truth.

1984

■■■■■ THE FUTURE IS PASSED

"It is bound to be a failure," Orwell wrote in 1946. "[E]very book is a failure," he added with typically Orwellian despondency. True to form—true, in fact, to the principles of doublethink—Orwell's wildly successful *1984* is a failure. It is all fragments, all details—rotten architecture but wonderful gargoyles.

Orwell was wrong about the telescreen. With *1984*—the year itself—fading into history, we can't seriously doubt that any more. Anyone who tries to argue otherwise is engaged in an act of doublethink as brazen as any described in *1984*.

Anthony Burgess, for example. In *The Novel Now* (1967), Burgess announced that "the ghastly future Orwell foretells will not come about, simply because he has foretold it: we have been warned." Burgess was wrong. *1984* is not a self-negating prophecy; it is a self-negating book. Orwell's vision is internally inconsistent: the science of Oceania is both fecund and sterile, the telescreen is both infinitely powerful and hopelessly weak. We did not need Orwell's prophecy to sidestep the Orwellian future; the future was a schizophrenic mirage from the outset. "[W]hat is it, this principle that will defeat us?" O'Brien asks Winston toward the end of *1984*. There is none, Orwell tells us: telescreen totalitarianism is stable and durable. But it isn't. If the Thought Police can use telescreens, so can others—that's just the

233

way telescreens work, if they work at all. Networks as powerful as Orwell imagined cannot be built any other way. The world of Stalin filled with Apple computers belongs to Apple, not Stalin.

Then there's the problem of Orwell's half-baked socialism, his conviction that central economic management is more efficient than competition. His defenders will insist that Orwell's socialism only reflected his deep empathy for the down and out. To write about the homeless, he went and lived with them. To learn that prison was less powerful than the market, he sent himself to prison—not as a reporter but as a common drunk. Orwell didn't just denounce fascism; he went and fought it in Spain, long before fighting fascism was popular; the Mauser bullet shot through his neck came within a millimeter of letting him die for the convictions that he lived. It is all true: Orwell was an almost suicidally decent man. And yet, with that said, Orwell's socialism was still half-baked. He never came close to grasping how inherently inefficient collectivism really is.

Other defenders of Orwell will remind us—correctly again—that Orwell had a brilliant sense, not only for what was important but for what would remain important years later. The entire telemachine debate today—spanning telephones, cable television, broadcast, pagers, cellular phones, vehicle locators, dispatch systems, telemetry, remote sensing, personal communication networks, and satellite reconnaissance—is crystallized in Orwell's writing. The choice between Orwell and Hayek, Orwell and Coase, Winston Smith and O'Brien, O'Brien and Blair—the choices between the market and the Ministry—are still the ones we grapple with today. Whatever his mistakes, Orwell is a sympathetic and intelligent observer; although his prophecies have not been fulfilled, they have not been made simply irrelevant by the passage of time.

And I agree, of course. In fact, I cannot imagine the day when an extended dialogue with the brilliant, fluid, doublethinking mind of George Orwell will no longer be profitable. He has taken on the issues that endure. If one has once read Orwell with attention, it is not easy to go a day without quoting him, because there are not many subjects of major importance that he does not discuss or at least mention somewhere or other, in his unsystematic but illuminating way. *Orwell's Revenge* is my own *Imaginary Dialogue with George Orwell*, my own drawn-out rewrite of Orwell's "Imaginary Interview with Jonathan Swift." It is a strange thing to have a 300-page conversation about contemporary problems with a man who has been dead for more than forty years; with most long-dead men, such an exercise would be a waste of time. But all of Orwell's important thoughts remain fresh, and his concerns still preoccupy us. With that said, Orwell was still wrong about the telescreen—completely, irredeemably, outrageously wrong.

Still others will reply that Orwell couldn't have been wrong, because he wasn't really prophesying. But Orwell himself was characteristically direct on that point. "I do not believe that the kind of society I describe [in 1984] necessarily will arrive," he wrote in a letter to Francis A. Henson, "but I believe (allowing of course for the fact that the book is a satire) that something resembling it could arrive." No, Orwell wasn't seriously prophesying that England would be renamed Airstrip One, or that the dominant political culture in Asia would be called Obliteration of Self. But Orwell was prophesying nonetheless, prophesying in a grand, allegorical way about what might be, what very well might be, when industrialism and electronics inevitably converged. As Michael Shelden notes, the picture Orwell paints in 1984 "is so realistic and compelling that readers from his day onward have come away from the novel feeling that they have been given a prediction." The book is satire, but it is also the distilled vision of a man who had been building a grand prophecy about the machine and the Ministry throughout his career as a writer.

It will also be said—correctly again—that whatever his failings as a social prophet, Orwell was a fine artist. "Beauty is meaningless until it is shared," Orwell wrote in *Burmese Days*. For any work of art there is only one test worth bothering about: survival. By this test Orwell's telescreen succeeded, even if the people who remember it hardly think of it as a machine at all. It is an electronic monster, but at any rate it exists. The emotional impact of 1984 is as strong today as it was when Orwell wrote the book in 1948. Orwell shared the beauty and the ugliness he saw as successfully as any other artist of his century.

Which means—as Orwell himself said of Dickens, Dalí, and Kipling—that Orwell was a "good-bad" artist, a genius and a fool too. Folly does not negate genius, of course. The views that a writer holds must be compatible with sanity, in the medical sense, and with the power of continuous thought; beyond that what we ask of him is talent, which is probably another name for conviction. Orwell did not possess ordinary wisdom, but he did possess a terrible intensity of vision, capable of picking out a single hidden truth and then magnifying it and distorting it. The durability of 1984 goes to show that if the force of belief is behind it, a worldview that only just passes the test of sanity is sufficient to produce a great work of art. Orwell was indeed a great artist. But he was still wrong about the entire technophobic scaffold on which 1984 is draped.

Orwell's defenders may perhaps reply, finally, that I am taking the details of 1984 too seriously. 1984 is satire, after all, and it's a waste of time to quibble about its footnotes. But the telescreen is not a detail in 1984, and to challenge Orwell's pessimism about its effect on society is not to quibble.

Misunderstanding the machine is—in Orwell's own view—a grave error, at least in a writer who is trying to make a serious social statement. Jonathan Swift's treatment of science and machinery in *Gulliver's Travels* is "irrelevant and even silly," Orwell writes, because for Swift, "science was merely a kind of futile muckraking and machines were nonsensical contraptions that would never work." Dickens "shows no interest either in the details of machinery or in the things machinery can do," Orwell complains, pointing to such things as the telegraph and the breech-loading gun, which first appeared in Dickens's lifetime and "made the modern world possible." Tennyson, like Dickens, "lack[s] the mechanical faculty," but he at least "can see the social possibilities of machinery." H. G. Wells and Bernard Shaw are "the 'progressives,' the yea-sayers, . . . always leaping forward to embrace the ego-projections which they mistake for the future."

Orwell attacks the techno-utopianism of H. G. Wells at some length. His main target is *The Sleeper Awakes*, which fails, according to Orwell, because Wells misconstrues the social effects of technology. The book portrays a privileged hedonistic class and slave laborers who "toil like troglodytes in caverns underground." Orwell rejects this as internally inconsistent:

[I]n the immensely mechanised world that Wells is imagining, why should the workers have to work harder than at present? Obviously the tendency of the machine is to eliminate work, not to increase it. In the machine-world the workers might be enslaved, ill-treated and even underfed, but they certainly would not be condemned to ceaseless manual toil; because in that case what would be the function of the machine?

Orwell has higher praise for Aldous Huxley's *Brave New World*. Huxley, at least, "has seen through the swindle of 'progress.'" His book "probably expresses what a majority of thinking people feel about machine-civilisation."

Orwell, in short, ranks, grades, and criticizes other writers according to how well they grasp the social implications of new technology. This is exactly as one would expect: the impact of technology on society is the central and most enduring theme of Orwell's own books and essays about the totalitarian state. Time and again in his writings, Orwell alludes to radios and bombs, machine guns and Hollywood films, gramophones and the secret police, with machine and misery invariably juxtaposed in just that way. The specter of the telescreen is central to *1984*; Big Brother without his electronic gadget is like the Wizard of Oz at the end of *Oz*: harmless, trivial, even silly once the curtain and the smoke-machine have been knocked aside. Orwell takes his machines very seriously indeed. In fairness to Orwell, we must too.

Finally, Orwell's misconceptions about electronic machines must be taken seriously if only because *1984* is such an important book, if only because Orwell's legacy is as serious as literary legacies come. To this day you cannot engage in any major debate about communication technology without stumbling across *1984*—the vocabulary, the imagery, the whole techno-dystopic vision, soup to nuts. "Kipling is the only English writer of our time who has added phrases to the language," Orwell once wrote. But Orwell has out-Kipled Kipling. If the word "Orwellian" is to remain a vitally evocative part of the English vocabulary—as it likely will for centuries to come—then we have a responsibility to ourselves, and to posterity, to understand just what that word evokes and why the real vision—the one behind the curtain, behind the "oblong metal plaque like a dulled mirror"—is so much less frightening than Orwell's original. We have a responsibility to examine with some care just how wrong Orwell really was.

And on the subject of the telescreen, Orwell was very wrong indeed.

■

He was wrong, to start with, about Ignorance and Strength. He believed that monopoly ownership of the electronic media was economically inevitable. But it wasn't, and isn't. "[T]he tendency of capitalism is to slow down the process of invention and improvement," Orwell wrote in 1937, "because under capitalism any invention which does not promise fairly immediate profits is neglected; some, indeed, which threaten to reduce profits are suppressed almost as ruthlessly as the flexible glass mentioned by Petronius." Flexible glass? For someone (like me) who first read those words in the year 1984, the irony is unusually rich. The telescreen revolution was in fact propelled by a radically new kind of flexible glass called optical fiber. Fiber was developed and commercialized in the late 1970s by a private, capitalistic, for-profit American corporation, Corning. But there is no monopoly anymore in the manufacture of flexible glass, still less in its telecommunicating uses.

Orwell was equally wrong about the socialists' advantage in developing powerful technology. He believed that "the rate of mechanical progress will be much more rapid once Socialism is established." But it was precisely because the capitalists did subject their technology to the discipline of the market that their machines advanced much faster. "Every strategic Plan, every tactical method, even every weapon will bear the stamp of the social system that produced it," Orwell writes in *The Lion and the Unicorn*. Precisely so. And the only social system capable of producing something as ingenious as a telescreen is Western liberalism. It is not Mao, not Stalin, not Kim Il Sung, not Big Brother who dwells inside the telescreen. Inside every telescreen live ten thousand free-minded hackers, wonks, nerds, and phone phreaks—young men and women who nursed as infants on empirical habits of thought, who thrive on science and objective truth, and who believe with unshakable conviction that two plus two equals four. They love gadgets and they understand freedom—understand it better, perhaps, than many a young aristocrat studying classics at Eton.

Orwell was wrong, too, about America's drift toward totalitarianism, though not as completely wrong as Americans might have wished. Joseph McCarthy began his unAmerican-Activities witch-hunts in 1950, a year after *1984* was published. Then came Vietnam. "Defenceless villages are bombarded from the air, the inhabitants driven out into the countryside, the cattle machine-gunned, the huts set on fire with incendiary bullets: this is called pacification." Orwell wrote that sentence in 1946. Still, Senate committees and napalm notwithstanding, Orwell overestimated the fascists in America, and he underestimated America's proles. "[W]hat instance is there of a modern industrialised state collapsing unless conquered from the outside by military force?" Orwell asked in 1943. Today we have our answer: Eurasia itself—Hungary, Poland, Rumania, Bulgaria, Czechoslovakia, Yugoslavia, Albania, and finally, the land of Stalin, the former Soviet Union. Whether "democratic socialists" like it or not, America's peaceful, steadfast, more-or-less liberal, free market capitalism was responsible for that historic, bloodless victory over the oligarchical collectivists.

Orwell was every bit as wrong about War and Peace. He believed that "only socialist nations can fight effectively." But the liberal capitalists, it turned out, could fight wars the same way as they developed machines and sold cereal—frugally, efficiently, with smarter weapons and fewer casualties, at least when one counted the casualties among their own ranks. They still can. Neither the atom bomb nor the cruise missile was developed by collectivists.

Finally, Orwell was wrong—fundamentally wrong—about Freedom and Slavery. He was wrong in thinking that the "miracles" of "electrical science" are "cheap palliatives" and useless "luxuries." It was television that exposed McCarthy, swarthy and sweating, as he hectored and slandered his witnesses. It was television again that showed us the naked little girl fleeing the napalm, and the picture of the Vietcong soldier with a pistol at his temple. As Orwell correctly anticipated in 1946: "People are . . . shot in the back of the neck or sent to die of scurvy in Arctic lumber camps: this is called elimination of unreliable elements." On television, however, the "unreliable element" cringing in front of the pistol looked too much like a man for proletarian American stomachs, and the killing stopped.

The man and the pistol brought home a fundamental fact about the technology of communication: better communicating machines produce more—not less—communication, more—not less—free expression, more—not less—political involvement, more—not less—freedom of thought. This is one of those plain, unmistakable facts so easily shirked by a man—especially a political man like Orwell—who in another part of his mind is aware of those facts. And if that last criticism of Orwell seems harsh, I can only say that the sentence (or at least a sentence very much like it) was written by Orwell himself, in a 1946 column titled "In Front of Your Nose." Orwell invented the telescreen long before the engineers had come close, and then stared at it for the better part of three years—and *still* missed its most salient feature. Telescreen technology gives far more freedom than it takes.

Orwell imagined the world of Stalin filled with Apple computers and concluded that it would be more horrible than any ever before imagined. He was wrong. Orwell understood Stalin perfectly. What he did not understand was the telescreen.

■

And that is still a very puzzling thing. Orwell, the man who always—*always!*—kept in mind that the first one now shall later be last, somehow never did grasp that the electronic sword would become a plowshare. Orwell saw the microphone-radio-gramophone-film machine statically. His telescreen was a machine that had stopped growing. It was already finished and perfect, set in a single unchangeable social structure, like a painting or a piece of furniture. His telescreen (one might say) had no mental life of its own. It did not evolve. It did not develop in unexpected ways. It contained no happy surprises. Orwell's attack on it was written from the standpoint—perhaps this seems a queer thing to say of the author of *1984*—of a man who lacked imagination.

With the telescreen, to put the matter bluntly, Orwell's failure was a failure of doublethink.

■■■■■ DOUBLETHINK

Man "is a noble animal and life is worth living," Orwell declares in his 1946 essay, "Politics vs Literature." Man also stands "aghast at the horror of existence." "The human body is beautiful: it is also repulsive and ridiculous." "The sexual organs are objects of desire and also of loathing." "Meat is delicious, but a butcher's shop makes one feel sick: and indeed all our food springs ultimately from dung and dead bodies, the two things which of all others seem to us the most horrible." Orwell loves writing sentences like these.

Indeed, he constructs paragraphs, pages, and entire books in much the same way. He is fascinated by artistic contradiction, the "good bad book" (like a Sherlock Holmes story), good-bad poetry (like Kipling's), the brilliant-disgusting art of Salvador Dalí. He wrestles with incongruities, he savors paradox, he recognizes the duality of everything. He engages, in other words, in the intelligent man's doublethink, which allows him "to hold simultaneously two opinions which cancel out, knowing them to be contradictory and believing in both of them, to use logic against logic." As one of his contemporaries acutely noted, "Mr. Orwell likes his friends no better than his enemies." That is in fact much of the fun in reading Orwell; if you read enough of him, he'll show you both sides of everything.

Consider Orwell's views about Adam Smith's England—the land of human blimps, decayed aristocrats, and bank officials with "prehensile bottoms." A terrible place, England, and also a blessed isle that Orwell loves better than any other place on the planet. When the revolution comes, when the stock exchange is pulled down and the Eton and Harrow match is forgotten, "England will still be England, an everlasting animal stretching into the future and the past, and, like all living things, having the power to change out of recognition and yet remain the same." That's doublethink, all right: the thing contains its own opposite, and the end of a nation is also its beginning.

And then there's America, the America of *1984*. Recall that the expanded America—Oceania—is the third sheaf of corn, the third totalitarian superstate, which by 1984 has replaced the pound with the dollar and renamed England Airstrip One. An evil place, America. Or is it? On the last page of *1984*, at the end of the Appendix on the structure of Newspeak, we suddenly stumble across a familiar text: "We hold these truths to be self-evident, that all men are created equal."* What on earth is *that* doing here? Well, Orwell's ostensible purpose is to explain how "it would have been quite impossible to render this into Newspeak while keeping to the sense of the original." But Orwell never chooses his texts by accident. So Orwell, the man who frequently sneers at the American speculator, embezzler, millionaire, cereal-eating hotel guest, tee-totaling missionary, and English-killing new-speaker, leaves us, on the last page of *1984*, with the words of Thomas Jefferson ringing in our ears. Orwell, we discover, admires American liberty. The theory at least. What he doesn't care for is the practice. American liberty begins with "a buoyant, carefree quality that you can feel . . . like a physical sensation in your belly." But in the end, American freedom is betrayed by "the rise of large-scale industry and the exploiting of cheap immigrant labour."

For Orwell, the glory of being human is to doublethink your way through everything, even human love. All the human relations in *1984* progress from trust to betrayal. Throughout the book, Winston is haunted by the memory of his adored mother, whose death he somehow caused when, as a child, he stole a piece of chocolate intended for

---

*Interestingly, Orwell *misquotes* the Declaration of Independence, omitting "just" from "governments . . . deriving their just powers." *1984*, p. 313.

his starving little sister. There is something about O'Brien that inspires intimacy; Winston confides in him; O'Brien is then unmasked as a faithful member of the Party. Charrington, the softly spoken, sixty-year-old owner of the junk shop, is "frail and bowed, with a long, benevolent nose, and mild eyes distorted by thick spectacles." He has "a vague air of intellectuality, as though he had been some kind of literary man, or perhaps a musician." He turns out to be a member of the Thought Police.

And how about Julia? At first Winston hates her as much as he desires her; his fantasy is to flog her with a rubber truncheon. Then they are ecstatically in love. "The one thing that matters," Winston says to Julia, "is that we shouldn't betray one another. . . . If they could make me stop loving you—that would be the real betrayal."

"They can't do that," Julia replies. "That's the one thing they can't do."

Winston agrees. "If you can feel that staying human is worth while, even when it can't have any result whatever, you've beaten them."

Later, when the two lovers confide in O'Brien, the question of loyalty comes up again. When pressed by O'Brien, both Winston and Julia agree to commit murder, to kill children, to betray their country, to commit any number of atrocities on behalf of the underground brotherhood. There is one last test.

"You are prepared, the two of you, to separate and never see one another again?" O'Brien finally asks.

"No!" replies Julia at once.

"No," replies Winston, after a pause.

In prison, Winston consoles himself with the knowledge that he has not betrayed Julia. "She betrayed you, Winston," O'Brien informs him. "Immediately—unreservedly. I have seldom seen anyone come over to us so promptly." A while later, O'Brien asks Winston: "Can you think of a single degradation that has not happened to you?"

"I have not betrayed Julia," Winston replies.

So O'Brien goes back to work. At the very last second, as the starving rats are about to tear into Winston's eyes and mouth, Winston understands what's expected of him. "Do it to Julia!" he screams. "Do it to Julia! Not me! Julia! I don't care what you do to her. Tear her face off, strip her to the bones. Not me! Julia! Not me!"

Orwell pulls it all together when Julia and Winston meet again at the very end of the book:

> "I betrayed you," she said baldly.
>
> "I betrayed you," he said.
>
> She gave him another quick look of dislike. . . .
>
> "[P]erhaps you might pretend, afterwards, that it was only a trick and that you just said it to make them stop and didn't really mean it. But that isn't true. . . . All you care about is yourself."
>
> "All you care about is yourself," he echoed.
>
> "And after that, you don't feel the same toward the other person any longer."
>
> "No," he said, "you don't feel the same."

The scene is as unspeakably miserable as the day itself, "a vile, biting day in March, when the earth was like iron and all the grass seemed dead and there was not a bud anywhere except a few crocuses which had pushed themselves up to be dismembered by the wind." And it is the last word on love and loyalty in *1984*.

Happily, however, it is not the last word. Orwell set out his doublethought on the subject a year later, shortly before he died. It appears in his magnificent essay, "Reflections on Gandhi." Orwell is talking about the perils of sainthood and the challenge of being human. He writes this single, wonderful sentence: "The essence of being human is that one does not seek perfection, that one is sometimes willing to commit sins for the sake of loyalty, that one does not push asceticism to the point where it makes friendly intercourse impossible, and that one is prepared in the end to be defeated and broken up by life, which is the inevitable price of fastening one's love upon other human individuals."

We should hardly be surprised, then, to find doublethink woven all through the writings of the man who invented the word. The market begins buoyant and free and ends with the parasitic monopolist. American liberty begins with Thomas Jefferson and ends with Airstrip One. Love begins with Julia and ends with rats. Life begins with friendship and ends with defeat. Poverty, socialism, England, America—Orwell loves them all, and hates them too, for they all begin beautiful and end ugly—or is it the other way around? Black is White, War is Peace, Freedom is Slavery, Ignorance is Strength. Doublethink is the whole point.

And that makes the big puzzle all the more puzzling. Ask the question once again: Why did the man who saw both sides of everything so clearly believe so unequivocally that *the machine itself is the enemy*? Why did Orwell never doublethink the telescreen?

■

Psycholiterary criticism is usually a waste of time, but with Orwell's views about machines and markets, it's inescapable.

Orwell's hero of *Keep the Aspidistra Flying* is an irritating poet called Gordon Comstock. Comstock has a thing about money: he hates it. And it's all because at school he was a poor boy among richer classmates. His life was miserable, of course. "Probably the greatest cruelty one can inflict on a child is to send it to school among children richer than itself." "Even twenty years afterwards the memory of that school made Gordon shudder."

But this is not Gordon Comstock who is speaking. It is George Orwell. Orwell uses almost the same words in an autobiographical essay—"Such, Such Were the Joys"—which was published (because of concerns about libel suits) only in 1968, two decades after his death. The essay describes in Dickensian detail the miseries of Orwell's own experiences at Crossgates, the boarding school he attended on scholarship before going on to Eton. "[T]he very rich boys were more or less undisguisedly favoured"; the "poor but 'clever'" scholarship boys didn't go riding, didn't get a cricket bat, didn't get a birthday cake, were caned more often, were publicly reminded of their poverty, and were expected to be snivelingly grateful to Crossgates for its charity.

The effects were predictable. "I despised anyone who was not describable as a 'gentleman,'" Orwell recalls in *Wigan Pier*, "but also I hated the hoggishly rich, especially those who had grown rich too recently. The correct and elegant thing, I felt, was to be of gentle birth but to have no money." Gordon Comstock amplifies in *Aspidistra*. "At an earlier age than most people [I] grasped that all modern commerce is a swindle. . . . What [I] realised, and more clearly as time went on, was that money-worship has been elevated into a religion."

For the rest of his days, Orwell blames the humiliations of his childhood on capitalism and the laws of inheritance. He lives his adult life in almost constant rebellion against the Crossgates money-culture. Like Comstock in *Aspidistra* and Flory in *Burmese Days*, Orwell infuriates his women friends by pursuing poverty as aggressively as most men pursue wealth. In *Burmese Days*, Elizabeth is a shallow, crassly commercial woman, who rejects the sensitive, beauty-loving Flory. Orwell has identical problems with his own women: he despises money; they don't. As Comstock puts it in *Aspidistra*, "[s]ocial failure, artistic failure, sexual failure—they are all the same. And lack of money is at the bottom of them all."

The rest is obvious. Money stinks, property is abominable, people who compete are tapeworms, corpses should not control property, capitalism is the enemy, and markets corrupt everything they touch. *The free market is the enemy too.*

■

If tapeworms and corpses will not control money and property, who will? The people, of course, which means the Ministry. Despite his deep distrust of Stalin and Hitler, Orwell the grown-up schoolboy loves the Ministry. Half of Orwell *wants* collectivism, wants it desperately, because "economic justice" does not arise spontaneously. Orwell knows that absent ministries, the natural economic order is Crossgates.

In *1984* itself, Orwell acknowledges that among men there are native inequalities of talent. He spends as little time as possible on this, and Blythe's book-within-a-book—while acknowledging these inequalities—strongly implies that equality would be inevitable but for the power-hungry oligarchy. In an earlier essay, Orwell even appeals to higher authority for support. His "Politics and the English Language" quotes a familiar verse from Ecclesiastes:

> I returned and saw under the sun, that the race is not to the swift, nor the battle to the strong, neither yet bread to the wise, nor yet riches to men of understanding, nor yet favour to men of skill; but time and chance happeneth to them all.

Orwell's ostensible purpose here is the same as with the Jefferson quotation in *1984*: he is simply going to illustrate how this magnificent language would be rendered in modern bureau-crap.* But Orwell never chooses his texts by accident, especially not his biblical texts, which he uses frequently. In choosing this verse of Ecclesiastes, Orwell is not just illustrating good and bad writing; he is making a political statement too. Orwell is a lilies-of-the-field kind of man. He does not *want* the race to go to the swift. Conveniently for Orwell, the Bible says that it doesn't have to.

But the Bible notwithstanding, the race normally *is* to the swift, and Orwell knows it. Some people are smarter, more industrious, honest, cooperative, entertaining, or agreeable than others, and those people usually get ahead. Most of the time, talent prevails, at least when freedom leaves talent to its own devices. As Damon Runyon observed, "The race may not always be to the swift nor the victory to the strong, but that's the way to bet it."

For Orwell, this creates a miserable dilemma. Freedom, for Orwell, begins with material sufficiency and economic equality. But it also means privacy and the "liberty to have a home of your own, to do what you like in your spare time, to choose your own amusements instead of having them chosen for you from above." Orwell knows that material equality in a world of unequal swiftness, strength, and wisdom requires something other than laissez-faire economics, capitalism, and the "obstructive nuisance" of private property. That something is a Ministry of Plenty. Which generally means another Ministry or two. Which means Big Brother.

Orwell runs into exactly the same problem with the wealth of nations. He desperately wants to treat all peoples and races fairly: the peasant soldier under his command in Spain, the "coolies" he oversees in Burma, the impoverished laborer he describes with deep compassion in an essay about Marrakech. The three totalitarian superstates in

---

*The passage emerges as: "Objective consideration of contemporary phenomena compels the conclusion that success or failure in competitive activities exhibits no tendency to be commensurate with innate capacity, but that a considerable element of the unpredictable must invariably be taken into account."

1984 maintain "cultural integrity," because if the average citizen were "allowed contact with foreigners he would discover that they are creatures similar to himself and that most of what he has been told about them is lies." With nations, as with individuals, Orwell wants to believe that time and chance happeneth to all. He *wants* to, but again he can't. "[T]he divisions between nation and nation are founded on real differences of outlook," he admits in a 1941 essay. It was once "thought proper to pretend that all human beings are very much alike," but Orwell concedes they aren't. So there isn't going to be any equality in the wealth of nations unless . . . unless what? World government is one possibility, but (as Orwell has remarked elsewhere) "it would be an outrage against the laws of God and Nature for England to be ruled by foreigners." The other road to national equality is *1984*: three sheaves of corn, three Parties, three Big Brothers.

War presents Orwell with the same intolerable choice once again. Nations and cultures are not merely unequal in talent and industry; some are downright evil. To resist them you need two things: superior weapons and political unity. Superior weapons are built by the same people who build telescreens. And political unity? In England, Orwell happily reports, "there can come moments when the whole nation suddenly swings together and does the same thing, like a herd of cattle facing a wolf." But such a nation, Orwell also knows, can be as "single-minded as the Gadarene swine" in times of peace. No matter. War is sometimes necessary, and war requires Ministries of Peace and Plenty. Which means a Party. Which means Big Brother.

So Orwell's brain is strangling in the coils of doublethink. For individuals, as for nations, he wants equality. The race-to-the-swiftest tendency is the problem; the Ministry is the solution. Crossgates is what descends on the nation that doesn't have the right Ministries. Hitler—the quintessential Ministry man—is what descends on the nation that does.

■

How then can we rid the world of Crossgates while still affirming "freedom" at every turn? We can't, except in French. And thus Orwell, the man who exhorts us to "drive out foreign phrases" from our writing, is quite unable to discuss economic theory without first crossing the English Channel.

Perhaps the Frenchism of laissez-faire capitalism can be forgiven, but what Orwell really loves to hate is the rentier. In essay after essay he excoriates "rentier capitalism," "the rentier-professional class," and the "rentier-intellectual." And what exactly is a rentier? My French-English dictionary defines it as "stockholder, fundholder; person of property, man of independent means; holder of an annuity; rentier. *C'est un petit rentier*, he has a small private income, he is a small investor." Orwell's definitions are more colorful. Rentiers, says Orwell, comprise "an entirely functionless class, living on money that was invested they hardly knew where." They are the "idle rich," "decayed throw-outs," "simply parasites, less useful to society than his fleas are to a dog." Brush aside Orwell's fine invective, and you come back to this: the freedom Orwell can't stand is the freedom to earn money, invest it in private property, and pass it on to your children. Which explains Orwell's French. If he talked about the "free" market, he would then have to murder "freedom." Linguistically, it is easier to liquidate a rentier.

But he doesn't fool anyone, not even himself. Equality—the kind of material equality that Orwell wants—and freedom—real freedom of effort, intellect, and personal industry—are irreconcilable. Like it or not, the free market is a big part of freedom—not just material freedom, but freedom of thought and speech and everything else. Some people produce newspapers, films, symphonies, operas, and plays; others pay to enjoy such things, and it's money that closes the loop. Crude as it sounds, spending money is a form of self-expression. Handing over cash is the most sincere way of declaring private preferences, whether they be crass, generous, foolish, wasteful, or ugly. Money talks. The rich (like Ravelston in *Aspidistra*) get to run nice little socialist magazines as a hobby. The poor (like Comstock) have to go off and work for horrible American advertising agencies. When it comes to freedom, mind and money walk hand in hand.

Orwell knows this. He also knows that it doesn't mean much to preach about higher forms of liberty to people who are digging coal fourteen hours a day and starving in the cold the other ten. He knows that the race-to-the-swift tendency pushes society away from "economic justice." He also knows you can't articulate any grand principles of freedom without grappling with economic freedom along the way. And he knows you can't talk serious economic socialism without drifting toward Big Brother. In *1984*, the Party has done many of the right socialist things. It has abolished private property and suppressed the free market. These are all things that Orwell the socialist believes *should* be done. Orwell knows that the Ministry of Plenty is a pillar of "oligarchical collectivism," which he hates, but he knows it is also a pillar of democratic socialism, which he loves.

So Orwell is stuck. Either he says something nice about Big Brother, which would ruin *1984*, or he says something nice about economic freedom, which means (more or less) free markets, which means (roughly) the rentier-capitalist—the other enemy. Orwell hates the Big Brotherhood of *1984*, but he is himself a socialist. He wants collectivism without Big Brother, and he doesn't know how to get it. The missing chapter in *1984*—the chapter on Freedom—is missing because of a completely unresolvable paradox in Orwell's own brand of Ingsoc politics.

◼

Now you may suppose that I have dwelled on Orwell's half-baked socialism to add some ad hominem weight to my rehabilitation of the telescreen. But I am not trying to discredit Orwell simply by painting him red. What Orwell believes about free markets explains, in the end, what he thinks about telescreen totalitarianism.

It's easy for people like Hayek and Coase to embrace the marketplace of ideas; the logic and the rhetoric of the free market is portable. It's equally easy for people like Hayek and Coase to be optimistic about things like telescreens. More and better communicating machines in more private hands will mean more commerce, more shopkeepers, more rentiers, and more free speech too. Collectivists—or, if you prefer, democratic socialists—have a much more difficult book to write. The collectivists demand that powerful, expensive machines be expropriated and ministerialized. For efficiency, you see. Efficiency and economic justice. So when it comes to newfangled things like telescreens, the libertarian-collectivists must somehow explain how they will collectivize the media of communication without collectivizing the message, how they will collectivize your purse without touching your mind, how they will woo the Ministry of Plenty without falling into the syphilitic embrace of the Ministry of Love. But they can't explain *that*. Because it can't be done.

Return then one last time to the question that led us to the market in the first place: Why didn't Orwell ever consider that telescreens might promote freedom? Why didn't he ever imagine that the slavery of a telescreened Ministry might be overwhelmed by the freedom of telescreens in private hands? That question led us to search for the missing chapter in *1984*—the chapter that would have set out Orwell's own, positive definition of Freedom. But all we found was another negative: freedom, whatever it is, is not the rentier-infested free market. The free market, after all, leads back to Crossgates, where the rich little bastards torture and humiliate the rest.

And oh yes, I forgot to mention this earlier. One typical indignity—one particularly memorable humiliation—for a scholarship boy at Crossgates was to be examined by richer boys on the size and power of his father's car—the car the scholarship boy's father of course did not own. Orwell himself remembered that, long, long afterward. A scholarship boy wouldn't seriously consider the possibility of owning a movie camera either. Recall that when Orwell thinks of a movie camera in "New Words," he reflexively conjures up some "millionaire" to own it. The private ownership of fancy machines evokes in Orwell almost unspeakably miserable memories. So, Orwell the adult concludes: one can defend (private) property only if one is more or less indifferent to economic justice. For Orwell, then, Freedom really *is* Slavery, at least when freedom extends to people who make money and then buy expensive gadgets with it. He simply cannot stand the thought of a world organized around fancy private possessions.

He spends his adult life declaring that tomorrow's world won't be. Hayek is wrong. Capitalism is finished. The one world even more horrifying (to Orwell) than *1984* is a world owned by the small rentier capitalists, a society like Crossgates, in which the scholarship boy is tormented forever because his father doesn't own a big personal computer. And that horror—his own, personal, childhood horror—is one that Orwell never does overcome. He sees everything perfectly, except for his own boyhood face in the mirror.

Who then will own the telescreens in the future according to Orwell? Surely not the rentier-capitalists who send their spoiled sons to

Crossgates. Motor cars, movie cameras, radios, telephones, dishwashers: in Orwell's economically just world, none of these things is going to be privately owned. They're all going to be owned by the Ministry of Crockery, or something much like it. That's the answer to horrible Crossgates. But Ministry ownership will be pretty horrible too. That's *1984*.

■

If Orwell had lived to the age of eighty-two, as his own father did, he would have died in 1985. A life that long would have allowed him to read history's own review of *1984* and given him time to compose his own letter-to-the-editor in reply. Perhaps his reply would have drawn from "New Words" and "Poetry and the Microphone." In any event, Orwell would have written, and written frankly, in a spirit of reflection and honest, self-critical inquiry. He was never a man afraid to face facts, even facts that contradicted what he himself had once believed. As often as not, he had already written the contradiction himself. Orwell thrived on doublethink.

In fact he lived it, and in the end he died it. He described himself as a "Tory Anarchist," by which (when describing Jonathan Swift with the same words) he meant a man despising authority while disbelieving in liberty. He began his adult career as a colonial policeman in Burma, running a network of spies, and ended it with *1984*. He hated the radio, and he spent two years broadcasting for the BBC. "One of the most horrible features of war," Orwell wrote in 1938, "is that all war propaganda, all the screaming and lies and hatred, comes invariably from people who are not fighting." Five years later he himself was part of England's wartime propaganda machine. "I suppose sooner or later we all write our own epitaphs," he observed, reflecting on that irony. Yes, Orwell would have written his own answer to *1984*—the book and the year too—if he had been given the time.

But Orwell's own epitaph was to be written long before the telescreen's. The pinnacle of doublethink in Orwell's own life comes during the writing of *1984* itself. In 1947, having completed only a very rough first draft of the book, Orwell learns he has tuberculosis. The best treatment is streptomycin, a new American drug that is still generally unavailable in England. David Astor, the son of an English lord, arranges through family connections in the United States to have a special shipment sent to Orwell's hospital. "I am a lot better," Orwell writes in a letter in April 1948. He sets feverishly to work completing his last novel. The first words of Winston Smith's diary—"April 4th, 1984"—are probably composed on April 4, 1948, or very close to that date. Orwell has been given another two years to live—just enough time to finish his greatest book and witness the beginning of its enormous triumph. Those two years have been given to him by the genius of American capitalism and the patronage of a rentier member of the English upper class.

Orwell died on January 21, 1950, at the age of forty-six.

■■■■■ THE MACHINE

> The Gestapo is said to have teams of literary critics whose job is to de-
> termine, by means of stylistic comparison, the authorship of anony-
> mous pamphlets. I have always thought that, if only it were in a better
> cause, this is exactly the job I would like to have.
>
> "As I Please" (1945)

"I wrote it. That is to say, I collaborated in writing it. No book is produced individually, as you know." O'Brien says this to Winston Smith
toward the end of *1984*. He is referring to *The Theory and Practice of
Oligarchical Collectivism*, the book ostensibly written by Kenneth
Blythe, which occupies the middle section of *1984*. But O'Brien didn't
write that book either. Blythe and O'Brien are, of course, inventions of
George Orwell. Whose real name was Eric Blair. So there we have it:
one book, four authors.

Or why not five? Upon reflection—upon careful reflection, after
reading *1984* many times—I came to realize that Orwell had made
some serious errors. He had also written my charge:

4.4.48 g.o. book malreported telescreen rectify forecasts misprints
malquotes doubleplusungood rewrite fullwise upsub antefiling.*

---

*In Oldspeak (or standard English) this would read: "The G[eorge] O[rwell] book of
April 4, 1948, included references, forecasts, quotes, and misprints relating to the telescreen that are extremely unsatisfactory. Rewrite it in full and submit your draft to higher authority before filing." Cf. *1984*, pp. 39, 45.

Yes, Orwell expected this to happen. By 1984, "[a]ll history was a palimpsest, scraped clean and reinscribed exactly as often as was necessary." By 1994, *1984* would be history too, and ready for the cleansing.

■

One of my own telescreens—the one used sometimes by my six-year-old daughter to play *Mixed Up Mother Goose*—is hooked up to a Hewlett-Packard flatbed scanner with an automatic document feeder. Inside the computer I've installed a circuit board manufactured by Calera Recognition Systems. I directed the HP, Calera, and my computer to devour the mutilated copy of *1984*. I fed the pages into the scanner, thirty or so at a time. The computer and scanner hummed and groaned for about five hours, after which the book had been scanned in its entirety and converted into electronic text. As I described in the Preface to this book, *1984* was on my hard disk, in an ASCII file, occupying 590,463 bytes of storage. The rest of Orwell's books, essays, and letters soon followed, along with Shelden's excellent biography.

I use a very fast word processor, XyWrite III+, running on what in 1993 was a reasonably fast machine—a 66 MHz 80486—with ample RAM (16 megabytes) to contain the entire book in dynamic memory. With *1984* loaded into my word processor, I am able to jump from the first word to the last in just over 1 second. I can search through the book at will for any particular word or phrase. I can move from one occurrence to the next as fast as I can hit a single key.

With the search power of my machine, I was able to track the patterns and themes Orwell developed in *1984* far more ambitiously than would ever have been possible by any other means. In a matter of seconds, for example, I was able to see how Orwell developed the theme of the church bells, or Winston Smith's fear of rats, or the imagery of a piece of coral embedded in glass, or the Chestnut Tree Cafe, or the idea of meeting some day "in the place where there is no darkness." It was now easy to trace out all of Orwell's recurring, interwoven metaphors of isolation and connection, hate and love, alienation and brotherhood. At times I felt as though I were looking over Orwell's shoulder as he knitted together the strands of his great classic novel. His intricate plan unfolded in front of me in a way that perhaps no one other than Orwell himself had ever seen before.

But I had a more concrete objective in mind. My telescreen was going to go after Orwell's handiwork. It was going to rewrite Orwell's book beginning to end.

■

At first, the thought of recreating Orwell seemed very intimidating. Orwell, after all, had great genius, and on top of that he had fifteen years of earlier Orwell to plagiarize from. And I? Well, I had . . .

And then I saw it: *I had Orwell's genius too.* Not in my head, but under my fingertips, in my computer. *I had Orwell's brain in a bottle.* If Orwell could cut and paste fifteen years of Orwell to produce *1984*, I could do the same for my book. Indeed, in matters of cutting and pasting I could almost certainly surpass Orwell, for my cut-and-paste tools were far superior to his.

The best part of it all, I soon realized, was that I had Orwell's express permission. In fact, I am sure Orwell would have demanded it. It is Orwell, after all, who had been chewing over the possibility of machine-written books years before any one else imagined such things. It is Orwell who seizes his moment as a BBC broadcaster to concoct an "Imaginary Interview with Jonathan Swift," and to produce a "Story by Five Authors," which is, quite literally, written by five separate authors. It is Orwell who gives us the Ministry of Truth in *1984* itself, where the poetry and literature of the past are revised beyond all recognition.

So, psychologically prepared by Orwell himself, I loaded *1984* into my computer and began to rewrite it line by line. My mission was simple: I would affirm *1984* even as I denied it. I would prove that Orwell was wrong by proving that he was right. It would be a triumphant act of doublethink. I owed Orwell no less.

As I assembled *Orwell's Revenge* from the bricks and mortar of Orwell's own writings, I relived Winston Smith's existence in the Ministry of Truth. I knew, for example, that Orwell despised the free market, whereas I planned to glorify it. No matter; Orwell had certainly provided some encouraging description of markets somewhere. In an instant, I could search for it through all his writings. Almost as fast as I could type the word "market" I would have in front of me a good passage to pirate. The machine in fact led me immediately to *Aspidistra*'s wonderful description of the fish market in Luton Road, the one in which the stalls glow with fine lurid colors, heavy-laden with hacked, crimson chunks of meat, piles of oranges, and so on. And it is Comstock who then reflects that "[w]henever you see a street-market you know that there's hope for England yet."

I could do the same with "wispy hair," or "top hat," or "drain," or "stank abominably," or "entrails," or "gramophone." How about Blair's girl? "Perhaps the most striking thing" about Orwell's early writing, Shelden's biography instantly informed me, "is that so much of it is concerned with prostitutes." Did I need text to paint a picture of O'Brien's decay? 1984 supplied some immediately, in passages describing the wrecks of former Party members who had been purged. And then my computer proposed some wonderful passages from Orwell's "Shooting an Elephant." The machine was right on the mark; the wrenching description of how an elephant dies when a bullet from a high-power rifle penetrates its brain seemed to work perfectly in describing O'Brien's own collapse. Did I need help with O'Brien's recollections as he prepares for yet another hanging? No better place to look than in Orwell's own essay, "A Hanging," one of the great, classic essays of English literature.

It was in doing this sort of thing that I discovered just how much of it Orwell had done himself. My computer was merciless. If I so much as paused, for example, to admire the "red velvet" simile that Orwell had used to describe the dying pachyderm in "Shooting an Elephant," my computer would whisper to me that Orwell had used it again in *Burmese Days*, and in a very similar context. As I show in the Notes, 1984 itself lifts phrases, sentences, metaphors, and scenes all but verbatim from Orwell's own earlier books and essays. Most of the quotes and paraphrases in the Preface to this book, which I presented as if they came from 1984, were in fact drawn from Orwell's other writings. They supply, nonetheless, a completely faithful summary of 1984. I also found that—perhaps as a little private joke—Orwell had made a point of including delicate (but obviously deliberate) allusions to his other works in a number of his own books and essays.

If Orwell could do it to Orwell, so could I. It was the most fun I've ever had at a keyboard. Instead of memory holes, I had a telescreen stuffed with memory: Orwell's literary memory, the whole of it, thousands of pages instantly accessible through the machine he hated most. When I wanted a scene, an image, or an idea, it could almost invariably be found in Orwell's electronically pickled brain, just waiting to be retrieved. My nonfiction pages on Orwell, including some of my most colorful commentary on his work, in this and all my other nonfiction chapters, likewise draw frequently from Orwell's own literary criticism. "Wonderful gargoyles, rotten architecture." "Compatible with sanity in the medical sense." "A man who lacked imagination." This is all Orwell, turned around to reflect on Orwell himself. The Notes provide a fairly complete record of how far all this went.

Let me add, finally, that I could easily have finished the job. Every decent word processor has a built-in thesaurus. Word by word, sentence by sentence, I could have dissolved away Orwell's text and replaced it with my own. I could easily have obliterated all evidence of what I had done. The final product would not have been Orwell's, or at least not identifiably so. Every word of any importance, every simile and metaphor, would have been just different enough to make my enormous debt to Orwell unrecognizable. My book would have been a sort of fossil, a mineralized facsimile of Orwell's, the carbon replaced, atom by atom, with sand. And yet, all the real work, the structure and arrangement of sentences and paragraphs, the logical flow, would still have been his. It would have been like painting by the numbers, but to the point where no one could have seen the original lines any more. I would have transformed Orwell into Huber, and no one would have been the wiser.

I declined to take the last step, however. I have kept the best of Orwell's allusions, images, and turns of phrase wherever they seemed to fit. I did this not because I was too lazy to finish what I had started but because *not* finishing was part of my point. I did not intend to vaporize Orwell completely. It was sufficient to make him love 1984 despite himself.

∎

I wrote my palimpsest with no sense of contrition; I make no apology for it here. All writing is allusion; all literature builds on common experience. The best Nonsense Poetry, Orwell once wrote, is written by communities, not individuals. Language itself, as Orwell points out in "New Words," is created collectively. To be sure, Orwell sometimes said that the *novel* would always remain a solitary endeavor. But Orwell never did fully understand the power of the telescreen.

In this, the age of the telescreen, it is not just possible but obligatory to integrate Orwell into any serious discussion of teletechnology. When you agree with him, you take his thought as your own. When you disagree, you stick his words into the mouth of an O'Brien or Burgess, and then you answer them. When Orwell is boring or pedantic, as he occasionally is, you cut. When Orwell is brilliant, as he very often is, you paste, and then answer him if you can. You spot something pretty—perhaps as small as a beautiful paperweight, say—and in a second it is sitting there on the mantlepiece of a chapter where it seems to fit best. However you use him, you must acknowledge Orwell's views on anything you write. There is no other choice. Orwell shapes your thoughts even when he is wrong, even when you disagree with him completely. Reading Orwell on (and about) the telescreen as one writes on (and about) the telescreen cannot be a passive business any longer.

"Who controls the present controls the past," Orwell wrote in *1984*. Whether we can alter what happened yesterday, we certainly can alter what yesterday's literary gents said would happen today. Yesterday's prediction of what will be today is ours to affirm or deny: 1984 belongs to us, who live it, and not to him, who wrote it. So too, then, should *1984*, and all books of prophecy beyond. The future is not a shall be, not a must be, not a will be. The future belongs to the living, not because they have the power to change what was but because they have the power in their own time to shape what is.

Timshel, it says in the Bible: not "Do thou," nor "Thou shalt," but *Thou mayest*. The future of the telescreen is a may be; it is a choice. It may yet be Orwell's. Or it may yet be mine.

■■■■■ LOOSE ENDS

[T]he bigger the machine of government becomes, the more loose ends
and forgotten corners there are in it. This is perhaps a small consola-
tion, but it is not a despicable one. It means that in countries where
there is already a strong liberal tradition, bureaucratic tyranny can perhaps never be complete.

"Poetry and the Microphone" (1945)

One was called Bell, the other Blue. The dark granite of Bell's headquarters towered vast and luminous above the crowded sidewalks in
the heart of New York City. Blue's operations were centered nearby, in
Armonk. Between them, B&B had 1.4 million employees. They controlled the two most lucrative and powerful businesses on earth. In an
age when most information—and indeed most of what the human
mind could create—was stored, edited, replicated, and distributed by
electronic means, B&B came as close as any power ever has to controlling thought itself.

The end, or at least the beginning of the end, came at one second
past the hour of midnight, on January 1, 1984. In a single stroke, the
Ministry shattered Ma Bell into eight pieces. Three weeks later, to the
booming strains of "Chariots of Fire," Steve Jobs stepped out on the
podium at the annual stockholders' meeting of Apple Computer and
unveiled the new Macintosh.

■

The idea of telephony, from the Greek "far speaking," has tantalized humanity since time immemorial. Nineteenth-century inventors were the first to explore the possibility seriously. In 1831, Michael Faraday demonstrated that a piece of iron vibrating in a magnetic field produces electrical pulses. Soon thereafter, in 1835, Samuel Morse invented the essential elements of a telegraph.

Alexander Graham Bell produced his first rough plans for a "harmonic telegraph" in 1872. Within a few years he had developed the phonautograph, which translated sounds into visible markings. In June 1875, Bell discovered the basic principles of the electromagnetic microphone and speaker, the key elements of a telephone. The famous words—"Mr. Watson, come here, I want you"—were transmitted from Bell to his assistant on March 10, 1876. Commercial telephone service was inaugurated in the United States the following year. Bell was confident that some day "a telephone in every house would be considered indispensable."

By 1878, Bell was installing two "telephones" at each station—one to talk into, the other for listening—so that the user wouldn't have to keep shifting the unit from mouth to ear. It was a phenomenal advance, of Orwellian implications: the new, two-tier telephone could both transmit and receive. Initially, however, telephones were linked in pairs, directly to each other. In 1878, the budding new telephone companies grasped the necessity of a telephone exchange. The exchange—a simple switchboard at first—radically increased a telephone's utility by enabling each telephone to reach every other telephone connected to the same exchange. Newark, New Jersey, boasted the first semiautomatic switching system in 1914.

The industry began as a monopoly of sorts, centered on Bell's patents. By 1894, however, the essential patents had either expired or been narrowly construed by the courts. Thousands of independent telephone companies took advantage of the opportunities offered by the newly available technology. Active competition and an explosive expansion of service ensued. By 1902, 451 out of the 1,002 cities with telephone service had two or more companies providing it. By 1907, when a telephone census was taken, the independents owned nearly as many telephone stations as Bell.

But the logic of the telephone exchange seemed to push the industry inexorably back toward monopoly. Competitive exchanges fragmented the market, drove up costs, and defeated the key advantage of a centralized switch—universal connection. Exchanges also raised the possibility of interexchange connections over longer distances, but the cost of running lines over great distances was huge. Two of the critical pieces of technology needed for long-distance service, loading coils and then the audion, the first vacuum tube amplifier, belonged to Bell. The specter of a Bell monopoly began to rise once again over the industry.

At about this time, Theodore Vail, a brilliant administrator, took over at Bell and resolved to recapture Bell's monopoly. The Bell System had lost its original patents on the telephone, but it had acquired new ones, which gave it a critical edge at the other end of the network, in providing good long-distance connections. Vail believed passionately in "universal service," to be supplied by one company: his own. Bell therefore offered its superior long-distance service exclusively to its own local affiliates. The company refused to sell equipment or to provide interconnection even to independents that did not directly compete with it. In rapid succession, telephone companies not affiliated with Bell either folded or were acquired.

Bell's activities attracted the attention of antitrust lawyers at the U.S. Department of Justice. In a 1913 agreement with the U.S. attorney general, a vice-president of Bell, N. C. Kingsbury, committed Bell to cease its acquisition of independent telephone companies and to permit the remaining independents to interconnect with Bell's long-distance service. But the "Kingsbury commitment" did nothing to promote competition in telephony. Local exchange monopolies were left intact, free to continue to refuse interconnection to other local competitors. Bell's monopoly long-distance service was accepted and indeed reinforced: Bell would be required to interconnect with all local exchanges, but there was no provision for any competition—or interconnection—among long-distance carriers.

Thus, markets were carefully carved up: one for each of the established monopoly local telephone exchanges and one for Bell's monopoly long-distance operations. Bell might not own everything, but some monopolist or other would dominate each discrete market. The ministries of the day had no objection. All they wanted was to keep the commercial monopolies at a size that they could manage.

Theodore Vail understood that perfectly. By 1915, when Bell had established transcontinental service, Vail could describe the Bell System as "an ever-living organism" that possessed "one of the largest laboratories of the application of science to industrial development in the world." Bell's slogan was: ONE POLICY, ONE SYSTEM, UNIVERSAL SERVICE.

According to the summer issue of his school magazine, in 1914 Eric Blair's cricket game was improving rapidly.

■

Bell had Theodore Vail; IBM had Thomas J. Watson. Watson trained as a salesman at National Cash Register, an organization that loathed competition and suppressed it almost as successfully as Bell. NCR's president, along with Watson and several other executives, were convicted of antitrust violations in 1912. The government later dropped the case on appeal.

In 1914, Watson became general manager of the Computing-Tabulating-Recording Company. Invented at almost the same time as the telephone to speed data analysis for the 1880 U.S. Census, the tabulating machine was an electromechanical device that processed information stored on punch cards. CTR's business boomed during World War I; by 1918, the company was selling more than 80 million blank cards a month. A few years later, Watson gained total control of the company. In early 1924 he changed its name to International Business Machines. Before long, IBM had established a complete monopoly in the market for commercial data processing.

Much of IBM's market power lay in the humble punch card itself. A large customer typically acquired millions of these a year. The investment in cards, and the plugboard configurations needed for processing them, grew in step with the business itself. After a certain point, replicating the data in some other format, retraining staff, and reworking procedures became prohibitively expensive.

This was exactly as Watson intended. IBM viewed business machines in much the same way as Bell viewed telephones. To function properly, calculating machines required central provision, maintenance, and oversight; one company was therefore better than many. Like Bell, Big Blue didn't sell its machines at all; it sold service, with the machines provided only under tight lease. There was no second-hand market in IBM tabulators. Like Bell, IBM had a motto, almost sinister in its simplicity: THINK.

In June 1922, nineteen-year-old Eric Blair took the civil service examination that would qualify him for the post of probationary assistant district superintendent of police in Burma.

■

By 1895, when Bell's major patents on the telephone had just expired, the new wonder of the technological world was not communication with wire but communication without it. That year, Guglielmo ("G.M.") Marconi produced the first practical radio. The following year Britain granted Marconi a patent on the device that was still known for precisely what it did not require—wires. It was the wireless telegraph, or wireless for short.

Radio appeared to be a major new competitive threat to the telephone. Marconi himself had conceived of it as a messaging system for ships. In short order, the wireless telegraph became a wireless telephone. Radio communication of human speech first occurred on Christmas Eve 1906, between Brant Rock, Massachusetts, and ships in the Atlantic Ocean. Soon the vacuum tube amplifier (the "audion") would improve radio transmission as dramatically as it improved telephony. In 1909, Bell's chief engineer sought research funds to put the company "in a position of control with regard to the art of wireless telephony, should it turn out to be a factor of importance."

The military was interested too. In a letter to Congress dated March 30, 1910, the U.S. Navy denounced the "chaos" prevailing in the airwaves. Various government departments had "for years sought the enactment of legislation that would bring some sort of order out of the turbulent condition of radio communication," the navy pointed out. The navy favored "the passage of a law placing all wireless stations under the control of the Government." A 1918 congressional bill to that effect would have given the navy exclusive control over all wireless communication for commercial purposes. Radio, a navy secretary would explain, was "the only method of communication which must be dominated by one power to prevent interference." "My judgment is that in this particular method of communication the government ought to have a monopoly." "There is a certain amount of ether, and you cannot divide it up among the people as they choose to use it; one hand must control it."

The navy's wishes were not met, however; private broadcasters multiplied. Fearing that Britain would become the world hub for radio, as it was already for undersea cables, the U.S. government backed the formation of a strong radio manufacturing company, the Radio Corporation of America (RCA).

With the early technologies, radio's great advantage was not in point-to-point messaging like telephone but in point-to-everywhere broadcast. David Sarnoff, who started as a telegraph operator for the Marconi Wireless Telegraph Company of America, was the first to recognize this potential. In 1916 he submitted his idea for a "radio music box" to the management of Marconi. Westinghouse inaugurated the nation's first true radio station, KDKA in Pittsburgh, in 1920. Bell put its own station, WEAF, on the air in New York City in 1922.

Hundreds of other new stations began broadcasting in the 1920s. With modest help from the courts, a spontaneous market order began to evolve. Once a broadcaster had occupied a certain frequency and begun to use it productively, the station's right to exclude interfering broadcasts would be affirmed. The early broadcasters were thus settling the airwaves in much the same way as pioneers on the prairies had created private property out of unbounded space, by settling on the land and putting it to use. The chaos of the airwaves began gradually to crystallize into an orderly, functioning market.

This spontaneous privatization met with fierce resistance from government officials. A 1925 Senate resolution declared radio spectrum to be "the inalienable possession of the people of the United States." In July 1926, a joint congressional resolution, expressly intended to prevent licensees from establishing property rights in frequencies, announced that no license should be granted for more than ninety days for a broadcasting station or for more than two years for any other type of station. The Radio Act of 1927 finished the job. The new Federal

Radio Commission was empowered to issue licenses only insofar as the "public interest, necessity or convenience would be served" by doing so. Licenses could not be bought or sold without the commission's approval.

The logic behind this sweeping assertion of governmental power seemed strong. Spectrum, it was said, was inherently scarce. Two radio stations could not broadcast simultaneously in the same area without interference, and there was some natural physical limit to how many radio stations could be on the air at the same time. So radio spectrum should be treated like a commons, a public park, to be managed exclusively by the federal government. Private rights to graze on the ether would be doled out sparingly, and only for short periods of time, to worthy, loyal citizens. The Radio Commission would be the national trustee of the scarcity and the reversionary owner of all rights to spectrum. Private stations would broadcast at the commission's pleasure, like peasants tending their cattle on the pastures of the crown.

In June 1927, shortly after celebrating his twenty-fourth birthday, Eric Blair boarded a train in Katha, Burma, heading for Rangoon. On July 14 he sailed back to England.

By the late 1920s, support had also begun to emerge for sweeping federal control of the telephone industry. Monopoly telephone service had become so familiar it seemed inevitable. Several ponderous studies officially confirmed that it was, a conclusion perfectly consonant with the New Deal political winds then blowing. Bell itself wanted to consolidate its dominant position and legitimize its monopoly. Vail spoke publicly in favor of regulation, sounding a theme ("cream skimming") that would become a Bell rallying cry for the next half-century. "If there is to be state control and regulation," Vail argued, "there should also be state protection—protection to a corporation striving to serve the whole community . . . from aggressive competition which covers only that part which is profitable."

On February 26, 1934, President Franklin Roosevelt asked Congress to create a separate Federal Communications Commission. By June 9 of that year, both houses had passed legislation. The president signed the Federal Communications Act of 1934 into law on June 18. The

Act's objective, as stated in its opening section, was to "make available, so far as possible, to all the people of the United States a rapid, efficient, Nation-wide, and world-wide wire and radio communication service with adequate facilities at reasonable charges." The Act incorporated the 1927 Radio Act, largely unchanged, leaving the federal government with absolute control of the airwaves. The Act also tilted strongly in favor of monopoly telephone service. New competitors would be permitted to enter telephone markets only if they could persuade the government that the "public convenience and necessity" so required.

In 1934, Eric Blair stopped writing magazine articles under his own name. He had published *Down and Out in Paris and London* under a pseudonym the year before. With the success of that book, Eric Blair died, and George Orwell was born.

∎

The monopoly owners of wire, spectrum, and calculating machines swelled and swelled from the 1930s until the 1970s. They accumulated corporate flesh as symbols of their greatness. They had once been obscure and hungry; now they grew fatter, richer, and more feared year by year. They grew swollen on the bodies of their enemies.

IBM's defining battle of the era was fought against cardboard. IBM customers were strictly forbidden to buy blank computer cards from anyone but IBM. In 1932, the federal government brought a first antitrust suit to overturn this practice. IBM responded that bad cards from independent suppliers would likely damage the machines IBM owned and serviced. The quality of service would deteriorate. Machines would jam. Businesses would fail.

In telephony, the FCC became a thoroughly servile agent of Bell's monopoly. The pinnacle of this collaboration came with the Hush-A-Phone, a small plastic device that snapped onto the mouthpiece of the telephone to provide some privacy and quiet in crowded office environments. The problem with the Hush-A-Phone was simple: it hadn't been invented or built by Bell. Bell, its lawyers argued to the commission, sold service—end-to-end service, with no loose ends, no forgotten corners. Service included all equipment on customer premises. Bell's tariffs expressly forbade any and all "foreign attachments." Such devices might send destructive pulses of electricity through the network, or degrade signal quality, or otherwise subvert the entire system. Moreover, Bell insisted, there was "no appreciable public demand" for the Hush-A-Phone. "[W]here privacy is needed," Bell assured the FCC, "it may be obtained . . . by cupping a hand around the transmitter and talking in a low tone of voice." The FCC agreed.

Meanwhile, in the radio business, the logic of scarcity expanded insatiably. Because of scarcity, the commission could direct radio stations to carry editorials, or responses to editorials, or political advertising. Because of scarcity, the commission could forbid stations from selling off blocks of airtime to the highest bidder. Because of scarcity, the commission could forbid stations to broadcast anything from tobacco advertising to children's cartoons. By the 1960s, the problem of scarcity would even supply the logic for regulating . . . abundance. The new technology of cable television offered limitless new transmission capacity. The FCC claimed jurisdiction over this capacious new medium anyway. The new abundance, the commission reasoned, threatened the well-being of established licensees of over-the-air scarcity, and that was reason enough to regulate it. Wealth was poverty. The courts agreed.

IBM's punch card case went up to the U.S. Supreme Court. In the end, IBM was forced to open the door to its market one small crack. A subsequent round of antitrust litigation, settled in a 1956 decree, required IBM to divest part of its card manufacturing operation. In a short opinion handed down the same year, a federal court of appeals threw out the FCC's ruling in the *Hush-A-Phone* case and affirmed "the telephone subscriber's right reasonably to use his telephone in ways which are privately beneficial without being publicly detrimental." In 1969, the scarcity rationale for regulating radio waves was embraced chapter and verse by the U.S. Supreme Court.

■

The genius of capitalism, as Lenin might have said, is that it develops its own rope, for hanging and other purposes. Even in the shelter of its anointed monopoly, the monstrous Bell System remained a for-profit enterprise. If it provided better, faster, and cheaper service, its revenues and profits would grow. The company had been founded on technology, and technology had remained its strength. In time, Bell would establish the greatest peacetime scientific research program the world has ever known, at Bell Laboratories in Murray Hill, New Jersey. Bell set its scientists in pursuit of better telephones, better networks, and better switches. The pursuit would span radio, then broadband communications, then telephone exchanges, and would end finally where the industry had begun: with the telephone box, which would come to be called a computer.

Bell had been barred from the radio broadcast business in 1927. But not all radio waves spread out like ripples on a pond. At sufficiently short wavelengths, radio signals move in straight lines, like beams of light. It became clear early on that electromagnetic waves, especially at higher frequencies, had enormous capacity to carry information accurately over long distances, at the speed of light. The broadcasters would push their way up the radio spectrum and by the 1950s would be transmitting the considerable volumes of information required for television. Telephone companies, especially Bell's long-distance arm, needed equally high-capacity (broadband) transmission systems, but systems that could operate over much larger distances, more securely, and more reliably.

Bell Labs began to investigate wave-guide transmission in 1931. The idea was to use the vast transmission capacities of high-frequency airwaves, but confined in ducts to maintain signal quality and ensure secure, point-to-point transmissions. By 1934, other researchers had developed a variation on the same idea: the coaxial cable, a copper sheath with a wire running down its center. "Coax," it turned out, could carry huge amounts of information with low attenuation. Within two years, Bell had installed its first coaxial cables in New York. Coax would supply many of the high-capacity trunks of the telephone network until the end of World War II.

Meanwhile, researchers at Bell Labs were laying the foundation for a second broadband technology: microwave. Harold T. Friis and his colleagues developed the horn-reflector antenna, now a standard fixture on microwave towers. Unlike their longer-wavelength cousins listed on the dial of any car radio, microwaves—short-wavelength radio waves—travel in straight lines and can be accurately focused. Because of their comparatively high frequency, microwaves can also carry far more information; even early systems were designed to carry up to 1,000 voice circuits. Their final advantage for long-distance transmission, especially in rural areas, was also the most obvious: microwave towers could be placed twenty or thirty miles apart, and a single license from the FCC could substitute for the cumbersome process of obtaining rights of way over the entire span. By 1959, microwave systems comprised 25 percent of Bell's long-distance network.

Coax and microwaves would transform more than the telephone industry. John Walson, Sr., of Mahanoy City, Pennsylvania, recognized that coaxial cable was the perfect medium for connecting homes in rural areas to a large master antenna. He began work on his first "community antenna" television network in 1948. Others took up the idea. Antennas were placed on hilltops, on tall buildings, and on masts. Distant signals were picked up and piped to viewers over coaxial cable. Before long, antenna operators began using microwave systems to beam in television signals to the master antennas from still farther afield. Thus, almost without design, cable television was invented. By 1955 there were 400 such systems in operation, serving 150,000 subscribers.

Still other Bell Labs scientists were leading research in yet another sphere. The technology of telephone exchanges had languished for some years after the first electromechanical switches began to be used. (As late as 1951, operators were still being used to connect almost 40 percent of domestic long-distance calls.) In 1936, when Orwell was publishing his third book, *Keep the Aspidistra Flying*, Bell Labs' director of research first discussed with physicist William Shockley the possibility of creating electronic telephone exchanges. Electronic switching, however, required a better amplifier than the vacuum tube technology. While each triode vacuum tube was capable of operating as a switch in a telephone exchange, an exchange needed thousands of such switches; tubes used too much power, and generated too much heat, to be packed together in the numbers required. Shockley and his Bell Labs colleagues Walter Brattain and John Bardeen set off in search of something better.

They found it in 1947, as Orwell was completing the first draft of *1984*. What they found was the transistor. A Nobel prize followed in 1956—the same year as the *Hush-A-Phone* ruling, the same year that

IBM agreed for the second time to let others into the punch card business.

The transistor, like the vacuum tube it displaced, was a compact, energy-efficient switch. Switches are the heart of a telephone exchange, for it is by opening and closing an appropriate set of switches that a single continuous line is created between Romeo in San Francisco and his Juliet in New York City. Switches are also the heart of a computer: by shifting on and off like beads moving on an abacus, switches can keep track of numbers, and numbers can keep track of everything. The first-generation computers in 1956 were still monstrous devices built around huge racks of vacuum tubes.

The new transistor soon came to the notice of Jack Kilby, an engineer who had been designing compact systems for hearing-aid companies. In 1958, Kilby moved to the Dallas headquarters of Texas Instruments and had a brainstorm. Transistors were being made on silicon by then. Why not make resistors and capacitors too on the same medium, and thus manufacture entire circuits all at once, in one process, on one substrate? Why not, in other words, manufacture an "integrated circuit"? Robert Noyce, another alumnus of Bell Labs then working at Fairchild Semiconductor, soon radically improved on Kilby's design. In 1968, Noyce and a colleague set up their own new company, Intel. Intel would eventually become master of the microprocessor, the computer on chip, which—like the audion before it—would fundamentally transform all of telephony, computing, and broadcast.

■

When microwaves, satellites, and developments in computers, radios, modems, fax machines, telephone handsets, and all the other varied progeny of the transistor began to make new competition feasible in the 1950s, the competitors arrived, first in ones and twos, then in legions, demanding permission to provide equipment and services around the periphery of the Bell empire.

At first Bell responded along the familiar *Hush-A-Phone* lines. By the 1960s, however, the pressure from the market had grown too intense for the FCC to ignore. Slowly, grudgingly, the FCC retreated from the

Hush-A-Phone mind-set and began authorizing all forms of electronic terminal equipment on private premises. Beginning with its *Carterfone* ruling in 1968 and ending in the late 1970s, the FCC eliminated all "foreign attachment" prohibitions from Bell's tariffs. Standard interfaces between customer equipment and the network were established. With the FCC's belated acquiescence, the market had won a historic victory over the monopoly. The way had been opened for a complete line of competitive products that would interconnect with the network on customer premises. To put the matter in Orwell's terms, it was now official Ministry policy that Bell would create, maintain, and support "loose ends and forgotten corners" on its network. The network now had something that it had not had before: jacks that any humble citizen could plug into, or disconnect from, without a by-your-leave from Bell or the FCC.

Virtually everything that was to follow in the dismantling of the Bell monopoly was a replay of *Carterfone*, a process of creating new "loose ends" on the network, new interfaces for the market. It required two more decades of regulatory and antitrust handwringing, but the rules permitting foreign attachments to the network created the market for enhanced services as well. If customers could connect their own telephones and answering machines to the network, private entrepreneurs could connect their own electronic publishing, data processing, voice mail, or dial-a-porn services too. All of these services simply involved connecting new equipment or new people to the existing wires.

Competing long-distance services developed in exactly the same manner. In the 1940s, long-distance service was provided exclusively over wires, and the same basic economics that seemed to preclude competition in local service applied equally to long-distance service. The development of microwave and satellite technologies radically changed that picture, making competition both practical and inevitable.

Initially, the pressure for competition came from large businesses, which sought to build microwave links solely to satisfy their own private communications needs. Then, in 1963, a small startup firm, Microwave Communications, applied to the FCC to construct a microwave line between St. Louis and Chicago. MCI told the FCC it would offer business customers "interplant and interoffice communications with unique and special characteristics." In fact, what MCI had in mind was head-to-head competition against Bell's long-distance operations.

Other MCIs came clamoring at the FCC's door, and the commission came under intense pressure to establish general conditions for entry by new long-distance carriers. In 1980 it formally adopted an open entry policy for all interstate services. It was *Carterfone* again, but this time on what engineers call the "trunk side" (as opposed to the "line side") of the local exchange.

Then, with almost no warning, a new generation of radio services burst on to the scene. When it first allocated frequencies for land mobile services in 1949, the FCC granted separate blocks to telephone companies and to "miscellaneous" or "limited" common carriers. The commission consistently maintained this procompetitive policy thereafter. When it began to issue cellular telephone licenses in the early 1980s, the FCC allocated two licenses for every service area, prohibited any licensee from owning a significant interest in both licenses, and thereafter encouraged the development of other radio technologies capable of providing directly competitive services. Most important, it required all landline telephone companies to provide unaffiliated mobile concerns with interconnection equal in type, quality, and price to that enjoyed by affiliates. Thus, a third set of loose ends to the network was created, this time at the interface between the traditional and still dominant landline telephone company and the new, much more competitive radio carriers.

Developing at the same time was an eclectic array of new telecommunicating exchanges and devices. Before the advent of the transistor, both computers and telephone exchanges had required large, cumbersome, costly, custom-configured, labor-intensive centers. With the new electronics, much more powerful telephone switches and computers could be built into more compact and reliable units—minicomputers and "private branch exchanges," which, as small, privately operated telephone exchanges, are telephony's equivalent to the desktop computer.

Larger institutions—hospitals, universities, corporate headquarters, and so on—had once relied on a few centralized mainframes to do their computing, and on "Centrex" services handled through public telephone exchanges, even for internal telephone calls. Now these same functions could be—and rapidly were—located in stand-alone units on private premises. Competing manufacturers of small, private exchanges and minicomputers proliferated. By the late 1970s, even Bell was systematically downgrading Centrex service and migrating its larger customers to private exchanges.

This dispersion of electronic intelligence created a host of new centers, held in private hands, capable of communicating by wire, and in need of connections to do so. As had happened almost a century earlier with the rise of the telephone itself, the new talking boxes created new demand. What was critically different about the new-generation local exchanges, whether true private exchanges or communicating computers, was that they were owned and controlled not by a small number of quasi-governmental, monopoly telephone companies but by a larger number of private, competitive institutions. For the most part, these private owners welcomed competitive bidding for their telecommunications needs. The telephone had created the original demand for a telephone network almost a century before. Now a new generation of transistor-based electronic equipment in private hands was creating demand for the kinds of competing long-distance services that MCI proposed to offer.

At the same time, the transistor was also fulfilling its original mission, which was to transform the public telephone exchange: a new generation of electronic switches was deployed in the 1960s and 1970s. These switches were far more efficient, powerful, and flexible than the old switches they replaced. They could support levels of interconnection—and thus offer customers a variety of choices—that would have been prohibitively slow, complex, and unreliable in the days when switching was accomplished by human operators or electromechanical devices. As MCI built up its business in the 1970s, the company resolved to carry competition back up the network—to compete not just in connecting private computers and switches but also between the public exchanges operated by the Bell and other public telephone companies. The capabilities of the new electronic switches made that aspiration quite realistic; as every telephone user knows today, such switches can be programmed with databases to route traffic automatically, Hatfield's to Bell, McCoy's to MCI, effortlessly and invisibly whenever either places a long-distance call.

The new array of players assembled around loose ends of the Bell network demanded truly equal interconnection on equal terms. When Bell declined to provide it, the newcomers responded with a blizzard of FCC petitions and private antitrust suits. Viewed in historical context, the federal government's antitrust suit that produced the final breakup of the Bell System was little more than a footnote to what had unfolded in the market and the FCC before. By late 1981, AT&T was ready to throw in the towel. It cut a deal with the federal antitrust prosecutors. The final breakup was scheduled for January 1, 1984.

■

For a time it appeared that Big Blue's hegemony would collapse long before Bell's.

Computers based on vacuum tubes rather than transistors had begun to displace tabulating machines in government and defense agencies during World War II. Two University of Pennsylvania scientists, J. Presper Eckert and John W. Mauchly, were the leading pioneers in the new field. Together they built ENIAC (Electronic Numerical Integrator and Computer), generally recognized as the first electronic computer.

Watson saw the ENIAC but failed to recognize its importance. In 1951, however, AT&T licensed the basic transistor patents to other companies. Philco, RCA, and General Electric quickly developed computers that were much more advanced than IBM's. In 1952, Remington Rand acquired the company founded by Eckert and Mauchly, and the following year it introduced the UNIVAC. IBM nonetheless continued to gain in the market, on the strength of its sales force and established business base. Before long, IBM had grasped the power of the new electronic technology and mounted a crash effort to recapture its technological lead. By the 1960s, there were eight major manufacturers of mainframe computers, but IBM was so dominant once again that the group came to be called Snow White and the Seven Dwarfs.

When IBM announced its new System/360 on April 7, 1964, it did so simultaneously in sixty-three U.S. cities and fourteen foreign countries. During the first two years of System/360, 9,013 computers (three times original projections) were ordered. By 1967, IBM 360 installations accounted for an estimated 80 percent of all new computer capacity in the world and approximately 70 percent of new computer installations in the major markets of Britain, France, Germany, Italy, and the United States. IBM's revenues mushroomed, from $1.7 billion to $7.5 billion.

The same economics that had secured IBM's market dominance in the era of punch cards and tabulating machines had apparently come into play again. Once a customer had committed to IBM, a switch to another vendor entailed prohibitive new investment in applications, training, and software. With the largest base of customers, IBM also offered the largest library of application programs. At the same time, IBM did all it could to freeze out the competition. The strategy was the same as Bell's. Computers then, as now, consisted of central processors, storage devices (disk drives, tapes, computer cards), and input-output devices (screens, printers, keyboards, and so on). IBM rigidly adhered to a policy of closed, proprietary architectures, a policy readily enforced when all its machines were supplied (like Bell's) only under lease. Would-be competitors were eager to sell "plug-compatible" peripherals—card readers, printers, disk drives, monitors, and so on—that would hook into the IBM machines. IBM was determined that they wouldn't. There were to be no loose ends on the IBM mainframe—none at all.

Outside IBM, there was much disagreement about precisely what should be done. In retrospect the debates seem absurd, but they were perfectly serious at the time. Many pundits still believed in Grosch's law, according to which the efficiency and power of an electronic computer would increase steadily with its size. You would always get more total computing power at less cost, it was thought, by building one larger computer rather than two smaller ones.

The implication was as obvious as it was ominous: computing was destined to end up in one or two machines, or perhaps a very small cluster of machines, located in a few, huge, central buildings, buildings that—every Orwellian expected—were bound to tower vast and white above the grimy landscape, enormous pyramidal structures of glittering white concrete, soaring up, terrace after terrace, three hundred meters into the air.

One possible solution would have been to unleash Bell and IBM to compete head to head. Bell, after all, had invented the transistor, the key to all electronic computers of the day; moreover, Bell was already manufacturing a lot of very powerful computers for its own uses. But as the government lawyers saw it, Bell was already too big and powerful for anyone's good, and in other arenas the entire government strategy had been to quarantine Bell from entering new markets like computing.

So instead of letting another established firm compete against IBM, the government resolved for a time to have IBM compete against itself. The objective: break up IBM. This required a mammoth antitrust suit. The following thirteen years of litigation would represent the slowest, most expensive, paper-clogged, and useless antitrust lawsuit ever undertaken by the federal government—an operation as monstrous and inefficient in its own way as the computer monopolist that it targeted. The suit came to be known as the Antitrust Division's Vietnam.

The agreement to break up AT&T was announced on January 8, 1982, the same day that the federal government agreed to dismiss its case against IBM. One of the eight fragments of the old Bell System—the surviving AT&T—was to be freed from all antitrust quarantines and so permitted to enter the computer business. Intel was already over a decade old. Apple was growing fast. And IBM had just introduced a brand-new machine, based on an Intel microprocessor. Big Blue's new machine—its "personal computer"—was small and beige.

■

The small beige machine was made possible by a single device: the integrated circuit, the microprocessor, the computer on a chip. The integrated circuit continued the transistor's restructuring of telephony but accelerated the pace of change a thousand-fold.

Intel, alongside other chip developers like Motorola and Texas Instruments, had taken a familiar device, the transistor, and made it smaller. Transistors were shrunk from the size of a fingernail to the size of a hair, to the size of a microbe and smaller. The power of the microprocessor grew as fast as its components shrank.

The economics of producing electronic equipment shifted dramatically. Designing a single, advanced microprocessor may require a billion-dollar investment. Thereafter, any number of copies can be stamped out at very little cost. The technology thus triggered an efflorescence of new desktop and office systems, as well as consumer electronics. All depended on the same fundamental component: the transistor. All operated digitally. All could be mass produced at little cost once the electronics for the first unit had been designed.

The result has been a radical technological transformation, characterized by two seemingly contradictory trends: fragmentation and convergence.

The first major trend today continues to be one of fragmentation. The once-centralized network is becoming decentralized. "Terminals"—dumb end points to the network—are giving way to "seminals"—nodes of equal power that can process, switch, store, and retrieve information with the agility that was once lodged exclusively in a few fortified centers' massive switches and mainframe computers. Residences and offices across the country are rapidly being equipped with a new generation of telephones: computers, facsimiles, electronic burglar alarms and meter readers, remote medical monitoring systems, and, soon, high-definition digital televisions. VCRs and videotapes are now, by a wide margin, the dominant medium for distributing movies. The "picturephone" that the Bell System unsuccessfully attempted to market in the 1960s is already owned by millions of Americans. It is called a video camera.

Fragmentation is most visible in the computer industry itself. In 1974, when Intel introduced its 8080 microprocessor, the computer on a chip matched the power of the IBM 704, a mainframe introduced twenty years earlier. It was in this environment that the Department of Justice had initiated its suits against AT&T and IBM, and the FCC had formulated its policies of "maximum separation" between telephone and computing services. By 1977, however, Zilog had cut the gap between centralized mainframes and microprocessors to fifteen years: the Zilog Z-80 microprocessor roughly matched IBM's 1962 Model 7094. By 1981, the gap had closed to six years, when Intel introduced its 8088 (the brains of the original IBM personal computer), which offered roughly the same computing power as a 1975 Digital Equipment machine, the PDP 11/70. Intel's 80386, introduced in 1987, had about the same raw power as Digital's VAX 8600, introduced in 1984. Intel's

1989 offering, the 80486, came close to matching IBM's 3090, introduced in 1985. Thus, in the space of a decade, the performance gap between microprocessors and mainframes was closed from twenty years to less than five. A $5,000 PC in 1990 had the processing power of a $250,000 minicomputer in the mid-1980s, and a million dollar mainframe of the 1970s. In a decade, 99 percent of computing power moved out of the central mainframe computer and on to the individual desktop. There has been a massive relocation of electronic power from the control of technicians, bureaucrats, and traditional system managers, into private hands.

The impact on IBM has been devastating. The only thriving parts of its hardware business today are at the bottom end, where Big Blue's small beige machines have been open, standardized, and widely copied from the day they were introduced. Between 1985 and 1992, IBM shed 100,000 employees. IBM's stock, worth $176 a share in 1987, collapsed to $52 by year's end 1992. In 1992, the *New York Times* would announce "The End of I.B.M.'s Overshadowing Role." "IBM's problems," the *Times* noted, "are due to its failure to realize that its core business, mainframe computers, had been supplanted by cheap, networked PC's and faster networked workstations." In a desperate scramble for survival, IBM is breaking itself into autonomous units and spinning off some of its more successful divisions. "The idea of open systems—that computers should easily share things and basically behave like friends—is what everyone is aiming for," IBM's advertising now declares. Instead of a computer screen, one ad shows two sliding glass doors opening out on a vast expanse of peaceful ocean.

As cheap storage and computing power move onto customer premises, the use of data communications has increased, but dependence on data communications has actually declined. Telephone users today routinely make such trade-offs when they opt to install a faster modem or fax machine, or to install a CD-ROM as a substitute for online electronic services, or to assemble a local area network of personal computers to replace on-line time sharing on a remote mainframe. In each instance, greater electronic power on a user's own premises becomes a strong substitute, at the margin, for greater usage of the telephone network. The link to the network is never severed; indeed, usage of the network increases steadily as businesses themselves become increasingly decentralized. But relations between consumers and providers of telephone service are nonetheless shifting profoundly, with the consumer's power increasing, while the telephone company's declines. Each new generation of equipment—computers, local area networks, metropolitan area networks, mobile switching offices, pay-per-view TV systems, and so on—offers a new cluster of possibilities for interconnection. Exchanges multiply and are dispersed; pathways across the network proliferate. Where once there was a monolithic provider of plain-vanilla service, there are now multiple providers offering an array of ever more exotic flavors.

This has triggered a further round of restructuring in the telco central office. The first-generation electronic switches were based on analog technology; the second-generation switches were digital. Digital switches entered the public telephone exchange in the late 1970s; by 1985, half of all telephone calls were digitally switched. The new switches were even more powerful and flexible than the analog electronic switches they replaced. The prior generation had been powerful enough to accommodate the rise of competition in interexchange services; the new generation was powerful enough to accommodate competition among myriad providers of communications and computing services of every description.

Prodded both by forward-looking regulators and providers eager to supply new services through the telephone network, equipment manufacturers and telephone companies have most recently begun to develop a new conception of the role and function of the public telephone exchanges. The regulatory mandate today is for open network architecture (ONA), which will disaggregate the individual components of a telephone connection—the line, the signaling (such things as dial and busy tones), switching, and so on—into basic service elements that can be priced and sold separately and integrated into a rich variety of enhanced services.

ONA is probably the inevitable technological culmination of the disaggregation and decentralization of telephony triggered by the electronics revolution. Theodore Vail's vision of universal service is not repudiated but instead carried to its logical conclusion. The telephone network will provide universal service not only to consumers but also to producers—to competing telephone companies (as already occurs in the long-distance markets), to radio-telephone competitors who need to interconnect their service with the landline network, and to a limitless number of competing providers of "enhanced" or "information" services, who will monitor burglar alarms, link together bank teller machines, transmit electronic mail, publish electronic newspapers, run shopping malls, or deliver on-line horoscopes.

So much for fragmentation. The second transcendent reality in the world of electronic thought is convergence. Telephony, television, and computing now share the same future. It is a future of switched, digital, broadband networks that combine the broadband carrying capacity of cable television, the digital power and flexibility of computers, and the switched addressability of telephones. In digital systems, a bit is a bit, whether it represents a hiccup in a voice conversation, or the price at which AT&T stock is selling at this particular instant, or a strand of hair in a rerun of "I Love Lucy." The lines between media formerly segregated by mode of transmission (radio vs. landline) and function (telephone, cable, broadcast, computer) are disappearing. We are moving toward a myriad of mixed media (radio/landline), integrated (digital), broadband networks, all interconnecting seamlessly to one another. As Ithiel de Sola Pool recognized in his landmark *Technologies of Freedom*, "the neat separations between different media no longer hold."

Perhaps the most vivid illustration of this convergence is cellular telephony, made possible by the synthesis of radio, telephone, and computers. The key problem with the early radio telephones, which persisted until the 1980s, was that there just didn't seem to be enough spectrum available to allow simultaneous use of very many of them. A few dozen stations pretty much fill up the dial of a radio—and radio telephone requires radio stations in pairs to sustain two-way conversation.

In the 1940s, researchers at Bell Labs proposed an ingenious solution. Radio telephones should be low-power, short-range devices. The same frequencies could then be used again and again (just as they are with cordless home telephones); a radio conversation at East Forty-second Street would not interfere with another one on the same frequency on West Fifty-first. A city would be divided into many separate "cells," each one served by its own low-power transmitter. The capacity of a cellular system could then be increased almost indefinitely by shrinking cells and increasing their number. But cellular telephony required, in exchange, highly sophisticated transmitters and receivers, and massive coordination among cells to "hand off" calls and coordinate frequencies as the car telephone on Forty-second Street moved toward Fifty-first. No one had the technology to perform this—until the advent of microelectronics.

After the FCC finally approved commercial cellular telephone systems in 1982, the market grew explosively. The new exchanges—mobile telephone switching offices—secured the right to interconnect with the established landline exchanges. By 1990, entrepreneurs and regulators were considering a second generation of over-the-air telephone systems—personal communications networks (PCNs)—based on microcells, with base stations linked to either private or public exchanges. Each new cluster of exchanges that appeared on the scene opened up new possibilities for service from competing networks. Cellular companies have quickly recognized the advantages of clustered service and established dedicated links between their own exchanges and those of the long-distance carriers. PCN operators have turned to cable companies to provide transport among the transceivers that will be used to support their service.

A less visible but equally revolutionary merger of radio and telephone technologies has occurred below ground, during almost exactly the same years as cellular systems were being deployed above. This too evolved directly from technological developments set in motion at Bell Labs several decades earlier.

The development of coaxial cable and microwave transmission marked a major advance in the continuing quest for ever more capacious, reliable, secure transmission systems. For telephonic purposes, microwaves represented an important advance over ordinary radio because they operated at much higher frequencies, capable of carrying much more information over focused paths. Push the frequencies higher still, and you get ultra-high-frequency radio waves, better known as light. A light beam can be shaped and modulated to carry information in much the same way as Marconi's radio waves, but in vastly larger amounts. It is best transmitted in a wave guide, similar (in principle) to those developed by Bell Labs in the 1930s. Extremely pure, hair-thin strands of glass serve admirably.

Fiber-optic systems represent today's pinnacle of telecommunications technology, the finest merger (so far) of radio, telephone lines, and electronics. Integrated circuits provide the highly sophisticated transmitters and receivers at each end of the line. The telephone line itself is now a strand of glass. The radio wave is now a beam of light, generated by a laser. A single strand of glass can transmit thousands of simultaneous telephone conversations, or hundreds of color television signals.

Fiber is now rapidly replacing copper, coaxial cable, and microwave everywhere in the telephone network, except (so far) in the short last stretch to the user's home. But competing local carriers have begun deploying independent fiber-optic systems in larger cities across the country, aiming to replay the MCI history again, with a new technology (fiber instead of microwaves) in response to enormously rapid increases in demand.

■

In the 1950s, competitors searched for forgotten corners in the shadow of B&B, where they might peddle such things as cardboard punch cards or plastic Hush-A-Phone cups. But that old world, Orwell's world, the world of computer and communications monopolies, will not be seen again in our lifetimes. The loose ends and the forgotten corners have taken over. The battle of the cardboard card and the plastic cup have been won; computers, telephones, and televisions are now riddled with slots, ports, jacks, joysticks, mice, and SCSI interfaces, and surrounded by compact disks, videocameras, VCRs, scanners, screens, optical character readers, facsimile interfaces, sound synthesizers, projectors, and radio antennas. The plugs and jacks and sockets have taken over the telescreen world; the Ministry is dead. Every unfilled plug, every unconnected jack, is a loose end, a new entry into the network or an exit from it, a new soap box in Hyde Park, a new podium, a new microphone for poetry or prose, a new screen or telescreen for displaying private sentiment or fomenting sedition, for preaching the gospel, or peddling fresh bread.

■■■■■ ABBREVIATIONS
IN THE NOTES

I have cited wherever possible paperback editions that are readily available.

Down and Out: Down and Out in Paris and London. Harcourt Brace Jovanovich, 1933.

Burmese Days: Burmese Days. 1934. Harcourt Brace Jovanovich, 1962.

A Clergyman's Daughter: A Clergyman's Daughter. 1935. Harcourt Brace Jovanovich, 1960.

Aspidistra: Keep the Aspidistra Flying. 1936. Harcourt Brace Jovanovich, 1956.

Wigan Pier: The Road to Wigan Pier. 1937. Harcourt Brace Jovanovich, 1958.

Homage to Catalonia: Homage to Catalonia. 1938. Harcourt Brace Jovanovich, 1952.

Coming Up for Air: Coming Up for Air. 1939. Penguin Books, 1990.

Lion: The Lion and the Unicorn. 1941. Penguin Books, 1941.

Animal Farm: Animal Farm. 1946. Harcourt Brace Jovanovich, 1946.

1984: Nineteen Eighty-Four. 1949. Harcourt Brace Jovanovich, 1977.

The Orwell Reader: The Orwell Reader. Harcourt Brace Jovanovich, 1956.

Essays, I: George Orwell: A Collection of Essays. Harcourt Brace Jovanovich, 1946.

Essays, II: The Orwell Reader: Fiction, Essays, and Reportage by George Orwell. Harcourt Brace Jovanovich, 1956.

Essays, III: The Penguin Essays of George Orwell. Penguin Books, 1984.

Essays, IV: George Orwell, Decline of the English Murder and Other Essays. Penguin Books, 1953.

Broadcast: Orwell, The War Broadcasts. W. J. West, ed. Duckworth/British Broadcasting Corporation, 1985.

CEJL, Vols. 1–4: The Collected Essays, Journalism and Letters of George Orwell. Martin Secker & Warburg, 1968.

Shelden: Michael Shelden, Orwell: The Authorized Biography. Harper-Collins, 1991.

■■■■■ NOTES

Preface

p. 1 *last two digits interchanged:* Shelden, p. 433. I refer to the book as *1984* rather than Orwell's original *Nineteen Eighty-Four.* The whole point of *Orwell's Revenge,* after all, is to rewrite Orwell in ways large and small.

... *New York Times reported:* Shelden, p. 430.

... *the New Yorker and the Evening Standard:* Shelden, p. 430.

p. 2 *one context or another:* "Charles Dickens" (1939), *Essays,* I, p. 91.

... *not so much a book, it is a world:* "Charles Dickens," p. 91.

... *quote him unconsciously:* "Charles Dickens," p. 92.

... *name to the English language:* "Rudyard Kipling" (1942), *Essays,* I, p. 126.

... *whole attitude to life:* "Books v. Cigarettes" (1946), *Essays,* III, p. 349.

... *the Washington Monument:* "Charles Dickens," p. 91 ("Nelson Column" in the original).

... *beneath is rotten:* "Charles Dickens," p. 96.

... *out of bed every morning: 1984,* p. 296.

p. 3 *occasional bomb crater: Coming Up for Air,* p. 30.

... *out of bedroom windows: Coming Up for Air,* p. 31.

p. 3 *and enormous faces on posters: Coming Up for Air,* p. 176.

... *telling you what to think: Coming Up for Air,* p. 186.

... *unbreakable system of tabus: 1984,* p. 70.

... *denouncing you to the secret police: Homage to Catalonia,* p. 147.

... *who disgusted him horribly:* Cf. "Inside the Whale" (1940), *Essays,* I, p. 210; "The Art of Donald McGill" (1941), *Essays,* I, p. 115 (in a totalitarian society art must therefore concentrate "on the unheroic in one form or another").

... *mutability of the past: 1984,* pp. 27, 157, 214.

p. 4 *and became truth: 1984,* p. 35.

... *well then, it never happened:* "Looking Back on the Spanish War" (1943), *Essays,* I, p. 199 (in the original, "the Leader, or some ruling clique" or "the Leader" instead of "Big Brother").

... *in 1984 is doublethink: 1984,* p. 36.

... *and accepting both of them: 1984,* pp. 215-216.

... *the reality which one denies: 1984,* pp. 215-216.

p. 5 *above a junk shop:* At another point, Winston and Julia meet in the belfry of a ruined church. *1984,* pp. 129, 131. The church is borrowed from *Homage to Catalonia,* p. 213.

... *overthrow the Party:* Resistance is necessary, O'Brien says, though hopeless. *1984,* p. 177. Or, as Orwell has already put in *Wigan Pier,* p. 158: "[E]very revolutionary opinion draws part of its strength from a secret conviction that nothing can be changed."

... *the arch-traitor Kenneth Blythe:* It's Emmanuel Goldstein in the original *1984,* of course. The Blythe, like the Orwell, is a river in England.

... *the middle of 1984:* The Book-of-the-Month Club wanted to cut them when it released *1984* in the United States. Orwell refused, risking the loss of 40 pounds sterling; as Orwell's authorized biographer reports, "the integrity of the book meant more to him than even this enormous sum." Shelden, p. 430.

... *egalitarian, classless society:* With allowances for the fact that everything is being overstated, "The Theory and Practice of Oligarchical Collectivism" clearly sets out Orwell's own political views. He repeats all its essential parts in many other essays, including several published at the same time as he was writing *1984.* See, e.g., "Toward European Unity" (1947), *CEJL,* Vol. 4, p. 370.

p. 5 *shared all around:* See *Wigan Pier,* p. 171; "Looking Back on the Spanish War," p. 203; "As I Please" (1946), *CEJL,* Vol. 4, p. 249 ("there is, or could be, plenty of everything for everybody . . . wealth might be so generally diffused that no government need fear serious opposition"). Cf. *1984,* p. 171.

By 1948, however, just as he was finishing *1984,* Orwell was beginning to rethink this notion. In one essay he criticizes Oscar Wilde for making "two common but unjustified assumptions." The first is that "the world is immensely rich and is suffering chiefly from maldistribution." In fact, Orwell now declares, the problem "is not how to distribute such wealth as exists but how to increase production without which economic equality merely means common misery." Wilde's second error, Orwell states, is to overestimate the potential of machines. There is in fact (says Orwell now) "a vast range of jobs—roughly speaking, any job needing great flexibility—that no machine is able to do." "The Soul of Man under Socialism by Oscar Wilde" (1948), *CEJL,* Vol. 4, pp. 426-428.

. . . *military strength decayed:* "Fascism is now an international movement," groping "towards a world-system" simultaneously in both communist and capitalist societies. *Wigan Pier,* p. 215. *Coming Up for Air,* p. 205, makes the same point more colorfully; that book places "all the soul-savers and Nosey Parkers, the people whom you've never seen but who rule your destiny all the same, the Home Secretary, Scotland Yard, the Temperance League, the Bank of England, Lord Beaverbrook, Hitler and Stalin on a tandem bicycle."

. . . *Orwell's earlier political essays:* "Second Thoughts on James Burnham" (1946), *Essays, II,* p. 335. The essay was originally printed in *Polemic* under the title "Second Thoughts on James Burnham," and later reprinted as a pamphlet, *James Burnham and the Managerial Revolution.* See *CEJL,* Vol. 4, p. 160.

. . . *the world is headed, and why:* Cf. *Wigan Pier,* p. 231: "Fascism is coming [to England]; probably a slimy Anglicised form of Fascism, with cultured policemen instead of Nazi gorillas and the lion and the unicorn instead of the swastika." See also "Not Counting Niggers" (1939), *CEJL,* Vol. 1, p. 398: with "prolonged war-preparation" England "may sink almost unresisting into some local variant of austro-Fascism. And perhaps a year or two later, in reaction against this, there will appear something we have never had in England yet—a real Fascist movement." Similarly, in *Coming Up for Air*, p. 176, Orwell writes: "It's all going to happen—the hate-world, slogan-world . . . the processions and the posters with enormous faces, and the crowds of a million people all cheering for the Leader till they deafen themselves into thinking that they really worship him, and all the time, underneath, they hate him so that they want to puke."

p. 6 *make that unthinkable:* By 1984 there has already been one more big war and at least one atom bomb dropped on England. The *1984* atom bomb had fallen on Colchester. *1984*, p. 33.

. . . *the educated, restless middle class:* In *Wigan Pier*, p. 226, Orwell has already explained how these types will be handled. "It is quite easy to imagine a middle class crushed down to the worst depths of poverty and still remaining bitterly anti-working class in senti-ment; this being, of course, a ready-made Fascist Party." Both Julia and Winston have streaks of this themselves: they are middle-class snobs. Winston despises the smell of Parsons' working-class sweat. And Julia sleeps with everybody—but "always with Party members" (not proles) and never with "those swine" from the Inner Party. *1984*, p. 126. As Orwell notes elsewhere, "One thing that often gives the clue to a novelist's real feelings on the class question is the attitude he takes up when class collides with sex. . . . [I]t is one of the points at which the 'I'm-not-a-snob' pose tends to break down." "Charles Dickens," p. 76.

. . . *molding the consciousness: 1984*, p. 209.

p. 7 *two gin-scented tears: 1984*, p. 300.

. . . *He loves Big Brother: 1984*, p. 300. In 1940, six years before he began *1984*, Orwell had already persuaded himself that that was how things were bound to end. "[W]e are moving into an age of totalitarian dictatorships—an age in which freedom of thought will be at first a deadly sin and later on a meaningless abstraction. The autonomous individual is going to be stamped out of exis-tence." "Inside the Whale," p. 249.

p. 7 *I want to write, he continues:* "Why I Write" (1946), *Essays*, I, p. 316.

... *his brain is not involved:* "Politics and the English Language" (1946), *Essays*, I, p. 166.

... *it was his larynx: 1984*, p. 55.

p. 8 *reliance on scissors and paste:* Compare "London Letter to *Partisan Review*" (1946), *CEJL*, Vol. 4, p. 189: "Scissors-and-paste anthologies and miscellanies continue to appear in great numbers."

... *in much the same way: 1984*, p. 11. See also "Review, *A Coat of Many Colours: Occasional Essays*, by Herbert Read" (1945), *CEJL*, Vol. 4, p. 50: "It is just thinkable that books may some day be written by machinery, and it is quite easy to imagine poems being produced partly by fortuitous means—by some device similar to the kaleidoscope, for instance."

... *swapped around by machine: 1984*, p. 107. Orwell himself had six novels to his name: *A Clergyman's Daughter, Burmese Days, Aspidistra, Coming Up for Air, Animal Farm,* and *1984.* (*Down and Out in Paris and London* is more diary than novel.)

... *without any human intervention whatever: 1984*, p. 139.

... *a child's Meccano set:* "The Prevention of Literature" (1946), *Essays*, III, p. 341. For other references to art by machine see "As I Please" (1944), *CEJL*, Vol. 3, p. 274; "As I Please" (1944), *CEJL*, Vol. 3, pp. 229-230 (the BBC and the film companies "manage to rob literary creation of its individual character and turn it into a sort of conveyor-belt process").

... *the end of the assembly line:* "The Prevention of Literature," p. 344. Anything so produced will of course "be rubbish," Orwell adds (p. 345).

p. 9 *at least elaborately rewritten:* "The Prevention of Literature," p. 345.

... *Michael Shelden, Orwell: The Authorized Biography:* (1991) (1,165,724 bytes).

... *like a sucked orange:* "Letter to A. S. F. Gow" (1946), *CEJL*, Vol. 4, p. 146.

... *using my brain or muscles: Wigan Pier*, p. 206. Flory, the sensitive, artistic, semiautobiographical hero of *Burmese Days*, is nonetheless "a fool about machinery" and quite willing to "struggle with the bowels of the engine until he [is] black with grease" (p. 200).

p. 9 *tenure at the BBC*: As W. J. West discusses in his introduction to the compilation of Orwell's wartime broadcasts, the British Ministry of Information oversaw the BBC. Its telegraphic address was MINIFORM. It was the highest building in London during the war and "towered above surrounding London in a way which we today, surrounded by skyscrapers, can hardly imagine." *Broadcast,* pp. 64-65. Orwell could see the building from the block of flats where he lived. The rhythmic chanting of "B.B." in *1984,* see p. 117, is an insider's joke about Bracken.

p. 10 *the Ministry of Information*: See *Broadcast,* p. 20.

. . . *Capitalism, Fascism and Socialism*: See *Broadcast,* p. 28. Bernal dropped out at the last moment, possibly at the secret behest of Guy Burgess, a colleague of Orwell's at the BBC. Bernal was an ardent Marxist, Burgess was a Soviet spy, and Orwell despised Russian communism (p. 30).

. . . *a Soviet spy*: As West points out: "If [Orwell] had wanted a person to act as a model for O'Brien in *Nineteen Eighty-Four,* a man who would betray him and anyone else for the Party, what better choice could he have made than his fellow-Etonian and fellow-veteran of Osterley Park, his former colleague and friend at the BBC, Guy Burgess." *Broadcast,* p. 67.

Ironically, another Burgess—Anthony—published his own alternative to *1984* in 1978. A. Burgess, *1985,* was published by Little, Brown, which happens to be the publisher of my legal treatise, *Federal Telecommunications Law* (coauthored with M. Kellogg and J. Thorne, 1992, Supp. 1993).

Chapter 1

p. 13 *dismembered by the wind*: *1984,* p. 293.

. . . *gray walls of the buildings*: Orwell loathes posters. Gordon Comstock, hero of Orwell's *Keep the Aspidistra Flying* (1936), "had his private reasons for hating them." *Aspidistra,* p. 6. In fact, "[h]e really hated them" (p. 14). The *Aspidistra* posters are "monstrous";

they are "plastered" all over London; one in particular is "torn at the edge; a ribbon of paper fluttered fitfully like a tiny pennant" (pp. 6, 230). In *1984*, Big Brother's "monstrous" posters are "plastered" everywhere, and one in particular, "torn at one corner, flapped fitfully in the wind." *1984*, pp. 4, 150.

p. 13 *Victory Mansions:* While working at the BBC during the war, Orwell lived in a room at Portland Place. See *Broadcast,* p. 65. In *1984*, these have become the "Victory Mansions."

p. 14 *production of pig iron: 1984*, p. 4.

. . . *no way of shutting it off completely: 1984*, p. 3.

. . . *watched at any given moment: 1984*, p. 4.

. . . *whenever they wanted to: 1984*, p. 4.

. . . *third most populous province of Oceania: 1984*, p. 5.

p. 15 *the three slogans of the Party: 1984*, p. 5.

. . . *turned from the window: 1984*, p. 6.

. . . *gulped it down: 1984*, p. 6.

. . . *line of sight: 1984*, p. 7.

. . . *trading was officially forbidden: 1984*, pp. 7-8.

. . . *the compendium of all heresies: 1984*, p. 15.

. . . *had passed through many hands: 1984*, p. 184.

. . . *Blair's bowels: 1984*, p. 8.

p. 16 *DOWN WITH BIG BROTHER: 1984*, p. 19.

. . . *greetings: 1984*, p. 29. One could organize a complete analysis, appreciation, and criticism of *1984* around this single, magnificent passage. Of almost biblical depth, it appears a few pages into Smith's diary, and it encapsulates the whole political point of the novel in two sentences. Men should not live alone, but they should not live uniformly like ants either. They should have privacy but not solitude; they should be different but not isolated; they should communicate but not live under the unblinking gaze of Big Brother. Truth must exist. The past must be immutable. The future must not be.

. . . *gazing stupidly at the page: 1984*, p. 9.

. . . *seconds were ticking by: 1984*, p. 9.

. . . *razor blades: 1984*, pp. 4, 8, 49, 61, 93, 176, 232, 234, 235, 241 (razor blades and more razor blades).

p. 17 *could be said to happen: 1984*, p. 11.

p. 17 *four-mile radius of the inner city:* "Some Thoughts on the Common Toad" (1946), *Essays*, III, p. 367.

. . . *'as 'er for a tanner:* "Hop-Picking" (1931), *CEJL*, Vol. 1, pp. 53-54.

p. 19 *like the smoke of a rubbish fire: 1984*, p. 123.

. . . *'Ullo, mate: Broadcast*, p. 99.

p. 20 *the significant thing had happened: 1984*, p. 18.

. . . *message had passed: 1984*, p. 18.

. . . *gin in his mouth: 1984*, p. 6.

p. 21 *contained all others in itself: 1984*, p. 20.

. . . *gangs of armed men: Homage to Catalonia*, pp. 147, 200.

. . . *seemed to grow cold:* Here's a little illustration of how an author's style can be dissected (unfairly perhaps) on a computer. From *Burmese Days* (pp. 152, 210, 237) come these sentences: "A chilly, desolate feeling had taken possession of his entrails"; "A pang like a blade of ice had gone through his entrails"; "Something happened in everybody's entrails." These are the counterparts in *1984* (pp. 18, 116, 222, 235): "Winston's entrails seemed to grow cold"; "For a moment it felt as though his entrails were being ground to pulp"; "Winston's entrails seemed to have turned into ice"; "Winston's entrails contracted"; "There was another spasm in his entrails."

. . . *heavily toward the door: 1984*, p. 21.

The Machine

p. 23 *sort of Chinese rice-spirit: 1984*, p. 6.

. . . *mouthful you drink: 1984*, pp. 291, 296.

. . . *in place of tears: 1984*, p. 296.

. . . *your bed overnight: 1984*, p. 296.

p. 24 *existed for the first time: 1984*, pp. 206-207.

. . . *ears with Party propaganda: 1984*, p. 74.

p. 25 *as if by accident: 1984*, p. 39. There are, by contrast, eighteen references to the dial on the pain machine O'Brien uses in Part III of *1984*.

. . . *explain how the gadget works:* Cf. "Charles Dickens" (1939), *Essays*, I, p. 85 (Orwell complains that one of Dickens's books involves the wonderful invention of a genial engineer but that Dickens never even tells us what that invention is).

Chapter 2

p. 27 *stupid thing to have done:* 1984, p. 21.

. . . *was standing outside: A Clergyman's Daughter,* p. 58.

. . . *It's got blocked up:* 1984, p. 21.

. . . *a foul drain-pipe: Wigan Pier,* p. 18. Orwell's original notes on this scene appear in "The Road to Wigan Pier Diary" (1936), *CEJL,* Vol. 1, p. 177.

p. 28 *seldom taken off: Wigan Pier,* p. 7; cf. 1984, p. 22.

. . . *a window pane for two years:* 1984, p. 22.

. . . *Vaunnie is:* 1984, pp. 22-23.

. . . *the stability of the Party depended:* 1984, p. 23.

. . . *blocked up the pipe:* 1984, p. 23.

. . . *devices as intricate as these:* 1984, p. 189.

p. 29 *prison or the scaffold:* I am quoting from A. Koestler, *Darkness at Noon* (New York: Bantam, 1989), p. 129: "Our engineers work with the constant knowledge that an error in calculation may take them to prison or the scaffold."

. . . *snooping into people's windows:* 1984, p. 4.

. . . *simple job on a printer:* 1984, p. 11.

. . . *through the body of a bird:* 1984, p. 157.

. . . *the Faroe Islands:* 1984, p. 25.

p. 30 *dark shirt and tie:* Shelden, p. 417.

. . . *to bust something open: Broadcast,* p. 99.

. . . *pale-blue, humorous eyes:* Shelden, p. 204.

p. 31 *the place where there is no darkness:* 1984, p. 26.

. . . *made much impression on him:* 1984, p. 26.

. . . *newsflash has this moment arrived:* 1984, pp. 26-27.

. . . *the continuity was not broken:* 1984, p. 28.

Brain in a Bottle

p. 33 *a brain in a bottle: Wigan Pier,* p. 201.

. . . *machinery-progress of the 1930s: Wigan Pier,* p. 208.

. . . *become a religion: Wigan Pier,* p. 189.

. . . *glutinously uplifting: Wigan Pier,* p. 193.

. . . *is that the machine itself may be the enemy: Wigan Pier,* p. 203.

p. 33 *The machine itself may be the enemy*: See also *Wigan Pier*, p. 191 ("The machine is the enemy of life").

. . . *clothes, books, and amusements*: *Wigan Pier*, p. 204.

. . . *the paradise of little fat men*: *Wigan Pier*, p. 193.

p. 34 *like Salvador Dalí*: "Benefit of Clergy: Some Notes on Salvador Dalí" (1944), *Essays*, IV, p. 20.

. . . *destroying the family*: "Review: *The Reilly Plan*, by Lawrence Wolfe" (1946), *CEJL*, Vol. 4, p. 91.

. . . *spiritual emptiness*: "Review, *Burnt Norton, East Coker, The Dry Salvages*, by T. S. Eliot" (1942), *CEJL*, Vol. 2, p. 239.

. . . *the demise of farming*: "On a Ruined Farm Near the His Master's Voice Gramophone Factory" (1934), *CEJL*, Vol. 1, p. 134.

. . . *Lower Binfield*: Bowling sets out to rediscover his childhood home and to return to the gloriously untouched fishing pond that he cherished as a boy. When he finally gets there, the pool has been utterly ruined. By gramophones. "As I got nearer the river I came into the sound—yes, plonk-tiddle-tiddle-plonk!—yes, the sound of gramophones." *Coming Up for Air*, p. 238. The pond is now "full of young fools with next to nothing on, all of them screaming and shouting and most of them with a gramophone aboard as well" (p. 239). Bowling departs in disgust: "Couldn't stick the noise of the gramophones any longer" (p. 239).

. . . *the gangster gramophone*: See *Coming Up for Air*, p. 171 ("You know the line of talk. These chaps can churn it out by the hour. Just like a gramophone. Turn the handle, press the button and it starts. Democracy, Fascism, Democracy"); *Wigan Pier*, p. 216 ["'Socialism' calls up . . . a picture of vegetarians with wilting beards, of Bolshevik commissars (half gangster, half gramophone)"]; *Homage to Catalonia*, p. 198 ("the 'good party man,' the gangster gramophone of continental Politics"); "Prophecies of Fascism" (1940), *CEJL*, Vol. 2, p. 30 ("the hero is the kind of human gramophone who is now disappearing even from Socialist tracts"); "Literature and the Left" (1943), *CEJL*, Vol. 2, p. 294 ("Numbers of them joined the Communist Party. . . . [W]hen it was found that they would not or could not turn themselves into gramophone records, they were thrown out on their ears"); "A New Year Message" (*Tribune*, 1945), *CEJL*, Vol. 3, p. 313 ("We hold that the most perverse human being is more interesting than the most orthodox gramophone record").

p. 34 *the gramophone mind*: Shelden, p. 365.

... *manufactured for us in Hollywood*: *Broadcast*, p. 73.

... *literature? Comstock wonders*: *Aspidistra*, p. 72.

... *behind the average book*: "London Letter to *Partisan Review*" (1941), *CEJL*, Vol. 2, p. 114.

... *a glass of inferior sherry*: *1984*, p. 376.

... *piece of rubbish*: Shelden, p. 324. Orwell does, however, admire Charlie Chaplin's *The Great Dictator* enormously. Even when Orwell is pointing out the limitations of the written word, he manages to make film seem worse. In a 1936 review of a book by Henry Miller, Orwell argues that writing fails when it attempts to describe the realm of "pure dream": "[W]ords are here being used to invade what is really the province of the film." But Orwell's example of how film escapes reality is a Mickey Mouse cartoon. "[T]he written word," by contrast, cannot really escape "the ordinary world where two and two make four." "Review, *Black Spring*, by Henry Miller" (1936), *CEJL*, Vol. 1, p. 231. In *1984*, the power to make two and two equal five belongs to the Party, and the pernicious implications of that power are a central theme of the book.

... *worst of all*: In a list of his own dislikes, compiled in 1940, Orwell itemized "big towns, noise, motor cars, the radio, tinned food, central heating, and 'modern' furniture." Shelden, p. 323.

... *productions as rubbish*: "Letter to A. S. F. Gow" (1946), *CEJL*, Vol. 4, p. 146.

... *bilge*: "Letter to Stafford Cottman" (1946), *CEJL*, Vol. 4, p. 149.

pp. 34–35 *purchased a wireless set*: *Coming Up for Air*, p. 182. Another piece of the ruin of Lower Binfield is that the old butcher's shop now sells radio parts (p. 236).

p. 35 *gramophones and radio*: Elizabeth, for example, in *Burmese Days*. See pp. 179-180.

... *the song of birds*: *Wigan Pier*, pp. 204-205. While convalescing from tuberculosis shortly after completing *1984*, Orwell described his pleasant surroundings in almost the same terms: "Not much noise of radios either—all the patients have headphones. . . . The most persistent sound is the song of birds." Shelden, p. 427.

p. 35 *for oppressed people:* Wigan Pier, p. 90.

. . . *the telegraph and radio:* Wigan Pier, p. 89.

. . . *and the Secret Police:* See Burmese Days, p. 9 ("the cinematograph, machine guns, syphilis, etc."); "Rudyard Kipling" (1942), Essays, I, p. 118 (Kipling fails to foresee "the tank, the bombing plane, the radio and the secret police, or their psychological results"); Coming Up for Air, p. 198 ("buses, bombs, radios, telephone bells"). The old gramophone works in Lower Binfield is now making bombs (p. 206).

. . . *Nosey Parker:* "England, Your England" (1941), Essays, I, p. 256.

. . . *chosen for you from above:* "England, Your England," pp. 255-256.

. . . *with tinny music:* Coming Up for Air, p. 22; 1984, p. 61 ("The announcement from the Ministry of Plenty ended on another trumpet call and gave way to tinny music"), p. 77 ("A tinny music was trickling from the telescreens"), p. 290 ("A tinny music trickled from the telescreens").

. . . *salmon canning factory in Moscow:* Wigan Pier, p. 230.

. . . *people nearer to the animals:* "Pleasure Spots" (1946), CEJL, Vol. 4, p. 81: "Much of what goes by the name of pleasure is simply an effort to destroy consciousness. . . . [T]he tendency of many modern inventions—in particular the film, the radio and the aeroplane—is to weaken [man's] consciousness, dull his curiosity, and, in general, drive him nearer to the animals."

Chapter 3

p. 37 *in front of the telescreen:* Burmese Days, p. 73. The "Physical Jerks" scene in 1984 is in fact lifted from Burmese Days, where pukka sahib Mr. Macgregor follows a strict daily routine of "Nordenflycht's 'Physical Jerks for the Sedentary'" (p. 73). By the end of the book, Macgregor "has grown more human and likeable"; "he has given up his morning exercises" (p. 287). Winston, just like MacGregor, goes through a miserable routine of "painful" "lunging" "in the direction of his toes." Burmese Days, p. 74: "Macgregor lunged painfully in the direction of his toes." 1984, pp. 35, 38: "[H]e forced his shoulders painfully backward . . . with a violent lunge, [he] succeeded in touching his toes."

p. 37   *woman's voice on the screen: 1984*, p. 32.

p. 38   *jointed truncheons: 1984*, p. 6.

p. 39   *thousands of throats: 1984*, pp. 17, 181, 182.

. . .   *talking by installments: 1984*, p. 129.

. . .   *Oceania, 'tis for thee: 1984*, p. 27.

. . .   *patriotic songs from the telescreens: 1984*, p. 101.

. . .   *without any human intervention at all: 1984*, pp. 44, 139.

. . .   *was always trite:* "Rudyard Kipling" (1942), *Essays*, I, pp. 130-131.

p. 40   *dim period of his early childhood: 1984*, p. 33.

. . .   *always been called London: 1984*, p. 33.

. . .   *Comrade Ogilvy: 1984*, p. 47.

. . .   *Charlemagne or Julius Caesar: 1984*, p. 48.

. . .   *controls the past: 1984*, pp. 35, 251.

p. 41   *exacting god behind the screen: Burmese Days*, p. 74.

. . .   *a little more genially: 1984*, p. 36.

. . .   *bellowed the woman: 1984*, p. 36.

. . .   *facecrime: 1984*, p. 62.

. . .   *completely expressionless: 1984*, p. 62.

. . .   *delicate enough to pick it up: 1984*, p. 79.

. . .   *physical torture: 1984*, p. 194.

. . .   *projects ever went anywhere: 1984*, p. 195.

. . .   *technical progress had ceased: 1984*, pp. 194, 199.

. . .   *strictly regimented society: 1984*, p. 190.

p. 42   *no need for science:* I am not in any way exaggerating the Party's hostility to science. Orwell really believed that doublethink could be raised to the point where a party maintained all of these beliefs and yet at the same time continued to operate a network of technologically brilliant telescreens. See *1984*, pp. 190, 194, 199, 267, 268, 270, 281, 312.

. . .   *no directories: 1984*, p. 160.

. . .   *plumber's blow-flame:* Cf. *1984*, p. 16: "[T]he rage that one felt was an abstract, undirected emotion which could be switched from one object to another like the flame of a blowlamp"; "Review: *The Totalitarian Enemy*, by F. Borkenau" (1940), *CEJL*, Vol. 2, p. 26: "Hatred can be turned in any direction at a moment's notice, like a plumber's blow-flame."

p. 42 *fingers under her toes: 1984,* p. 37.

   ... *for the first time in several years: 1984,* p. 38.

The Ministry

p. 43 *That's better, comrade: 1984,* p. 37.

   ... *photographs, telescreen broadcasts, and so on: 1984,* p. 40.

   ... *really frightening one: 1984,* p. 6.

   ... *three hundred meters into the air: 1984,* p. 5.

   ... *corresponding ramifications below: 1984,* pp. 5-6.

p. 44 *gets 75 mentions in 1984:* I include in the count references to "ministries" and also to the shortened names Minitrue, Miniluv, Minipax, and Miniplenty.

   ... *a frying-pan which has had fish in it:* "As I Please" (1945), *CEJL,* Vol. 3, p. 329.

   ... *is appallingly concentrated:* E.g., *Homage to Catalonia,* p. 50. See also "The English People" (1944), *CEJL,* Vol. 3, p. 12: "The much-boasted freedom of the British press is theoretical rather than actual. To begin with the centralised ownership of the press."

   ... *as two-penny postcards:* "The Art of Donald McGill" (1941), *Essays,* I, p. 109.

   ... *and Boys' Weeklies:* "Boys' Weeklies" (1939), *Essays,* I, pp. 280, 281, 306.

   ... *and most of all, the radio:* "Boys' Weeklies," p. 281. Similarly, the military and imperialist middle class have been destroyed by the telegraph, which has created a "narrowing world, more and more governed from Whitehall." "England, Your England" (1941), *Essays,* I, p. 273.

   ... *by a conniving monopolist: Wigan Pier,* p. 207: "Some years ago someone invented a gramophone needle that would last for decades. One of the big gramophone companies bought up the patent rights, and that was all that was ever heard of it."

p. 45 *Orwell declares in a 1945 book review:* Review, *A Coat of Many Colours, Occasional Essays,* by Herbert Read (1945), *CEJL,* Vol. 4, p. 49.

   ... *some form of collectivism: Wigan Pier,* p. 188.

   ... *vital industries like coal mining:* "London Letter to *Partisan Review*"

(1944), *CEJL*, Vol. 3, p. 125: "It is, in fact, obvious that without centralising the industry it would be impossible to raise the enormous sums needed to bring the mines up to date."

p. 45   *give claws to the weak:* "You and the Atom Bomb" (1945), *CEJL*, Vol. 4, p. 7. See also Shelden, p. 328, quoting Orwell: "That rifle hanging on the wall of the working-class flat or labourer's cottage is the symbol of democracy."

. . .   *toward collective ones:* As it grows more centralized, civilization grows more vulnerable to outside enemies. "[T]he German bombers," Orwell gloomily predicts in 1937, "could probably reduce England to chaos and starvation in a few weeks." "Review, *The Men I Killed*, by Brigadier-General F. P. Crozier" (1937), *CEJL*, Vol. 1, p. 283.

. . .   *dividing the world between them:* "You and the Atom Bomb," p. 8.

. . .   *in fewer hands than ever before:* "You and the Atom Bomb," p. 8.

. . .   *the slave empires of antiquity:* "You and the Atom Bomb," p. 9.

. . .   *recent years has accelerated it:* "You and the Atom Bomb," p. 9.

Chapter 4

p. 47   *flung it at the screen:* 1984, p. 15.

. . .   *decrepit chair up to his desk:* 1984, p. 38.

. . .   *like a sucked orange:* "Letter to A. S. F. Gow" (1946), *CEJL*, Vol. 4, p. 146.

. . .   *due for destruction:* 1984, p. 41.

p. 48   *sharp-faced man:* Orwell has known men who looked like that all his life. In an autobiographical essay about his early years at boarding school, Orwell recounts how he had sneaked off campus to a sweet shop to buy some forbidden candy: "As I came out of the shop I saw on the opposite pavement a small sharp-faced man who seemed to be staring very hard at my school cap. Instantly a horrible fear went through me. There could be no doubt as to who the man was. He was a spy placed there by [the headmaster] Sim! . . . Sim was all powerful, and it was natural that his agents should be everywhere." "Such, Such Were the Joys" (1947), *Essays*, I, pp. 15–16.

. . .   *named Connolly: Coming Up for Air*, p. 254.

p. 48 *hostile flash in Blair's direction: 1984,* p. 42.

p. 49 *at short intervals in every corridor: 1984,* p. 38.

p. 50 *to men like these: Wigan Pier,* p. 193.

p. 51 *chunk of their consciousness: Wigan Pier,* p. 197.

p. 52 *nicknamed him in his own mind: 1984,* p. 67.

. . . *saving stupidity: 1984,* p. 55.

p. 53 *empirical approaches in these two areas: 1984,* p. 194.

. . . *a rubbish heap of detail: 1984,* p. 91.

. . . *another species of insect: 1984,* p. 93.

. . . *the labyrinthine corridors of Ministries: 1984,* p. 61.

The Enemy

p. 55 *Second Thoughts on James Burnham:* "Second Thoughts on James Burnham" (1946), *Essays,* II, p. 335.

. . . *technicians, bureaucrats, and soldiers:* "Second Thoughts on James Burnham," pp. 335-336. Cf. *1984,* p. 206: "The new aristocracy was made up for the most part of bureaucrats, scientists, technicians, trade-union organisers, publicity experts, sociologists, teachers, journalists, and professional politicians."

. . . *in Europe, Asia, and America:* "Second Thoughts on James Burnham," p. 336. Cf. *1984,* p. 186: "The splitting-up of the world into three great superstates was an event which could be and indeed was foreseen before the middle of the twentieth century." "Second Thoughts on James Burnham," p. 336: "These super-states will fight among themselves for possession of the remaining uncaptured portions of the earth, but will probably be unable to conquer one another completely." Cf. *1984,* p. 188: "It is for the possession of these thickly populated regions, and of the northern ice cap, that the three powers are constantly struggling."

. . . *a mass of semi-slaves at the bottom:* "Second Thoughts on James Burnham," p. 336. Cf. *1984,* p. 266: "The Party seeks power entirely for its own sake."

. . . *Orwell summarizing Burnham:* The essay addresses two books by Burnham, *The Managerial Revolution* and *The Machiavellians,* and some of Burnham's other writings, all published between 1940 and 1945.

p. 56   *in Wigan Pier: Wigan Pier,* p. 231; "Not Counting Niggers" (1939),
          CEJL, Vol. 1, p. 398.

. . .   *Coming Up for Air: Coming Up for Air,* p. 176.

. . .   *do not disprove Burnham's theory:* "Second Thoughts on James
          Burnham," p. 348.

. . .   *if human society is to hold together at all:* "Second Thoughts on
          James Burnham," pp. 353-354.

. . .   *tyrannies eventually collapse:* "Review, *Power: A New Social Analysis,*
          by Bertrand Russell" (1939), *CEJL,* Vol. 1, pp. 375-376.

p. 57   *of motor cars in 1850:* "Second Thoughts on James Burnham," p.
          352.

. . .   *Orwell had written then:* "Review, *The Calf of Paper,* by Scholem
          Asch" (1936), *CEJL,* Vol. 1, p. 249.

p. 58   *know how successful it will be:* "Review, *Russia under Soviet Rule,* by
          N. de Basily," (1939) *CEJL,* Vol. 1, p. 381. See "Notes on the Way"
          (1940), *CEJL,* Vol. 2, p. 17: "What we are moving towards at this
          moment is something more like the Spanish Inquisition, and prob-
          ably far worse, thanks to the radio and the secret police."

. . .   *H. G. Wells' The Sleeper Awakes:* Published 1900.

. . .   *Jack London's The Iron Heel:* Published 1907. London's book does
          however contain this passage: "We had planned to strike our first
          blow at the nervous system of the Oligarchy. The latter had re-
          membered the general strike, and had guarded against the defec-
          tion of the telegraphers by installing wireless stations, in the
          control of the Mercenaries. We, in turn, had countered this move.
          When the signal was given, from every refuge, all over the land,
          and from the cities, and towns, and barracks, devoted comrades
          were to go forth and blow the wireless stations. Thus at the first
          shock would the Iron Heel be brought to earth and lie practically
          dismembered" (p. 195).

. . .   *Zamyatin's We:* Published 1923. Orwell first read this in the mid-
          1940s, however. Shelden, p. 434.

. . .   *Aldous Huxley's Brave New World:* Published 1930.

. . .   *Arthur Koestler's Darkness at Noon:* Published 1941.

. . .   *E. M. Forster's "The Machine Stops":* reprinted in *The Collected
          Tales of E. M. Forster* (New York: Knopf, 1947), p. 144. *1984* does,
          however, contain many echoes of Forster's short story. In the

futuristic world Forster describes, people live in absolute, technology-maintained isolation. The central character "knew several thousand people; in certain directions human intercourse had advanced enormously" (p. 145). People communicate by way of a "round blue plate" (p. 145), a "cinematophote" (p. 157), very much like Orwell's telescreen. One "mustn't say anything against the Machine" (p. 146). There is "the button that produced literature" (p. 150). But there is only one real book left; "[t]his was the Book of the Machine" (p. 151). "The Central Committee published it" (p. 152). In Forster's story, "the Machine hummed eternally" (p. 152). The central character "knew all about the communication-system . . . the universal establishment of the Machine" (p. 153). "[T]hanks to science, the earth was exactly alike all over" (p. 155). Society endures so "that the Machine may progress, that the Machine may progress, that the Machine may progress eternally" (p. 167). "[T]he only thing that really lives is the Machine. . . . The Machine develops—but not on our lines. The Machine proceeds—but not to our goal" (p. 176). "[T]he Machine is omnipotent, eternal" (p. 184). "Year by year [the Machine] was served with increased efficiency and decreased intelligence" (p. 185). "[P]rogress had come to mean the progress of the Machine" (p. 186). "The Machine still linked them. Under the seas, beneath the roots of the mountains, ran the wires through which they saw and heard, the enormous eyes and ears that were their heritage, and the hum of many workings clothed their thoughts in one garment of subserviency" (p. 191). The whole thing is run by a "central power station . . . far away in France" (p. 193). It all ends when "the entire communication-system broke down, all over the world" (p. 192). "[B]eautiful naked man was dying, strangled in the garments that he had woven" (p. 196).

Orwell was undoubtedly familiar with Forster's story. See Shelden, pp. 177, 342-343, 399. They were contemporaries at the BBC and even collaborated in writing a "Story by Five Authors." See Broadcast, pp. 32, 41.

p. 58 a voice on the telescreen: 1984, p. 209.

Chapter 5

p. 59 *carpeted passages in the building:* 1984, p. 168.

. . . *a mane of greasy gray hair:* 1984, p. 76.

p. 60 *fifteen minutes to die:* "As I Please" (1946), *CEJL*, Vol. 4, p. 239.

. . . *other channels of communication closed:* 1984, p. 207.

. . . *from the very moment of his release:* 1984, p. 77.

. . . *as a warning to posterity:* 1984, p. 77.

. . . *twenty-four hours a day under the eyes of the police:* 1984, p. 207.

. . . *formidable, intelligent face:* 1984, p. 169.

p. 61 *not far from Waterloo bridge:* Down and Out, pp. 131, 132, 134, 161.

p. 62 *morasses and sickly weeds:* "Review, *Alexander Pope,* by Edith Sitwell" (1930), *CEJL*, Vol. 1, p. 22.

. . . *all other channels of communication closed:* 1984, p. 207.

p. 64 *for a half starved people:* Wigan Pier, p. 90.

. . . *that dreaded thing, thought:* "Pleasure Spots" (1946), *CEJL*, Vol. 4, p. 80.

. . . *had to be as few as possible:* "Lear, Tolstoy and the Fool" (1947), *Essays*, III, p. 413.

p. 65 *he was hugely fat:* Coming Up for Air, p. 166.

. . . *something very near poetry:* Burmese Days, p. 14.

Doublethink

p. 67 *against those who know the facts:* "Review, *Power: A New Social Analysis,* by Bertrand Russell" (1939), *CEJL*, Vol. 1, p. 376.

. . . *when the Leader says so:* "Review, *Power: A New Social Analysis,* by Bertrand Russell," p. 376.

. . . *asked himself that question many times:* No state can deny the truth "in ways that impair military efficiency. . . . [S]o long as parts of the earth remain unconquered, the liberal tradition can be kept alive." "Looking Back on the Spanish War" (1943), *Essays*, I, p. 200. See also "The Prevention of Literature" (1946), *Essays*, III, p. 346: "At this stage of history, even the most autocratic ruler is forced to take account of physical reality, partly because of the lingering-on of liberal habits of thought, partly because of the need to prepare for war. So long as physical reality cannot be altogether ignored, so long as two and two have to make four when you are, for example, drawing the blue-print of an aeroplane, the scientist has his function, and can even be allowed a measure of liberty."

Cf. *1984*, pp. 198-199: "In the past . . . war was one of the main instruments by which human societies were kept in touch with physical reality. All rulers in all ages have tried to impose a false view of the world upon their followers, but they could not afford to encourage any illusion that tended to impair military efficiency. . . . In philosophy, or religion, or ethics, or politics, two and two might make five, but when one was designing a gun or an airplane they had to make four."

p. 68   *forgotten doublethink: 1984*, p. 269.

. . .   *conquer the whole world simultaneously:* "Looking Back on the Spanish War," p. 200.

. . .   *liberal societies will no longer exist:* See also "Letter to H. J. Willmett" (1944), *CEJL*, Vol. 3, p. 149: "[T]he exact sciences are endangered as soon as military necessity ceases to keep people up to the mark. Hitler can say that the Jews started the war, and if he survives that will become official history. He can't say that two and two are five, because for the purposes of, say, ballistics they have to make four. But if the sort of world that I am afraid of arrives, a world of two or three great superstates which are unable to conquer one another, two and two could become five if the fuehrer wished it."

. . .   *not distinguishable at all: 1984*, p. 198.

. . .   *like three sheaves of corn: 1984*, p. 198. "[W]e [in England] believe half-instinctively that evil always defeats itself in the long run," Orwell writes. "What evidence is there that it does? And what instance is there of a modern industrialised state collapsing unless conquered from the outside by military force?" "Looking Back on the Spanish War," p. 200. O'Brien puts exactly the same question to Winston at the end of *1984* (p. 273).

p. 69   *The Gutenberg Galaxy:* Toronto: Univ. of Toronto Press, 1962.

. . .   *England, Your England:* "England, Your England" (1941), *Essays*, I, p. 254.

. . .   *namely literature:* "England, Your England," p. 264. And Orwell doesn't think all that much of painting in any event. "Painting is the only art that can be practised without either talent or hard work," Orwell informs us in *Burmese Days*, p. 89.

p. 69 *separation and communication*: *Wigan Pier*, p. 156; *A Clergyman's Daughter*, p. 17; *Aspidistra*, pp. 28, 71, 133, 136; *Down and Out*, p. 93; "As I Please" (1947), *CEJL*, Vol. 4, p. 267.

. . . *Orwell writes in a 1946 piece*: "Why I Write" (1946), *Essays*, I, p. 316.

. . . *essay on Charles Dickens*: "Charles Dickens" (1939), *Essays*, I, p. 103.

. . . *Orwell and his writing*: Shelden, p. 314.

p. 70 *as clear as one can through pictures*: "Politics and the English Language" (1946), *Essays*, I, p. 169. See also "The English People" (1944), *CEJL*, Vol. 3, p. 27: "The people likeliest to use simple concrete language, and to think of metaphors that really call up a visual image, are those who are in contact with physical reality. . . . [T]he vitality of English depends on a steady supply of images."

See also "Tobias Smollett: Scotland's Best Novelist" (1944), *CEJL*, Vol. 3, p. 244: "A 'realistic' novel is one in which the dialogue is colloquial and physical objects are described in such a way that you can visualise them."

. . . *German Science and Jewish Science*: "Looking Back on the Spanish War," p. 199.

. . . *sufficiently covered by the word Ingsoc*: *1984*, p. 194: "The empirical method of thought, on which all the scientific achievements of the past were founded, is opposed to the most fundamental principles of Ingsoc." See also *1984*, p. 312.

. . . *a high level of mechanical civilisation*: "Review, *The Martyrdom of Man*, by Winwood Reade" (1946), *CEJL*, Vol. 4, p. 119.

p. 71 *once Socialism is established*: *Wigan Pier*, p. 206. He also concedes that "the idea of Socialism is bound up, more or less inextricably, with the idea of machine-production" (p. 188).

. . . *as in earlier essays*: *1984*, p. 205. "[A]ll sensitive people are revolted by industrialism and its products," Orwell declares in "Writers and Leviathan" (1948), *Essays*, III, pp. 462-463. But Orwell is quite sure that the machine also contains a promise of economic salvation. "[T]he conquest of poverty and the emancipation of the working class," he concedes in the same sentence, "demand not less industrialization, but more and more."

p. 71 *stolen literature's thunder: Wigan Pier,* p. 190.

... *technology of television: Broadcast,* p. 27. Another talk was on the connection between science and literature (p. 30).

... *Orwell writes in Wigan Pier: Wigan Pier,* p. 206.

... *using my brain or muscles: Wigan Pier,* p. 206. Flory, the sensitive artistic, semiautobiographical hero of *Burmese Days,* is nonetheless "a fool about machinery," and quite willing to "struggle with the bowels of the engine until he [is] black with grease" (p. 200).

... *tremendously prescient about technology:* This is all the more remarkable because we know (from Orwell himself) that his early education was at a school where science was "so despised that even an interest in natural history was discouraged." "Such, Such Were the Joys" (1947), *Essays,* I, p. 8. At Crossgates (Orwell's lower school), natural history "smelt of science and therefore seemed to menace classical education" (p. 18).

p. 72 *have very important effects: Broadcast,* p. 215.

... *the police of totalitarian regimes: Broadcast,* p. 215.

... *essay that Orwell wrote in 1940:* "New Words" (written 1940?), *CEJL,* Vol. 2, p. 3.

... *all of his inner life known:* "New Words," p. 10.

... *to erode class differences:* "The English People" (1944), *CEJL,* Vol. 3, p. 23.

... *lying more and more difficult:* "London Letter to *Partisan Review*" (1941), *CEJL,* Vol. 2, p. 113. And again in "As I Please" (1944), *CEJL,* Vol. 3, pp. 128-129: "[T]he BBC is a better source of news than the daily papers, and is so regarded by the public. . . . Social surveys show the same thing—i.e. that as against the radio the prestige of newspapers has declined. . . . [I]n my experience the BBC is relatively truthful and, above all, has a responsible attitude towards news and does not disseminate lies simply because they are newsy."

p. 73 *will never be enforceable:* "London Letter to *Partisan Review,*" p. 119.

... *for intelligent programmes:* "London Letter to *Partisan Review*" (1946), *CEJL,* Vol. 4, p. 190.

p. 73 *possibilities of radio have not yet been explored*: "London Letter to *Partisan Review*," p. 190.

... *can listen to nothing else*: "As I Please" (1944), *CEJL*, Vol. 3, p. 146. Orwell referred back to this column (and reiterated its point) some months later: "[M]odern scientific inventions have tended to prevent rather than increase international communication. . . . [T]he radio [is] primarily a thing for whipping up nationalism. Even before the war there was enormously less contact between the peoples of the earth than there had been thirty years earlier, and education was perverted, history rewritten and freedom of thought suppressed to an extent undreamed of in earlier ages. And there is no sign whatever of these tendencies being reversed." "As I Please" (1945), *CEJL*, Vol. 3, pp. 328-329.

Orwell says much the same thing again in "You and the Atom Bomb" (1945), *CEJL*, Vol. 4, p. 9: "The radio was once expected to promote international understanding and cooperation; it has turned out to be a means of insulating one nation from another." Elsewhere, however, Orwell firmly concludes that wartime radio propaganda on both sides had almost no impact at all, at least not on the enemy. See "Letter to George Woodcock" (1942), *CEJL*, Vol. 2, p. 268. German radio propaganda was "an almost complete flop." "London Letter to *Partisan Review*" (1942), *CEJL*, Vol. 2, p. 182. BBC propaganda was "just shot into the stratosphere, not listened to by anybody." Shelden, p. 348.

In the Preface to the Ukrainian edition of *Animal Farm*, written in March 1947, Orwell reports learning "how easily totalitarian propaganda can control the opinion of enlightened people in democratic countries." "Author's Preface to the Ukrainian Edition of *Animal Farm*" (1947), *CEJL*, Vol. 3, p. 404.

... *hopefully titled 1945 essay*: "Poetry and the Microphone" (1945), *Essays*, III, p. 245.

... *anything except tripe*: "Poetry and the Microphone," p. 250.

... *have failed to return*: "Poetry and the Microphone," p. 250.

... *or great monopoly companies*: "Poetry and the Microphone," p. 250.

p. 74 *in every country of the world*: "Poetry and the Microphone," p. 250.

p. 74 *run its propaganda machines:* "Poetry and the Microphone,"
p. 250.

. . . *bureaucratic tyranny can perhaps never be complete:* "Poetry and the
Microphone," p. 251.

p. 75 *obscured by the voices of Professor Joad:* Cyril Edwin Mitchinson
Joad, Irish-born philosopher, pacifist, and socialist, was a promi-
nent radio personality on the BBC's "Brains Trust" program from
1941 to 1947.

. . . *and Doctor Goebbels:* "Poetry and the Microphone," pp. 251-252.

Chapter 6

p. 79 *If there is hope it lies in the proles: 1984,* p. 69. Resistance is necessary, O'Brien says to Smith later in *1984,* but hopeless. "You will
have to get used to living without results and without hope. . . .
There is no possibility that any perceptible change will happen
within our own lifetime" (p. 177). Or, as Orwell has already put it
in *Wigan Pier,* p. 158: "[E]very revolutionary opinion draws part of
its strength from a secret conviction that nothing can be changed."

. . . *how they smelled:* See *Wigan Pier,* pp. 127, 129.

p. 80 *mysteriously transmuted into something nobler: Aspidistra,*
p. 239.

. . . *assertively at her companion: 1984,* p. 82.

. . . *That's the truth:* Contrast *1984,* pp. 82-83.

. . . *they are loyal to one another: 1984,* p. 166. Here again we see how
different Orwell's world view might have been if he had shared
Hayek's faith in spontaneous order and the marketplace. Despite
all his pessimism, Orwell believed deeply in the inherent loyalty of
the ordinary English. He returns to the theme of private loyalty
and trust repeatedly in *1984,* particularly in his discussion of family and the proles. See, e.g., p. 31 ("conception of loyalty that was
private and unalterable"), and p. 166 ("they were governed by private loyalties"). The same theme appears briefly in *Aspidistra,* in
the language I quote earlier in this chapter, see *Aspidistra,* p. 239.
But as *1984* plainly reveals, Orwell simply didn't believe that pri-

vate loyalty could overcome public betrayal. In Orwell's universe, the Ministry is always more powerful than the sum of the individuals beneath it.

p. 81 *a mystical truth and a palpable absurdity:* 1984, p. 82.

... *deep in conversation:* Contrast 1984, p. 84.

... *the status of a major industry: Wigan Pier,* p. 89. Here is another example of how 1984 synthesizes themes and arguments that Orwell had first developed years earlier in other writings. And it shows again the very pessimistic side of Orwell's view of the proles. The proles are perfectly capable of keeping financial accounts, but only on futile things like the lottery, never in productive business.

... *even though they never were:* 1984, p. 85. I quote this sentence whole because it is so wildly implausible. In the age of the telescreen, with "intercommunication" perfected to the point where there is no privacy left at all, Orwell would have us believe that there is, at the same time, no "real intercommunication" at all.

p. 82 *hope for England yet: Aspidistra,* p. 105. As I make clear in both text and notes later, much of this wonderful paragraph from "The street was so crowded . . ." to "hope for England yet" is lifted with only minor alteration from *Aspidistra.* (A quite similar market scene appears in *Burmese Days,* pp. 126-127.) It is an important text, for it again illustrates Orwell's own ambivalence about markets and commerce. He loves them at the retail level, the level of little stalls and shopkeepers. He loves stallkeepers, but he despises capitalism, advertising, banks, private property. He loves the marketplace, but he loathes "the free market."

... *criminality among the proles:* See 1984, p. 72.

... *abolished long ago:* See 1984, p. 207.

... *property had been an obstructive nuisance:* "Charles Dickens" (1939), *Essays,* I, p. 65.

... *officially labeled a swindle: Coming Up for Air,* p. 13.

p. 83 *Fronky:* As a child, Eric Blair "invented an imaginary friend with whom he could play freely. For some unknown reason he called the friend 'Fronky.'" Shelden, p. 19.

The Market

p. 87 *like guardsmen naked on parade:* I am quoting from *Aspidistra,*
p. 105.

. . . *generally crowded and noisy: 1984,* p. 128.

. . . *staggering feats of memory: 1984,* p. 85.

. . . *forecasts, and lucky amulets: 1984,* p. 85.

p. 88 *then the handle came off: 1984,* p. 70.

. . . *shopping means rations: 1984,* pp. 27, 40, 59, 71, 163, 270.

. . . *and vouchers: 1984,* p. 32.

. . . *private property has been abolished: 1984,* p. 207.

. . . *criticism of markets, money:* In Orwell's socialist utopia, "[m]oney,
for internal purposes, ceases to be a mysterious all-powerful thing
and becomes a sort of coupon or ration-ticket, issued in sufficient
quantities to buy up such consumption goods as may be available
at the moment." *Lion,* p. 75.

. . . *money-business, and money-morality: Aspidistra,* pp. 14, 48-49. According to my computer, "money" appears some 366 times in the
book, an average of one and a half times on every page.

. . . *are a huge racket: Coming Up for Air,* p. 13.

. . . *insurance is a swindle: Coming Up for Air,* p. 13.

. . . *frantic struggle to sell things: Coming Up for Air,* p. 149.

. . . *is an obstructive nuisance:* "Charles Dickens" (1939), *Essays,* I,
p. 65.

. . . *torture millions of one's fellow creatures:* Private property cannot be
reconciled with "economic justice." "Review, *Communism and
Man,* by F. J. Sheed" (1939), *CEJL,* Vol. 1, p. 384.

. . . *by means of idiotic wills:* "Charles Dickens," p. 51.

. . . *Orwell writes in a 1940 letter:* "Letter to Humphry House" (1940),
CEJL, Vol. 1, p. 532.

. . . *he declares in a 1946 essay:* "Some Thoughts on the Common Toad"
(1946), *Essays,* III, p. 368.

. . . *Capitalism is a tyranny:* "Writers and Leviathan" (1948), *Essays,*
III, p. 461.

. . . *Tweedledum and Tweedledee:* "Spilling the Spanish Beans" (1937),
CEJL, Vol. 1, pp. 273-274; see also "Review, *Russia under Soviet
Rule,* by N. de Basily" *CEJL,* Vol. 1, p. 381: "If even a few

hundred thousand people can be got to grasp that it is useless to overthrow Tweedledum in order to set up Tweedledee, the talk of 'democracy versus Fascism' with which our ears are deafened may begin to mean something."

Indeed, for many years Orwell's every mention of capitalism is paired with one of fascism. For example: Fascism "is only a development of capitalism, and the mildest democracy, so-called, is liable to turn into Fascism when the pinch comes." Quoted in Shelden, p. 218. Fascism is simply capitalist democracy with the "barriers down" and with the "motives out in the open." "Raffles and Miss Blandish" (1941), *Essays,* I, p. 144. "It is futile to be 'anti-Fascist' while attempting to preserve capitalism." "Letter to Geoffrey Gorer" (1937), *CEJL,* Vol. 1, p. 284. The liberal bourgeoisie "are the supporters of Fascism when it appears in . . . modern form." *Homage to Catalonia,* p. 48.

p. 89 *the one is robbing the other:* "Review, *The Communist International,* by Franz Borkenau" (1938), *CEJL,* Vol. 1, p. 350.

. . . *the capitalist affluence of his patrons:* "Benefit of Clergy: Some Notes on Salvador Dalí" (1944), *Essays,* IV, p. 30. Indeed, Dalí's art casts a "useful light on the decay of capitalist civilisation" (p. 26).

. . . *nothing but saleable drivel:* "As I Please" (1944), *CEJL,* Vol. 3, p. 250. See also "The Prevention of Literature" (1946), *Essays,* III, p. 336 ("The independence of the writer and the artist is eaten away by vague economic forces").

. . . *money controls opinion:* "Why I Joined the Independent Labour Party" (1938), *CEJL,* Vol. 1, p. 337.

. . . *that capitalism has yet produced: Aspidistra,* p. 51. Advertising, which accounts fully for the "silliness" of the English press, "arises from the fact that newspapers live off advertisements for consumption goods." "The English People" (1944), *CEJL,* Vol. 3, p. 35. "While the journalist exists merely as the publicity agent of big business, a large circulation, got by fair means or foul, is a newspaper's one and only aim," he writes in a "A Farthing Newspaper" (1928), *CEJL,* Vol. 1, p. 14.

. . . *monopoly on radio and the films:* "The Prevention of Literature," p. 335.

p. 89 *who are only one degree better:* "As I Please" (1946), *CEJL*, Vol. 4, p. 242.

... *theoretical rather than actual:* "The English People" (1944), *CEJL*, Vol. 3, p. 11.

... *the same way as a state censorship:* "Freedom of the Park" (1945), *CEJL*, Vol. 4, pp. 39-40.

... *an instinctive hatred of intelligence:* "The British Crisis" (1942), *CEJL*, Vol. 2, p. 209.

... *the flexible glass mentioned by Petronius: Wigan Pier*, pp. 206-207.

... *Gordon Comstock reflects bitterly in Aspidistra: Aspidistra*, p. 54.

... *that it kills thought: Aspidistra*, p. 49.

... *The free market is the enemy too:* "Review, *Workers' Front*, by Fenner Brockway" (1938), *CEJL*, Vol. 1, p. 305.

pp. 89–90 *high degree of economic equality:* In *1984*, p. 190, he declares (through Blythe) that social inequality would largely disappear (and "freedom" would materially advance) in "a world in which everyone worked short hours, had enough to eat, lived in a house with a bathroom and a refrigerator, and possessed a motorcar or even an airplane."

p. 90 *freedom of speech and the press:* "Democracy in the British Army" (1939), *CEJL*, Vol. 1, p. 405.

... *censorship or the Secret Police:* "Review, *The Calf of Paper*, by Scholem Asch" (1936), *CEJL*, Vol. 1, p. 249: "You can't ignore Hitler, Mussolini, unemployment, aeroplanes and the radio." The theme of Mark Twain's books, says Orwell, is: "This is how human beings behave when they are not frightened of the sack." "Mark Twain— The Licensed Jester" (1943), *CEJL*, Vol. 2, p. 325. Regular employment as a "cog" in the capitalist machine is equally bad. "Review, *Red Spanish Notebook*, by Mary Low and Juan Brea" (1937), *CEJL*, Vol. 1, p. 287.

... *industrial America that was to follow:* See also "Riding Down from Bangor" (1946), *Essays*, III, p. 406: Nineteenth century America "was a better kind of society than that which arose from the sudden industrialization of the later part of the century . . . uncorrupted."

... *wildness of spirit:* "Review, *Herman Melville*, by Lewis Mumford" (1930), *CEJL*, Vol. 1, p. 21.

p. 90   *a buoyant, carefree feeling:* "Riding Down from Bangor," p. 406.

. . .   *may not be again for centuries:* "Mark Twain—The Licensed Jester," p. 325.

. . .   *irresponsible, ungenteel ways:* "Review, *Herman Melville,* by Lewis Mumford," p. 21. See also "Riding Down from Bangor," p. 407: "There was room for everybody, and if you worked hard you could be certain of a living."

. . .   *had hardly come into being:* Thus, "nineteenth-century America was capitalist civilisation at its best." "Riding Down from Bangor," p. 407.

Chapter 7

p. 93   *servant in a white jacket: 1984,* p. 169.

. . .   *the soundless carpet: 1984,* p. 169.

. . .   *towered over the smaller man: 1984,* p. 170.

. . .   *seconds marched past: 1984,* p. 170.

. . .   *cringing love at the first smile:* "Such, Such Were the Joys" (1947), *Essays,* I, p. 25.

. . .   *his somersault when there was no whip:* "As I Please" (1944), *CEJL,* Vol. 3, p. 181.

pp. 93–94 *the vagueness of his own motives: 1984,* p. 170.

p. 94   *elimination of Blytheism: 1984,* p. 54.

. . .   *a line of type cast solid: 1984,* p. 54.

. . .   *two blank discs instead of eyes: 1984,* p. 54; see also "Politics and the English Language" (1946), *Essays,* I, p. 166.

. . .   *The lessons . . .: 1984,* p. 47.

. . .   *assumed personality even for a moment: 1984,* p. 171.

. . .   *glasses on his nose: 1984,* p. 170.

p. 97   *the Polynesian islander swam: Wigan Pier,* p. 206.

The Ministry

p. 99   *in a planned centralised society:* "Review, *A Coat of Many Colours: Occasional Essays,* by Herbert Read" (1945), *CEJL,* Vol. 4, pp. 48-49.

. . .   *could be enormously accelerated: Wigan Pier,* p. 207.

p. 100 *is in decay:* "No, Not One" (1941), *CEJL,* Vol. 2, p. 171.

p. 100 *dissolving*: The blurb on the 1941 dust jacket of *The Lion and the Unicorn* stated: "This original book is a study of England and of England's special problems in an age when private capitalism is dissolving into a classless, ownerless society." This was written by Orwell himself. See *Lion*, p. 30.

... *disappearing*: "The Proletarian Writer: Discussion between George Orwell and Desmond Hawkins" (BBC broadcast, 1940), *CEJL*, Vol. 2, p. 41; "Second Thoughts on James Burnham" (1946), *Essays*, II, p. 335.

... *doomed*: "London Letter to *Partisan Review*" (1942), *CEJL*, Vol. 2, p. 235 ("obviously doomed"); "Literature and Totalitarianism" (1941), *CEJL*, Vol. 2, p. 135 ("the period of free capitalism is coming to an end").

... *and dead*: "London Letter to *Partisan Review*" (1941), *CEJL*, Vol. 2, p. 117; *Lion*, p. 118: "Laissez-faire capitalism is dead."

... *and it will not return*: "London Letter to *Partisan Review*," p. 117.

... *monopoly spreads year by year*: "The British Empire," one of Orwell's characters declares, "is simply a device for giving trade monopolies to the English rather than to gangs of Jews and Scotchmen." *Burmese Days*, p. 40. Orwell's own father, Richard Blair, spent a lifteime dutifully maintaining the monopoly opium trade in colonial Bengal and China. Shelden, p. 14.

... *Orwell writes in 1928*: "A Farthing Newspaper" (1928), *CEJL*, Vol. 1, p. 13. In his 1945 essay on antisemitism, the first thing Orwell does is defend Jews against the charge that they have monopolized British business: "The Jews seem, on the contrary, to have failed to keep up with the modern tendency towards big amalgamations and to have remained fixed in those trades which are necessarily carried out on a small scale and by old-fashioned methods." "Antisemitism in Britain" (1945), *Essays*, III, p. 285.

... *the milkman out of existence*: "Bookshop Memories" (1936), *Essays*, III, p. 34.

... *It cannot deliver the goods*: *Lion*, p. 73.

... *Orwell announces in 1940*: "Notes on the Way" (1940), *CEJL*, Vol. 2, p. 16.

... *and in fact cannot happen*: "Notes on the Way," p. 16.

p. 100 *much appeal any longer, he writes elsewhere:* "London Letter to *Partisan Review*," p. 120.

... *in a BBC broadcast:* "Literature and Totalitarianism," p. 137. See also "London Letter to *Partisan Review*," pp. 117-118: "Centralised ownership and planned production are bound to come."

... *waste and obstruction, is obvious:* Lion, pp. 74-76.

... *embraces a form of socialism:* "Either we turn this war into a revolutionary war . . . or we lose it. . . . [I]t is certain that with our present social structure we cannot win. Our real forces, physical, moral or intellectual, cannot be mobilized." *Lion*, p. 114. See also "London Letter to *Partisan Review*," p. 113: "Nearly the whole of the press is now 'left' compared with what it was before Dunkirk—even *The Times* mumbles about the need for centralised ownership and greater social equality."

... *stronger than a planless one:* Lion, p. 74. See also "The British Crisis" (1942), *CEJL*, Vol. 2, p. 209: "It means that our military weakness goes beyond the inherent weakness of a capitalist state"; p. 214: "We can't win the war with our present social and economic structure"; "London Letter to *Partisan Review*," p. 236: "[E]ither we introduce Socialism, or we lose the war"; *Lion*, p. 79: "[W]hile England in the moment of disaster proved to be short of every war material except ships, it is not recorded that there was any shortage of motor cars, fur coats, gramophones, lipstick, chocolates or silk stockings."

... *British capitalism does not work:* Lion, p. 77.

p. 101 *quite so ghastly again:* Lion, pp. 79-80.

... *established a collectivist economy:* "London Letter to *Partisan Review*" (1944), *CEJL*, Vol. 3, p. 294.

... *towards a planned economy:* "London Letter to *Partisan Review*," p. 294. See also "London Letter to *Partisan Review*" (1946), *CEJL*, Vol. 4, p. 186: "[T]he drift is towards Socialism, or at least towards state ownership. Transport, for example, is being nationalised."

... *to laissez-faire capitalism:* "Review, *The Democrat at the Supper Table*, by Colm Brogan" (1946), *CEJL*, Vol. 4, p. 97.

... *revert to a past phase:* "Letter to the Reverend Herbert Rogers" (1946), *CEJL*, Vol. 4, p. 103.

p. 101 *to what they had before:* "London Letter to *Partisan Review*" (1945), *CEJL*, Vol. 3, p. 384.

... *he writes in 1948:* "The Soul of Man under Socialism by Oscar Wilde" (1948), *CEJL*, Vol. 4, p. 427.

Chapter 8

p. 103 *the atmosphere of a dream: 1984*, p. 161.

... *came for you at night:* See *1984*, p. 20.

... *as the masters of the world:* "Notes on the Way" (1940), *CEJL*, Vol. 2, p. 15.

... *a summer evening after rain: 1984*, p. 161. I quote this passage for a reason. The most important metaphor in *1984* is the metaphor of light. And as with almost everything else in the book, it is a subject of *doublethink*. On the one hand, the "place where there is no darkness" is the most evil, privacy-destroying, self-destroying room in all London, a place of torture, confession, and brainwashing. But Orwell's heaven, his Golden Country, is also suffused with light; it is vast, open, luminous, place where one can see "interminable distances" (p. 161).

p. 104 *a flowering chestnut tree:* Orwell develops this metaphor throughout the book too. See *1984*, pp. 56, 76, 290, 295 (Chestnut Tree Cafe); 77, 296 ("Under the spreading chestnut tree, I sold you and you sold me"). Here again, the imagery is wonderfully apt. A chestnut tree in flower is a vast, subdividing network, almost like a fractal drawing, with each flower on the tree a tiny replica of the entire tree.

... *growing ever finer and more intricate:* This is another recurring image in *1984*. Visually, the coral is like the chestnut tree, an intricate, subdivided, interconnecting system, a network of networks. See pp. 95, 148, 224.

... *see into interminable distances: 1984*, p. 161.

... *the cold had descended: Aspidistra*, pp. 69-70.

... *for a bottle of gin:* See *1984*, p. 65.

p. 105 *wrote letters any more: 1984*, p. 112.

... *the ones that were inapplicable: 1984*, p. 112.

... *flanks showed supple and trim: Aspidistra*, p. 103.

p. 106 *to make them brighter: 1984*, p. 143.

. . . *She was a prole:* In *1984*, Julia and Winston are members of the same class. Both are middle-class snobs. Julia, for example, sleeps with everybody but "always with Party members" (not proles) and never with "those swine" from the Inner Party (p. 126). Winston despises the smell of Parson's working-class sweat. As Orwell writes in "Charles Dickens": "One thing that often gives the clue to a novelist's real feelings on the class question is the attitude he takes up when class collides with sex. This is a thing too painful to be lied about, and consequently it is one of the points at which the 'I'm-not-a-snob' pose tends to break down." "Charles Dickens" (1939), *Essays*, I, p. 76.

Orwell has already explained how the Outer Party will be handled in *Wigan Pier*, p. 226: "It is quite easy to imagine a middle class crushed down to the worst depths of poverty and still remaining bitterly anti-working class in sentiment; this being, of course, a ready-made Fascist Party."

. . . *with a grin as he passed:* "Clink" (1932), *CEJL*, Vol. 1, p. 92.

p. 107 *the second replied:* "Clink," p. 92.

. . . *getting into very different company:* Paraphrased and quoted in Shelden, p. 145.

. . . *made the plane trees rattle: Aspidistra*, p. 70.

. . . *"I love you," he would say: 1984*, p. 109. Orwell proposed to his first wife the first time he took her out to dinner. Shelden, p. 209.

p. 109 *only two or three hours before: 1984*, p. 225. I wonder if Orwell, when writing these pages of *1984*, knew that he was putting together two very vivid and painful memories of his own childhood—one of bedwetting, the other of being caned for it by his sadistic headmaster, Vaughan Wilkes. See Shelden, pp. 26, 29, 36.

Chapter 9

p. 111 *one of the seedier parts of town:* In *1984*, Winston wanders into a pub. This scene is from *Aspidistra*. The landlady of the *Aspidistra* pub has "powerful forearms"; the barman in the *1984* pub has "enormous forearms" (*1984*, p. 87). Both pubs reek of "sour" beer; both have sawdust on the floor; both are filthy; both have an ongoing game of darts; in both the glasses are not washed, just "rinsed in beery water"; in both there is "a moment's hush" when a member of the upper class enters. In *Aspidistra* the intruder asks for a pint of ale, but the pub has only half-pint bottles. In *1984*, an old man demands a pint but can only get a half-liter. Compare *Aspidistra*, pp. 86, 89, and *1984*, pp. 84, 87, 88. The old man in *1984* in fact demands a pint of "wallop" (p. 88). Orwell had written a little paragraph on how that word suddenly came into fashion in 1940 and had gone out again by 1945. "As I Please" (1945), *CEJL*, Vol. 3, p. 326.

p. 113 *on a corner in a side street: Aspidistra*, p. 86. Compare *1984*, pp. 86-93.

. . . *smell revolted him: Aspidistra*, p. 86.

. . . *a game of darts: Aspidistra*, pp. 86-87.

p. 114 *reeked of gin: 1984*, p. 34.

. . . *straightening his shoulders: 1984*, p. 88.

. . . *presence was forgotten: 1984*, p. 88.

pp. 114–115 *set his glass gingerly down: Aspidistra*, p. 87.

p. 115 *the wines of Burgundy: Aspidistra*, p. 87.

. . . *half a dozen times during the night: Down and Out*, p. 131.

. . . *changes since you were a young man: 1984*, p. 88.

. . . *He took up his glass: 1984*, p. 88.

. . . *some guts in it: Coming Up for Air*, p. 48.

. . . *the lords of the earth: 1984*, p. 90.

Chapter 10

p. 119 *Chapter 10*: Orwell was very interested in dreams and what they meant. One of the last things he recorded in his diary was a description of one of his own dreams, which he believed portended his death. In this short chapter I illustrate what can be done in generating new prose out of old in the age of the machine. I've picked fragments of Orwell's writing on dreams from a wide range of his books and essays and combined them to craft new Orwell out of the old.

. . . *solid light, like snow: Burmese Days*, pp. 176-177.

. . . *dense masses like women's hair: 1984*, p. 31.

p. 119 *forbidden to dream of such things:* "Why I Write" (1946), *Essays*, I, p. 314.

.... *deepest recesses of his unconsciousness: A Clergyman's Daughter*, p. 109.

.... *talking of peaceful things: 1984*, p. 278.

.... *Big Brother had vanished: Animal Farm*, p. 22.

p. 120 *private and unalterable: 1984*, pp. 31, 166.

.... *a Golden Age:* "Arthur Koestler" (1946), *Essays*, III, p. 277.

.... *thoughts, images, and feelings:* "New Words" (1940?), *CEJL*, Vol. 2, p. 4. There is an echo of this same language in *1984* itself: "'I dreamt,' he began, and stopped short. It was too complex to be put into words" (pp. 160-161).

.... *gradually lightening abysses: A Clergyman's Daughter*, p. 96.

.... *uncontrollable chattering of teeth: A Clergyman's Daughter*, p. 185.

.... *and of waking in sunlight:* Shelden, p. 442.

.... *overpowering happiness:* Cf. *1984*, pp. 161, 164 (gestures of Winston's mother).

.... *a single movement: 1984*, p. 32.

.... *drew her arm round him: 1984*, p. 164.

Doublethink

p. 121 *freedom of speech is a Socialist regime:* "Why I Joined the Independent Labour Party" (1938), *CEJL*, Vol. 1, p. 337. See also "As I Please" (1944), *CEJL*, Vol. 3, p. 255: "State patronage is a better guarantee against starvation than private patronage, but . . . this implies [censorhip]." Or, as Orwell puts it (only somewhat tongue in cheek) in *Lion*, pp. 113-114, a democratically socialist England "will crush any open revolt promptly and cruelly, but it will interfere very little with the spoken and written word." In an essay published not long after, Orwell refers respectfully to "the liberty of the individual." He then hastens to add: "But this has nothing to do with economic liberty, the right to exploit others for profit." "England, Your England" (1941), *Essays*, I, p. 256.

.... *free capitalism is coming to an end:* "Literature and Totalitarianism" (1941), *CEJL*, Vol. 2, pp. 134-137. He still expects that "[w]ith that, the economic liberty of the individual, and to a great extent his liberty to do what he likes, to choose his own work, to move to and fro across the surface of the earth, comes to an end."

p. 122 *admit that these ideas have been falsified:* "Literature and Totalitarianism," p. 135.

. . . *the executioner blows your brains out from behind:* See also "Notes on the Way" (1940), *CEJL,* Vol. 2, p. 16.

. . . *tried out in a western country:* "Letter to Victor Gollancz" (1940), *CEJL,* Vol. 1, p. 409.

. . . *would destroy human individuality:* "Review, *The Unquiet Grave: A Word Cycle,* by 'Palinurus'" (1945), *CEJL,* Vol. 3, p. 320.

. . . *centralised economy is liable:* "Letter to Francis A. Henson" (1949), *CEJL,* Vol. 4, p. 502.

. . . *without hand, eye, or brain: Wigan Pier,* p. 197: "Is it work to dig, to carpenter, to plant trees, to fell trees, to ride, to fish, to hunt, to feed chickens, to play the piano, to take photographs, to build a house, to cook, to sew, to trim hats, to mend motor bicycles? All of these things are work to somebody, and all of them are play to somebody. There are in fact very few activities which cannot be classed either as work or play according as you choose to regard them." The obvious response—that the line between work and play is the same as the line between choice and compulsion—is never considered.

p. 123 *The Cost of Letters, illustrates what I mean:* "The Cost of Letters" (1947), *CEJL,* Vol. 4, pp. 201-203.

p. 124 *Orwell is sure of it:* Orwell is still certain, for example, that "totalitarianism, leader worship, etc." are on the increase; Hitler's demise will only strengthen "(a) Stalin, (b) the Anglo-American millionaires and (c) all sorts of petty fuehrers of the type of de Gaulle." "Letter to H. J. Willmett" (1944), *CEJL,* Vol. 3, pp. 148-149. "The only question is whether [collectivism] is to be founded on willing cooperation or on the machine-gun." "Notes on the Way," p. 16. See also *Lion,* p. 118: "The choice lies between the kind of collective society that Hitler will set up and the kind that can arise if he is defeated"; "London Letter to *Partisan Review*" (1941), *CEJL,* Vol. 2, p. 117: "The whole question is who is to be in control of the collectively owned machines of production."

p. 124 *in an economic sense:* "Letter to H. J. Willmett," p. 149.

. . . *railways, public utilities, and banks:* "London Letter to *Partisan Review*" (1945), *CEJL*, Vol. 3, p. 396.

. . . *class privilege under English capitalism:* "Preface to Ukrainian Edition of *Animal Farm*" (1947), *CEJL*, Vol. 3, pp. 404-405.

. . . *the British Labour Party (of which I am a supporter):* "Letter to Francis A. Henson," p. 502.

. . . *hence of freedom of thought:* "The Prevention of Literature" (1946), *Essays*, III, p. 339.

. . . *like Britain's Ministry of Information:* "The Prevention of Literature," p. 335.

. . . *are killing the arts too:* "As I Please" (1944), *CEJL*, Vol. 3, pp. 229-230.

. . . *not worth saving anyway:* "As I Please" (1946), *CEJL*, Vol. 3, p. 230.

. . . *must necessarily disappear with it:* "As I Please," p. 229: "[I]f one thinks of the artist as an Ishmael, an autonomous individual who owes nothing to society," he writes in the same column, "then the golden age of the artist was the age of capitalism. He had then escaped from the patron and not yet been captured by the bureaucrat" (p. 229).

p. 125 *who cares for literature can cling:* "Literature and Totalitarianism," p. 137. See also "Letter to H. J. Willmett," p. 148: "I believe very deeply, as I explained in my book *The Lion and the Unicorn*, in the English people and in their capacity to centralise their economy without destroying freedom in doing so."

. . . *frantic struggle to sell things: Coming Up for Air,* p. 149.

p. 126 *contrive to keep their decency: Aspidistra,* p. 239.

. . . *too expensive: 1984,* p. 96.

. . . *bred out in a couple of generations:* "As I Please" (1944), *CEJL*, Vol. 3, pp. 189-190.

. . . *filled with a wildness of spirit:* "Review, Herman Melville, by Lewis Mumford" (1930), *CEJL*, Vol. 1, p. 21.

. . . *there will be room for everybody:* "Riding Down from Bangor" (1946), *Essays*, III, pp. 406-407.

p. 127 *strength [will] change into consciousness: 1984,* p. 221.

. . . *blow the Party to pieces: 1984,* p. 70.

p. 127 *collectivist logic of the Party: 1984*, p. 267: "[I]f a man can escape from his identity, if he can merge himself in the party so that he is the Party, then he is all-powerful and immortal."

Chapter 11

p. 132 *DOWN WITH BIG BROTHER: 1984*, p. 19.

p. 133 *nothing to set beside it:* "England, Your England" (1941), *Essays*, I, p. 252.

. . . *emotional unity:* "England, Your England," p. 266.

. . . *found himself in a new section: 1984*, pp. 185-186.

. . . *fired them at ourselves:* Compare *1984*, p. 154.

. . . *to destroy the products of human labor: 1984*, p. 191.

. . . *we preserve the Party's control: 1984*, p. 192.

. . . *the natural, unavoidable condition of survival: 1984*, p. 192.

p. 134 *in ways that impair military efficiency:* "Looking back on the Spanish War" (1943), *Essays*, I, p. 200.

. . . *they have to make four:* See *1984*, p. 198.

. . . *kilometers away in space:* See *1984*, p. 195. Here, as elsewhere, Orwell proves prescient about where technology may head. Forty years after he first metioned the "lens" weapon, "Star Wars" technology was very much in vogue.

. . . *not in fact advancing at all:* See *1984*, pp. 196, 199.

. . . *like three sheaves of corn: 1984*, p. 198. "[W]e [in England] believe half-instinctively that evil always defeats itself in the long run," Orwell writes. "What evidence is there that it does? And what instance is there of a modern industrialised state collapsing unless conquered from the outside by military force?" "Looking Back on the Spanish War" (1943), *Essays*, I, p. 200. O'Brien puts exactly the same question to Winston at the end of *1984* (p. 273).

. . . *cause comparatively few casualties: 1984*, p. 187.

. . . *maintain our cultural integrity:* See *1984*, p. 197.

. . . *which direction is up and which is down: 1984*, p. 199.

p. 135 *There would be a bloody struggle:* See *Homage to Catalonia*, pp. xxi (introduction by Lionel Trilling); pp. 121-22.

. . . *grinding them down in exploitation:* See *Broadcast*, p. 62 (quoting Churchill).

p. 135 *differs enormously from country to country:* "England, Your England" (1941), *Essays*, I, pp. 252-253.

p. 136 *ceases to be an enemy of any account:* Cf. *Wigan Pier*, p. 219: "A country like England . . . could be reduced to chaos by a few thousand well-placed placed bombs."

. . . *mostly highly trained specialists:* See *1984*, p. 187.

. . . *in which people rule themselves:* Cf. "Looking Back on the Spanish War," p. 210: "No bursting bomb can ever shatter the crystal spirit of democracy."

. . . *firmness in the truth:* "Reflections on Gandhi" (1949), *Essays*, I, p. 177.

Chapter 12

p. 137 *all had to be organized:* See *1984*, p. 149.

. . . *suddenly appeared all over London: 1984*, p. 150.

. . . *unworthy of their attention:* "As I Please" (1944), *CEJL*, Vol. 3, p. 98.

. . . *like monstrous horizontal ears: Aspidistra*, p. 128.

p. 138 *in the corner of her room:* The *1984* lovers find a hiding place in a dilapidated room above a junk shop. The room awakens in Winston "a sort of nostalgia, a sort of ancestral memory. It seemed to him that he knew exactly what it felt like to sit in a room like this, in an armchair beside an open fire with your feet in the fender and a kettle on the hob, utterly secure, with nobody watching you, no voice pursuing you, no sound except the singing of the kettle and the friendly ticking of the clock." *1984*, p. 96. This echoes a very similar passage in *Wigan Pier* (pp. 117-118). At another point, Winston and Julia meet in the belfry of a ruined church. *1984*, pp. 129, 131. The church is borrowed from *Homage to Catalonia*, p. 213.

. . . *in her arms: 1984*, p. 121.

. . . *rosy in the early morning light: Aspidistra*, p. 97.

pp. 138–139 *cracking their whips and cursing: Coming Up for Air*, p. 47.

p. 139 *they are loyal to one another: 1984*, p. 166.

. . . *evolved spontaneously from their loyalties:* See *Aspidistra*, p. 105. A similarly upbeat market scene, equally rich in color and detail, appears in *Burmese Days*, pp. 126-127.

p. 139 *It was a political act: 1984,* p. 128.

p. 140 *glass and water are not the same thing:* "As I Please" (1947), *CEJL,* Vol. 4, p. 267.

. . . *fawn jacket, and a mac:* Shelden, p. 223.

. . . *his emaciated torso:* Shelden, p. 322.

. . . *a mischievous, amused look:* Shelden, p. 273.

p. 141 *She adored cats:* See Shelden, p. 197.

. . . *can carry on where we leave off: 1984,* p. 156. Again, one wonders how Orwell managed to ignore the relationship between musings like this one and telescreen technology. As *1984* makes abundantly clear, these "small groups . . . banding together" don't stand a chance against the Ministry, the large group linked by telescreen. But why not? Orwell has to assume, at every turn, that only the Ministry knows how to use telescreens, not the dissidents.

. . . *rebel from the waist downward: 1984,* p. 157.

. . . *conscious beings must one day come: 1984,* p. 222.

p. 142 *laying its coralline beak upon them: Burmese Days,* p. 57. There is, of course, a very similar scene in *1984,* p. 125.

. . . *a torrent of song: 1984,* p. 125.

. . . *she had been asleep:* In *1984,* Julia is a synthesis of other Orwellian women. In *Aspidistra,* "Julia" is the hero's sister. *1984's* Julia lives in an unpleasant women's hostel, just like the heroine in *Aspidistra.* "Whenever there was nothing particular to do," *Aspidistra's* Hermione "always fell asleep as promptly as an animal" (p. 96). *1984's* Julia is "one of those people who can go to sleep at any hour and in any position."

By contrast, Winston's estranged wife, Katharine, was "[t]he human sound track." *1984,* p. 67. Orwell's favorite insult for orthodox Party hacks in other books is the "gangster gramophone." See *Homage to Catalonia,* p. 198 ("the gangster-gramophone of continental politics"); and *Wigan Pier,* p. 216 (Bolshevik commissars are "half gangster, half gramophone.").

p. 143 *the bells of Shoreditch: 1984,* pp. 97-100, 147, 179. A bell is a telegadget too, of course. Indeed, a church bell is the original "telephone," or "far speaker" in Greek.

. . . *a crimson silence:* Shelden, p. 67.

Chapter 13

p. 145 *nothing to set beside it:* "England, Your England" (1941), *Essays*, I, p. 252.

. . . *in moments of supreme crisis:* "England, Your England," p. 266.

. . . *an invisible chain:* "England, Your England," p. 266.

. . . *it must close its ranks:* "England, Your England," p. 267. See also "Notes on the Way" (1940), *CEJL*, Vol. 2, p. 17: "If whole armies had to be coerced, no war could ever be fought. Men die in battle—not gladly, of course, but at any rate voluntarily—because of abstractions called 'honour,' 'duty,' 'patriotism' and so forth."

p. 146 *in perfect unison:* "England, Your England," p. 264. See also *Homage to Catalonia*, pp. 28, 59. Cf. "Review: *The Totalitarian Enemy*, by F. Borkenau" (1940), *CEJL*, Vol. 2, p. 25: "[A] country . . . which is waging or preparing for 'total' war must be in some sense socialistic." *Lion*, p. 22: "War creates a consciousness of fraternity. Above all, war brings home to the individual that he is not altogether an individual." "Notes on the Way," p. 17: "People sacrifice themselves for the sake of fragmentary communities—nation, race, creed, class—and only become aware that they are *not* individuals in the very moment when they are facing bullets."

. . . *the spirit of the church:* Cf. "Review: *The Spirit of Catholicism* by Karl Adam" (1932), *CEJL*, Vol. 1, p. 79.

. . . *Industrialism requires coordinated control: Wigan Pier*, p. 188.

. . . *constant stimulation from other people:* "As I Please" (1944), *CEJL*, Vol. 3, p. 133: "If Defoe had really lived on a desert island he could not have written Robinson Crusoe, nor would he have wanted to. Take away freedom of speech, and the creative faculties dry up."

. . . *by communities rather than by individuals:* "The Prevention of Literature" (1946), *Essays*, III, p. 334.

. . . *an index to majority opinion:* "Lear, Tolstoy and the Fool" (1947), *Essays*, III, p. 421: a poem "defends itself by surviving, or it is indefensible."

. . . *a creation of common experience:* "New Words" (1940?), *CEJL*, Vol. 2, p. 9.

p. 146 *meaningless until it is shared: Burmese Days*, p. 57: "Beauty is meaningless until it is shared."

. . . *truth is indeed statistical: 1984*, pp. 219, 280.

. . . *then a lunatic: 1984*, p. 80.

. . . *need not greatly trouble him: 1984*, p. 80.

. . . *the belief might also be wrong: 1984*, p. 80.

. . . *must be written in solitude:* "The Prevention of Literature," pp. 342-343: "Certain kinds of poems, such as ballads, or, on the other hand, very artificial verse forms, can be composed cooperatively by groups of people. Whether the ancient English and Scottish ballads were originally produced by individuals, or by the people at large, is disputed, but at any rate they are non-individual in the sense that they constantly change in passing from mouth to mouth. . . . In prose, this kind of intimate collaboration is quite impossible."

. . . *eternal guardians of the weak: 1984*, p. 265.

p. 147 *cutthroat equality:* See *Homage to Catalonia*, p. 61.

. . . *Gadarene swine in times of peace:* "England, Your England" (1941), *Essays*, I, p. 265.

. . . *so that he might then run to friends for help:* When the Spanish police were pursuing Orwell, they arrested his wife Eileen "as a decoy to help them apprehend . . . her husband." Shelden, p. 270.

. . . *was a beehive: Wigan Pier*, p. 216.

. . . *a handful of stoats: Wigan Pier*, p. 216.

. . . *as a sort of keystone:* "London Letter to *Partisan Review*" (1944), *CEJL*, Vol. 3, p. 81.

. . . *really a waxwork:* "London Letter to *Partisan Review*," p. 81.

. . . *the price of civilization: 1984*, p. 205.

. . . *hierarchy and regimentation: 1984*, p. 205.

p. 148 *quickly merged into large ones:* See "England, Your England," p. 269.

. . . *hosts of petty traders:* "England, Your England," p. 273.

. . . *steel and concrete nests:* "Review, *Angel Pavement*, by J. B. Priestley" (1930), *CEJL*, Vol. 1, p. 25.

. . . *Obliteration of the Self:* See *1984*, p. 198.

p. 149 *actually not possible to keep them:* "Such, Such Were the Joys" (1947), *Essays*, I, p. 5.

... *unrelated and unintelligible facts:* "Such, Such Were the Joys," p. 9.

... *only true feeling was hatred:* "Such, Such Were the Joys," p. 26.

... *did not teach science in any form:* "Such, Such Were the Joys," pp. 8, 18.

... *principles of Ingsoc: 1984,* p. 194.

... *a dual system of astronomy: 1984,* p. 269.

p. 150 *no weeds, no poverty, no pain: Wigan Pier,* p. 189. See also Orwell's own summary of Oscar Wilde's utopianism in "The Soul of Man under Socialism by Oscar Wilde" (1948), *CEJL,* Vol. 4, pp. 426-428.

... *an efficient world: Wigan Pier,* p. 190.

... *more organization, more telescreens: Wigan Pier,* p. 193.

p. 151 *uniformity of opinion on all subjects: 1984,* p. 207.

... *had ever forged unity before:* Orwell believed this completely. He had said it many times before. The new totalitarianism was different because it was backed by more powerful technology. "[W]e are different from the persecutors of the past," O'Brien boasts. In *Coming Up for Air,* George Bowling saw that too. "Old Hitler's something different. So's Joe Stalin. They aren't like these chaps in the old days who crucified people and chopped their heads off and so forth, just for the fun of it. . . . They're after something quite new—something that's never been heard of before." *Coming Up for Air,* p. 185. What they're after, of course, is man's mind. They are the Thought Police.

Cf. "Some Thoughts on the Common Toad" (1946), *Essays,* III, p. 341: "The despotisms of the past were not totalitarian. Their repressive apparatus was always inefficient, their ruling classes were usually either corrupt or apathetic or half-liberal in outlook, and the prevailing religious doctrines usually worked against perfectionism and the notion of human infallibility."

... *that machines made history:* Orwell himself embraces this view in the Blythe essay in the middle of *1984.* He has presented this argument before. The steady advance of "the machine" was creating wealth for all, which might readily have been shared all around. *Wigan Pier*, p. 171; "Looking back on the Spanish War" (1943), *Essays*, I, p. 203; "As I Please" (1946), *CEJL*, Vol. 4, p. 249.

p. 152 *and yet still not live alone: 1984*, p. 29.

. . . *self-contained space:* A. Koestler, *Darkness at Noon* (New York: Bantam, 1989), p. 211.

. . . *start out on his backbone: Coming Up for Air*, p. 271; *1984*, p. 62.

. . . *a ruling group can fall from power:* See *1984*, p. 208.

. . . *fecundity and industriousness of its inhabitants:* See *1984*, p. 187.

p. 153 *the great nebula in Orion:* Cf. *Broadcast*, p. 80.

. . . *discontent can now become articulate: 1984*, p. 208.

. . . *journalists, and professional politicians:* See *1984*, p. 206.

p. 154 *the linking together of opposites:* See *1984*, p. 217.

. . . *this principle that will defeat us: 1984*, p. 273.

p. 155 *touching to see such love:* See *1984*, p. 259.

. . . *the suspicions he had long possessed: 1984*, p. 218.

. . . *I have almost ignored: 1984*, p. 218.

p. 156 *definitely pleasant thrill:* "Such, Such Were the Joys," p. 27.

Chapter 14

p. 157 *on the sixth day: 1984*, p. 180.

. . . *Big Brother had been overthrown:* Compare *1984*, p. 180.

. . . *admission that any change had taken place: 1984*, p. 181.

p. 158 *slipped into the speaker's hand:* See *1984*, pp. 181-182.

. . . *understanding rippled through the crowd: 1984*, p. 182.

. . . *thrown into the melting pot:* See "Politics and the English Language" (1946), *Essays*, I, p. 164.

. . . *governed by love and reason:* "Politics vs Literature: An Examination of *Gulliver's Travels*" (1946), *Essays*, III, p. 385. Also, "[t]hey had reached, in fact, the highest stage of totalitarian organisation, the stage when conformity has become so general that there is no need for a police force" (p. 385).

. . . *without even breaking the syntax: 1984*, p. 182.

. . . *shooting out slogans:* In *1984*, Winston attends a huge rally. It's both a mesmerizing scene and a wonderfully clever parody of Party propaganda. It is also lifted pretty much word for word from *Com-*

ing Up for Air, p. 175, written ten years earlier. *Wigan Pier*, pp. 175-176, contains another much shorter account of what may be the same episode.

Orwell, who stood six feet two, did not particularly care for short people. See, for example, *Coming Up for Air*, p. 14: "The floor-manager was an ugly little devil, undersized, with very square shoulders and a spiky gray moustache. . . . Do you notice how often they have undersized men for these bullying jobs?"

p. 159 *her dreams were slogans*: *Coming up for Air*, p. 172.

. . . *stick inside a swill-bucket*: *Aspidistra*, p. 50.

p. 160 *the same old invective*: "Politics and the English Language," p. 161.

. . . *dump of worn-out metaphors*: "Politics and the English Language," p. 159.

. . . *a prefabricated hen house*: "Politics and the English Language," p. 159.

. . . *lackey-flunkey-mad-dog-jackal-hyena-hydra-headed*: "As I Please" (1944), *CEJL*, Vol. 3, p. 109.

. . . *all the factories, and all the money*: *1984*, p. 73.

. . . *blood-bath*: "As I Please," pp. 108-109.

. . . *the lifeline of the network*: *1984*, p. 90.

. . . *Fascism ... Democracy...*: *Coming Up for Air*, p. 153.

p. 161 *malfunctioning old gramophone*: Cf. *Homage to Catalonia*, p. 198 (the "good party man," the "gangster-gramophone of continental politics"); *Wigan Pier*, p. 216 ("Bolshevik commissars (half gangster, half gramophone)").

. . . *hammering down on your brain*: *Coming Up for Air*, p. 156.

. . . *in the tone of her voice*: *Coming Up for Air*, p. 156.

. . . *won't smash our poor ones*: See also "Lear, Tolstoy and the Fool" (1947), *Essays*, III, p. 420.

. . . *principles of Blytheism—that, etc. etc.*: *1984*, p. 54.

p. 162 *The stinking corpse*: "As I Please," p. 109.

. . . *offal from a rentier class*: "Benefit of Clergy: Some Notes on Salvador Dalí" (1944), *Essays*, IV, p. 31.

. . . *poisoned the imagination—on life itself*: "Benefit of Clergy: Some Notes on Salvador Dalí," p. 24.

. . . *filthy stew of words*: "As I Please," pp. 109-110. See also "Politics and the English Language," p. 166: "[B]estial atrocities, iron heel, bloodstained tyranny, free peoples of the world, stand shoulder to shoulder."

p. 163 *through a viscous sea: Burmese Days*, p. 252.

. . . *menacingly above her head: 1984*, p. 181.

Chapter 15

p. 165 *with unmerciful clarity:* "The Spike" (1931), *CEJL*, Vol. I, p. 39.

Winston Smith of course lands in a cell in *1984*. We've read about that cell before. Orwell himself in fact occupied it, in London's Bethnal Green police station. There are several descriptions of the same cell in *Down and Out* (p. 146), in Orwell's essay "Clink" (1932), *CEJL*, Vol. 1, p. 87, and in *Aspidistra*. The walls are "glittering white porcelain," and the prisoners while away time by counting the bricks. They sit on a plank "shelf" rather than a bench or a bed. There's a spy-hole in the steel door. There's a single open toilet in the cell, which prisoners use abundantly; they "can't help it." The toilet doesn't flush properly. The cell then stinks "abominably." It's all exactly the same in each of Orwell's three accounts. See *1984*, pp. 223, 225, 229, 233, 237; compare *Aspidistra*, pp. 179, 183, 187; "Clink," pp. 87, 89, 90. See also *Homage To Catalonia*, p. 31 ("The position stank abominably, and outside the little enclosure of the barricade there was excrement everywhere"); *Burmese Days*, p. 75 ("It was very dark, stifling hot, and quite unfurnished, except for an earth latrine that stank to heaven"); *Burmese Days*, p. 217 ("It [the badly cured leopard skin] also stank abominably"); *Down and Out*, p. 199 (a tramps' hostel has a "common chamber-pot" that "stank abominably"). Compare *1984*, p. 237 ("Parsons used the lavatory, loudly and abundantly. It then turned out that the plug was defective, and the cell stank abominably for hours afterwards").

Even one of the other inmates—a man dying of starvation—is a repeat. He's "a commonplace, mean-looking man who might have been an engineer or technician of some kind." *1984*, p. 238: "But what was startling was the emaciation of his face. . . . The man was dying of starvation." Here he is in *Down and Out*, p. 156: "I had time to see his face, and it looked agonised. Quite suddenly I realised, from the expression of his face, that he was starving."

p. 165 *eyes looked disproportionately large:* 1984, p. 238; compare *Down and Out,* p. 97.

. . . *said the voice:* 1984, p. 239.

p. 166 *solitude, and persistent questions:* See 1984, pp. 102, 167.

. . . *I have almost ignored:* 1984, p. 218.

. . . *that makes freedom inevitable:* 1984, p. 218.

. . . *reach the central secret:* 1984, p. 218.

p. 168 *churned up within him: Down and Out,* p. 131.

. . . *a cough that almost tore him open: Coming Up for Air,* p. 30.

. . . *blood-streaked mucus on his hand:* "How the Poor Die" (1946), *Essays,* II, p. 89.

p. 171 *chosen for you from above:* "England, Your England" (1941), *Essays,* I, p. 256.

. . . *conscious of anything outside their daily lives:* 1984, pp. 202-203.

. . . *films oozing with sex:* 1984, p. 44.

. . . *peddled furtively to their youths:* 1984, p. 132.

. . . *horse shaking off flies:* 1984, p. 70.

p. 172 *without any impulse to rebel:* 1984, p. 211.

. . . *the range of their vision:* 1984, p. 92.

p. 173 *mixed with repulsion and bewilderment:* See 1984, p. 265; "Lear, Tolstoy and the Fool" (1947), *Essays,* III, p. 407.

. . . *the depths of his bones: Burmese Days,* p. 35.

p. 175 *almost no friction:* Cf. *Broadcast,* p. 79.

. . . *no longer requires collectivism:* Cf. *Wigan Pier,* p. 188.

. . . *a high level of technical development:* "Review, A Coat of Many Colours: Occasional Essays, by Herbert Read" (1945), *CEJL,* Vol. 4, p. 48.

. . . *Cooperation can be by consent:* Cf. "Review, The Unquiet Grave: A Word Cycle, by 'Palinurus'" (1945), *CEJL,* Vol. 3, p. 320: the error of the book lies "in assuming that a collectivist society would destroy human individuality."

. . . *except for the information it conveys:* Cf. *Broadcast,* p. 73: "We have learned now, however, that money is valueless in itself, and only goods count."

p. 177 *ration books, and coupons:* 1984, pp. 27, 32, 40, 59, 270.

334   NOTES

p. 177 *Lighthouses for ships:* Cf. R.H. Coase, "The Lighthouse in Economics," *Journal of Law and Economics* 17 (1974): 357. Coase ends as follows: "[E]conomists wishing to point to a service which is best provided by the government should use an example which has a more solid backing" (p. 376). With technology available today, it is far easier than Coase ever imagined to privatize the services that a lighthouse (or an air traffic control center) provides.

... *for air, water, or land:* See, generally, R. H. Coase, "The Problem of Social Cost," in Coase, *The Firm, the Market, and the Law* (Chicago: University of Chicago Press, 1988), pp. 95, 114-119. Coase, "Notes on the Problem of Social Cost," in *The Firm,* pp. 157, 174-179.

... *the right instincts: 1984,* pp. 8, 212. See also "Who Are the War Criminals?" (1943), *CEJL,* Vol. 2, p. 319: "To begin with, what crime, if any, has Mussolini committed? In power politics there are no crimes, because there are no laws"; "As I Please" (1943), *CEJL,* Vol. 3, p. 66: "How could there be, when legality implies authority and there is no authority with the power to transcend national frontiers?"

... *reborn spontaneously in a telescreened society:* Cf. "The English People" (1944), *CEJL,* Vol. 3, p. 9: "[T]he efficiency of the English police force really depends on the fact that the police have public opinion behind them." See also "Freedom of the Park" (1945), *CEJL,* Vol. 4, p. 40: "Whether [the laws] are carried out, and how the police behave, depends on the general temper of the country. If large numbers of people are interested in freedom of speech, for example, there will be freedom of speech, even if the law forbids it; if public opinion is sluggish, inconvenient minorities will be persecuted, even if laws exist to protect them."

p. 178 *he slouched forward: Aspidistra,* p. 72.

... *a printing press or a broadcast station:* Cf. "London Letter to Partisan Review" (1941), *CEJL,* Vol. 2, p. 118: "[I]n England there is a great respect for freedom of speech but very little for freedom of the press."

... *even if the law forbids it:* "Freedom of the Park," p. 40.

p. 179 *leisure creates literacy: 1984,* p. 191.

p. 180 *were all stagnant oligopolies*: "Boys' Weeklies" (1939), *Essays*, I, pp. 280-281.

. . . *this will now disappear*: Cf. "The English People," p. 23: mass-produced amusements "have to appeal to a public of millions and therefore have to avoid stirring up class antagonisms."

. . . *and often several*: "Boys' Weeklies," p. 280.

. . . *a single national network cannot possibly do*: "Boys' Weeklies," p. 281.

. . . *and crossword puzzle fans*: "England, Your England," p. 255.

p. 181 *the whole of Hyde Park*: Cf. *Burmese Days*, p. 191: "He told Flory not to start talking like a damned Hyde Park agitator."

. . . *Hitler to be Jesus Christ*: "Freedom of the Park," p. 39.

. . . *in the physical world*: "Freedom of the Park," p. 39.

. . . *irresponsible, ungenteel ways*: "Review, *Herman Melville*, by Lewis Mumford" (1930), *CEJL*, Vol. 1, p. 21.

. . . *a buoyant, carefree feeling*: "Riding Down from Bangor" (1946), *Essays*, III, p. 406.

. . . *capitalist civilization at its best*: "Riding Down from Bangor," p. 407.

p. 182 *buy them back in private, among friends*: *Burmese Days*, p. 69.

. . . *chosen for you from above*: "England, Your England," p. 256.

. . . *like the quacking of a duck*: *1984*, pp. 51, 54-55, 311.

. . . *fastening one's love upon other human individuals*: "Reflections on Gandhi" (1949), *Essays*, I, p. 176.

Chapter 16

p. 183 *a quarter bottle of gin*: Cf. Shelden, p. 151.

. . . *with darkness all above*: *Coming up for Air*, p. 173.

. . . *peered meaningfully from several doorways*: *Aspidistra*, p. 166.

p. 184 *vulgarer versions of Kate's*: *Aspidistra*, p. 172.

. . . *a broad-lipped smile*: *Aspidistra*, p. 72.

. . . *the same bed, probably*: *Aspidistra*, p. 174.

. . . *fear and sadistic exaltation*: Shelden, p. 214.

. . . *Come closer*: *Aspidistra*, p. 175.

pp. 184-185 *violently sick, three or four times*: *Aspidistra*, p. 177.

p. 185 *I'm going to be sick*: *Aspidistra*, p. 179.

Chapter 17

p. 187 *in the corner of the room:* See *1984*, p. 243.

. . . *like a mountain crumbling:* See *1984*, p. 77.

. . . *fierce and watchful: 1984*, p. 274.

. . . *costly piece of machinery:* "Shooting an Elephant" (1936), *Essays*, I, pp. 151-152.

. . . *hypodermics and the pain machine:* Many of the prison exchanges between O'Brien and Smith in *1984* are reworked from Orwell's prior essays.

For example: In language lifted straight out of Orwell's earlier essays, O'Brien explains why the torture is necessary. O'Brien: "Can you not understand, Winston, that the individual is only a cell? The weariness of the cell is the vigor of the organism." *1984*, p. 267. Compare "Notes on the Way" (1940), *CEJL*, Vol 2, p. 317: "Man is not an individual, he is only a cell in an everlasting body." See also "Review, *Communism and Man*, by F. J. Sheed" (1939), *CEJL*, Vol. 1, p. 383: "Either this life is a preparation for another, in which case the individual soul is all-important, or there is no life after death, in which case the individual is merely a replaceable cell in the general body."

Similarly, O'Brien explains that power is everything: "The Party seeks power entirely for its own sake." Compare "Raffles and Miss Blandish" (1944), *Essays*, I, p. 139: There is "only one motive," which is "the pursuit of power." See also "Rudyard Kipling" (1942), *Essays*, I, p. 118: "No one, in our time, believes in any sanction greater than military power; no one believes that it is possible to overcome force except by greater force. There is no 'law,' there is only power." "Charles Dickens" (1939), *Essays*, I, p. 65: "The central problem how to prevent power from being abused remains unsolved."

O'Brien reduces this to a single metaphor: "If you want a picture of the future, imagine a boot stamping on a human face forever." *1984*, p. 271. Compare "England, your England" (1941), *Essays*, I, p. 259: "The goose-step . . . is simply an affirmation of naked power; contained in it, quite consciously and intentionally, is the vision of a boot crashing down on a face." See also "Raffles and

Miss Blandish," p. 139: "[T]he hero . . . is described as stamping on somebody's face."

p. 188 *down his face from cheek to chin:* Shelden, p. 212.

. . . *Do you understand that:* 1984, pp. 248-249.

. . . *the overthrow of the Party:* 1984, p. 265.

. . . *who could pronounce their aitches:* Wigan Pier, p. 50.

p. 189 *you happen to be insane:* 1984, p. 262.

. . . *resettled his spectacles thoughtfully:* 1984, p. 249.

. . . *persuade rather than to punish:* 1984, p. 249.

. . . *human drudgery had disappeared:* 1984, p. 190.

. . . *living standards of the average human being improved steadily:* 1984, p. 190.

. . . *wealth would confer no distinction:* 1984, p. 190.

. . . *only possible on a basis of poverty and ignorance:* 1984, p. 191.

p. 190 *incompatible with equality:* "The English People" (1944), CEJL, Vol. 3, p. 23.

. . . *in their native talents:* 1984, p. 205.

. . . *in ways that favored some individuals over others:* 1984, p. 205.

. . . *impossible for mechanical reasons:* "Second Thoughts on James Burnham" (1946), Essays, II, p. 351.

p. 191 *thicker than my thighs:* 1984, p. 274.

. . . *the weight of my skull:* 1984, p. 275.

. . . *six guards to pry him loose:* "A Hanging" (1931), Essays, II, p. 10. See also "As I Please" (1944), CEJL, Vol. 3, p. 267.

. . . *an unbreakable system of tabus:* Burmese Days, p. 69.

p. 192 *admire the man's impudence:* Burmese Days, p. 255.

. . . *American breakfast cereal:* Down and Out, p. 82.

p. 193 *blackmail, fraud, and libel:* Cf. Homage to Catalonia, p. 65.

. . . *compositor, author, and bookseller:* I am paraphrasing here from Orwell's "Review of Penguin Books" (1936), CEJL, Vol. 1, pp. 165-167. Like so many others, this essay demonstrates that Orwell does not understand economics at all. He is sure that cheaper books are "an advantage from the reader's point" and accepts that they don't "hurt trade as a whole." But he is equally sure that "for the publisher, the compositor, the author and the bookseller," cheaper books are "a disaster" (p. 166). In effect, then, Orwell assumes that the demand for books is completely inelastic, so that lower prices invariably mean lower revenues. McDonald's, however, sells cheaper beef than Maxim's, and yet makes its owners far richer.

p. 194 *walking down a wet street:* Shelden, p. 325 (quoting Stephen Spender's description of Orwell).

. . . *all shall be forgiven you:* "Benefit of Clergy: Some Notes on Salvador Dalí" (1944), *Essays,* IV, p. 26.

. . . *gained by private sponging:* "Review, *The Rock Pool,* by Cyril Connolly" (1936), *CEJL,* Vol. 1, p. 226.

. . . *the song of birds: Wigan Pier,* pp. 204-205.

p. 195 *news the Party supplies today: 1984,* p. 44.

. . . *every form of diseased intelligence:* "Benefit of Clergy: Some Notes on Salvador Dalí," p.27.

. . . *what they do not want to hear:* "The Freedom of the Press," quoted in Shelden, p. 235.

p. 196 *better that he should be a policeman than a gangster:* "Raffles and Miss Blandish," p. 144.

p. 197 *on the side of the criminal:* "No, Not One" (1941), *CEJL,* Vol. 2, pp. 166-167.

. . . *picking pockets at the races:* "Benefit of Clergy: Some Notes on Salvador Dalí," p. 26.

. . . *high sentiments make no appeal:* "The Art of Donald McGill" (1941), *Essays,* I, p. 114.

p. 198 *neatly as a skinned rabbit:* "Shooting an Elephant" (1936), *Essays,* I, p. 151.

. . . *hedonistic utopia that Winston Smith imagined: 1984,* p. 270.

p. 199 *only a polite name for capitalism: Homage to Catalonia,* pp. 60, 69.

p. 200 *phesbian leminists of England: Wigan Pier,* p. 174.

. . . *hierarchies of talent and nothing else:* "Such, Such Were the Joys" (1947), *Essays,* I, p. 41.

. . . *pull in opposite directions:* "Review, *A Coat of Many Colours: Occasional Essays,* by Herbert Read" (1945), *CEJL,* Vol. 4, p. 49.

p. 201 *for each other's mutual benefit:* "Review, *A Coat of Many Colours: Occasional Essays* by Herbert Read," p. 49.

. . . *Everyone had laughed:* "A Hanging," p. 13.

. . . *bubbling sound deep down in his belly: Burmese Days,* p. 13.

. . . *journalists, and professional politicians: 1984,* p. 206.

p. 201 *running up his right leg: 1984*, p. 275.

p. 202 *the Party controls you: 1984*, p. 257.

. . . *to find a window somewhere: 1984*, p. 235.

. . . *You are dead:* In the *1984* prison scenes, Orwell returns to a question he has explored throughout *1984*, the death of body and soul. A man dies when he rejects the Party. From the moment Winston begins to write his diary he knows he is "already dead" (p. 29). "We are the dead," Winston intones to Julia time and again during their affair (p. 222). But a man also dies when he embraces the Party. "We shall crush you down to the point from which there is no coming back," O'Brien tells Winston. "Everything will be dead inside you" (pp. 259-260). So you're dead if you do and dead if you don't.

Just as in *Coming Up for Air.* The men who fought in World War I are all dead (p. 133). But somehow those who didn't fight are dead too. A poet who just can't believe that "Hitler matters" is dead. "He's a ghost. . . . Perhaps a man really dies when his brain stops, when he loses the power to take in a new idea" (p. 188).

Gordon Comstock thinks similar thoughts in *Aspidistra.* "My poems are dead because I'm dead. You're dead. We're all dead. Dead people in a dead world" (p. 83).

. . . *one of the two would be gone:* "A Hanging," p. 11.

p. 203 *cut down to a minimum: 1984*, p. 304.

. . . *one clearly understood instruction: 1984*, p. 304.

p. 204 *Now it is known as Newspeak:* See *Broadcast*, p. 62.

. . . *one long struggle not to be laughed at:* "Shooting an Elephant" (1936), *Essays*, I, p. 153.

. . . *like the tolling of a bell:* "A Hanging," p. 12.

. . . *legs sagging and head drooping:* "Shooting an Elephant," pp. 154-155.

p. 205 *like red velvet:* "Shooting an Elephant," p. 154; *Burmese Days*, p. 28.

Chapter 18

p. 207 *a foul, musty smell: 1984*, p. 288. Rats are always popping up in Orwell's books. In *Homage to Catalonia*, Orwell returns repeatedly to the soldier's never-ending battle with rats (p. 106). Orwell also twice quotes an "old army song" about rats (pp. 78, 106). In one barn in particular, Orwell recounts, "[t]he filthy brutes came swarming out of the ground on every side. If there is one thing I hate more than another it is a rat running over me in the darkness" (p. 183). Those same "[f]ilthy brute[s]" reappear to terrify Winston in *1984* (p. 145).

p. 207 *it had become unbearable agony*: Wigan Pier, pp. 25-27.

p. 208 *too dreadful to be faced*: 1984, p. 286.

. . . *he despised rats the most*: 1984, pp. 145, 287-288.

. . . *devour his tongue*: 1984, p. 288.

p. 209 *a screaming animal*: 1984, p. 289.

. . . *away, away, away from the rats*: 1984, p. 289.

. . . *such beautiful things could be found*: Shelden, p. 284, quoting Orwell's thoughts about the leaves of silver poplars that brushed against his face as he was being hauled out of slippery trench after being shot through the neck.

p. 210 *he was no longer afraid of dying*: Shelden, p. 442: "I begin to despair of ever recovering. What I can never understand is why, since I am not afraid of death (afraid of pain, & of the moment of dying, but not extinction)."

. . . *one of simple resentment*: "Review, Burnt Norton, East Coker, The Dry Salvages, by T. S. Eliot" (1942), CEJL, Vol. 2, p. 238.

. . . *certainty that it was possible*: Homage to Catalonia, p. 89.

p. 211 *their awakening will come*: 1984, p. 221.

. . . *restoring confidence by the fact of being spoken*: 1984, p. 17.

p. 212 *coral plucked from the Indian Ocean*: 1984, pp. 95, 148, 224.

p. 213 *she said baldly*: 1984, p. 294.

. . . *the tunnel, and the rat*: 1984, p. 289.

. . . *you don't feel the same toward the other person any longer, she said*: "Reflections on Gandhi" (1949), Essays, I, p. 176.

. . . *clinging to him like a child*: Aspidistra, p. 119.

. . . *still soft, still warm*: Compare 1984, pp. 16, 124-125, 294.

p. 214 *knew that he loved Big Brother*: 1984, p. 300. This is how *1984* ends too, but the words there mean something quite different. In 1940, six years before he began *1984*, Orwell had already told us this was going to happen. "[W]e are moving into an age of totalitarian dictatorships an age in which freedom of thought will be at first a deadly sin and later on a meaningless abstraction. The autonomous individual is going to be stamped out of existence." "Inside the Whale" (1940), *Essays*, I, p. 249.

p. 214 *exactly as often as is necessary: 1984*, p. 41.

p. 215 *stretched away into inconceivable distances: Homage to Catalonia*, p. 40.

. . . *there too will always be Eden:* Or, as Mark Twain put it, "[a]fter all these years I see that I was mistaken about Eve in the beginning; it is better to live outside the Garden with her than inside it without her. At first I thought she talked too much; but now I should be sorry to have that voice fall silent and pass out of my life." M. Twain, *Adam's Diary* (Oakland, CA: Star Rover House, 1984), p. 89.

. . . *it would do the job:* Shelden, p. 294.

. . . *nitwits wanting only to be doped:* "As I Please" (1944), *CEJL*, Vol. 3, p. 250.

Doublethink

p. 217 *compared with that of the capitalist:* "Clink" (1932), *CEJL*, Vol. 1, p. 90; Shelden, p. 164.

p. 218 *like the rules of grammar:* See generally F. A. Hayek, "Notes on the Evolution of Systems of Rules of Conduct," in Hayek, *Studies in Philosophy, Politics and Economics* (Chicago: University of Chicago Press, 1967), p. 66; Hayek, "The Results of Human Action But Not of Human Design," in Hayek, *Studies in Philosophy*, pp. 96-105.

p. 219 *sliding down the road to serfdom:* E.g., "Politics and the English Language" (1946), *Essays*, I, p. 156.

. . . *by coercion and central planning:* For a marvelous recent essay on this theme, see Steven Pinker, "Grammar Puss," in *New Republic*, January 31, 1994, pp. 19-26, based on Steven Pinker, *The Language Instinct* (New York: Morrow, 1994).

. . . *the English language:* "As I Please" (1947), *CEJL*, Vol. 4, p. 305: "English is well fitted to be the universal second language, if there ever is such a thing. It has a large start over any natural language and an enormous start over any manufactured one."

p. 219 *contrive to keep their decency: Aspidistra*, p. 239.

. . . *alongside another book by K. Zilliacus:* "Review, *The Road to Serfdom*, by F. A. Hayek; *The Mirror of the Past*, by K. Zilliacus" (1944), *CEJL*, Vol. 3, p. 117.

p. 220 *dedicates its issue to Orwell's works:* Orwell was himself at least an occasional reader of the magazine. See "As I Please" (1945), *CEJL*, Vol. 3, p. 318.

p. 221 *something verging on it:* See R. Manvell, "Review, R. Coase, *British Broadcasting: A Study in Monopoly*," *World Review* (June 1950): 73 (quoting Coase).

p. 222 *Orwell loved Wells:* See "Such, Such Were the Joys" (1947), *Essays*, I, p. 17.

. . . *his troubles would be ended:* "The Rediscovery of Europe" (1942), *CEJL*, Vol. 2, pp. 201-202.

. . . *Coase could:* Coase wrote about a number of other related issues that I touch on in this book. "The Nature of the Firm," in R. H. Coase, *The Firm, the Market, and the Law*, (Chicago: University of Chicago Press, 1988), discusses why people abandon the market to form corporations—which are fundamentally *collectivist* institutions. In a nutshell, the reason is to reduce transaction costs. It's cheaper to have a boss set a secretary's salary than to have an arms-length market transaction every time a letter has to be typed. Coase comes close to making a big mistake, however. He declares: "Inventions which tend to bring factors of production nearer together, by lessening spatial distribution, tend to increase the size of the firm. Changes like the telephone and the telegraph, which tend to reduce the cost of organising spatially, will tend to increase the size of the firm" (p. 46). Coase is very wrong about that, but he saves himself in a footnote: "It should be noted that most inventions will change both the costs of organising and the costs of using the price mechanism. In such cases, whether the invention tends to make firms larger or smaller will depend on the relative effect on these two sets of costs. For instance, if the telephone reduces the costs of using the price mechanisms more than it reduces the costs of organising, then it will have the effect of reducing the size of the firm" (p. 46, n. 31).

p. 223 *Euripides and others perished:* "As I Please" (1944), *CEJL,* Vol. 3, p. 178.

. . . *passed into history and became truth: 1984,* p. 35.

p. 224 *the police of totalitarian regimes: Broadcast,* p. 215.

. . . *cheap motor cars: Lion,* p. 68.

. . . *an important part of the solution:* "The English People" (1944), *CEJL,* Vol. 3, p. 34.

. . . *along the arterial roads: Lion,* p. 68.

. . . *invents better machines: Wigan Pier,* p. 206: "[T]he tendency of capitalism is to slow [invention] down, because under capitalism any invention which does not promise fairly immediate profits is neglected."

. . . *and wages war more effectively:* "England, Your England" (1941), *Essays,* I, p. 266.

p. 225 *the shadow of any central Ministry:* In *Wigan Pier,* p. 188, Orwell argues that industrialism and socialism are siblings, and that socialism depends on "constant intercommunication and exchange of goods between all parts of the earth." But "constant intercommunication and exchange" does not require Ministries. What these things require is a telescreen.

. . . *willingness to share and cooperate:* See generally Michael Schrage, *Shared Minds: The New Technologies of Collaboration* (New York: Random House, 1990). Mitchell Kapor unconsciously echoed *1984* in his dust jacket blurb: "*Shared Minds* is an agile account which tells us how the new tools and methods for collaboration in the workplace make 1 + 1 = 3." See also *Globalization, Technology, and Competition: The Fusion of Computers and Telecommunications in the 1990s,* ed. Stephen P. Bradley, Jerry A. Hausman, and Richard L. Nolan (Boston: Harvard Business School Press, 1993); Tom Peters, *Liberation Management: Necessary Disorganization for the Nanosecond Nineties* (New York: Knopf, 1992); Shoshana Zuboff, *In the Age of the Smart Machine: The Future of Work and Power* (New York: Basic Books, 1988); Anon., "The Fall of Big Business," *Economist* (April 17, 1993), p. 13.

p. 225 *mainly on herrings and potatoes*: *Wigan Pier*, p. 159. "Under the capitalist system," Orwell writes in *Wigan Pier*, p. 159, "in order that England may live in comparative comfort, a hundred million Indians must live on the verge of starvation."

. . . *first thought of writing 1984*: "Letter to F. J. Warburg" (1948), *CEJL*, Vol. 4, p. 448.

. . . *the Empires of the Mind*: *Broadcast*, p. 62, introduction by W. J. West, quoting speech by Winston Churchill.

. . . *a very fashionable concern around then*: *Broadcast*, p. 7, introduction by W. J. West.

. . . *an enthusiast for a while*: *Broadcast*, p. 47. As a BBC broadcaster, Orwell commissioned a talk on Basic.

. . . *the part Orwell liked*: "As I Please" (1944), *CEJL*, Vol. 3, p. 210: "One argument for Basic English is that by existing side by side with Standard English it can act as a sort of corrective to the oratory of statesmen and publicists. High-sounding phrases, when translated into Basic, are often deflated in a surprising way. . . . In Basic, I am told, you cannot make a meaningless statement without its being apparent that it is meaningless—which is quite enough to explain why so many schoolmasters, editors, politicians and literary critics object to it."

pp. 225–226 *led Orwell to 1984's Newspeak*: Orwell likewise rejected "Nu Speling" and any attempt to change the British system of weights and measures. "As I Please" (1947), *CEJL*, Vol. 4, pp. 304-306.

p. 226 *Orwell's 1944 column on capitalism and art*: "As I Please" (1944), *CEJL*, Vol. 3, pp. 228-230.

. . . *there must be a solution*: "As I Please," p. 230.

p. 227 *the electronic equivalents of Boys' Weeklies*: "Boys' Weeklies" (1939), *Essays*, I, p. 279.

. . . *farthing newspapers*: "A Farthing Newspaper" (1928), *CEJL*, Vol. 1, p. 12.

. . . *and the comic art of Donald McGill*: "The Art of Donald McGill" (1941), *Essays*, I, p. 10.

. . . *garret he occupies in Brewer's Yard*: *Aspidistra*, p. 205.

. . . *it is vast and anonymous*: *Wigan Pier*, p. 79: "London . . . is so vast that life there is solitary and anonymous."

p. 227 *restaurant, pub, and inn:* Shelden, p. 403.

... *as the largest metropolis:* See Howard Rheingold, *The Virtual Community: Homesteading on the Electronic Frontier* (Reading, MA: Addison-Wesley, 1993); Ithiel de Sola Pool, *Technologies without Boundaries* (Cambridge: Harvard University Press, 1990).

... *island off the coast of Scotland:* Shelden, p. 402.

... *the possibilities in a 1947 column:* "As I Please" (1947), *CEJL,* Vol. 4, p. 310.

p. 228 *conveyed to those in power:* Curiously, when Orwell quotes Jefferson at the end of *1984,* he leaves out the word "just" (p. 313).

... *dislikes standardised education:* "Letter to Geoffrey Gorer" (1939), *CEJL,* Vol. 1, p. 381.

... *a private school on every desktop:* See Lewis J. Perelman, *School's Out: Hyperlearning, The New Technology, and the End of Education* (New York: Morrow, 1992); Seymour Papert, "The Children's Machine," *Technology Review,* 30-3 (July 1993).

... *listened to by no one:* Orwell might have imagined *that* very easily indeed. He himself was quite sure that the wartime radio propaganda—the huge volume of "filth . . . flowing through the air"—had no impact at all. *Letter to George Woodcock* (1942), *CEJL,* Vol. 2, p. 268. German radio propaganda was an almost complete flop. London Letter to *Partisan Review* (1946), *CEJL,* Vol. 2, p. 182. BBC propaganda was "just shot into the stratosphere, not listened to by anybody." Shelden, p. 34.

... *the technologies of freedom:* Ithiel de Sola Pool, *Technologies of Freedom* (Cambridge: Harvard University Press, 1983), pp. 26-27.

p. 229 *he first thought of writing 1984:* "Letter to F. J. Warburg," p. 448.

... *Orwell writes an essay for Partisan Review:* "London Letter to *Partisan Review*" (1944), *CEJL,* Vol. 3, p. 298.

... *original defiler of civilization's purity: 1984,* p. 13.

Part 4

p. 231 *one leap ahead of the truth: 1984,* p. 216.

The Future Is Passed

p. 233 *with typically Orwellian despondency:* "Why I Write" (1946), *Essays,* I, p. 316.

. . . *wonderful gargoyles:* "Charles Dickens" (1939), *Essays,* I, p. 96.

. . . *we have been warned:* Anthony Burgess, *The Novel Now* (New York: Norton, 1967), p. 43. Burgess goes on to publish his own answer to Orwell's *1984* a decade later, in 1978. A. Burgess, *1985* (Boston: Little Brown, 1978). Burgess's *1985* begins with an imaginary dialogue between Burgess and Orwell and concludes with a novelette that sets out Burgess's own little prophecy. His theme is that trade unions are going to take over the world. Burgess turns out to be an even worse prophet than Orwell. Within a year or two after *1985* was published, organized labor entered into rapid decline in both England and America.

p. 234 *Apple, not Stalin:* This fact has not been lost on Apple Computer itself. See "Why 1984 wasn't like '1984'" (advertisement), *Wall Street Journal,* January 24, 1984, p. A7. The ad displays a large picture of a Macintosh. In the bottom left corner is a picture of the cover of 1984 with the caption: "George Orwell's classic science fiction novel '1984.' It turned out to be more fiction than science." Apple was perhaps unaware that a similar ad had been run a decade before by Olivetti. It is reproduced in John Rodden, *The Politics of Literary Reputation: The Making and Claiming of "St. George" Orwell* (New York: Oxford University Press, 1989), p. 257. The Olivetti ad (for Olivetti's M20 Personal Computer) is head-lined, "1984: Orwell Was Wrong." For the story of the Macintosh itself, see Steven Levy, *Insanely Great: The Life and Times of Macintosh, the Computer That Changed Everything* (New York: Viking Press, 1993).

. . . *for the convictions that he lived:* Shelden, p. 268.

. . . *irrelevant by the passage of time:* "The Soul of Man under Socialism by Oscar Wilde" (1948), *CEJL,* Vol. 4, p. 426.

. . . *his unsystematic but illuminating way:* "Lear, Tolstoy and the Fool" (1947), *Essays,* III, p. 419.

p. 235 *something resembling it could arrive:* "Letter to Francis A. Henson" (1949), *CEJL,* Vol. 4, p. 502. In prior writings, of course, Orwell had set forth his prophecies a lot less tentatively than that. See, e.g., "Why I Joined the Independent Labour Party" (1938), *CEJL*, Vol. 1, p. 337: "[T]he era of free speech is closing down. . . . The time is coming—not next year, perhaps not for ten or twenty years, but it is coming—when every writer will have the choice of being silenced altogether or of producing the dope that a privileged minority demands." See also "The Prevention of Literature" (1946), *Essays*, III, p. 335: "Everything in our age conspires to turn the writer, and every other kind of artist as well, into a minor official, working on themes handed to him from above and never telling what seems to him the whole of the truth."

p. 235 *they have been given a prediction*: Shelden, p. 432.

. . . *throughout his career as a writer*: Moreover, in several of his other books, Orwell himself uses the word "prophecy," albeit self-deprecatingly, to describe what he is doing. For example: "Sneaking off to Lower Binfield to try and recover the past, and then, in the car coming home, thinking a lot of prophetic baloney about the future." *Coming Up for Air*, p. 270. "And this kind of prophetic feeling that keeps coming over me nowadays, the feeling that war's just round the corner and that war's the end of all things, isn't peculiar to me. We've all got it, more or less" (p. 29). "It was as though the power of prophecy had been given me. It seemed to me that I could see the Whole of England, and all the people in it, and all the things that'll happen to all of them" (p. 268).

"I still believe that—unless Spain splits up, with unpredictable consequences—the tendency of the post-war Government is bound to be Fascistic. Once again I let this opinion stand, and take the chance that time will do to me what it does to most prophets." *Homage to Catalonia*, p. 182.

"All prophecies are wrong, therefore this one will be wrong, but I will take a chance and say that though the war may end quite soon or may drag on for years, it will end with Spain divided up." "Spilling the Spanish Beans" (1937), *CEJL*, Vol. 1, p. 275.

. . . *Orwell wrote in Burmese Days*: *Burmese Days*, p. 57.

. . . *test worth bothering about: survival*: "Charles Dickens," p. 98.

. . . *at any rate it exists*: "Charles Dickens," p. 98. See also "Lear, Tolstoy and the Fool," p. 421: a poem "defends itself by surviving, or it is indefensible."

p. 235 *artist of his century:* "England is lacking . . . in what one might call concentration-camp literature," Orwell wrote in "Arthur Koestler" (1946), *Essays,* III, p. 275. "The special world created by secret-police forces, censorship of opinion, torture, and frame-up trials is, of course, known about and to some extent disapproved of, but it has made very little emotional impact" (p. 275). Orwell changed that all right, once and for all.

p. 236 *produce a great work of art:* "Politics vs Literature: An Examination of *Gulliver's Travels*" (1946), *Essays,* III, pp. 392-393. My text here—"The views that a writer . . . great work of art"—is verbatim Orwell, except that Orwell was writing about Jonathan Swift and *Gulliver's Travels.*

. . . *nonsensical contraptions that would never work: Wigan Pier,* p. 190.

. . . *made the modern world possible:* "Charles Dickens," p. 85. Dickens's "unscientific cast of mind" is "damaging"; for Dickens, "[s]cience is uninteresting and machinery is cruel and ugly" (p. 86).

. . . *social possibilities of machinery:* "Charles Dickens," p. 85.

. . . *which they mistake for the future:* "Inside the Whale" (1940), *Essays,* I, p. 243.

. . . *the social effects of technology: Wigan Pier,* p. 202.

p. 237 *the function of the machine: Wigan Pier,* p. 202.

. . . *people feel about machine-civilization: Wigan Pier,* p. 203.

. . . *Orwell once wrote:* "Rudyard Kipling" (1942), *Essays,* I, p. 126.

. . . *metal plaque like a dulled mirror: 1984,* p. 3.

p. 238 *the flexible glass mentioned by Petronius: Wigan Pier,* pp. 206-207.

. . . *once Socialism is established: Wigan Pier,* p. 206.

. . . *Orwell writes in The Lion and the Unicorn: Lion,* pp. 82-83.

. . . *wonks, nerds, and phone-phreaks:* For more on phreaks and hackers, see Bruce Sterling, *The Hacker Crackdown: Law and Disorder on the Electronic Frontier* (New York: Bantam, 1992).

. . . *a year after 1984 was published:* It is worth noting, however, that in 1949 Orwell himself began to assemble a "private list of people in the West whom he suspected of being 'crypto' Communists. He was fearful that 'enormous mischief' could be done by 'apologists of the Stalin regime' who pretended to be politically independent." Shelden, p. 428. "His notebook lists over a hundred names of possible 'cryptos,' many belonging to people he did not know personally." Orwell had also written at least one column on "crypto-communism" that would have pleased McCarthy immensely. See "Two Letters to the Editor of *Tribune*" (1947) *CEJL*, Vol. 4, pp. 191-193 (Orwell's Reply to Konni Zilliacus MP): "the substance of it boils down to this: that he says he is not a 'crypto-Communist.' But of course he does! What else could he say?"

p. 239 *this is called pacification:* "Politics and the English Language" (1946), *Essays*, I, p. 166.

. . . *Orwell asked in 1943:* "Looking back on the Spanish War" (1943), *Essays*, I, p. 200.

. . . *bloodless victory over the oligarchical collectivists:* "Our economies are propelled by information technologies," Margaret Thatcher said in a speech given shortly before the final collapse of the Soviet Union. "Theirs are fueled by Vodka." Victory Gin, she might have said. I don't know if Thatcher realized that she was echoing *1984*, but in any event, Thatcher was right, and Orwell was wrong.

. . . *only socialist nations can fight effectively:* "England, Your England" (1941), *Essays*, I, p. 266.

. . . *elimination of unreliable elements:* "Politics and the English Language," p. 167.

. . . *and the killing stopped:* "Unfortunately I had not trained myself to be indifferent to the expression of the human face," Orwell once wrote about the natives he had seen punished in Burma. Shelden, p. 112.

p. 240 *is aware of those facts:* "In Front of Your Nose" (1946), *CEJL*, Vol. 4, p. 123: "[P]lain, unmistakable facts being shirked by people who in another part of their mind are aware of those facts."

. . . *a 1946 column titled In Front of Your Nose:* "Closely allied to [schizophrenia] is the power of ignoring facts which are obvious and unalterable, and which will have to be faced sooner or later." "In Front of Your Nose," p. 123.

p. 240 *film machine statically:* "Charles Dickens," pp. 82-83.

. . . *It contained no happy surprises:* "Charles Dickens," p. 99.

. . . *a man who lacked imagination:* Wigan Pier, p. 190.

Doublethink

p. 241 *all others seem to us the most horrible:* "Politics vs Literature: An Examination of *Gulliver's Travels*" (1946), *Essays,* III, p. 391.

. . . *like a Sherlock Holmes story:* Shelden, p. 219; "Inside the Whale" (1940), *Essays,* I, p. 212.

. . . *art of Salvador Dalí:* "Benefit of Clergy: Some Notes on Salvador Dalí" (1944), *Essays,* IV, p. 25.

. . . *to use logic against logic: 1984,* p. 36.

. . . *likes his friends no better than his enemies:* Quoted by Bernard Crick in Introduction to *Lion,* p. 28. The reviewer was V.S. Pritchett, writing in the *New Stateman and Nation,* March 1, 1941.

p. 242 *bank officials with prehensile bottoms: Lion,* p. 103.

. . . *and yet remain the same: Lion,* p. 70.

. . . *tee-totaling missionary:* I am not being unfairly selective in what follows. An electronic search for "America" through all of Orwell's major books and essays comes up with cracks like these on almost every single hit. We encounter "cheap American dentists" (*Coming Up for Air,* p. 21); American embezzlers (*Down and Out,* p. 26); and "that little American doctor who dismembered his wife (and made a very neat job of it by taking all the bones out and chucking the head into the sea, if I remember rightly)" (*Coming Up for Air,* p. 54). We meet "an ass of an American missionary, a teetotal cock-virgin from the Middle West" (*Wigan Pier,* p. 146). Americans staying in fancy Paris hotels are "easy to swindle"; Americans "know nothing whatever about good food." They "stuff themselves with disgusting American 'cereals,' and eat marmalade at tea, and drink vermouth after dinner, and order a poulet á la reine at a hundred francs and then souse it in Worcester sauce. . . . Perhaps, it hardly matters whether such people are swindled or not" (*Down and Out,* p. 82). The American apple is "a lump of highly-coloured cotton wool" with a "shiny, standardised, machine-made look," whereas the English apple has "superior taste" (*Wigan Pier,* p.

204). Even American tramps are a lesser breed: they reflect "delib-erate, cynical parasitism," not like English tramps, who are im-bued with "a strong sense of the sinfulness of poverty" (*Down and Out*, p. 202). "American soul-mate slop" is the American eu-phemism for adultery (*Aspidistra*, p. 104). The typical American paper is "mainly adverts with a few stories lurking apologetically among them"—a "panorama of ignorance, greed, vulgarity, snob-bishness, whoredom and disease" (*Aspidistra*, p. 234). "The Amer-icans always go one better on any kind of beastliness, whether it is ice-cream soda, racketeering or theosophy" (*Aspidistra*, p. 235). And on his very favorite subject Orwell writes gloomily: "When I think of what the book trade is like morally, I wonder why we don't go the whole hog and organise it into a proper racket on American lines" (Shelden, p. 294).

There is, Orwell suggests, a distinct (and clearly inferior) "Amer-ican language" ("Raffles and Miss Blandish" (1941), *Essays*, I, pp. 138, 140). Orwell excoriates the "enormous literature" in America "plainly aimed at sadists and masochists" ("Raffles," p. 140). He regrets the "great numbers of English people who are partly Americanised in language and, one ought to add, in moral, outlook" ("Raffles," p. 141). See also "Decline of the English Murder" (1946), *Essays*, IV, p. 13: "The most talked-of English murder of recent years should have been committed by an Amer-ican and an English girl who had become partly Americanized"; "As I Please" (1944), *CEJL*, Vol. 3, p. 169: "In America even the pretence that hack reviewers read the books they are paid to crit-icise has been partially abandoned"; "As I Please" (1946), *CEJL*, Vol. 4, pp. 234-235: "[T]o a casual glance he looks as though he were kissing the hem of the woman's garment—not a bad sym-bolical picture of American civilisation, or at least of one impor-tant side of it."

Ironically but quite predictably, Orwell becomes somewhat more favorably disposed toward America when English public opinion grows more hostile—which is to say, during the war years, when boisterous American troops are stationed in large numbers in Eng-land. See, e.g., "London Letter to *Partisan Review*" (1945) *CEJL*, Vol. 3, p. 298: "I would like to add, without flattery, that judging from such American periodicals as I see, the mental atmosphere in the USA is still a good deal more breathable than it is in England." "In Defence of Comrade Zilliacus" (1948), *CEJL*, Vol. 4, p. 397: "*Tribune's* anti-Americanism is not sincere but is an attempt to keep in with fashionable opinion. To be anti-American nowadays is to shout with the mob. Of course it is only a minor mob. . . . I do not believe the mass of the people in this country are anti-American politically, and certainly they are not so culturally." "In Defence of Comrade Zilliacus," p. 398: "[W]e shall be obliged, in the long run, to subordinate our policy to that of one Great Power or the other. . . . And in spite of all the fashionable chatter of the moment, everyone knows in his heart that we should choose America."

p. 242 *and English-killing new-speaker:* In a 1944 criticism of American English, Orwell supplies a clear preview of the Newspeak Appendix to *1984*, complete with the promise of "a huge loss of vocabulary" if American habits are adopted. Americans form verbs "by adding ise to a noun," they ignore the differences between transitive and intransitive verbs, they "replace strong primary words by feeble euphemisms." American English is "terribly poor in names for natural objects and localities." The American tendency is "to lump the lady-bird, the daddy-longlegs, the saw-fly, the water-boatman, the cockchafer, the cricket, the death-watch beetle and scores of other insects all together under the inexpressive name of bug." "The English People" (1944), *CEJL*, Vol. 3, pp. 28-29. Cf. *1984*, p. 51: "We're destroying words—scores of them, hundreds of them, every day," Syme happily informs Winston Smith in *1984*.

. . . *exploiting of cheap immigrant labour:* "Inside the Whale," pp. 217-218.

p. 243 *or perhaps a musician: 1984*, pp. 93-94.

p. 244 *you don't feel the same: 1984*, p. 294.

. . . *to be dismembered by the wind: 1984*, p. 293.

. . . *fastening one's love upon other human individuals:* "Reflections on Gandhi" (1949), *Essays*, I, p. 176.

p. 245 *among children richer than itself: 1984*, p. 41.

. . . *made Gordon shudder: 1984*, p. 42.

. . . *It is George Orwell:* "Charles Dickens" (1939), *Essays*, I, p. 54.

p. 245 *two decades after his death:* "Such, Such Were the Joys" (1947), *Essays,* I, p. 1.

... *before going on to Eton:* The school's real name was St. Cyprian's, see Shelden, p. 23. *Clergyman's Daughter* develops the same theme at length.

... *but to have no money: Wigan Pier,* p. 137.

... *elevated into a religion: Aspidistra,* p. 43.

p. 246 *the Crossgates money-culture:* Cf. *Lion,* p. 107: "We could start by abolishing the autonomy of the public (for American readers 'private') schools and the older universities and flooding them with State-aided pupils chosen simply on grounds of ability."

... *the sensitive, beauty-loving Flory:* Elizabeth's "whole code of living was summed up in one belief, and that a simple one. It was that the Good ('lovely' was her name for it) is synonymous with the expensive, the elegant, the aristocratic; and the Bad ('beastly') is the cheap, the low, the shabby, the laborious." *Burmese Days,* p. 90. In *Aspidistra,* p. 97, Hermione is the perfectly self-centered, rich girl-friend of a rich (but otherwise sensitive) magazine editor whose hobby is socialism. "Of course I know you're a Socialist," she tells him. "So am I. I mean we're all Socialists nowadays. But I don't see why you have to give all your money away and make friends with the lower classes. You can be a Socialist and have a good time, that's what I say."

... *at the bottom of them all: Aspidistra,* p. 78.

... *Orwell wants collectivism:* Orwell, for example, generally approved of the wartime economy, in which free market commerce had been replaced by central command. Here's his socialist summary of the change: "Before the war there was every incentive for the general public to be wasteful, at least so far as their means allowed. Everyone was trying to sell something to everyone else, and the successful man, it was imagined, was the man who sold the most goods and got the most money in return. We have learned now, however, that money is valueless in itself, and only goods count." *Broadcast,* p. 73.

... *native inequalities of talent: 1984,* p. 205.

... *His Politics and the English Language quotes:* "Politics and the English Language" (1946), *Essays,* I, p. 163.

p. 247 *biblical texts, which he uses frequently*: The front page of *Keep the As-pidistra Flying*, for example, is 1 Corinthians 13: "Though I speak with the tongues of men and of angels, and have not love . . ." but with the word "money" substituted all the way through for "love."

... *that's the way to bet it*: Quoted in Russell Baker, "Usuality as Usual," *New York Times*, March 14, 1992, p. 25.

... *material sufficiency and economic equality*: "All that the working man demands," Orwell says in a 1943 essay, is "enough to eat, freedom from the haunting terror of unemployment, the knowledge that your children will get a fair chance, a bath once a day, clean linen reasonably often, a roof that doesn't leak, and short enough work-ing hours to leave you with a little energy when the day is done"— the "indispensable minimum without which human life cannot be lived at all." "Looking back on the Spanish War" (1943), *Essays*, I, pp. 207-208. *1984*, p. 190, contains a very similar passage: "In a world in which everyone worked short hours, had enough to eat, lived in a house with a bathroom and a refrigerator, and possessed a motorcar or even an airplane, the most obvious and perhaps the most important form of inequality would already have disap-peared."

... *chosen for you from above*: "England, Your England" (1941), *Essays*, I, p. 256.

p. 248 *has been told about them is lies*: *1984*, p. 197.

... *Orwell concedes they aren't*: "England, Your England," p. 252.

... *ruled by foreigners*: "The English People" (1944), *CEJL*, Vol. 3, p. 7.

... *superior weapons and political unity*: "Looking Back on the Spanish War," p. 204; "England, Your England," p. 255.

... *a herd of cattle facing a wolf*: "England, Your England," p. 264.

... *as the Gadarene swine*: "England, Your England," p. 265.

... *foreign phrases from our writing*: "Politics and the English Lan-guage," p. 169.

p. 249 *he excoriates rentier capitalism*: "Looking Back on the Spanish War," p. 191.

... *the rentier-professional class*: "Inside the Whale," p. 222.

p. 249 *and the rentier-intellectual:* "Inside the Whale," p. 230.

. . . *he is a small investor: The New Cassell's French Dictionary* (1971), p. 639. Orwell describes the rentier thus: "A rentier is part of the possessing class, he can and, almost without knowing it, does make other people work for him, but he has very little direct power." "Charles Dickens," p. 53. Orwell usually has in mind the "second-generation rentier" who is "living on inherited money." "Review, *Personal Record,* by Julian Green" (1940), *CEJL,* Vol. 2, p. 20. But he has quite as much disdain for the first-generation fortune of the "American millionaire." See, e.g., "Letter from England to *Partisan Review*" (1943), *CEJL,* Vol. 2, p. 282: "[T]he dreary world which the American millionaires and their British hangers-on intend to impose upon us begins to take shape"; "Letter to H. J. Willmett" (1944), *CEJL,* Vol. 3, p. 148: "Hitler, no doubt, will soon disappear, but only at the expense of strengthening (a) Stalin, (b) the Anglo-American millionaires and (c) all sorts of petty fuehrers of the type of de Gaulle." By 1943, Orwell is in fact describing the economic enemy as the "American millionaires and their British hangers-on." "Letter from England to *Partisan Review*" (1943), *CEJL,* Vol. 2, p. 282.

. . . *decayed throw-outs: Coming Up for Air,* p. 139. Orwell sees colonialism—Britain's "looting of Asia and Africa"—as just another manifestation of rentier capitalism, a scheme for boosting national income with "interest from foreign investments." "Writers and Leviathan" (1948), *Essays,* III, p. 462.

. . . *fleas are to a dog:* "England, Your England," p. 269. They are also "too civilised to work, fight or even reproduce themselves." "Review, *Burnt Norton, East Coker, The Dry Salvages,* by T. S. Eliot" (1942), *CEJL,* Vol. 2, p. 238. In his Dickens essay Orwell states: "But in these books [by Dickens] the good rich man has dwindled from a 'merchant' to a rentier. This is significant." "Charles Dickens," p. 53.

. . . *mind and money walk hand in hand:* He was equally interested in how the economic environment affected the progress of science. While at the BBC he asked one prospective speaker for a talk on the "effects of capitalism on science, the extent to which it has stimulated its development, and the point at which it becomes a retarding influence." *Broadcast*, p. 185. Another BBC talk he commissioned was on 'The Economic Basis of Literature" (p. 31).

p. 250 *without drifting toward Big Brother:* As Orwell acknowledges in his 1946 essay on Burnham, "it has always been obvious that a planned and centralised society is liable to develop into an oligarchy or a dictatorship." "Second Thoughts on James Burnham" (1946), *Essays*, II, p. 338.

p. 251 *boy's father of course did not own:* "Such, Such Were the Joys," p. 35.

. . . *indifferent to economic justice:* "Review, *Communism and Man*, by F. J. Sheed" (1939), *CEJL*, Vol. 1, p. 384.

. . . *boyhood face in the mirror:* "In Front of Your Nose" (1946), *CEJL*, Vol. 4, p. 123.

p. 252 *going to be owned:* During the Spanish civil war, Orwell himself even participates in a gunfight for control of the telephone exchange in Barcelona. *Homage to Catalonia*, p. 121.

. . . *as his own father did:* Shelden, p. 312. Eric Blair was born June 25, 1903. His father, Richard, was born January 7, 1857, and died on June 28, 1939, aged 82 years and 5 months.

. . . *as a Tory Anarchist:* Shelden, p. 219. See also Bernard Crick's Introduction to *The Lion and the Unicorn*, p. 10. Crick explains that Orwell "was an individualist who resented one man or one culture imposing its values on another, and above all resented servants of the state moralizing their power with talk of 'responsibility.'" But neither Shelden nor Crick notes that Orwell gave the phrase a somewhat more cynical (and pessimistic) definition of his own when applying it to Jonathan Swift.

. . . *while disbelieving in liberty:* "Politics vs Literature: An Examination of *Gulliver's Travels*," p. 386.

. . . *people who are not fighting:* Homage to Catalonia, p. 65.

. . . *reflecting on that irony:* "War-time Diary" (1942), *CEJL*, Vol. 2, pp. 415-416.

. . . *Orwell learns he has tuberculosis:* Shelden, p. 332.

. . . *unavailable in England:* Shelden, p. 424.

p. 253 *shipment sent to Orwell's hospital:* The drug arrives in early 1948 and Orwell is given regular doses of it. Shelden, p. 424. Meanwhile, in February 1948, Orwell writes another letter in which he states: "If anything should happen to me I've instructed Richard Rees, my literary executor, to destroy the [manuscript of *1984*] without showing it to anybody." "Letter to F. J. Warburg," p. 404.

p. 253 *completing his last novel:* Shelden, p. 425.

The Machine

p. 255 *the job I would like to have:* "As I Please" (1945), *CEJL*, Vol. 3, p. 357.

. . . *produced individually, as you know: 1984*, p. 215.

. . . *Or why not five:* As a broadcaster for the BBC Orwell himself engineered the writing of a "Story by Five Authors." They were: Orwell himself, Inez Holden, L.A.G. Strong, Martin Armstrong, and E. M. Forster. *Broadcast*, p. 41.

p. 256 *as often as was necessary: 1984*, p. 41. Orwell himself is fond of doing this sort of thing to others, particularly to religious texts. See, e.g., *Burmese Days*, p. 18: "He began to sing aloud, 'Bloody, bloody, bloody, oh, how thou art bloody' to the tune of the hymn 'Holy, holy, holy, oh how Thou art holy'"; *Burmese Days*, p. 79: "What shall it profit a man if he save his own soul and lose the whole world?"; *Aspidistra* (frontpiece): "Though I speak with the tongues of men and of angels, and have not money," etc.; *A Clergyman's Daughter*, p. 214: "[I]f you took I Corinthians, chapter thirteen, and in every verse wrote 'money' instead of 'charity'"; "The Prevention of Literature" (1946), *Essays*, III, p. 336: "To bring this hymn up to date one would have to add a 'Don't' at the beginning of each line."

p. 257 *rewrite Orwell's book beginning to end:* I realized this in late 1991. It seemed like a propitious time to undertake the job, as we approached the tenth anniversary of April 4, 1984, the day on which Winston Smith began his seditious diary. If Orwell had stuck with his original plan, his book would in fact have been called *1994* rather than *1984*. The title of the book came from reversing two digits in 1948, when Orwell actually finished writing it. But the book was not published until 1949.

p. 258 *concerned with prostitutes:* Cf. Shelden, p. 9.

p. 258 *a number of his own books and essays:* For example: *Coming Up for Air*, p. 163, includes a capsule summary of *A Clergyman's Daughter:* "She lives on some kind of tiny fixed income, an annuity or something, and I fancy she's a left-over from the old society of West Bletchley, when it was a little country town, before the suburb grew up. . . . It's written all over her that her father was a clergyman and sat on her pretty heavily while he lived."

Down and Out, p. 192, includes a mention of Lower Binfield, which is the center of the story in *Coming Up for Air*.

Burmese Days, p. 58, contains discrete references to "magnified aspidistras" and describes a woman's frustration at meeting "a veritable artist who was willing to work penniless all his life rather than sell himself to a bank or an insurance company." This is, of course, a capsule summary of *Keep the Aspidistra Flying*.

p. 259 *all literature builds on common experience:* As *Orwell's Revenge* went into galleys I stumbled across this in the Sunday edition of the *New York Times:* "There's nothing scandalous about this sort of borrowing. The history of literature is a history of appropriation. Shelley's gothic novel, 'Zastrozzi,' is a deliberate pastiche of novels and stories by his well-known predecessors Monk Lewis and Mrs. Radcliffe, right down to the characters' names. Joyce plundered the entire canon of English literature, adapting it for his purposes. Literature, like property, is theft." J. Atlas, "Who Owns a Life? Asks a Poet, When His Is Turned into Fiction," *New York Times*, February 20, 1994, p. E14.

p. 260 *always remain a solitary endeavor:* "The Prevention of Literature" (1946), *Essays*, III, p. 343: "Serious prose, in any case, has to be composed in solitude."

. . . *Orwell wrote in 1984: 1984*, p. 35.

. . . *time to shape what is:* For further philosophical reflections on the hyper-intelligent future, see Albert Borgmann, *Crossing the Postmodern Divide* (Chicago: University of Chicago Press, 1992), pp. 102-109.

. . . *but Thou mayest:* John Steinbeck, *East of Eden* (Penguin Books ed., 1986), pp. 395, 399.

Loose Ends

p. 261 *tyranny can perhaps never be complete:* "Poetry and the Microphone" (1945), *Essays*, III, p. 245.

... *1.4 million employees:* At its apogee, just prior to divestiture, the Bell System had annual revenues of $58 billion and total assets of $138 billion; it employed over 1 million people. By 1986, IBM had 407 employees. "The End of I.B.M.'s Overshadowing Role," *New York Times*, December 20, 1992, 3: 2.

p. 262 *would be considered indispensable:* Robert W. Garnet, *The Telephone Enterprise: The Evolution of the Bell System's Horizontal Structure, 1876-1909* (Baltimore: Johns Hopkins University Press, 1985), p. 12.

... *shifting the unit from mouth to ear:* See George David Smith, *The Anatomy of a Business Strategy: Bell, Western Electric, and the Origins of the American Telephone Industry* (Baltimore: John Hopkins University Press, 1985), pp. 20-22.

... *directly to each other:* Garnet, *The Telephone Enterprise*, p. 15.

p. 263 *inexorably back toward monopoly:* See Garnet, *The Telephone Enterprise*, p. 23, for a discussion of these problems and rationale.

... *either folded or were acquired:* See Robinson, "The Federal Communications Act: An Essay on Origins and Regulatory Purpose," reprinted in *A Legislative History of the Communications Act of 1934* (Paglin ed., 1989), p. 7; Burch, "Common Carrier Communications by Wire and Radio: A Retrospective," *Federal Communications Law Journal* 37 (1985): 85, 87; Warren G. Lavey, "The Public Policies That Changed the Telephone Industry Into Regulated Monopolies: Lessons from Around 1915," *Federal Communications Law Journal* 39 (1987): 171.

p. 264 *cricket game was improving rapidly:* Shelden, p. 39.

... *name to International Business Machines:* Richard Thomas DeLamarter, *Big Blue: IBM's Use and Abuse of Power* (New York: Dodd, Mead, 1986), p. 15.

... *the humble punch card itself:* Card sales would account for almost a quarter of IBM's net income in the two decades after 1930. Robert Sobel, *I.B.M.: Colossus in Transition* (New York: Times Books, 1981), p. 210.

p. 264 *became prohibitively expensive:* DeLamarter, *Big Blue,* pp. 19-20.

p. 265 *superintendent of police in Burma:* Shelden, p. 81.

. . . *a messaging system for ships:* Edward Anton Doering, *Federal Control of Broadcasting Versus Freedom of the Air* (Washington, D.C., 1939), p. 4.

. . . *a factor of importance:* Quoted in Ithiel de Sola Pool, *Technologies of Freedom* (Cambridge: Harvard University Press, 1983).

. . . *The military was interested too:* My summary here is taken from R. H. Coase, "The Federal Communications Commission," *Journal of Law and Economics* 2 (1959), and from Thomas W. Hazlett, "The Rationality of U.S. Regulation of Broadcast Spectrum," *Journal of Law and Economics* 33 (1990).

p. 267 *he sailed back to England:* Shelden, p. 111.

. . . *and legitimize its monopoly:* See Richard McKenna, "Preemption under the Communications Act," *Federal Communications Law Journal* 37 (1985): 1, 8; Sen. Larry Pressler & Kevin V. Schieffer, "A Proposal for Universal Service," *Federal Communications Law Journal* 40 (1988): 351, 356; Robinson, "The Federal Communications Act," pp. 6-7.

. . . *covers only that part which is profitable:* Statement of Theodore Vail, Bell chairman, quoted in Gerald W. Brock, *The Telecommunications Industry: The Dynamics of Market Structure* (Cambridge: Harvard University Press, 1981), pp. 158-159.

. . . *create a separate Federal Communications Commission:* S. Doc. No. 244, 73d Cong., 2d sess. (1934).

. . . *had passed legislation:* See *Congressional Record,* June 9, 1934, pp. 10,912, 10,995.

. . . *into law on June 18:* *Congressional Record,* June 9, 1934, p. 12, 451.

p. 268 *adequate facilities at reasonable charges:* Communications Act of 1934, ch. 652, sec. 1, 48 Stat. 1064 (1934), (codified as amended at 47 U.S.C. sec. 151 (1988)). The new commission was to regulate radio as well as wire communications and, hence, replace the Federal Radio Commission established by the Radio Act of 1927, 44 Stat. 1162 (1927).

. . . *under his own name:* Shelden, p. 165.

p. 268 *on the bodies of their enemies: Burmese Days*, p. 14.

. . . *cards from anyone but IBM:* DeLamarter, *Big Blue*, pp. 21-22.

. . . *crowded office environments:* Hush-A-Phone, 20 F.C.C. 391 (1955); 238 F.2d 266 (D.C. Cir. 1956); *on remand*, 22 F.C.C. 112 (1957).

. . . *all foreign attachments:* A typical such provision reads as follows: "No equipment, apparatus, circuit, or device not furnished by the Telephone Company shall be attached to or connected with the facilities furnished by the Telephone Company, whether, physically, by induction or otherwise, except as provided in this tariff. In case any such unauthorized attachment or connection is made, the Telephone Company shall have the right to remove or disconnect the same; or to suspend the service during the continuance of said attachment or connection; or to terminate the service." Jordaphone, 18 F.C.C. 644, 647 (1954).

p. 269 *for the Hush-A-Phone:* Hush-A-Phone, 20 F.C.C. at 397.

. . . *talking in a low tone of voice:* Hush-A-Phone, 20 F.C.C. at 398.

. . . *went up to the U.S. Supreme Court:* DeLamarter, *Big Blue*, p. 22.

. . . *settled in a 1956 decree:* DeLamarter, *Big Blue*, p. 23; Sobel, *I.B.M.*, p. 142.

. . . *without being publicly detrimental:* Hush-A-Phone, 238 F.2d 266, 269 (D.C. Cir. 1956).

. . . *and verse by the U.S. Supreme Court:* Red Lion Broadcasting Co. Inc. v. FCC, 395 U.S. 367 (1969).

p. 271 *Bell's long-distance network:* Richard H. K. Vietor, "AT&T and the Public Good: Regulation and Competition in Telecommunications, 1910-1987," in *Future Competition in Telecommunications*, ed. Stephen P. Bradley and Jerry A. Hausman (Boston: Harvard Business School Press, 1989), pp. 27, 52.

. . . *television network in 1948:* Morton I. Hamburg, *All About Cable*, rev. ed. (New York: Cambridge Univ. Press, 1985), pp. 1-6.

. . . *domestic long-distance calls:* John Brooks, *Telephone: The First Hundred Years* (New York: Harper & Row, 1975), p. 244.

p. 272 *on one substrate:* See T. R. Reid, *The Chip: How Two Americans Invented the Microchip and Launched a Revolution* (New York: Simon & Schuster, 1984).

p. 273 *between St. Louis and Chicago:* The following relies primarily on Peter Temin, *The Fall of the Bell System* (New York: Cambridge Univ. Press, 1987), pp. 47-54.

p. 274 *unique and special characteristics:* Quoted in Temin, *Bell System*, p. 50.

. . . *limited common carriers:* General Mobile Radio Serv. Allocation of Frequencies between 25 & 30 Megacycles, 13 F.C.C. 1190, 1228 (1949).

. . . *significant interest in both licenses:* See Amendment of the Commission's Rules, 98 F.C.C.2d 175, 218 (1984).

. . . *enjoyed by affiliates:* See, e.g., An Inquiry into the Use of Bands 825-845 MHz & 870-890 MHz for Cellular Communications Systems, 86 F.C.C.2d 469, 495-496 (1981); Amendment of Part 21 of the Commission's Rules with Respect to the 150.8-162 Mc/s Band to Allocate Presently Unassignable Spectrum to the Domestic Public Land Mobile Radio Service by Adjustment of Certain of the Band Edges, 12 F.C.C.2d 841, 849-850 (1968), aff'd, sub nom. Radio Relay Corp. v. FCC, 409 F.2d 322 (2d Cir. 1969).

p. 276 *failed to recognize its importance:* Regis McKenna, *Who's Afraid of Big Blue? How Companies Are Challenging IBM—and Winning* (Reading, MA: Addison-Wesley, 1989), p. 18.

p. 277 *from $1.7 billion to $7.5 billion:* DeLamarter, *Big Blue*, p. 349.

. . . *library of application programs:* McKenna, *Who's Afraid of Big Blue?*, p. 22.

. . . *three hundred meters into the air: 1984*, p. 5.

p. 278 *to enter the computer business:* In 1991 it purchases NCR, the former National Cash Register, where Tom Watson first learned how to sell business machines.

p. 280 *IBM's 3090, introduced in 1985:* Intel, "The Next Revolution," *Business Week*, September 26, 1988, p. 74. To be sure, a microprocessor, no matter how fast, is not a full working computer; a crude MIPS comparison somewhat overstates the advance of the microprocessor. But only somewhat.

. . . *a million dollar mainframe of the 1970s:* Peter H. Lewis, "Chips for the Year 2," *New York Times*, June 19, 1990, p. C8.

. . . *IBM shed 100,000 employees:* "Deconstructing the Computer Industry," *Business Week*, November 23, 1992, p. 90.

p. 280 *collapsed to $52 by year's end 1992:* "The End of I.B.M.'s Overshadowing Role," *New York Times*, December 20, 1992, 3: 2.

. . . *the New York Times would announce "The End of I.B.M.'s Overshadowing Role":* *New York Times*, December 20, 1992, 3: 2.

. . . *and faster networked workstations:* "The End of I.B.M.'s Overshadowing Role," *New York Times*, December 20, 1992, 3: 2.

. . . *IBM's advertising now declares:* IBM advertisement, *Forbes*, November 23, 1992, p. 202.

p. 281 *were digitally switched:* Vietor, "AT&T and the Public Good," p. 52.

p. 282 *different media no longer hold:* Pool, *Technologies of Freedom*, pp. 26-27. A major study by Congress's Office of Technology Assessment reached identical conclusions in 1990. "With digitalization all of the media become translatable into each other—computer bits migrate merrily—and they escape from their traditional means of transmission. A movie, phone call, letter, or magazine article may be sent digitally via phone line, coaxial cable, fiber optic cable, microwave, satellite, the broadcast air, or a physical storage medium such as tape or disk." Office of Technology Assessment, U.S. Congress, *Critical Connections* (Washington, D.C.: U.S. Government Printing Office, 1990), p. 50.

p. 284 *hundreds of color television signals:* Although the present capacity is 24,000 simultaneous conversations, "[e]xperts suggest a theoretical carrying capacity of about 600 million [simultaneous] conversations." Marshall Yates, "The Promise of Fiber Optics," *Public Utilities Fortnightly*, August 16, 1990, p. 14.

■■■■■ ACKNOWLEDGMENTS

My telecommunications work has been generously funded by the Markle Foundation and the Manhattan Institute for Policy Research. I am deeply indebted to Bill Hammett for his most patient support and encouragement.

Janey Huber Reacher provided extensive help with the fiction parts of this book, particularly the scenes of London. My friends and colleagues Michael Kellogg and John Thorne read and provided invaluable comments on early drafts. The three of us are also coauthors of *Federal Telecommunications Law* (1992) and *The Geodesic Network* (1993), in which we jointly developed, albeit at a more down-to-earth level, many of the ideas presented in *Orwell's Revenge*. I am also indebted to Fred Siegel, Lewis Bateman, and Martin Kessler, who all read and commented on various drafts of the book. Fred Siegel in particular offered encouragement when I needed it most.

In the summer of 1992 I was invited by John O'Connor to present my views in a lakeside talk at the Bohemian Grove. The feedback and expressions of interest I received from John and the very generous audience there gave me the stamina to complete what I might otherwise have abandoned.

Some months later, George Gilder kindly read my manuscript and put me in touch with Erwin Glikes, editor of The Free Press. Erwin agreed to take a chance on my unorthodox creation. He then patiently steered my book through a raft of lawyers and agents, on both our side of the Atlantic and Orwell's. Erwin Glikes died suddenly in May 1994, as my book was going to press. I am forever in his debt.

I am indebted as well to Erwin's assistant at The Free Press, Marion Maneker, who helped see the book through to completion. My copy editor, Beverly Miller, suggested many useful changes, and meticulously cleaned up the notes. The book's elegant design was the work of Carla Bolte. Loretta Denner of The Free Press patiently coordinated the production. My mother, Dorothy Huber, and my research assistants, Karin Albani, Olga Grushin, Laura Haefner, Penny Karas, Lynn Kelley, Rosemary McMahill, B. J. Min, T. J. Radtke and Gary Stahlberg, Jr. helped proofread the manuscript; my secretary Danelle Lohman worked many long hours to put it in final electronic shape.

Finally, I am grateful to Orwell's literary executors at A. M. Heath & Company (London) for their agreement to let me use Orwell's work as I have. The estate is receiving a share of the royalties earned on this book, which of course it fully deserves.

INDEX